Unpopular Education

also by CCCS and published by Hutchinson

Resistance through Rituals
On Ideology
Women Take Issue
Working Class Culture
Culture, Media, Language

Authors of Unpopular Education

Steve Baron
Dan Finn
Neil Grant
Michael Green
Richard Johnson

Unpopular Education

Schooling and social democracy
in England since 1944

Education Group
Centre for Contemporary Cultural Studies

Hutchinson
London Melbourne Sydney Auckland Johannesburg

in association with
The Centre for Contemporary Cultural Studies
University of Birmingham

Hutchinson & Co. (Publishers) Ltd
An imprint of the Hutchinson Publishing Group
24 Highbury Crescent, London N5 1RX

Hutchinson Group (Australia) Pty Ltd
30-32 Cremorne Street, Richmond South, Victoria 3121
PO Box 151, Broadway, New South Wales 2007
Hutchinson Group (NZ) Ltd
32-34 View Road, PO Box 40-086, Glenfield, Auckland 10
Hutchinson Group (SA) (Pty) Ltd
PO Box 337, Bergvlei 2012, South Africa

First published 1981

Set in IBM Press Roman

Printed in Great Britain by The Anchor Press Ltd
and bound by Wm Brendon & Son Ltd
both of Tiptree, Essex

British Library Cataloguing in Publication Data

Unpopular education.
    1. Educational sociology — England
    2. Education, secondary — England — History
    — 20th century
    I. University of Birmingham. Centre for
    Contemporary Cultural Studies
    373.42   LC191.8.G7

ISBN 0 09 138960 7 cased
        0 09 138961 5 paper

Contents

What national education is going to mean: a class at an open-air school in Leicester
The children have plenty of space between them. They are all near the big, open windows.
They work in plenty of air and light. The teacher gives them interesting, creative things to
do. The pupils are absorbed in their jobs.

Source: *Picture Post* 403, 4 January 1941
Reproduced by permission of the BBC Hulton Picture Library

Free schooling system
in growing danger

Free education, the fine principle enshrined in the 1944 Education Act, is now sounding increasingly hollow. Growing numbers of parents and children are being asked to pay for schooling as spending cuts take their toll on textbooks, paper and equipment. Bingo evenings raise cash for sports equipment, girls go modelling to pay for books and parents clean, paint and repair their children's schools.

Scandal as parents foot bills for books

Source: TES special survey, 9 May 1980, p. 10

Preface

This book has been a long time in the writing, longer than we or some of our readers ever anticipated. What began as a manageable project which could be completed with relative ease, was transformed by our chosen mode of collective writing into something which necessarily was more extended. The geographical dispersal of the authors as well as the pressure of recent political events also combined to protract the actual process of writing as we attempted to consider the ramifications of these events.

Readers will see that we have chosen to offer a collective authorship for the text, and this is appropriate. Every part of the book has been written by more than one person, although it will be apparent that individual styles will predominate in sections where one person has undertaken the major or final responsibility of authorship.

The project of which this book is a product has a specific history which extends back over the five years during which the Education Group has worked in the Centre for Contemporary Cultural Studies. From the first stage of our work, in which we owed much to the suggestions of Simon Frith and Paul Corrigan, a long article was produced dealing with the relationship of social democracy to the contemporary 'crisis' in educational policy and practice.[1]* The more recent history of our work has therefore coincided with a period of rapid change in the nature of educational politics and indeed national politics as a whole. As we have been writing this book, the challenge to social democratic orthodoxies, which we discussed in our article, has become a wholesale demolition following the success in the 1979 General Election of a new and radical Conservatism. The failure of the Labour Party to muster more than a minimal opposition either to the challenge to or subsequent dismantling of the post-1944 consensus has dramatically confirmed our major theses — that the old repertoire of Labour Party policies is largely exhausted in the forms in which it is currently conceived and presented.

Our efforts to keep pace with recent events have not merely served to delay, but also to caution us about the political implications of anything we might choose to say. The last thing which we would wish is that our critique would in any way serve the Conservatism of the 1980s.

This book, like the article which preceded it, is not intended to be an account

*Superior figures refer to the Notes on pages 267-99.

which is distanced from the processes and events it describes. As individuals we are also involved in political struggles, and we offer here an account which is informed by a socialist perspective. We therefore hope that our work will contribute to the furtherance of socialist and feminist struggles, not only in education but also more widely.

The purpose of this book has been to understand the ways in which educational politics have been constructed in England (and to some extent in Britain more generally) during the post-second world war period. The process of researching and writing about this period has been, for us, a form of political education in itself, and one which we hope to share with a larger audience. It is not, however, a definitive account or a set of prescriptions for political action. Readers, who expect us to deliver a set of solutions in this sense, will, we fear, be necessarily disappointed. This is well beyond our competence or the scope of any one book; it is also in direct opposition to what we see as the role of analytical texts, or of one small group of researchers. In fact, as we point out, the work is 'by no means concluded'. Rather, our book is an attempt to further a redefinition of the way in which a more widely based socialist and feminist educational politics must progress, if it is to constitute an effective or possible opposition to the dominance of capitalist and patriarchal definitions of educational means and ends.

We hope that we will inform those who are involved in struggles but also that they will in turn comment critically on what we have to say. There are two areas where we are already aware of deficiencies or absences in what we have written, and where we anticipate (justified) criticism. First, our treatment of the themes of race and gender as constitutive and organizing elements of educational politics is clearly inadequate. In these areas especially we would welcome suggestions about the integration of such themes into the analysis we have presented, or alternatively, about the incompatibilities between our analysis and a more adequate account. Second, we have not addressed, in detail, the changing character of the grass-roots situation in the schools and therefore the immediate context of the classroom, the curriculum and the everyday world of the teacher. We have, however, drawn heavily on recent research on the cultural character of schooling and the forms of resistance to be found there among groups of school pupils, boys and girls. We present these forms of resistance as springing directly from the patriarchal and capitalist context of schooling. To take the argument further — to present a view of a popular and a socialist education — is an important task but beyond our brief and our competence. We have no past or contemporary models to hand although we do draw attention to a long but discontinuous tradition of popular counter-education, outside and in opposition to the state or philanthropic agencies. Our concluding chapter, then, stops short of presenting a full account of an alternative. It concentrates, rather, on analysing the conditions under which such an alternative could be produced.

The book is organized in three parts: the first, 'Social democracy: the making', deals with the origins and the formation of a social democratic hegemony in education with its point of culmination in the 1960s. Part Two, 'Social democracy: the limits', is a critical examination of the forms of knowledge and the contradictory assumptions that informed policy in this phase. In Part Three, 'Social democracy: the breaking', we return to a detailed history of the 1970s, the main organizing theme of which is the collapse of the 1960s' settlement and the disintegration of the social alliance on which it was based. The argument of our concluding chapter is that there can be no simple return to the orthodoxies of the 1960s. We seek to establish some of the conditions for a new popular politics of education, in opposition both to social democracy and the harsh instrumental orthodoxies of the 1980s.

We have one main suggestion for readers about the way this book might be read. Chapter 1 is the most theoretical part of the book: it outlines the general features of our approach, which was formed, in part, in the theoretical debates, among sociologists and Marxists, of the last ten years. In particular, our approach developed from a critical examination of theories of social reproduction. The problem with many such theories, despite the real deepening of knowledge which they represent, is that they are insufficiently alive to the *contested* nature of such processes and therefore to the centrality of political struggles. We hope that the formulations we have now agreed combine explanatory force with a more activist, less pessimistic employment of theory. Readers concerned with these theoretical developments will wish to start their reading with Chapter 1: others may wish to start with Chapter 2 and return to the first chapter after they have read the other, more substantive parts.

In the course of writing such a book, especially over so long a time, many debts are incurred. To previous members of the education group at this centre we offer thanks and gratitude for their many and varied contributions. We thank, especially, Angela McRobbie and Henry Miller; also Marilyn Crutcher whose work on the popular press and education provided material for our discussion of the media in Chapter 9. Thanks too for the assistance provided by Wendy Bradshaw, Rajinder Bhogal, Berit Kosterlitz, Irene Lindsay, Kath Sheehan, Pam Thompson and Joan Goode. We also thank Claire L'Enfant of Hutchinson for her help and encouragement in seeing the project to fruition in its book form. Finally to all those past and present associates of the Centre for Contemporary Cultural Studies, thanks not only for ideas and encouragement but also for making the Centre such a stimulating environment in which to work.

Steve Baron
Dan Finn
Neil Grant
Michael Green
Richard Johnson
September 1980

Part One
Social democracy: the making

'Now let this discussion on Demobilization and Social Security be a lively one, with a spirited interplay of ideas, even if we have to be a half-minute late for tea.'

Source: *Punch*, 29 November 1944, p. 457
Reproduced by permission of Punch Publications Ltd

'Don't stop him, darling! It's his form of self-expression.'

Source: *Punch*, 8 August 1945, p. 113
Reproduced by permission of Punch Publications Ltd

1 Perspectives on schooling and politics

In this opening chapter we explore some of the general problems of writing a critical study of post-war schooling. We do not want to produce, in advance, a general, formal theory of education, but to sketch some key features of our own approach. These have been formed in a three-sided engagement. We have learnt, first, from the theoretical debates of the last ten years, especially from the proliferation of sociologies of education, old and new, and from the revival of Marxist analysis. Second, we have drawn on these theories to the extent that they have helped us to make sense of the pattern of post-war changes. We have valued or criticized them for their explanatory power or weakness. Third, our approach has been formed by the very events we describe, especially, of course, by the developments of the 1970s. Like all students of social developments, we stand inside the social relations we describe, not outside them. We have consciously taken sides and have not held back from arguing political preferences. In particular, we have been influenced by a growing sense of the need for a more adequate socialist politics of education.

Chapter 1 is the most theoretical part of this book, but we will not spend a great deal of time describing the arguments of other theorists; we will concentrate instead on saying what, from our point of view, has proved useful or problematic in them.[1]

Approaches to policy

There is a large literature on state education policy and policy-making. Until recently most of the historical writing on education has focused on these topics at the expense of a more social history of schooling.[2] There are many similar studies for other policy areas and similar paradigms operate in orthodox political science.[3] The main feature of most of this work is that it is written from a standpoint internal to the policy-making process itself. Our attention is directed to the most apparent generative processes — to legislation, administration and the formal politics of education — and towards the most immediately responsible persons and organizations: politicians, civil servants, departments and boards of government, local authorities and the various organized interest groups. We stand at the elbow of the policy-maker; certainly the policy-makers' voices reach us most insistently from the sources. It is difficult to emancipate ourselves from their assumptions, or transcend their limitations of vision. So politics tend to be treated as a specialist, expert realm into which the rude noises of 'the population' rarely intrude, or, if they do, they do so mainly as 'constraints' on policy-makers' solutions or through accredited representatives or the media. As I. G. K. Fenwick has put it, in a useful study of the politics of comprehensive schooling:

For the most part it is necessary to concentrate on interested groups, parties, Parliament, bureaucrats and the Press as being, in this country, the most active and well-established gatekeepers of the political system.[4]

In the older histories of education reconstructions of the intentions of authors may stand in for more complicated accounts of why changes happened. Active and concerned persons deal with passive but potentially dangerous problems (which are actually constituted in the life activity of the underlying social groups and classes). Events are characteristically coupled with key authors: from Forster's or Fisher's or Butler's Education Acts to the Geddes Axe. Even the best histories of policy-making resemble the most traditional, conservative and widely read of historical genres: biographies or autobiographies of leading public figures.[5]

Certainly it is important not to lose a sense of authorship or agency, or of the rush and muddle of decision-making 'at the top'. Both are correctives to the tendency to ascribe perfect knowledge and conspiratorial intent to politicians or to 'the state'. But this type of account is deeply problematic, theoretically and politically. It excludes the living, active force of the vast majority of historical populations and tends, qualitatively, to take the side of the dominant and articulate minorities. This can happen even where there is no deliberate attempt to uphold the *status quo*. It follows from accepting, as given, features of politics, 'education' or social conditions in general, which ought to be appraised critically and which have an intricate history of their own. One example is the tendency to identify the peculiar British post-war combination of parliamentary democracy and bureaucratic statism with 'democracy' or 'the modern political system', and therefore to accept as given the political *dis*organization which occurs when 'the gates' are kept only too well. It is not enough to note, as Fenwick does, 'the largely negative role played by large numbers of legitimate participants' and to concentrate, therefore, on 'the major elements of the population actively interested in education, the education public'.[6] We have to ask how and why educational politics have been constructed in this way, why there has been no vigorous post-war popular politics and what, in the absence of such movements, the more diffused forms of resistance have been.

Another example of the same conservative form is the tendency to identify 'education' with the work of schools, colleges and other formal 'educational' institutions. As we shall see, this reduction was characteristic of the 'old' sociology of education, but it has also been a persistent feature of public debates, as everyday language testifies: 'education system', 'education cuts', 'education debates', etc. It is, in fact, very important to distinguish more carefully between 'education' and 'schooling'; the first term refers to all forms of learning, the second to that specific historical form which involves specialized institutions and professional practitioners. Mass, public, compulsory, state schooling is a still more specific educational form, limited historically to the last 150 years or so.

The identification of schooling and education is very conservative in its effects. It tends to present schools as natural rather than as historical products. It tends to devalue and marginalize the more spontaneous and more diffused ways of learning. It constructs a very sharp divide between school-like institutions (where we learn/are educated) and life outside these walls (where we work/play). It enhances the professional teacher and the organized curriculum over other sources of wisdom and, often, over practical knowledge as such. Above all, it hides from view a whole history of the construction of schooling – or encourages the belief in some simple history of progress, a history with no costs, no struggles, no ambiguities. Throughout this book, we shall explore the gap between capitalist schooling and education. We shall also present modern educational arrangements in the form of state schooling as particular historical products.

There are, more generally, three main ways of breaking out of the conservatism which we have described. Each involves a more critical or 'external' way of writing about policy or about the state. The first strategy is to continue to inhabit the world of the policy-makers but with a more critical eye. This approach reads policy statements, public debates and professional discourses not as they present themselves (as a humanitarian concern for 'the poor' or as a preoccupation with 'equality') but according to the underlying logic or ideological character of a practice or a text. The focus is less on intent than on tendency; less on what is said than what is hidden or implied. Critiques of this kind have been common within the radical sociology and social history of the last decade or so,[7] but it is worth looking, briefly, at a very sophisticated variant, the work of the French historian Michel Foucault.[8]

In his more historical work, Foucault is especially interested in areas which are often taken to be natural but which, as he shows, have been socially constructed: the definition and regulation, for instance, of sexuality, of childhood, of criminality or of madness. The subjects of Foucault's histories are not individual politicians, authors or even social classes or groups, but what he calls 'discourses' or 'discursive practices'. In using these terms Foucault insists on the intimate connection between knowledge and power, between the defining of a practice and its regulation. 'Discourse' includes worked-up forms of knowledge, usually those associated with a professional practice such as law, medicine or religion, but also the material or bodily concomitants of such power: imprisonment, hospitalization or the act of the confessional. These 'modalities' of control and incitement are minutely described, each discourse having its own peculiar character. Foucault thus preserves and explores the complexity of regulative disciplines without accepting their legitimacy, either as scientific knowledge or a necessary means to social order. Foucault is interested in the knowledges of policy-makers not because they are true but because they create 'regimes of truth' and are part of the operation of a 'micro-physics of power'.

Foucault's histories suffer, however, from problems common to all abstracted or decontextualized studies of ideologies or policy statements. The micro-physics of power are supposed to work in the way described in the official manuals of method or the authoritative descriptions of 'the system'.[9] Foucault retains a place – in theory — for relations or forces that exist outside the discourses he describes, but in his histories these are rarely elaborated. Recent work in Britain, owing much to Foucault's method and style, has tended to accentuate this problem rather than solve it.[10] In such work we stay *inside* discourses, unconcerned with their adequacy as knowledge and ignorant of the forms of resistance to them. We stay, in other words, in the fool's paradise of the powerful. It is impossible to explain, from this perspective, why regulative practices and their attendant knowledges collapse or are forced to innovate. A Foucauldian critique of post-war educational policy could certainly show us how certain professional knowledges and practices were implicated in a logic of domination. It could not tell us why the 1960s' policies fell apart or were transformed. This was not a product of discourse alone, but also of powerful social forces which the dominant knowledges failed to anticipate. Certainly a non-purist Foucauldian method may *contribute* to a history of policy but it provides no complete model. We do have to attend closely to the internal logic of public knowledge, but we also have to move it away from the centre of the stage to consider agencies and determinations which it does not describe. We need accounts of these too, as complex and subtle as Foucault's own histories of discursive formations.

A more common riposte in Britain to state-orientated research, and the second main tendency on which we draw, has been to take the side of 'the people'. The writing of popular, working-class or labour history has been a longstanding preoccupation of intellectuals within, or to the left of, the Labour Party. The tradition of sympathetic social histories of popular experiences and movements goes back at least as far as John and Barbara Hammond and the inter-war founders of 'labour history'. It remains a lively and growing historiographical presence today.[11] The focus here is upon the experiences of the governed. In itself this standpoint renders problematic a view from 'above', but much more is involved than an inversion of perspective. The popular histories have often been written by socialists or Marxists who have seen the struggle of classes as the principal historical dynamic. E. P. Thompson's polemical and historical writing, for example, is a sustained exploration of these themes.[12] The emphasis is on the working class or the populace as an active force which has shaped social institutions and values. Far from being a docile object of policy, popular struggle constitutes the policy-makers' problems in the first place. It builds its own resistances, modifies the direction of social development and sometimes forces the law to perform in practice what its rhetoric of impartiality declares. Without abandoning a notion of the state as a means of control, Thompson presents popular struggles as actually constitutive of state policies and state forms. They are a principle of movement in the whole system.

We have taken a great deal from the popular histories and from radical sociologies with a similar perspective. We have tried to view post-war history from a standpoint on the side of subordinated or oppressed classes and social groups. We have stressed the formative influence of popular interests and experience as the ground or basis of politics itself. We have looked at a long history of popular educational struggles, including working-class counter-education of an independent kind. In general, taking the popular standpoint seems to us a prerequisite for any socialism worth the name.

Yet, taking the viewpoint of the people is a much more complex business in analysis today than, for example, in writing about the counter-revolution in the 1790s or the Chartist insurgency of the 1830s and 1840s. It necessarily involves lengthy evaluations of the agencies that claim to represent working-class people, especially, nearer the present day, the Labour Party and the trade unions. It involves the recognition that whole sections of the population, with specific and important interests in education – most working-class mothers for instance – are not represented adequately at all. It necessarily involves looking at struggles, in and around the schools, that are not normally regarded as political, but exercise their own force on outcomes at an individual or structural level. It may involve, in the end, a quite fundamental questioning of what passes as politics today – of the content of policy, but also of its peculiar political forms. Such questions are best discussed in particular cases. The problem of the popularity of the Labour Party, for example, is a key issue for this book and the whole question of the nature of popular interests in education and of the ways in which they might be represented is, similarly, central to the argument.

Although there are important and interesting examples, notably the work of Brian Simon, [13] popular histories have not been the most common way of writing about education in the 1970s. The dominant tradition, especially on the left, has been more 'sociological'. We do not intend, in this introduction, to review the field of the sociology of education – partly because sociologists will figure as active makers of history in the account that follows! We want, however, to stress our debts to, and our quarrels with, a third body of critical writing relevant to our theme: Marxist, neo-Marxist or Marxist-feminist accounts of the state, the state's ideological functions and of the relation between state policy and the requirements of capitals.

If the historian's question has been 'how was this system produced?' these theorists have concentrated on the question 'how does the education system function?' or 'what work does it perform for other institutions or interests?' This investigation has rarely been concerned with the experiences of the policy-makers or of the dominated: it has rested on a more external appraisal of the structures of domination. Since most of the theorists have been Marxist or Marx-influenced, they have been interested mainly in the functions which education performs for capital, capitalism or for the reproduction of social classes. The intellectual pedigree of much of the writing can be traced back to Marx's discussion of 'reproduction' in *Capital*, especially the discussion of the reproduction of labour power and of the working class, texts to which we will return.

We have, then, accounts of how the schools, as 'ideological state apparatuses' reproduce capitalist relations of production.[14] We have an important history of schooling in the USA, organized around the argument that schools replicate, in their social relations, the conditions and mentalities of capitalist labour.[15] We have an extended sociological investigation of schooling as a form of 'symbolic violence', reinforcing the unequal distribution of cultural resources and securing the existing relations of power.[16] As part of a long British tradition of the investigation of schooling and class, we have Bernstein's arguments that schools reproduce inequalities by institutionalizing the cultural criteria of sections of the dominant class.[17] Latterly, similar questions have been posed by feminists and Marxist-feminists concerned to understand the systematic disadvantages of girls in schooling, or to relate an analysis of sex—gender relations or 'patriarchy' to the traditional Marxist categories of class and exploitation.[18] Work on schooling has formed a relatively small part of a more general revival of Marxist theory and research. Much of this has focused on the labour process and the conditions of work, on the nature of the state in 'late capitalism', on the meaning of welfarism in the post-war period and on the character of the political crises of the 1970s.[19]

Our approach has been formed, in large part, by debates within these currents. Specific debts will become clear in the course of the argument, but we also share a rather widespread dissatisfaction with some features of this theoretical work, despite the real deepening of knowledge which it represents. With notable exceptions, much of the work has been very abstract and very unhistorical. It has often been informed by the grand ambition of presenting working models of large social totalities — hence a stress on the systematic logic or structure of social processes. A strongly conservative, or, more correctly, pessimistic strand has been present in the theories, coexisting oddly with a more hopeful tone. The force of the arguments often makes it very difficult to see how a popular politics (of education or of anything else) may interrupt or modify the work which schools carry out in the reproduction of capitalist relations, of political domination, or of existing structures of material and cultural inequality. Paradoxically, the critical power of these theories reinforced their pessimism. In a sense, indeed, pessimism was the mission of the theorists. In Britain, North America and France, main targets have been liberal or social democratic expectations about progress through schooling. The older 'utopianism' was replaced by a realism bordering on despair. Capitalist societies were seen as deeply and intrinsically unfair; schooling mirrored these inequalities, reinforcing or reproducing them, making change more difficult by hiding injustice or rendering it legitimate. There was no lack of sympathetic identification with the subordinated populations in these accounts, but there was a virtual suppression of the possibility of struggle. Very often, indeed, agency and politics, as such, disappeared, or was supplied in a postscript.[20] Those who looked to theory for practical guidance were told mainly about the constraints on their action and the huge and marvellously intricate apparatus of social control. They learnt plenty about what was *not* worth doing, much less about what to do.

All this poses considerable dilemmas for anyone wanting to understand recent developments in a way that may help to inform political practice. If we are interested in the explanation of continuity and change in the history of schooling, modern Marxism offers very powerful tools of analysis. Politically, however, this contribution is problematic: much of the knowledge has remained too abstract and too purely critical to help in the development of alternative practices. The problem is now to draw on these insights in a way that gives a central place to struggle and to a conscious willed politics, to disorganized and diffuse resistances, but also to more organized political forces with their own theories and strategies. More abstractly, the problem is to combine a concern with structural conditions, and the logic of process or function, with a concern with agency, will and active human energies. We do not attempt to solve this problem in this chapter (or this book), but it is worth presenting, in advance, some of the general arguments which underpin our more detailed historical accounts. [21]

Conditions, needs and requirements

A useful starting point is to consider the uses made of notions like conditions, needs and requirements. They are often discussed in the context of the problem of reproduction, or of the way in which societies, particular social relations or institutions are perpetuated or maintained. This form of analysis is not necessarily conservative (as in structural-functionalism) or pessimistic (as in much Marxist theory). It allows us to identify certain structural features or mechanisms (in capitalism the subordination of the labourer to the capitalist) and therefore to envisage how such a society might be transformed. The argument takes this form: 'if this condition and that condition continue to be met, the society will remain a capitalist one; if this set of relations is no longer sustained, then some of the conditions of transition are present'.

This is a common way of arguing in Marx's *Capital.* [22] Capitalism requires fresh supplies of labourers, appropriately skilled and willing to labour. The reproduction of the working class implies not only biological procreation (about the conditions of which Marx has very little to say), but also 'the transmission and accumulation of skills from one generation to another'. [23] It involves the reproduction of a whole class of wage labourers and a particular social relation between labourer and capitalist which Marx calls 'the capital-relation itself'. [24]

This very abstract, simplified discussion of what Marx calls 'simple reproduction' is helpful for more concrete analysis. It draws attention to one set of connections that link educational arrangements to the conditions of capitalist production. It shows us that capital, or more correctly, different capitals, have stakes in the cultural forms in which labour is reproduced. Historically we find an almost continuous concern, especially in debates about schooling, with the quantity and quality of labour power. There is a recurrent image of the perfect worker, from the self-respecting 'mechanic' of the mid nineteenth century, through the militaristically marshalled mass workers of the 1890s or the upskilled comprehensively educated school leavers of the 1960s, to the modern subjects of the Manpower Services Commission complete with 'employability' and 'social and life skills'. [25]

However we cannot go on to construct a whole account of the development of schooling from these very slender materials. This is clear from a second type of discussion of conditions in *Capital*, which takes the form of 'historical sketches'.

The objects here are not the logical conditions of capital accumulation, but the detailed circumstances in which these needs were met, or transformed. Marx's account of 'the so-called primitive accumulation' traces how the conditions for early capitalist development were established through bitter and prolonged social struggles over the concentration of capital and the expropriation of small independent producers.[26] His account of the Factory Acts and the limitation of the length of the working day shows how popular struggles actually modified the way in which capital employed labour, giving rise to *new* requirements and needs. [27] These two forms of analysis — the logical and the historical — are distinct but interdependent: the first gives us knowledge about what is at issue if capitalism is to survive or develop; the second gives us an account of how certain outcomes actually occurred.

Our point here is to indicate some pitfalls in arguments about requirements which are not always avoided in the theoretical writing on education. The chief danger is to move imperceptibly from one form of analysis to the other, without fully marking the difference: from conditions to outcomes, from theory to history. Two main transformations may then occur. First, it is assumed that *conditions are continuously met* and that the 'system' reproduces itself in the same old forms. 'Conditions', in other words, cease to be conditional: they become functional *necessities*. The sense that their realization depends on the outcome of struggles, which include but are not limited to forms of willed and conscious politics, may be altogether lost. Second, there is too swift a move from simple description, theory, or abstraction to the full account of complex, concrete historical events and determinations. The relations described in a logical, simplified and schematic way are held to work, *just like that* in the historical sequences, uncomplicated by *further* relations and determinations, many not yet grasped theoretically. Theory is realized in history without additions to and transformations of the categories. This tendency, which we would call in a general way 'functionalist', involves a drastic simplification of history. It also tends to make historical social relations more or less self-reproducing, eternal and immune to collective human control. According to Marxist accounts, the system which is reproduced is fundamentally unfair and contradictory — whereas in structural-functionalist sociology or pluralist political science, the system is basically liberal, progressive and easily reformed. But as critics have often pointed out, particular forms of functionalism are indeed common to both traditions, or to tendencies within them. [28]

One corrective to all this is to write and think more 'historically'. By historically, we do not merely mean in a way that is concerned with the past, though this longer historical reach is important. We refer to two main features of the best historical work: first, a concern with close and detailed description and analysis, firmly set in time and place and, second, a preoccupation with continuity and especially with change, with crisis and with transformations. There is, in our view, a close association between historical understanding in *this* sense and a hopeful, progressive, politics.

Historical work should not however be thought of as antithetical to theory.[29] All historical accounts have premises of their own about the nature of knowledge and about the general characteristics of societies or of social relations. It is equally important to close the gap between theory and history from the other, theoretical, side: to make theories more complex as well as histories more theoretical. The more subtle and more complex our general thinking becomes, the better we are able to make sense of the confusion and muddle of everyday life and immediate appearances. In the context of this book, we aim for a complex Marxism, modified by what can be learned from other traditions and from the theorization of *further* contingencies. This means, among other things, that it is useful to think about determinations on or within 'education' aside from capital's requirements for self-reproduction. Only when we have done this can we return to 'capital's needs' with a more developed sense of their conditionality and their dependence on struggle.

In the rest of this chapter, we try to make explicit our view of these other determinations on schooling's outcomes, some of which can be considered within the terms of a Marxist tradition, others of which require theoretical innovations. Our account here is bound to be somewhat truncated because our priority is to deliver a critical history. But there are four main areas of elaboration:

1 A more complex view of capital's needs and strategies.
2 A view of the place of schools in society which stresses the relations of the family to the school and the centrality, in schooling, of age and gender relations.
3 A drawing out of the implications of the structural location of school for the popular politics of schooling, especially the political importance of representations of parenthood and the centrality of cultural and ideological processes.
4 The dependence of educational politics on the conditions of formal politics more generally.

A more complex view of requirements

In any specific historical situation industry's needs for labour power are themselves extremely complex: these are not so much a question of the 'requirements of capital' as the needs of different, coexisting capitals. A different 'educational' logic attaches to different forms of capitalist business, depending on technical organization and the hierarchies of labour. Labour-intensive industries, employing large numbers of routine labourers, have diffcrent needs to those of highly automated technically sophisticated industries. Both forms, however, may be served by the same set of institutions. There is therefore a problem, of satisfying or approximating to different demands, which is resolved only by political means. State agencies, where these conflicts are condensed, become a site of struggles between different sections of capital.

Demands in relation to labour power are never simply a matter of skill or technique. Recent analyses, including those developed later in this book, stress the subjective aspects of the preparation of labour power, the 'need' to win the consent of the human bearers of labour power to tasks which rob them of control over their labour, over their life activity itself.[30] If schooling is to contribute to reproducing the hierarchies of control, it faces acutely contradictory demands: to develop in some the desire to manage the labour of others, in others a limited technical mastery and, for the great majority of young people, to ease the transition towards essentially subordinate positions in the hierarchies of labour.

Capital's needs moreover are not adequately grasped from this viewpoint alone, the viewpoint of labour and production. Capital also has requirements in relation to consumption: expanded consumption involves the creation of new needs, new pleasures, new desires, If schools 'produce' labourers, do they not 'produce' consumers too?[31]

A similar argument applies to the conditions of the production of fresh labourers and consumers, to biological procreation, to sex—gender relations and to particular forms of the family. As we shall be arguing, the significance of gender relations in education is by no means exhausted by their intersections with capital's requirements, but the connections are, nonetheless, very close. Since at least the late nineteenth century, the figure of the perfect worker (usually male) has been accompanied by the figure of the perfect reproducer of labour power, the 'mother' as constructed by discourses about 'population' or 'national efficiency'. In the era of mass consumption, women have also acquired a key significance as buyers and consumers, while capital's labour forces have been deeply structured by sexual divisions especially as more women have entered waged work since the war.[32] Again, in concrete analyses, the picture is extremely complex, but capitals certainly have a stake in the forms of sex—gender relations and therefore have 'needs' in relation to them too.

There are two further sets of relations to be considered. We have assumed so far that what capitals 'need', schools and colleges can indeed deliver. It will be one of the themes of this book that, especially in the 1960s, the tightness of this relation was enormously exaggerated. Schools are very specific kinds of institutions, capable only of very specific effects. They cannot, for instance, 'reproduce the relations of production'.[33] Schools do not themselves create the complex structures of labour and management, or the social places of shopkeeper and technician, mother and father. These are reproduced in other social sites in quite other processes.[34] The characteristic contribution of school systems is to 'prepare' persons to occupy these places, but even this 'function' has to be understood complexly. As we shall see, much more is involved in schooling than that.

Beyond a certain point, the language of requirements and needs is itself likely to mislead. If we view the matter from the standpoint of an agent of capital, we will find different possible strategies for accumulation rather than singular, inflexible requirements. Some of these may involve educational solutions; but most will not. Some possible solutions, ideal perhaps from the perspective of production requirements, will be limited or blocked by the need to attend to other considerations, notably the resistance of workers, or consumers, or conservative family forms. Historically, capitalism has always attempted to remove inhibitions to its self-expansion, but finds limits to it both in those social spaces it has not yet fully transformed and in those groups whom it dispossesses and threatens to throw hither and thither in conformity with its needs. Our ideal capitalist agent (nowadays a panel of experts perhaps) must attend to all these features and contradictions, but we should not assume that a perfect knowledge of them is possessed. Some solutions, which are possible structurally, may not yet have entered the conscious knowledge of the panel, nor of the high-powered think-tank that advises government ministers planning for a higher rate of growth. Experts are often simply wrong. It is, however, in the course of such calculations that a particular regime of needs is defined. It becomes part of a conscious strategy for expansion or survival and may be pursued and argued for in appropriate political forms.

This may be clearer if we return to our historical cases of the perfect worker and the perfect mother. These historical constructs have always been accompanied by others which reveal the presence in workers, in parents and in children of qualities quite the reverse of those required. The distance between ideal and reality is testimony to capital's 'need' to put up with adverse conditions, to adapt around them, to find another route to expansion. In this context, the definition of 'need' belongs also to political processes, designed to convince fellow managers, or politicians, or populace that desirable outcomes really are absolute necessities. All this is not to abandon a more careful analysis of conditions which may show, precisely, the limits of adaptability — but it is a major theoretical and political error to give to every feature of society that seems favourable to a capitalist future the status of a necessary condition. One effect of this ascription is to deny the possibility of major structural change and to abandon what, for socialism and feminism alike, is an important ground of argument: that current problems can be solved only if certain fundamental conditions are transformed. We may say that although schools do not simply function for capitals, and could never do so without contradictions, capitals certainly have stakes in schooling. How real these stakes become, how tightly schools are reduced to their training functions, how far education *becomes* capitalist schooling depends on the strength of resistances and the resultant balances of forces. It is to these non-capitalist or popular elements in schooling that we must now turn.

Schooling in society

Just as historical accounts depend upon theoretical positions (which should be openly argued), so more abstract thinking always refers to historical situations (of which theory should always be conscious). In what follows we assume broadly 'modern' conditions — for Britain mainly post second world war, except where we specifically refer to earlier periods. We assume a developed system of state schooling at primary, secondary and tertiary levels, with universal (but unequal) access to the first two. We assume compulsion to attend school and a developed 'democratic' educational climate in which access to schooling is seen as a universal right of citizenship. We assume a formally democratic political system with its own developed relations of power and legitimation. We also assume the massive post-war expansion of the means of public communication as an organic part of broader political processes. We assume, finally, the characteristic modern separation, in terms of geographical place and dominant social relations, of the social sites of the family, the school and waged labour.

('Site' indicates a particular *social* space but also has useful connotations of institutional or material hardness — literally 'the school down the road'. The play on building [as in 'building site'] is also intended: sites have always been constructed, always have a history, involving destruction and renovation. They are also sites of particular kinds of labour. Sites may be analysed in their relations to economic activity — hence the sites of production or consumption or reproduction — but may also be defined by legal and other regulative practices. We find this notion useful — if still underdeveloped and imprecise. When we refer to schools as sites we want to draw attention to all these features. Central to the question of the place of schooling in society, then, is its relation to other social sites from which, historically, it has already been distinguished.)[35]

By making these assumptions we do not wish to imply that what has occurred historically is natural, necessary or desirable. One of our recurrent arguments will be that it is necessary to question separations such as these, in thought and practice, in order to act constructively for better *educational* (in the broader sense) solutions. This will relate closely to our criticism of dominant left strategies in education which, initially for good reasons, have deepened these divisions so that they have come to tyrannize over us. The equation of schooling with education, and even with knowledge as such, is a case in point. Another is the tendency to believe, on the basis of the very existence of 'the education system', that education is a matter which concerns mainly teachers, children and adolescents and concerns other adults only in their capacities as parents. As we shall see, there have been historical alternatives to these ways of thinking which it is important to recover.

We may start from the recognition that the modern school faces two ways: towards wage labour and the tasks of housewife and mother on the one side, and towards the child's family of origin on the other. We have seen that capitals have a stake, particularly, in the relation of school to wage labour. There are popular interests too in this relation, but as with all popular interests in education, they usually find expression in a highly mediated or indirect form. Direct popular organization around the school—work relationship has, historically, been quite rare and, in this significant absence, attention to the school—work relation tends to *mean* attention to the needs of capital and of organized bureaucracies in the professions and in the state. Much more commonly, popular interests have been expressed in relation to the family, and particularly through the crucial figure of 'the parent'. It is for this reason that we wish to stress the importance of the family in the school—family—production complex.

As we suggested earlier, social sites may be distinguished in part by the dominant social relations to be found there. These differences are never exclusive and, in historical analysis, social relations of different kinds are hard to disentangle especially in their combined effects. Nonetheless, it is useful to think of 'the factory' (in shorthand) as the main site of the reproduction of class relations, and the family as strongly organized around relations of gender, sexuality and age. By 'gender' we mean the socially constructed forms of masculinity and femininity. By 'sexuality' we mean the bodily capacities of males and females for sexual pleasure and for procreation as these too are shaped by social relations and by culture. By age we refer mainly to child—adult relations, which, though they have a physiological aspect, have also been historically very varied. The child—adult difference, for example, has been more or less accentuated, or defined in different ways.

The main historical form of both sex—gender and child—adult relations has been patriarchal. The forms of patriarchy have differed historically and, within the same society, by class, status and ethnic group. They are continually modified, even in the intimacy of 'the couple', by what an older common sense used to call 'the battle of the sexes'. There are common elements across these diverse situations, however, which warrant the (sparing) use of a single general category — 'patriarchy'. Complexly different arrangements have produced similar results: the dominance of the husband—father—male and, more specifically, his control of the labour, the means of subsistence, the procreative capacity and the sexuality of other members of the family—household. These are certainly some of the main structural supports of the persistent historical fact of the subordination of women.[36]

It is important that we are not misunderstood at this point. We are *not* saying that relations of class have no influence on the forms of familial organization (or, for that matter, that patriarchy has no effects on women's waged labour!). Gender is intimately connected with class. Gender differences, indeed, are partly constructed in relation to the class organization of economic life. The salience of waged labour for the construction of working-class masculinity and the salience of 'work' (or its refusal) for all men is a case in point. Rather we want to assert the absolute centrality of patriarchal relations for the family and to insist that this accentuating of gender and age has effects in other social sites.[37] The family is not, therefore, a merely dependent institution, with no determinacy of its own. It is not merely transformed by capitalism and by the development of schooling: it, or its salient relations, also contribute to the complex of determinations on schooling in absolutely central ways. Indeed, it has systematically shaped the very conception of 'education' itself.

We can now look at this from the vantage point of the history of schooling and the modern character of the school. Historically, a useful illustration is compulsory attendance. Compulsory attendance, generally enforced in Britain between the 1870s and 1900s, was certainly a breach of the father's right to dispose of the labour of his children. It also radically reorganized the family economy, especially of the poor. But the authority of the modern school was also founded upon the father's authority. The first official image of the professional schoolteacher was the substitute parent;[38] even now the authority of the school over the child is exercised *in loco parentis*. [39] The actual practice of enforcement, in past and present, has also been deeply influenced by the different familial roles of boys and girls, not only by official definitions, but also by a popular common sense.[40]

Similarly, schools now take something of their character from each adjacent site. On their homely side, they are places for the care of children and the development of aptitudes and sociality. This involves practices that are thought appropriate for women and are, in fact, commonly performed by them. Nursery, infant and junior schools are especially appropriate foci for the development of child-centred and humanistic educational ideas which have, as Bernstein has suggested, a definite relation to the family life of sections of the professional middle class. Age and sex—gender relations organize schools, including secondary schools, in almost every aspect of their operation, shaping the school experience quite as powerfully as relations of class. Working-class girls are bound into a particularly tight circle here: from dependent, but often 'responsible' positions in their family of origin, by way of a characteristically feminine path through school, to a destiny that is usually thought of in primarily gendered terms as 'girlfriend', 'housewife' and 'mother'.[41]

Relations of age are equally important in structuring the experience of school. They are intimately involved, for instance, in the way education prepares a future work force. We have already argued against an abstract functionalism here, but school is certainly one site, perhaps the most important one, where young people acquire an orientation towards places in the adult world. These subjective orientations are marked out by examination results and certificates which become signs for employers. There is a growing body of research which argues that the subjective identifications of young people constitute the decisive moment of preparation for different forms of labour. Even resistance in school, for boys and girls alike, takes the form of the assertion of adulthood.[42]

Political implications of the structural location of school

The politics of schooling are deeply influenced by the family—school connection, and, more specifically, by the social construction of childhood as a stage of dependence on adults and by that semi-possession of a child which is parenthood. The salience of child—adult relations means that there are always two levels of struggles in relation to schooling: there are struggles *within* the schools, in which children and teachers are the most active participants, and there are struggles *over* schooling from which children and adolescents are excluded and in which the figure of the parent carries the full weight of popular interests. It is parents who are directly addressed in debates about schooling; it is their consent, on behalf of 'their' children, which is won or lost.

There is, however, nothing self-evident about the character and content of parental interests in education. Versions of parenthood differ greatly. Parents may be addressed, as in discussions of 'parental choice', as individuals responsible for *their children.* But they may also appear as a group with a larger social responsibility for *'our' children*, even for *all the children.* In the 1940s, for example, parents were addressed as active, participating citizens, contributing not just to their own child's welfare, but the shape and character of the system of schooling as a whole.[43] The content of parental wishes may also differ radically. One common polarity, for example, is that between humanistic views of education (wanting an all-round development of faculties) and a stress on future occupation (wanting an appropriate training). Similarly, the definition of parental interests may take an oppositional and even a socialist form, or be more or less in conformity with capitalist requirements.

The construction of parenthood will be a recurrent preoccupation throughout this book, but it is a specific instance of a more general problem: the relation between popular knowledge and experience on the one hand, and the representation of educational issues in public debates on the other.

Culture, ideology and the field of public representations

We will be centrally concerned, in this book, with these three key terms and with the processes they designate. By *culture* we understand the shared principles of life, characteristic of particular classes, groups or social *milieux.* Cultures are produced as groups make sense of their social existence in the course of everyday experience. Culture is intimate, therefore, with the world of practical action. It suffices, for most of the time, for managing everyday life. Since, however, this everyday world is itself problematic, culture must perforce take complex and heterogeneous forms, 'not at all free from contradictions'.[44]

This usage is close to those of the founding texts of 'cultural studies' and much recent social history.[45] It is also similar to what Antonio Gramsci, the theorist and leader of Italian communism in the 1920s and 1930s, called 'common sense' — 'the "spontaneous philosophy" which is proper to everyone'. Under common sense Gramsci included 'language itself' as 'a totality of determined notions and concepts', popular religion and 'the entire system of beliefs, superstitions, opinions, ways of seeing things and of acting, which are collectively bundled together under the name of "folklore" '.[46]

By *representations* we understand conceptions of the world which in a different moment of their circulation take on a different form.[47] Ideas and feelings may be distanced from immediate practical activity. They may appear, for example, in popular television programmes or as academic books. This depends in part on a social division: the division of mental and manual labour, and the emergence of what Marx called 'the thinkers of the class', 'active, conceptive ideologists' and 'producers of ideas': in other words, 'intellectuals' of different kinds.[48] Gramsci makes a similar point when he distinguishes 'common sense' and 'philosophy', associating the latter with coherent and developed intellectual forms, though for Gramsci the term 'intellectual' is much wider than its ordinary English usage.[49] In modern societies this division of labour has acquired very elaborate forms: whole sets of institutions are organized around the production of ideas, especially education

systems and the modern media. If we are interested in the ways in which
consciousness is formed, we cannot stop at the level of lived beliefs. Beliefs,
conceptions and feelings are not only carried in the minds of human subjects;
they are also written down, communicated, 'put into circulation', inscribed in
physical objects, reproduced in institutions and rituals and embodied in all kinds
of codes. They can be studied in 'texts' of all kinds; not only books, pamphlets
or newspapers, but also visual images and aural media. Indeed, there is hardly a
human product that cannot be analysed in this way since all have a symbolic or
communicative value whatever else they are useful for.[50]

Certain forms of representation are closely associated with formal politics and
'public life'. This is especially the case with the press and television. It is this
sphere, the sphere of 'public opinion', which we call the field of public representations. It has its own characteristic practices and its own patterns of inclusion and
exclusion. Those who are involved in practical activity may find their own activity
re-presented back to them by the media, not simply inverted or reflected as in a
mirror, but always systematically transformed according to the practices of the
medium itself.

By *ideology* we refer to particular forms of such transformations. Ideas are
properly called ideological when they can be shown to conceal or to resolve in an
idealistic or imaginary way the problematic character of social life. In the process
of presenting a particular social order as harmonious, natural or in need of rescue
from subversion or decay, ideological accounts serve also to secure the position of
dominant social groups. Ideology is necessarily, in this view, a critical concept with
a particular and limited scope of application.[51] In this book, we are especially
interested in the ideological aspects of the field of public representations about
'education'.

In the 1970s, as recurrently before, schools figured very largely in public debates —
as news in the media, as issues in party politics. The actual workings of the schools
(including the cultures of schooling) were represented to teachers and pupils, to
industrialists, to 'parents' and to the 'public'. We shall be looking at this process
in more detail in Chapter 10, but we should note, in advance, two main features.
First, public representations of schools are constructed at some distance from the
processes they are meant to describe. The media fix on a particular example. They
rip it from its concrete context. They connect it, as a signal instance, to a whole
field of pre-formed arguments. It becomes a *cause célèbre* or further evidence of a
generalized malaise. Such representations are always highly constructed and may
be heavily ideological. Yet, our second main point is that we have to take
seriously the effects of such representations and their attendant ideologies. They
are intimately linked to political processes and ultimately to policy. The history
of the last fifteen to twenty years is an example of this: over this period the whole
field of debate about education has been transformed and this has been accompanied
by an equally dramatic shift in the direction of state policy.

Charting this history, we have looked closely at public discourses of all kinds:

political programmes and debates ('great' and puny), media representations and the professional knowledges of the field, especially the sociology and economics of education. The nature of this work produces a characteristic temptation: to infer the state of popular opinion about schooling from the field of public representations. There are several reasons, however, why this is a completely illegitimate procedure.

First, we know enough now about processes of cultural struggle and reproduction to say that all models which assume a system of perfect communication or transmission are hopelessly crude. Work on education processes, for example, the paradigmatic case of the transmission model, shows that all pedagogies involve transformations, blockings, inversions and complex reproductions, never simple teaching and learning.[52] We can now see that cultural moments which were previously thought of as passive, including the stereotypical case of 'watching television', involve active appropriations and transformations of meaning. 'Reading' itself (which in this context includes listening and watching) is a process of cultural *production,* or the production of meanings. There is, perhaps, nothing particularly surprising in this discovery; if we think hard for five minutes about what happens in our heads when we (not some mythical passive other) read a book, the active character of reading can be swiftly recalled.

Second, to infer popular knowledge from public representations, as if the first were an effect of the second, is to neglect the possibility that the causal sequence may run the other way. The media themselves may (and in fact commonly do) appropriate elements of common sense understandings, transform them and offer them back to 'the public' in this different form. We have, in fact, to think of these transformations as part of a complex circuit running *either* way, not as a one-way sequence.

Third, inferences of this kind take no account of the different social positions occupied by collective 'audiences'. It is a feature of public representations that they conceal these differences, especially differences of class, gender and race. A good example is the figure of the parent itself as it appears in public discourses. It is a deeply ideological figure. It systematically conceals the different relations to schooling of middle-class and working-class parents.[53] It disguises the very particular stake which mothers have in the education of their children, the way in which schooling regulates the mother's own life at every turn. It homogenizes the 'parental community' in a way that is completely misleading. It also makes it difficult to think freshly and clearly about child—adult relations themselves, naturalizing the non-citizenship of the child and the exclusive public responsibility of the parent. After all, why should it mainly be parents who, on the popular side, have a right to a say in educational arrangements? Should not all citizens, irrespective of their familial status, have such a say? What appears as a 'democratic' image in education debates, is in fact a very restrictive one, which defines and regulates at the same time as it gives 'rights'. One problem for an adequate popular politics is to break out of 'parentdom' or transform the category itself.

Education and formal politics

We can look at popular interests in education from the point of their (more or less ideological) definition, but we can also consider their 'representation' in another but allied sense of this word: the extent to which they are expressed in formal political arrangements. It is useful to think of formal politics too as a social site with its own characteristic social organization. By formal politics we mean political arrangements in the narrow sense: the apparatuses of parliament, political parties, electoral procedures, voting and party-political combat.

We can look at these political arrangements with two related questions in mind: the extent to which parties represent the range of relevant interests, and the extent to which the rules of formal politics exclude whole areas of legitimate struggle and define them as 'non political'.

Clearly, some relevant educational interests are not represented at all. Children and 'young people' are a very clear case. The political position of persons under 18 is still that of women before 1918. Other groups are formally represented (they have the vote) but not effectively. They are lumped in with other constituencies in a way that makes it impossible for their distinctive interests to be expressed. We have already noted the case of mothers, especially working-class mothers, but this argument would also apply to black people as a whole. Feminist and black organizations have started to raise such issues, but politics tends to be dominated by masculine and white middle-class definitions of political significance: by principles of policy and 'great public issues' rather than the daily grind. [54]

Historically, the Labour Party has played the most important role in representing popular educational interests. From its foundation to the end of the second world war it formed part of a progressive educational alliance (discussed in Chapter 2), demanding the expansion of schooling. The Conservative Party was, by contrast, the party of educational reaction in this period. [55] That these associations were a matter of history and contingency and not a matter of an inexorable class logic comes out very clearly from the post-war story. The erosion of the Labour Party's popular base and the rise of an educational Toryism claiming popular support are among the organizing themes of this book.

If we are thinking of the connection between political parties and popular interests (which parties also help to define), we need to consider and to qualify the general adjective 'popular'. So far we have used this term mainly in opposition to others: to mean, in fact, 'not directly related to the needs of capital'. But we have also suggested, in the discussion of parentdom, that unspecific terms like this may be very treacherous. Their advantage is that they allow us to include constituencies usually excluded from consideration altogether, not just 'the working class', but also black people, women in different classes and ethnic groups, children, 'intermediate' social groups (like teachers) and so on. There may also be a sense in which all these groups — 'the people' — do have certain interests in common against, say, large capital and the state bureaucracies.

In what follows we use the term 'popular' to refer to such constituencies. We use the term 'populist' with its somewhat pejorative connotations to designate forms of politics which systematically disguise the complex and antagonistic formation of popular forces. For there are undoubtedly major *differences* of interest between these forces too; witness the way gender-based struggles cut right through any popular alliance of this kind. In education differences of interest by class, race and gender are particularly important.

Finally, in this section, we want to draw attention to the strategic location of certain social groups in the popular politics of education: narrowly, those who perform predominantly intellectual functions in the society, and, more broadly, groups we will refer to as the professional middle class.

Intellectual functions (thinking about politics) are important in all political struggles. Education is peculiar, however, in actually being *about* the social constitution and distribution of intellectual functions: the production of 'intellectuals'. Schooling is a particular form of such production and reinforces the strong division of labour between intellectuals and not-intellectuals-at-all which is especially sharply accentuated in cultural life in Britain. Struggles over the education system are struggles over intellectual functions, monopolies, distribution, qualification and access, and also over the dominant forms of intellectualism itself.[56]

Teachers, especially where they are also active in trade unions and professional bodies, are obviously central to the popular politics of schooling, not least because they combine the two levels of struggle: struggles in and struggles over schools. Their relation to other popular constituencies, especially working-class parents, is peculiarly contradictory. But this goes for other professionals too, especially educational researchers and educational experts in universities — academics who make a profession of the study of pedagogy or curricula. This 'educational interest' belongs to a broader social *milieu* with two major characteristics: first, a relative distance from the management and control of economic activity, whether financial activity or productive industry; second, a high degree of dependence on personal skills which are closely associated with formal education and certification.[57] Such groups have a particularly intimate stake in the education system, both in terms of their own employment (many are employees of the state if not of the education system) and in terms of family strategies for their own children. They are likely to be more knowledgeable than others about the internal working of schools and about the complexities of individual advancement by this route. They are likely to play a particularly important — and also highly ambiguous — role in educational politics as a whole.

Hegemony, settlement and crises

We can now see something of the complexity of the determinations on educational policy. As we shall be arguing, throughout this book, but especially in relation to the 1970s, the needs of capitalist industry do exercise a major influence on the character and structure of the education system. This influence operates in a number of different ways: through the commitment of governments to secure national economic goals in capitalist terms, through the political pressures exercised by representatives of capitalist business, through the structural over-representation of dominant interests in the apparatuses of the state and, at a deeper level, through the life experience of parents, pupils and teachers whose educational expectations are necessarily shaped by the social relations in which they stand. These relations involve power and dependency. They confer unequal powers to achieve desires or satisfy needs: class over class, men over women, white over black, adult over child. These inequalities are condensed and reinforced in formal political processes and in the apparatuses of the state, but they have, as we shall see, a deep influence on the aspirations and subjectivities of those in dependent positions. The sheer solidity of capitalist social organization and of the structural subordination of women has itself a massive 'educational' influence.

Human beings are implicated in these social relations, but *actively*; because the relations are unequal or asymmetrical, activity involves struggle. For this reason, the power of dominant interests is never secure; it always has to be won. Following Gramsci, we use the term 'hegemony' to sum up this process on a societal level.[58] Hegemony involves securing both the conditions for future capitalist production and the consent of the subordinated population to the social and cultural implications of 'progress'. It is exercised not only through law and coercion, but also through 'educative' processes in a larger sense, including schooling, the media and, centrally, political parties. It necessitates the building of alliances that may be active in promoting new solutions. Hegemony is not uniquely a product of 'the state' but involves the institutions of 'civil society' too.

If hegemony refers to the overall relations of force in a society, we wish to use the term 'educational settlement' to refer to the balance of forces in and over schooling. Settlements entail, at this 'regional' rather than 'global' level, some more or less enduring set of solutions to capital's educational needs, the putting together of a dominant alliance of forces, and a more widespread recruitment of popular support or inducement of popular indifference.

Settlements are highly unstable and deeply contradictory arrangements which easily pass into crises. One way of understanding the history of educational policy is in terms of the succession of crises and settlements. In the post-war period, we identify four such phases: the educational settlement of 1944 and of the 1950s, with origins going back to the 1930s, and a generative moment in the war itself; the critique of this settlement, and especially of tripartitism that developed in the late 1950s and early 1960s; the installation of educational expansion of an avowedly egalitarian kind in the 1960s; and the collapse of the 1960s' settlement and of its associated alliance in the 1970s. One of the purposes of the later sections of this book will be to consider the forms of and the conditions of struggle over, the emergent educational settlement of the 1980s.

2 Popular dilemmas, radical strategies and the inter-war Labour Party

The range of historical phenomena representing popular educational aspirations and dilemmas has been huge. It has included forms of popular activity usually regarded as neither 'educational' nor 'political': the forms of resistance of working-class pupils in schools, the use of non-school facilities as educational resources (all the informal ways of learning in the home, peer group, neighbourhood, or place of work) and the patterns of behaviour associated with school attendance, especially revealing of popular attitudes to schooling before the coming of compulsory attendance. In this chapter, however, we are mainly concerned with organized forms of popular politics and, in particular, with a definite historical succession usually summed up in such terms as 'the Labour movement' or 'the working-class movement'.

We will consider some of the main forms of organized popular struggle over education from the early nineteenth century to the period before the second world war. No full history is possible here, but there are several reasons why a longer historical perspective is important. It is essential that our general understandings are not limited by the particular features of the period most closely in view: from the mid 1930s to the present day. We shall argue later that a feature of the 1950s and 1960s was the failure of formal educational politics, especially of the Labour Party, to address the educational dilemmas of the popular constituencies, especially those of the working class. From a standpoint in the post-war period and within Labour's tradition, it is easily assumed that there are no distinctive popular interests in education, or none that cannot easily be catered for in the 'usual' routines of formal educational politics. Within a longer historical view, this assumption can be challenged, the specific features of the post-war decades grasped and new possibilities more easily imagined. Contemporary or near-contemporary historians lack the full benefits of hindsight, but they may compensate by comparing their own period with earlier formations.

Once a long history of popular struggles over education has been brought to view, we may compare the various strategies that have been adopted and relate them to current dilemmas. We can place modern educational strategies, especially those of the left, in a larger comparative context. We may be able to see their strengths and limitations, what is necessary about them and what can be and needs to be transformed.

A further reason for looking at earlier periods concerns the centrality of the Labour Party in our later argument. The period from the early 1920s to the mid

1930s is especially important here. The inter-war politics of education form the
immediate pre-history of the story we want to tell in more detail. It was the
politics of *this* phase that were thrown into crisis in the events leading up to the
passage of the 1944 Act. But some of the key features of later Labour Party
policy were also formed in this phase, especially the commitment to educational
progress through state policy and the neglect of a more direct popular educational
connection. Later Labour Party policy was, in many ways, an elaboration of this
early stance in profoundly changed circumstances. We will end this chapter, then,
with a closer look at early Labour Party policy, especially through R. H. Tawney,
Labour's leading educational philosopher.

From counter-education to state education

The history of working-class educational politics spans four main phases: the popular
radicalism, Chartism and Owenism of the first half of the nineteenth century; the
popular Liberal working-class politics of the mid and late Victorian eras; the revival
of socialism and the growth of feminism in the years up to the first world war; and
the emergence of something like the modern configuration of the Labour Party,
fragments of the left and trade unions in the inter-war years.

If we look at the history of these movements, we find a recurrent educational
dilemma.[1] On the one hand, the active radical minorities valued the acquisition of
knowledge very highly. Knowledge appears again and again as a good in itself and
as a means to political emancipation. This passion can be traced through the autobiographies of working-class activists, through the forms of organization and
political programmes of the movements themselves, and in the movements' own
media, from the radical 'unstamped' press of the early nineteenth century to the
socialist magazines and newspapers of the 1880s to the 1920s.

At the same time working-class radicals were acutely conscious of the poverty of
educational resources to hand and the limitations on their use. Especially before
the growth of state regulation and municipal provision in the late nineteenth
century, this poverty was partly quantitative: lack of schools, lack of books, lack
of energy, lack of time. But there were always qualitative questions involved too.
The quality of what was on offer never matched the aspirations. Radicals in the
1830s and 1840s, facing the attempt to preach and teach *down* their movements
with tracts, schools and mechanics' institutes, saw provided education of all kinds
as a kind of tyranny or, at best, as a laughable irrelevance. They coined the phrase
'really useful knowledge' both as a satire on the Society for the Diffusion of Useful
Knowledge (a liberal middle-class educational association), and to express their
own educational ideas.[2] Similar criticisms were made of the public elementary
schools run by school boards between 1870 and 1902 and, especially, of the
continued existence of religiously organized voluntary schools.[3]

This view of education was typical among those who had gained an educational
experience of a positive kind through politics, and in the oppositional cultural
worlds of popular radicalism, socialism or feminism.[4] One key moment in the

'conversion' to socialism or feminism was an energetic and passionately pursued self-education through the texts and journals of the movement: in the earlier radical period, Tom Paine's *Rights of Man,* Cobbett's addresses and journalism, or later, the educational fare of the Chartist newspaper *The Northern Star*; in the socialist revival of the late nineteenth century, the works of Ruskin, Carlyle, and of the modern socialist writers like William Morris, the early Fabians, Edward Carpenter or Robert Blatchford.[5] Men and women who gained some taste of really useful knowledge felt the blocks and disappointments of formal education all the more keenly, on behalf of themselves, their children and their class or sex as a whole.

This radical current in popular educational opinion has often spanned working-class, artisanal and lower middle-class groupings.[6] It has always coexisted with other educational orientations: we certainly cannot identify it with popular or working-class opinion as such.[7] It has often been accompanied, for example, by the desire of relatively privileged or socially aspirant parents to secure individual educational advantages for their children. This has been a feasible individual strategy, the route into schoolteaching aside, only after the establishment of scholarship systems and free places at secondary schools in the early twentieth century. Before that it was possible to buy your children petty educational advantages but the opportunities for social mobility by this route were not large.[8] A much more common working-class response has been a kind of realism about schooling. Certain limited but tangible benefits have been sought from schooling, judged from the viewpoint of the average labourer under capitalist conditions, or the average woman destined to work for a wage but mainly to look after her husband and bring up her children. From this perspective, schooling must offer something useful that can be cashed in the labour or marriage markets. Since, for ordinary manual labour, schooling has actually offered rather little, it has often seemed important to minimize its costs in terms of time (hence patterns of early leaving), or of energy and emotional commitment (hence counter-school cultures). There is a long history of (mainly incomprehending) middle-class comment on this parental scepticism from nineteenth-century schools inspectors and assistant commissioners to the following characteristic research finding of 1972:

Parents in the manual occupational group show signs of alienation from the schools their children attend. They provide the weakest educational support for their children . . . their homes show least evidence of literacy . . . . Some of these parents' other attitudes are out-of-step with those of the school. Of all the parents, they are most likely to be in favour of their children having part-time jobs . . . .[9]

This history is paralleled by another: a long history of pupil resistance in school, some but not all forms of which have been related to the irrelevance of educational curricula and its distance from working-class experience and needs.[10]

The radical, pro-education elements within the working class have often been directly at odds with the sceptical pragmatic majorities.[11] These two positions share, however, a sense that the offer of schooling for working-class people under existing social conditions is very problematic. They share too a sense that individual solutions, aiming at social mobility or a private self-realization are illusory as a *class* or *group* strategy. What solutions, of a collective kind, have radicals offered to these dilemmas?

It is useful to draw a distinction between two broad forms of strategy which we will call 'substitutional' and 'statist'. Substitutional strategies concentrate on building an independent popular educational provision more or less in contestation with philanthropic or state agencies. The solution is to do it ourselves, drawing on resources that already exist within communities, but improvising new, more flexible forms. There has been a close historical association between socialist movements in Britain and the proliferation of alternative media, alternative forms of schooling, alternative ideas and practice which centre around specifically socialist pedagogy and (more problematically) around a socialist educational content.

Statist strategies, on the other hand, have centred on agitation over the public provision of educational facilities and the state's regulation of adjacent spheres (for example, the length of the working day, children's employment, child health). The strategy here has been to adopt the state system or a part of it as 'the people's schools' and work to improve its quality and accessibility. We call this strategy 'statist' because one effect has been to fuel successive expansions of the state education system, usually in a broadly egalitarian direction. The demand for fairness, an elementary grass-roots egalitarianism, has been one strand in working-class and socialist attitudes, perhaps the fundamental form of socialist criticism of public education.

It is tempting to identify substitutional strategies with a revolutionary or transformative educational politics, and to regard statist forms as necessarily 'reformist' or 'corporate'. There is some truth in this. Substitutional strategies may take a 'counter-educational' form and, where successful, constitute a challenge to established modes of cultural reproduction that is open, broad, combative and capable of a really close connection with popular educational needs. Statist strategies are much more dependent on the existing forms of state provision, the detailed configuration of which will determine the sites of popular struggle. They often involve acceptance of the separations constructed by the school system itself – for example, the separation of school and work, the identification of learning with childhood, the professionalization of teaching – which counter-educational movements may challenge. Statist strategies may, as we shall argue throughout this book, be exceedingly contradictory from the viewpoint of a socialist conception of popular interests.

So simple an opposition, as though there was an equally weighted choice in all historical periods, is, however, very misleading. Substitutional and statist strategies have been alternatives only in a very limited sense. This is partly because statist strategies have been dominant from the 1850s to the present day. In fact there have only been two periods when substitutional activity was organized on a large scale. The stress on 'organized' is important here, since there has never been a period in which formal educational provision has monopolized the means of learning. These periods of organized substitution were the first half of the nineteenth century, and the period of socialist revival from the 1880s to the early 1920s. Both periods saw exceptionally widespread radical mobilizations. Counter-education was sustained by the belief in the imminence of fundamental social change: the Chartists' charter, the Owenites' 'new moral world', the 'new life' of the late nine-teenth-century socialists or the Marxists' revolution.[12] In the wake of failure, especially of Chartism in the 1850s, radicals found the best way of pursuing democratic goals at a lower level of expectation in statist agitations. For the later socialists, statist and substitutional strategies were not alternatives at all but complementary strategies: the one addressed especially to the needs of children; the other to the political—educational needs of adults and of the movement.

It has been argued that the Chartist and Owenite phase, which depended on popular traditions established since the 1790s, was not a fully working-class phenomenon, but rather a feature of economic and cultural transition.[13] Working people, who still had some margin of independence from capitalist control, fought to defend these areas against both capital's encroachments and a growing state and philanthropic apparatus of cultural intervention. Counter-education, in this phase, built on indigenous popular educational traditions, gave them a radical and often anti-capitalist inflection and improvised new educational forms. If this argument is correct, it is only for the period after the 1850s or thereabouts that we can speak of a more fully proletarian working class in Britain, and to such a transition is linked the growth of a more statist form of educational strategy. From the 1850s onwards, and more surely from 1870, the choice was not between counter-education and public education, but between some form of combination of the two and a more abjectly statist route.

An understanding of this early, pre-proletarian history is important for educational politics today. Early radical practices challenged much that was to be taken for granted in later socialist agitations. This is partly because of the novelty of the situation in the early nineteenth century which saw the beginnings, but only the beginnings, of a public educational system.[14] In opposition to mass schooling, radicals insisted that education was something that happened all the time and at all ages. It had a value only if the process was fully controlled by those who sought knowledge themselves — education could not, by definition, be a gift or an imposition.

If it was imposed, it was not education at all, but what Cobbett called, in an indispensable coinage, 'Heddekashun'.[15] 'Really useful knowledge' was a knowledge of everyday circumstances, including a knowledge of why you were poor, why you were politically oppressed and why, through the force of social circumstance, you were the kind of person you were, your character misshapen by a cruel competitive world.[16] Radicals in this phase refused the distinction between liberal and utilitarian conceptions of education, between 'truth' and 'usefulness'. They insisted that from a popular radical standpoint these things were identical: that in order to change the world, you needed to be able to explain everyday experience, to account for 'all known facts'.[17] Education was a natural or human right, but it was also a way of achieving justice. This pointed to a profound suspicion of all provided education which was usually justified in openly controlling terms. State systems, under these circumstances and in the absence of any form of democratic control, were to be resisted.

The substitution–statist distinction marks an historical transition and is not just a formal difference; but it may be misleading unless we make distinctions within each category. Substitution may take compensatory or more oppositional forms: 'self-education' or 'counter-education'. Since the pursuit of personal desires must also be recognized as a politics, the distinction is not, in practice, an easy one to draw. There have, however, been plenty of examples of conflicts between these tendencies in the history of adult education. They have usually taken the form of battles between a strongly political and agitational conception of adult education, identifying a distinctively socialist or working-class curriculum, and a more philanthropic, humanistic and radical–liberal tradition which has often been more open. The conflict between the Workers' Educational Association (founded in 1903) and the groups that broke away from Ruskin College in 1907 and became the Plebs League is the best known example.[18]

There are also different dimensions to statist strategies, and these differences are crucial to much of the post-war analysis. Statist agitations may be pursued on broader or narrower fronts. They may take more or less popular forms. There are different grounds of struggle against or within state systems. Existing public provision may be criticized on grounds of *access* and the systematic exclusion or disadvantaging of the majority of children. Much of the Labour Party's educational repertoire has revolved around this point, from the party's original demand for 'secondary education for all' to the espousal of the common school. In itself, we will be arguing, this is a narrow demand, whose radical challenge is relatively easily contained by real or apparent structural changes in the state system. But access-related struggles have often been accompanied by a concern with educational *content,* with the constitution of knowledge and the modes of acquiring it. Agitations of a statist kind may also raise questions of *control*: who decides the forms and contents of schooling? What does democracy mean in this sphere? In what sense are state schools the people's own? Finally, statist strategies may embrace some explicit understanding of the *context* of schooling, especially of the place of school, as determined and determining, within the family–school–production complex. They may have a more or less adequate grasp of what shapes educational outcomes, both at the level of schooling systems and at the level of the individual or class. All strategies necessarily work with assumptions about this, implicitly or explicitly.

Four subordinate categories — struggles over access, content, control and context — allow us to discriminate between different forms of statist strategy. Attempts to change the pre-existing system of public education are by no means necessarily narrow or conservative. The point is best stressed by looking at the popular politics of schooling in the period from the 1870 Act to the first decade or so of the new century. The fascinating aspects of this period, which speak to socialist dilemmas today, are the breadth and relative popularity of statist struggles and their coexistence, especially after 1880, with a marked counter-educational upsurge.[19]

From the 1870s to 1902, popular educational politics revolved around the creation, extension and finally defence of locally elected, single-purpose elementary education authorities called 'school boards'. Initially this was a liberal rather than a socialist politics. It hinged less on opposition to capital or the capitalist state and more on hostility to squire and parson and the Anglican—Tory alliance. School boards were valued for the width of their franchise and the promise of an education that would be secular and free. Later they became a testing-ground for socialist and feminist politics. The battle to preserve the boards in the face of the 1902 Act was a late example of the classical popular Liberal alliance of nineteenth-century politics, with the addition of a distinctively Labour voice, articulated by the Trades Union Congress.[20]

This politics and its immediately succeeding forms was both wide and popular. It was as much a politics of the street corner as of the committee room. Control was centrally involved: the democracy of the boards was prized in comparison with the proprietory rights of the clergy over the voluntary schools. Questions of content were continuously present through the issue of religion and the radical demand for secularization. Some of the most vigorous campaigns, particularly later in the period, concerned the context of schooling, especially the health of children and the regulation of child labour. Questions of access were centrally raised, but there was a tendency to see the board schools as 'the people's own', and to attempt to extend opportunities within the elementary system, rather than build ladders to higher levels.[21]

Statist strategies, then, do not necessarily involve a loss of popular involvement or a narrowing of the issues raised. Much of the vigour of educational politics, especially after the 1880s, depended upon the political education of adults within the socialist societies, through the socialist press, in the growing feminist movement and in the diffused cultural politics of the period. Socialists even began, again, to improvise their own means for the education of children, as the growth of socialist Sunday schools testified. In some areas of exceptional socialist strength these oppositional educational traditions continued well into the inter-war period, to be remembered by older people today:

My father was a strong socialist by that time, with the reading he had done in Belfast. He was a Co-operator and he was an atheist as well . . . Dad sent me right away to the Partick Socialist Sunday-school . . . I was taken down at four years of age to the Sunday-school and that was the happiest time of my life right up until I was fourteen . . . It was very well organized in Glasgow and all of the socialist — the Labour voters as you would call them nowadays — they were really early socialists who wanted a change of society and their children to learn as much as possible about these things. They didn't want to have to — they didn't want to just vote Labour. They wanted their children to learn that socialism was a good way of life and what was good for one was good for all, and so this was a moral attitude they had.[22]

What is interesting and important about these popular socialist memories is not only the counter-educational energies they record, but also the deep sense of loss in comparison with today, especially the loss of excitement, vision and idealism:

People often say to me 'How would things be different under socialism?' I think it is sad, that capitalism has even obscured our capacity for visions. Nobody can imagine what a better life would be like, because we are always being told this is the best possible life.[23]

The period from 1870 to the first world war illustrates one further feature of statist strategies — their dependence on the existing forms of state provision. Popular agitations certainly had effects on educational structure. It was popular support for Liberal educational policy in the 1860s that finally shifted the Tory–Anglican bloc sufficiently to permit a public state education system at all.[24] Trade union and socialist agitation, the competition of ruling parties for popular support, the grass-roots pressure for post-elementary education and eventually the mobilization of the first world war underlay the popular gains of the period up to 1920.[25]

The actual structure of provision also formed the shape of educational politics. Throughout this period and beyond, the education system was conspicuously class-based: it involved the manifest exclusion of the majority of children from all forms of education deemed 'secondary'. The objects of a popular statist strategy were therefore much clearer than they became after 1944 or in the 1970s: 'secondary education for all', or at least an extension of working-class opportunities within the elementary school system. The connection was more detailed, more binding even than this. The strengths and weaknesses of popular strategies shadowed the forms of administrative and educational arrangements. School board politics was popular, in part, because of a relatively extended franchise and the opposition between 'democratic' public provision and the voluntary schools, dominated by the Anglican parsons. School board politics kept alive the issue of control. Similarly, the question of content remained an issue between radicals (who favoured a secular curriculum) and conservatives (who wished to retain religion). When the structure of educational administration was changed in the 1902 Act towards the familiar multi-purpose local authorities, the Liberal politics of education had to change too. The popular labourist politics of the inter-war period took its stamp from the sharply institutionalized division between secondary and elementary education which was installed after 1902. The central issue became how to break down this division, or how to gain access for working-class children to its 'upper' levels. A similar sequence, as we shall see, was to be repeated in the period before and after 1944. One persistent problem with statist agitations is that, even at the point of 'victory', they may be radically disorganized by changes in the state system itself. Unless popular movements develop educational repertoires of their own, these victories (or defeats) may take decades to recoup.

The Labour Party and education before the war

What were the typical forms of educational politics in the two decades before the 1944 Act? What elements of the Labour Party's post-war educational policies had already been formed? The 1920s and 1930s saw a particularly bitter struggle between two contending alliances. The first, oppositional alliance was organized around the demand for egalitarian forms of educational expansion; the second, dominant alliance resisted these demands and sought, where possible, to reverse expansionist tendencies. The progressive alliance was described by R. H. Tawney, its leading intellectual, as 'educationalists and teachers, economists and social workers, administrators, and not least, the parents themselves'.[26] The parents were represented, in a largely masculine form, in the organizations of the Labour movement, but also by the Workers' Educational Association which Tawney saw as a vehicle for the opinions of 'plain people' on educational policy.

We should look more closely at the constituents of this alliance in order, especially, to make comparisons with the 1960s. The inter-war pro-education forces included those specifically concerned with the field as teachers and as educationalists, sections of the professional middle class, and a large popular constituency, addressed and organized in specifically class terms. The 1960s' alliance was to include similar elements, especially the professionals, but the nature of its popular basis was to be much less clear. The other major difference was the conspicuous exclusion of all representatives of capitalist business, for Tawney's progressive movement was explicitly organized to combat industrial interests not, as in the post-war period, to woo them. The Federation of British Industries (the inter-war CBI) was, indeed, Tawney's main polemical target.[27] The other main enemies, constituents of the dominant bloc, were Conservative and national governments and the officials of the Board of Education.

The nature of the contending alliances can also be traced in Brian Simon's accounts of the high-points of the inter-war struggles.[28] At each point that educational expenditure was cut (the major form of educational reaction), Conservative politicians faced the wrath of teachers' unions, local administrators, and working-class organizations, local and national. Government policy was solidly supported by business. On two occasions leading businessmen were prominent on the committees actually recommending retrenchment.[29] Educational politics was seen as an overtly class politics, even by Tawney, who was a tough-minded Christian socialist and no Marxist. He denounced the justifications of cuts by the May Committee of 1931, for example, as 'a declaration of class war in the schools', even as 'counter-revolution'.[30] Employers, for their part, did not see educational expansion as part of their repertoire of solutions. Most favoured the educational settlement of 1902, with its rigid elementary—secondary education division and its limited access to the latter.[31]

These battles had much of the character of the broader class struggles of the period. They were defensive campaigns. Like the General Strike itself, they were part of a pattern of hard-fought working-class defeats. Of course these features must be seen against the general adversities of the inter-war years, especially the economic power of capital in a period of mass unemployment and recurrent crisis.

It is important, however, to note the narrowness of this class-based politics as compared with the pre-first world war forms of statism already analysed. Popular politics tended to narrow down to questions of access and the immediate physical environment of the child. The concern with content and control was lost. There was a different relation too between socialist adult education (which continued on a smaller scale) and the agitation over schooling. Far from fuelling each other, these forms of struggle tended to be held separate, often organized by different agencies. The connection might have been made by the Labour Party itself, properly regarded as the political agency of the working class in this phase. But, as we shall see, the party was too firmly wedded to a narrow statism to take its broader 'educative' responsibility more seriously.

These points can best be developed by looking at a central text of inter-war social democracy — Tawney's *Secondary Education for All* (1922).[32] This is an obvious choice because of Tawney's importance as a philosopher of British socialism, its genesis in one of the post-war Labour advisory committees and its status, in Rodney Barker's phrase, as 'a perfect illustration of the character of the Labour Party'.[33] If any one document summed up earlier working-class demands and shaped Labour's inter-war policy, this text did.

Tawney's pamphlet was shaped, morally and politically, by a thorough-going form of socialist egalitarianism. It expressed a popular sense of insult. Of the work of the WEA Tawney had already written:

'What,' said an educated man to the writer, 'you teach history and economics to miners and engineers? Take care. You will make them discontented and disloyal to us.' That division of mankind into those who are ends and those who are means, whether made by slave-holders or by capitalists, is the ultimate and unforgivable wrong, with which there can be truce neither in education nor in any other department of social life.[34]

Tawney showed how these principles of class organization were enshrined in the secondary school—elementary school division as established in 1902.[35] True, some bridges had been built since, through scholarships and free places, but they tended to perpetuate the structural class-based division. The answer was to secure 'a living and organic connection' between elementary and secondary education, reclassified as successive age-defined stages through which every child should go. Only thus could the illegitimate intrusions of 'class' into education be ended.

We should note, at this stage, the main features of Tawney's conception of class; also his neglect of non-class relations and particularly of gender. His was a particular view of class, but one that was to recur throughout the tradition which he helped to found. A fuller account is contained in his socialist classic, *Equality* (1931).[36] Here he presented class as, in part, a matter of economic function: the population was divided between 'the majority who work for wages, but who do not own or direct, and the minority who own and direct the material apparatus of industry

and determine industrial organisation and policy'.[37] But he stressed much more
the social and cultural aspects of class which he saw as relatively independent from
'the necessary diversity of economic functions'. It was possible to envisage a society
in which occupations and incomes varied, in which captains gave orders and
managers managed, but in which there were common standards of health, education
and environment, an openness of social intercourse, a freedom from poverty and
want, and a shared culture. However the 'historical structure and spirit' of English
society preserved a tradition of differentiation not by function alone, but by
wealth, status and oligarchic power. Necessary hierarchy was overlaid by inappropriate discrimination which ignored 'the common element in human requirements'.[38]
In writing of class, then, Tawney's stress characteristically concerned what later
sociologists were to call 'status', a term with a curious and flirtatious relationship
with the older Marxist category.[39] Class, in this sense, was detachable from the
social division of labour and from necessary and rationally justifiable hierarchies
of ability and function. In this form, it was a relatively weak though certainly
pervasive influence on educational structure, an 'irrelevance', a vulgar intrusion
into matters concerning our common humanity.[40] This is why Tawney could argue
that, while Conservatives and businessmen stoked up class conflict, Labour's mission
had a supra-class quality: 'not for the advantage of any *single class*, but to develop
the human resources of the whole community'.[41] Tawney was, then, a class warrior
only by force of circumstance. Class was something he earnestly hoped would
wither away.

This conception certainly has political strengths, preserving the idea of a non-class
utopia. But, as we shall see, this and similar social democratic and sociological
conceptions tend seriously to underestimate the effects which class (and other
social relations) persistently have on educational outcomes, individual and
collective. They also seriously overestimate the power of educational expansion
and reform to mitigate the effects of class relations. The history of Labour's
educational policy, especially after 1944, might be understood as a gradual discovery
of these facts.

The actual proposals of 1922, which became Labour's official programme,
centred exclusively on matters of access. Tawney's writing is chock-full of
metaphors which underline this concern: landings and staircases here, *cul de sacs*,
bridges, greasy poles and handrails there. There is even, in a reference to primary
schools, 'a rope which the Indian juggler throws in the air to end in vacancy'.[42]
The answer was to ensure universal access to secondary education. This meant
the reorganization of all schools into primary or secondary, the abolition of fees
in secondary schools, the increase of maintenance allowances, and an expansion
of secondary school places. Most of the pamphlet concentrated on the detail and
the costing of this, under the slogan 'idealistic but not visionary'.

Tawney's discussions of content, control and context were, by contrast,
cursory. The discussion of educational content was brief and tautological, defining
secondary education by 'the stage of life for which it provides'.[43] The significance
of this (apart from Tawney's acceptance of a nature-based conception of adolescence)

was in its opposition to narrowly vocational conceptions: 'Labour must reject the vulgar commercialism which conceives of the manufacture of efficient typists and mechanics as the primary object of adolescent education.' The doctrine of the determinacy of occupation was 'fundamentally vicious'.[44]

The problem here is two-fold. No positive conception of education was forthcoming to place in opposition to capitalist imperatives, only a conception of culture, which Tawney inherited from Matthew Arnold, which was presented as being outside or above classes. Second, Tawney's struggle in his writing and in his political practice to disengage education from class determinations made it very difficult for him to think constructively about the actual relations between education and other social sites. His view of the context of education implied total autonomy, or at least a unilateral declaration of independence by the educators! Parents and children, it seems, were required to make the same altruistic move. It is interesting that the process of disengagement was accompanied by a strong stress on 'biological and psychological realities' and on the importance of professional expertise.[45] Next to metaphors of access, metaphors of organic growth and biological process proliferate most lushly in his educational writing.

It is important to set Tawney and *Secondary Education for All* in a wider context of Labour's educational thinking before 1935. The most striking feature perhaps is the heterogeneity of this tradition. As several commentators have noted, Labour's repertoire here, as in other spheres, displayed a persistent duality. On the one hand, the party, or its leftish elements, embraced a broad ethical egalitarianism, critical of capitalist society in its social and moral effects; on the other hand, the repertoire included the tradition of Fabian social engineering, a tendency not incompatible with a collectivist liberalism or a more efficient and just capitalist order. This dichotomy has certainly been a feature of Labour's educational policies and the arguments by which they have been promoted. We will analyse the whole formation in much more detail in Chapter 4, having looked at its post-war transformations. For the moment, we may follow Rodney Barker in noting the opposition between an educational egalitarianism and a more elitist or meritocratic concern with 'equality of opportunity'.[46] It is this combination, the attempt to serve popular interests in a socialist or democratic form *and* to secure a progressive capitalist adaptation that distinguishes what, throughout this book, we shall call 'social democracy'.[47]

Tawney was well aware of the opposition we have described, wrote eloquently of the difference between 'practical equality' and 'equality of opportunity' and stigmatized Sidney Webb's London County Council policies as inegalitarian.[48] We can place him, fairly unambiguously, on the egalitarian side of Labour's repertoire, on the terrain of 'British socialism'. Yet there were features of Tawney's thinking that rendered both it and the early Labour programmes relatively easy to incorporate in a version in which the Fabian elements were dominant, especially the failure to think through the relation between schools and the adjacent social sites. In general, the programme of 1922, through its exclusive stress on access at the expense of content, control and context was a narrowing, even an impoverishment, of an inherited popular radical tradition.

It is important to stress one further feature of this phase, a tendency which deepened in the years after 1944: the loss of an organic connection between political education and agitation (or the broader educative function of parties or groups) and the campaigns around schooling. Substitutional activity, if connected to Labour's mainstream politics, might have compensated for or even transformed its statism; it might have connected policy with popular experience of a more positive and qualitative kind, in addition to the experience of exclusion; it might have provided a practical forum for the development of an alternative socialist conception of educational content similar to the 'spearhead knowledge' of the Chartists and Owenites;[49] it would certainly have raised, much more centrally, the question of control.

These questions were in fact raised in the inter-war years, but mainly by groups that operated to the left of the party's political centre of gravity, especially by the Marxist adult educators of the Plebs League and the National Labour College and, in connection with schooling, by the short-lived and proscribed Teachers' Labour League.[50] The Labour Party as a whole was never a counter-educational agency of this kind. It had more affinity with the liberal, compensatory tendencies in the WEA. In its origins it rested on the educative activity of the socialists, feminists, Marxists and syndicalists of the pre-war period. After 1918, however, it failed to reproduce the very conditions on which its growth had depended, resting already upon a type of class support similar to the loyalties of an official trade unionism. Its more agitational elements — the Independent Labour Party, the *Daily Herald*, the Labour Research Department and, in general, socialist intellectuals — were rendered marginal within the party's structure or subordinated to the routines of electioneering.[51] Such a party could not produce intellectuals out of the classes and groups which gave it support. The intellectuals which it had recruited, via Liberal politics or an orthodox academic route, often gave the party faithful but not uncritical service. But men like Tawney and G. D. H. Cole also noted the party's failure to 'make socialists'. As Tawney put it (in fundamentally optimistic terms), 'its function is not merely to win votes; it is to wake the sleeping demon'.[52]

All this was part of a much larger political adaptation, part of the unqualified parliamentarianism that had become the strongest reflex of Labour's leadership.[53] Labour indeed was carefully tutored in these older political ways by the leaders of the older parties, welcomed into (minority) office, stigmatized as Bolshevik when it got out of line. The comparison between a radical past and a Labourist present has to be seen, though, against the background of changes in political structure.

As formal political rights were won at last by women and by all working-class men, the older forms of 'pressure from without' declined. Formal politics, the individualized casting of the vote itself or the marshalling of voters *en masse*, could now be represented as 'politics' as such, extending even to the socialist heartlands of the localities. The primary exclusions, which had fuelled the agitations around school boards and boards of poor law guardians, lost much of their clarity and force. The pattern of containment, established in formal politics in the inter-war years, was to be repeated in education in the decades that followed.

Here too the whole of Labour's energies was devoted to changing the formal machinery. The main cost of this was the systematic reproduction of the characteristics of state education and the non-popular statist evolution of the party as a whole. At its best, the Labour Party remained the educational provider *for* popular groups and classes, not an educative agency *of* and *within* them. The full significance of these inter-war changes was not to become clear until the oppositional alliance of the 1920s became, in a new form, the dominant educational orthodoxy of the post-war period. It is to the first stages in this transformation that we must now turn.

3 Conservatism, citizenship and the 1944 settlement

Introduction

In this chapter we examine the politics of education from the 1930s to the early 1950s: a period dominated by the genesis and effects of the 1944 Education Act, often called the Butler Act. This was the last major attempt to restructure the English educational system, and has remained largely intact during the post-war years (though there are signs of considerable encroachments upon it as this book is completed). Its assumptions and provisions have been central in framing much subsequent debate about education policy, and it is therefore a legislative moment which cannot be ignored.

The moment of 1944 was however but one dimension of a much broader political settlement, whose winning inaugurated a developing post-war consensus. We are seeking to locate the specific role of educational debates in the wider politics of the period. The origins of the 1944 Act lay in the emergence of forces which began to acquire a coherence and influence as new political and intellectual groupings in the years before the war. It was under the influence of the war itself that a consensus around planning, state intervention and universal forms of social provision came to define a new political middle ground — in which, in contrast to the exclusion and restriction of the inter-war years, educational provision assumed a particular prominence. The 1944 Act was constructed as a political intervention designed to secure the maximum support, with a concomitant marginalization of other options and strategies. With it was associated the demobilization of the popular expectations which were a marked feature of domestic politics during the war. Educational politics in the years after the war were dominated by the forms of the Act's implementation.

Several rich issues arise here. In the context of this argument, we wish to concentrate on the ways in which Labour now lost touch, decisively, with its distinctive concern to represent working-class interests. Around 'citizenship' there came new, classless notions of a shared 'nationhood'. The 1944 Act was at once the realization, in important ways, of Labour's traditional objectives, and the decisive breaking up of older kinds of struggle.

We discuss these phases in turn. First, we review the old Conservative policies and attitudes against which the new middle ground groups began to assert education's importance. Next, we outline the place of education policy in the strategy of these groups, and in particular their espousal of the cause of education for citizenship. The discourse of citizenship is then treated as an organizing theme in the politics of wartime Britain, both in relation to the different dimensions of war radicalism and as a concern of the reforming wing of the Conservative Party. Last, we look at Labour's implementation of the Act and the Conservative appropriation of the initiative in educational policy.

Education and the inter-war Conservatives

In the last chapter, we described the general pattern of politics, during the period, as a dour struggle between two sets of political forces, a pattern reproduced in the narrower arena of educational politics. A tightly utilitarian definition of education with an attendant restriction of access was upheld by the Federation of British Industries and the Conservative Party. Ranged against this entrenched orthodoxy of exclusion and restriction was a broadly 'progressive' alliance composed not only of the Labour Party, but also of teachers and intellectuals of the field.

While education had only a low priority as an area of reform, it would be incorrect to suggest that Conservative dominated governments of the period simply set their faces against it. But the limits of their ambitions for reform resulted in a persistent narrowness of conception. To cite one example, a 1928 Conservative publication contained a neat summary of the party's perspective. Stanley Baldwin, as Prime Minister, provided an introduction which began:

One of the strongest bonds between men is a common education, and England has been the poorer that in her national system of schooling she has not in the past fostered this fellowship of mind.[1]

The pamphlet proposed as a service to the 'social life' of the nation to reform the education system in favour of a unitary system of state schooling. The divisions of schooling provision, represented in the existence of elementary schooling as a separate route for working-class children, were seen as antipathetic to the interests of social unity. The pamphlet outlined a logic of reform, in a magical resolution of class antagonisms:

1 A house divided against itself may stand — but it will not prosper.
2 We cannot prosper while we have class divisions based on social prejudice.
3 These distinctions have been perpetuated by the horizontal stratification of our schools.
4 The vast majority of *the people* have been educated only in schools classed as 'elementary'.
5 This inequality has been a source of grievance.
6 The 'elementary' system is being scrapped and *the worker's* sense of inequality will disappear (our emphasis).

This simple equation of class divisions with social attitudes, of 'the people' with 'the worker', was matched by a naivety about the amelioration of the problem, as the easy invocation of a shared set of social assumptions indicated:

With a more liberal education and consequently better opportunities to get on employee and employer can work together without periodical setbacks due to class misunderstandings.

The direct subordination of schooling to the requirements of employers was taken as axiomatic, whether it involved the release of children from school to meet the requirements of a local labour market, or their retention in school to ease the burden of local unemployment: 'the longer school life inevitable under the new system will keep children out of the labour market, where they are not wanted'. It was also the employer's perspective which was advanced in relation to the actual content of schooling, with a stress on the utility of vocational preparation: 'the fetish of book-learning has been the bane of the school from the employer's point of view'. The school's support for practical work would 'invest manual labour with dignity at least equal to that of the sedentary occupations, and will give the manual worker a status hitherto denied him'.

Yet this narrowness of view was not completely representative as Conservative supporters of educational expansion sought to demonstrate. Cyril Norwood commented that investment in education could be considered as a form of self-interest, as a bulwark against the spread of communism:

I hope that those who attribute the scarcity of domestic servants to the unreasonable institution of elementary education, by which they are made to pay for the teaching of other people's children, will lay in the other scale this other service which has made of Bolshevism only a bogy which sits by their pillows and frightens them in the night. [2]

Although the point was not lost, the subsequent actions of the Conservative dominated governments did little to move even as far as maintaining existing educational provision. In the retrenchment of 1931 the national government chose social expenditure as a prime area for savings, and subsequent years brought no sign that education's priority would increase.

Forging a new consensus

It was in the wake of the debacle of 1931, with the minority Labour government replaced by a Conservative controlled national government, that a recomposition of political forces became evident.

The political impasse which confronted the Labour Party, reduced to a mere fifty-two seats in the post-election parliament of 1931, brought little comfort to those outside the party who also regarded the prospect of a national government with dismay. A bankruptcy of political issues reinforced fears of a more general social breakdown.

In these conditions there emerged a series of groupings which offered a reassessment of the role of the state from an interventionist viewpoint. Such groups maintained a political distance from the Labour Party, but were hostile to the refusal of the Conservatives to adopt any long-term planning policies in the economic and social spheres. Indeed, existing policies seemed woefully inadequate for the maintenance of democratic parliamentary government. Thus it was in a new style of politics, involving a partial recomposition of older tendencies, that both a critique of state inaction and a blueprint for policy changes were elaborated. Moreover, education was to be increasingly stressed as a central component of a new strategy for political and economic reconstruction.

The groups we have referred to above took different forms, and related to different constituencies of support, though there was frequently an overlap in membership.[3] What united them was an acute awareness of new political conditions, exemplified by the strength of fascist totalitarianism as a force to be reckoned with both nationally and internationally. Simultaneously, the prospect of an active socialist movement which might move in the direction of the Soviet Union posed another set of unwelcome possibilities.

What was positively sought was a form of political and economic intervention which would pre-empt and contain any movement to what were characterized as the politics of the extremes. The quest for an activist 'middle road' as a focus for the consolidation of countervailing political forces was therefore the priority. Inspired by the thinking of the Liberal Party's Yellow Book of 1928 *(Britain's Industrial Future)*, by the contemporary writings of Keynes, and by the example of Roosevelt's 'New Deal', the preferred perspective was summed up by an *Economist* article of 1934 which projected:

a possible halfway house, namely, a reformed capitalism utilising the immense driving force, elasticity and experimentalism of private enterprise, while at the same time limiting it within the requirements of the public interest.[4]

The political drive to establish this new perspective in policy stressed a number of major themes, in particular the need to reconstruct and modernize both the economic organization and social relations of British capitalism. In this respect the role of planning in the service of democracy was seen as an indispensable counter to the imposition of planning in more overtly totalitarian directions. Although the whole question of leadership was explosive in the 1930s, it is clear that the proponents of the 'middle road' considered themselves equipped for the task ahead.

One such group, cast in a Fabian mould, was Political and Economic Planning, founded prior to the formation of the national government in 1931. It pursued a strategy of conducting social research whose findings were so disseminated as to achieve influence within the corridors of power. According to its first secretary, Kenneth Lindsay, its influence could be measured through its contact with over '300 leading persons in the 1930s'.[5] Its perspectives also achieved some more public prominence through an organization founded in 1934 and later known as the Next Five Years Group. This was supported by members of all political parties (notably Harold Macmillan) and by numerous writers, scientists and educationalists such as Hadow and Percy Nunn. It was more overtly propagandist than PEP and its programme *An Essay in Political Agreement* (1935) stated:

We believe that the present situation offers a new opportunity and a new challenge: a challenge to give leadership in organizing a world order freed from the menace of war, a challenge to develop an economic system which is freed from poverty and makes full use of the resources of the age for the general advantage, and a challenge to safeguard political liberty and to revitalize democratic government.[6]

Such leadership was to be found, according to the group, in the middle ground between the traditional political polarities:

The historic controversy between individualism and socialism — between the idea of a wholly competitive capitalistic system and one of State ownership, regulation, and control — appears largely beside the mark, if regarded with a realistic appreciation of immediate needs. For it is clear that our actual system will in any case be a mixed one for many years to come; our economy will comprise, with great variety of degree and method, both direct State ownership and control, and management by public and semi-public concerns, and also a sphere in which private competitive enterprise will continue within a framework of appropriate public regulation.[7]

The publication of Keynes's major book *The General Theory* in 1936 suggested a social and economic strategy which was broadly in line with that proposed by the Next Five Years Group and the work of PEP. But the reception of his work within the Labour Party was also significant as it was seen to vindicate a policy of state intervention and direction on a hitherto unknown scale. A. L. Rowse, in his *Mr Keynes and the Labour Movement,* argued that *The General Theory* was 'the complete justification, on the best theoretical grounds, for a practical and moderate English socialism, as it is in theory, the foundations for a socialist economics'.[8] This ground for rapprochement between labourism and a reforming liberalism in the field of economic policy, offering a strategy for reconstruction within a mixed economy and a constitutional framework, was to consolidate a communality of interest and perspective which would achieve a real ascendancy within a short time at the onset of the war. A great deal of groundwork had already been done. Moreover it could be appropriated to the 'moderate' and respectable side of labourism, thereby enabling the maintenance of a strictly constitutional politics with an eschewal of class struggle versions of transformation.

The stress on regulation and the integration of social and economic planning lacked, in itself, any direct appeal to the population at large. So while programmes could be produced and plans drawn up there remained the necessity of actually mobilizing and winning political support. The picture of the future had to be painted in sufficiently bright colours to convince people that it could be realized. Assumptions underpinning the plans had to be broadcast widely and consent secured:

Unless we can convince the man in the street, and keep him convinced, that we are making a juster and fairer world, for him as well as for his children, we might as well spare our efforts to increase the efficiency of the economic mechanism. For any system, however productive of wealth, however much it may increase the consumption of the masses, is doomed unless the plain man can feel in his bones that he is getting a square deal. 9

The winning of political consent from 'the plain man' would involve active persuasion that a better future could be realized without recourse to anti-democratic forms of politics. Here the role of education was identified as central as a means of transmitting democratic principles:

The principle of government by consent and free discussion must be made more fully operative through the extension of education — that cardinal function of a democratic state; through the improvement of the system of representation, and through the further breaking down of barriers of class and privilege.10

The Next Five Years Group were anxious to promote a revitalized notion of political leadership, but the very concept of leadership was fraught with connotations of totalitarianism — hence the need for the reassurance that 'leadership and democracy are not incompatible . . . the surest foundation for creative leadership is an educated democracy'. But when the group located education as a major force in securing that educated democracy, the question of what schools should actually do was absolutely central. Democracy could be assisted through 'the inclusion in the educational system, of teaching in the duties and responsibilities of citizens and their governments in relation to the world community'.

Schooling and citizenship

To propose a set of general principles was one thing, to secure their acceptance in schools another. The stronger definition of political objectives within schools could not be undertaken without encountering and indeed generating resistances. For schools to prepare pupils directly for their political role was a necessary component of middle ground strategy but required a redefinition of curriculum content and purpose. This was no simple task. In the words of a contemporary writer, Professor F. A. Cavanagh, the curriculum was 'a hornets' nest to disturb. All sorts of vested interests and prejudices are aroused which make dispassionate treatment very difficult'.11 In the wake of the General Strike, and the proscription of the Teachers' Labour League from the Labour Party, there had been considerable debate about the activities of politically motivated teachers. Though the criticisms of political bias originated primarily from Conservative politicians, the Labour Party was equally anxious to establish the content of schooling as something outside the sphere of political decisions — a matter to be left to the professional judgment of teachers. It was this autonomy of the teacher, or rather the head teacher, which presented a major stumbling block to political intervention in the actual content of schooling. Teacher autonomy was jealously guarded by the teacher organizations. One of the founding principles of the NUT had been to secure for teachers 'freedom from obnoxious interference',12 an aim shared by other teachers' associations.

Following the Nazi seizure of power in 1933, the example of German schools subordinated to the political purpose of one party prompted discussions in the educational press — in particular *The Times Educational Supplement* — about the role of education in the service of the 'national interest'. On the one hand, any political intervention into the curriculum could be represented as totalitarian in intent and practice. On the other the lack of action could result in totalitarianism triumphant. The necessity felt for an intervention in the curriculum which would promote 'democratic' rather than 'extremist' goals was to some extent resolved by an initiative formulated in specifically educational terms.

The Association for Education in Citizenship was formed in mid 1934, and can be seen as a model of middle ground political intervention into questions of education. As with other groups, its intention was to unite as wide a range of support as possible. In this respect both politicians and educationalists provided support for its aims, as well as a means of disseminating its work to a wider audience. The aim of the association, as set down in its formal statement of objectives, was to:

advance the study of training and citizenship, by which is meant training in the moral qualities necessary for the citizens of a democracy, the encouragement of clear thinking in everyday affairs.[13]

Its more specific political objective was, however, more openly acknowledged, as Oliver Stanley (president of the Board of Education) made clear in his foreword to an early publication:

The decay of democracy abroad has led many people to the conclusion that, if those democratic institutions, which we in this country agree are essential for the full development of the individual, are to be preserved, some systematic training in the duties of citizenship is necessary.[14]

In endorsing the association *The Times Educational Supplement* provided its own inflection, relating the kind of preparation to the types of children who would enter the social and political relations of adult life:

It will be generally agreed that democratic institutions can only succeed if citizens are politically educated to carry out each his own function, whether this be that of a voter only or the more responsible task of leadership.[15]

The clear inference here was that, although citizenship education might be universally required, its content would not be universally the same. Rather it would be constructed in different ways for the appropriate class of child and future adult.

Such a view was not characteristic of the association's membership as a whole, where, typically of the new middle groupings, diverse views held together around ambiguous concepts. A more complete study of the discourse of citizenship would follow up Laclau's view of 'what is most specific to the ideological class struggle — the attempt to articulate the same interpellations in antagonistic discourses'.[16] Here we can note only that citizenship could point one way towards conformist imperatives of duties, another towards the exercise of rights. For G. D. H. Cole, a council member of the association and secretary of the New Fabian Research Bureau, the need for co-operation against fascism overrode all else:

I feel that the present must be of sheer necessity my main concern. I am a socialist, as I have been since I began to think politically, or to know anything about the world and its affairs. But I say frankly that, in the present situation, I am less concerned about the need for passing socialist measures in the immediate future than about saving democracy from total eclipse.[17]

For these reasons, citizenship became ubiquitous, and by the early years of the war the middle ground priorities — planning, reconstruction, education for citizenship — were at the centre of the political stage. Yet in education, as in other areas of reform, the full entry into 'modern' conditions was inaugurated only through an active popular politics which had been notably absent in the defensive struggles of the 1930s.

War radicalism

From the earliest stage of the war, the question of what kind of society would follow was contested in virtually every public discussion of war aims. What the country was supposed to be fighting for, as opposed to what was being fought against, involved the setting of objectives which both the government and other groups sought to command. Debates about the nature of reconstruction were at the centre of opposed perspectives on the conduct of the war at home and abroad.

In the context of domestic politics, the fact of war and the grim years preceding it were almost automatically laid at the door of the Conservative Party. Viscount Hailsham, writing much later, commented with some annoyance:

Between 1939 and 1945, a stream of 'yellow backs', written by political agitators often posing as ancient Romans, pinned responsibility for the war upon the Conservative Party and, by vilifying the domestic past, pointed the way to the Socialist future.[18]

Hailsham's 'agitators' were the authors of books such as *Guilty Men*[19] and *Your M.P.*[20] written under the pen-names of 'Cato' and 'Gracchus'. These books enjoyed a huge circulation inside the distinctive yellow dust jacket of the Gollancz publishing house. The fact that the authors took seriously an injunction of Churchill's must have been galling for Hailsham, since it was Churchill who had remarked that 'the use of recrimination about the past is to enforce effective action at the present'. The size of the books' circulation confirmed the scale of the constituency interested in such recriminations, but also the interest in proposals for 'effective action at the present'.

The requirements of the war economy for the direction of labour on an un-precedented scale, and the need to mobilize the active consent of the working population, posed novel problems for a government which, despite its basis in a formal coalition, was overwhelmingly Conservative. Although the trade unions and Labour Party were represented in the government as a way of reducing political and industrial conflict, something more than the general promise of a better future was required.

From an early stage of the war, while the official preparation of reconstruction schemes was under way (with Beveridge reporting in 1942, and an Education White Paper in 1943), there was also an unprecedented involvement of much wider groups in debates about the political future. The reconstruction of the educational system, with more open access to schooling and a longer school life for children, was a central issue in such discussion of the post-war world. Plans for reorganization proliferated:

1942 and 1943 were memorable for the number of semi-official schedules of reform. Committees of the three leading political parties threw out their suggestions. So did the Trades Union Congress, the National Union of Teachers, the Association of Directors, the churches and a hundred and one private organizations . . . England's appetite for a new deal in education was whetted as never before.[21]

The forces mobilized are not simply summarized in the listing of major organizations which prepared reports and policy blueprints. H. C. Dent, the wartime editor of *The Times Educational Supplement*, pointed out in 1943 that:

it would be giving a wholly wrong impression to suggest that anything like a full picture of the movement for educational reform can be gathered from a study of the reports and memoranda prepared by the executives of the interested bodies. In fact, the real movement, the genuinely popular movement, has taken place very largely outside the closed doors behind which these executives have formulated their proposals and drafted their programmes.[22]

The major attempt to win support for a programme from a popular audience, through open meetings and conferences, came from an alliance formed in 1942. The Council for Educational Advance represented four organizations — the Trades Union Congress, the Co-operative Union Education Committee, the National Union of Teachers and the Workers' Educational Association. Together they comprised an original combination of forces, both from the labour movement and the educational field, which an NUT president celebrated as 'the first direct and official alliance between the NUT and the working-class movement'.

The CEA called for:

immediate legislation to provide equality of educational opportunity for all children, irrespective of their social and economic conditions, in order to equip them for a full life, and for democratic citizenship.[23]

In pursuit of this aim, hundreds of meetings were called, at which a twelve-point programme was presented for discussion, and resolutions of support sent to the Board of Education's president. Many of the points of the CEA programme were subsequently incorporated into legislation but these were concerned chiefly with questions of access and administration, and in many ways reproduced contemporary

Labour Party objectives. The question of curriculum content was not addressed. The National Council of Labour Colleges was also excluded from any direct participation in the council's work. This was a significant move since the NCLC, committed to independent working-class education, was deeply concerned with the class nature of educational content over and above the administered forms in which it was presented. Despite the exclusion, the CEA could still be attacked by Dent as too narrow in its social base:

The campaign organized by the Council has had so far a limited success. It has held many successful meetings at which considerable enthusiasm has been shown, but it has not yet succeeded in fanning to a mighty blaze the enthusiasm I know to be everywhere smouldering. Why not? First, the organizations, being all specifically representative of the 'working classes', have not attracted much support from those in the higher income ranges — that is, in positions from which effective influence could be radiated.[24]

In indicating his own preference for a politics of influence rather than of a more 'grass-roots' struggle, Dent pointed to a persistent duality in the perspectives of the CEA, as in the Labour Party. While working-class interests could be advocated, and their support canvassed, the accepted mode of operation was one of negotiation. Parliament remained the cockpit of decision-making, and the state the neutral provider.

Meanwhile some important forms of educational provision outside schooling were being expanded. The armed forces, given their increased training commitment, also established non-vocational programmes whose emphasis was firmly on current affairs. In 1941 the Army Bureau of Current Affairs was established under a civilian director, W. E. Williams of the British Institute of Adult Education. The bureau circulated a weekly bulletin to army units as the basis for a weekly discussion group which would be conducted by officers. One hour a week was to be set aside for this purpose, although evidence suggests that this was far from universal. The formal aim was to develop the soldier as a 'citizen in uniform', while maintaining morale and improving relations between the ranks. The scheme at once met with opposition from officers and politicians who feared the possibility that the opportunity to discuss politics could open a forum for the left. Calder remarks that:

where ABCA was taken at all seriously the discussion was bound to range on to the controversial points which could not be cleared up by reference to the bulletins, and where the officer in charge was not always competent to intervene. If he did intervene, ABCA would be dismissed as more 'bullshit'. If he did not, an opinionated Marxist private could sweep all before him.[25]

The existence of such a session however provided the space for political discussion, and legitimated debates which might otherwise have been proscribed. Where there was the likelihood of a more radical interest developing in the armed forces, the authorities were quick to contain it. The 'Cairo Parliament', where soldiers organized a mock parliament to conduct political debates, was closed down in 1944 after only a short time.[26] (Ironically, since the parliamentary model for debating sessions was advocated in a publication of the Association for Education in Citizenship, as an ideal method of conducting citizenship education!)[27] Commenting on the outcome of the subsequent general election of 1945, one Conservative thought that:

the forces' vote, in particular, had been virtually won over by the left-wing influence of the Army Bureau of Current Affairs. Socialism provided them with a vision and doctrine to which we had no authoritative answer or articulated alternative.[28]

War radicalism involved both a new communality ('we are all the people as long as we are willing to consider ourselves the people',[29] said Priestley) and *Picture Post*'s 'democratization of the subject'.[30] Of its new moral energies, the Labour Party became the primary political beneficiary, converting the war impulses of working together into a new consensus around state management of the economy with a parallel intervention in the field of social policy. At the same time, more radical possibilities were latent.

The Conservative stake in the drawing-up of an agenda for reconstruction then involved the pre-empting of those possibilities around a limited set of changes. Conservative education proposals retained the policy initiative in preparing (as Butler's senior civil servant advised him) for a 'major measure of educational reform' which would be 'demanded in quarters which will make the demand irresistible'.[31]

Liberal Conservatism and the 1944 Act

As early as November 1940 the Board of Education was preparing plans for reconstruction, and by 1941 a memorandum *Education after the War* was in circulation. This 'Green Book' set out the main lines which were incorporated in the White Paper on Educational Reconstruction in 1943. It

amounted to an updating and adapting of immediate pre-war policies and aims to meet the growing demand for a more radical approach. Among the officials themselves there were traditionalists who were above all anxious to preserve what they believed essentially sound, and there were others who saw a need — and an opportunity — for radical change.[32]

R. A. Butler, the politician who was to oversee these plans for educational reconstruction, went to the Board of Education as president in 1941.

Butler's role as a liberal Conservative is doubly significant since he also headed the Conservative Party's own Central Committee on Post-War Problems. He was therefore to play an important role both in the construction of educational policy and in developing Conservative thinking on broader questions of social and economic policy. Butler's assessment of education as an area of strategic importance, which would 'influence the future of England', endorsed the need for a policy which would command maximum support. Aware of the range of forces which claimed

or exerted an influence over education, he determined to avoid controversy where-
ever possible. He was warned by Churchill to minimize discussion over the question
of private education while the prospect of a confrontation with the churches posed
similar problems. The strategy was therefore to anticipate areas of opposition and
where possible circumvent them. Similarly, the thought that 'in a period of
convulsion any plan which was ready and thought out, was apt to be accepted and
put into force by the ruler or rulers of the day'[33] underlined his determination to
secure a wide base of consent: to this end it was also necessary to confront opposition
within the Conservative Party which feared the political ramifications of major
reforms, and of an expanded role by the state. In addition to addressing
constituencies within the party whose opposition could have disrupted the basis of
agreement about reform, Butler also commissioned research to assess the extent of
'public feeling' about education. The two issues which were reported to dominate
the 'public mind' were those of school fees and the school leaving age. The basic
demand was for an extended and free system of schooling, a minimal set of issues
around which reconstruction proposals could be focused.

Official inquiries which would present 'considered' views on more controversial
questions were also to prove effective in defusing any wider political controversy.
The Fleming Committee, established in 1942 at the request of the public schools,
considered the relationship of public schools to the state system. The Secondary
Schools Examination Council undertook the task of reporting on the need for
changes in the secondary school curriculum and examinations. Both were to play
significant roles in the structuring of subsequent debate. In these circumstances,
controversial elements were handled outside the immediate reconstruction proposals.
Although the situation of the churches was a major point of contention between the
Board of Education and the various church bodies, a degree of unanimity was
eventually achieved over the financing of church schools, despite residual opposition
from Catholics. As for the White Paper on Reconstruction which was presented to
Parliament, its principles had already been agreed to by the Labour dominated
reconstruction group, even before it had been presented to the Cabinet.

The subsequent adoption of the Bill by the government therefore at once
conceded the essential Labour demand of 'secondary education for all' and removed
the single most controversial issue from any debate between the major parties. The
Education Bill was introduced into the House of Commons in December 1943 and
passed into law in August 1944. Its major provisions included the abolition of
tuition fees at all state-maintained schools; abolition of the distinction between
'elementary' and 'higher' schooling with its replacement by a continuous system of
provision divided into the stages of primary, secondary and further education; and
the raising of the school leaving age to 15 and ultimately (thirty years later, in
practice) to 16. The Board of Education was upgraded to a ministry responsible for
overseeing the local authorities which would implement the Act's provisions.

No specific form of secondary school organization was stipulated in the Act,
although the Board of Education favoured the prosposals of the Norwood Committee
for a tripartite structure. The Norwood Report (1943)[34] endorsed the idea of three

types of school which were intended to cater for three different 'types' of child. According to a psychological notion of 'capacities' children would variously proceed to a secondary modern, a secondary technical or a grammar school. The question of what constituted an appropriate education for a child of allegedly determinate and determinable capacities was one which would continue to dominate the secondary school debate. The change from pre-war discussions was that instead of a simple opposition between a politics of exclusion and demands for access, the new politics were concerned with internal school forms — a narrower debate. The provision of three types of school which were then said to enjoy 'parity of esteem' obscured the retention of the social divisions inherent in the older forms of provision.

The separate issue of private education was the subject of the Fleming Report [35] published shortly before the 1944 Act became law. No real change was proposed in the relation between the state and the public schools, beyond the suggestion that a quarter of all places should be available for local authorities to use for scholarship places. Despite some complaint, the bulk of Labour MPs appeared to consider the issue one which could be postponed. A warning by the WEA in 1943 that there 'might be a strong inclination to arrive at a compromise' [36] on this issue proved correct, as did its conclusion that such a compromise would not solve the wider political problems raised by the continuance of the system. Butler wrote of the triumph that the issue could be so peacefully managed with the 'first class carriage' removed from view. [37]

In retrospect, it is clear that the moment of 1944 constituted the inauguration of a new settlement in education politics, with a considerable degree of agreement over major ends and means of educational policy. The impact of universal educational provision should certainly not be underestimated. It constituted a major victory for the Labour movement, experienced as such — the realization of a long struggle. The passing of the Education Act did not exhaust the range of possibilities for reconstruction, but it removed certain bases for confrontation. The extent to which the Act met with the wish for change would depend greatly on its mode of operation. The judgment that the 1944 Act was constructed in predominantly conservative forms, which endured in subsequent years, can be secured through an examination of the way in which the terms of the Act were taken up in its implementation by the Labour government.

The 1944 Act under Labour

The major decisions under the Act about the actual structure of schools, and the accompanying forms of control over them were those taken by the new Labour government. In the event, the forms of implementation adopted were of the most conservative kind, while the commitment to a solely administrative mode of operation disorganized those forces which had been so important in generating popular involvement in educational debate.

The Labour government selected the tripartite proposals of the Norwood Report as the system of organization for secondary schools. This in itself illustrated the persistence of longer term divisions within the party. Throughout the 1930s and the war, party policy had remained unclear — whether it was in favour of a common school for all in secondary education, or some other differentiated system:

On the one hand it admired the grammar school tradition and sought to make it available for all children irrespective of parental means. On the other, it was associated with support for the multi-lateral school which, if made the basis of a complete system of adolescent education, could only lead to the elimination of the grammar school in its traditional form.[38]

That ambivalence persisted into the policy adopted, though not without strong opposition from within the party conference. The National Association of Labour Teachers' motion condemning the government's plans as set out in a document titled *The Nation's Schools*[39] was carried against the wishes of the minister for education, Ellen Wilkinson. Despite the government concession that local authorities could experiment with multilateral or comprehensive schools, the overall position of difference between kinds of school remained largely unchanged.

What was striking in Labour's interpretation of the Act was the confidence in administration as the vehicle for achieving reform. The administrative perspective was caught in Ernest Green's opposition to the integration of private schools by compulsion:

The solution lies in the state providing education opportunities of such wide variety, encouraging experiments so comprehensive in character, and planning and staffing its schools, to provide such high standards of teaching and amenities that no parent, however rich or however snobbish, could gain any advantage either in prestige or social opportunity by paying £315 per year to maintain his son at Eton.[40]

In this view the development of the state system would itself be quite sufficient to provide both economic inducements for the abandonment of private education and a form of moral example. Any conception of the political role of public schools was abandoned. A better state system would straightforwardly persuade parents to move their children into it.

The characteristic separation of leaders and led inherent in the administrative and statist approach of Labour, entailed the demobilization of the popular dimension of wartime struggle. The idea of direct parental involvement in discussions about the course of educational reconstruction had been proposed by NUT leaders both as a means of ensuring the implementation of the Act's expansionist aspects and to retain and develop the level of interest generated during the war. At the 1945 NUT Conference 20,000 parents' meetings were called for as a means of pursuing this principle.[41]

We can take one specific example. The Birmingham CEA produced a pamphlet for the Birmingham Education Week of 1947 and its tone captured the slightly apologetic stance of an organization which from being at the forefront of a campaign found itself faced with its consequences. In an explanation of what happens in secondary education, the language of individual capacities and dispositions speaks loud:

Under the New Act, all children, no matter who they are, go on to secondary school at the age of eleven. This raises many problems, the most thorny that of individuality and personality. Heretofore children have all been learning in broadly the same way to cope with the world they have found themselves in. But from now on, each will begin to branch off on his own, according to his particular personality. Just as we each have our own individual thumb print and our own individual blood count, so we have our own individual aptitude.[42]

This combination of a psychologistic discourse invoking the individual's interest, with a universalizing 'no matter who they are', summarizes the major elements of the debate about school organization. Whether it proved persuasive is another question. The TUC had pointed out, in opposition to tripartism, ten years previously, that social divisions would be maintained by the separation of schooling along the lines of the division of labour. [43] Psychological terms were, however, increasingly familiar as a result of assessment procedures employed both in the armed services and in other areas during the war. Their apparent legitimacy, and hence their strength, lay at least partly in the wartime victory. Assessment and differentiation in the service of some greater good was a proposition not easily challenged in the absence of any adequate contemporary criticism.

The overarching ideology of citizenship also structured much of the thinking that went into redefining the relationship between schooling and the economy, and provided the basis for a new conception of curricular purpose. The Central Advisory Council's report *School and Life,* published in 1947, provided one rationale for this new conception, as well as observing the changing nature of the labour process:

The young workers, when they come to be employed as adults, may no longer require the all-round skill of their predecessors, but what they will require is a greater degree of adaptability to changes of industrial technique. Even if many have less scope for initiative, their work will require a more widespread sense of responsibility to the whole of which they are a part.[44]

This suggested an education which was essentially social in character and could not be provided by a narrow kind of curriculum knowledge:

While the old type of apprenticeships' training is less required, there is an equal if not greater need for workers who can take responsibility for a job — a more important distinction than manual skill. These may not have the skill of their predecessors, but have to be trusted with appliances and materials worth perhaps thousands of pounds. Again, certain qualities which are social as much as industrial are called for. [45]

Such a diagnosis distanced schools from any requirement to serve industry directly: it stressed the social rather than the technical preparation of labour as the proper domain of the school, and because such qualities as 'responsibility' were to be developed, it sanctioned a more informal pedagogy. These proposals therefore justified the take-up of social studies and citizenship courses on a much greater scale. Social antagonisms were often reduced to the need to form appropriate pupil attitudes of 'responsibility to the whole of which they are a part'.

Labour's investment in education as a major site for securing social change elsewhere still saw the area, in Tawney's formulation, as a means of overcoming the barrier of class-based attitudes. Questions of content and structure remained unresolved. The achievement of universal provision was coupled to a sense of purpose in removing outmoded or old-fashioned views.

It had as its other side — the reconstitution of the legal and political relations of the state. Where those relations were established on the basis of universal rights but vitiated by persisting inequality, the scope for a different politics existed. This possibility was realized in the mode of critique adopted by the Conservative Party in the later 1940s — in a politics which took advantage of divisions inherent in the tripartite structure, and of the distance between the Labour Party in government and the popular base which had helped bring it to power.

Redefining the problems: the right and 'standards'

The struggle within the Labour Party for a move away from tripartism and into forms of comprehensive education made considerable advances in the late 1940s. At the 1949 party conference, delegates heard the pledge that 'comprehensives will be encouraged wherever possible'. This prospect was not welcomed by the right, even if the government's practice was more restrictive than public statements suggested. A media critique of the concept of comprehensivization was already under way. In December 1948, a report on the American schooling system prompted the comment from *The Times* that:

the chief argument for comprehensives is not educational, but social. It is argued that they will break down class distinctions — though there is no evidence that in America they have done anything of the kind. [46]

It cautioned that during the war there had been complaints that American schools had failed to maintain maths and science teaching at a sufficient level. A week later *The Times* reported a teacher's allegations that misbehaviour among young people was increasing and this corresponded to 'the decline of old-fashioned teaching and the rise of that form of juvenile freedom so beloved of the educational psychologist'.[47] The day before, readers would also have heard of the Archbishop of York's allegations that the state's increased role in providing for the education, health and nutrition of the child was having a damaging effect on the influence of the parent.[48] A general argument about the consequences of educational change was becoming apparent, which would serve as a focus for those opposed to any extension of more egalitarian ambitions for education. The advent of comprehensives was represented as exacerbating a decline in standards, of which the concentration on non-traditional subjects was symptomatic. *The Times Educational Supplement* offered an editorial arguing:

today we are aware that over-emphasis on the humanizing and civilizing aspects of school life may result — some think is already resulting — in under emphasis on, or even neglect of the sterner and more exacting disciplines which distinguish the older traditions.[49]

This contribution was in the context of a much wider call for control over teachers. The alleged openness of the curriculum was thought vulnerable to the activities of communist teachers and others, a state of affairs which prompted demands for tighter controls from both Labour and Conservative MPs.

The Conservative Party attack on the course of post-war education followed the same pattern. A major intervention was the Conservative Political Centre's pamphlet *One Nation* (1950), which strongly argued for the state's role and the centrality of education, confirming the shift in the balance of forces within the Tory party since 1945.

Of all the services, we believe education to be second only to housing. In the long run these two services, more than any other, will determine the health, prosperity and morale of the British people. Indeed, so long as the 'cold war' against communism continues, education is more than a social service; it is part of defence.[50]

In order to justify concern, the authors argued that standards were, in many schools, 'lower than before the war', despite increased spending. The 'new' could now be set against older and more familiar practices. The remedy was clear:

The '3 Rs' will always remain the basic elements of schooling, for without them full citizenship in the modern world is impossible. Too many children, despite the raising of the school leaving age still finish their school life without knowing enough of these subjects.[51]

Such arguments had a wide currency, since the typical experience of schooling held by adults could be counterposed to the esoteric nature of educational 'progressivism'.

The Korean war was also to support further allegations that schools were 'simply not doing their job', as charges were made of low levels of literacy among army recruits.[52] Here the *One Nation* authors could offer another target, the educational experts whose support for 'progressivism' gave it added legitimacy, and whose role in arguing for comprehensivization on educational grounds was having increasing importance. Rehearsing the combination of arguments which have become familiar in the 1970s, they argued that:

the new host of 'experts', each with a specialist axe to grind, must be held in check. Too often they waste the time of overburdened teachers, and deflect the energies of their pupils from the pursuit of basic knowledge. We believe, for example, that the provision of better teachers and more staffing ratios would result in a more rational attitude towards the present expensive craze for elaborate 'visual aids'.[53]

The pamphlet defended tripartism and traditional teaching methods and a narrowing of the curriculum, adding the idea of an 'end of school test' for those children who did not go to grammar school.

For all that, the confrontations of the late 1940s and early 1950s were muffled. They took place within the guidelines of the 1944 Act from whose framework neither party departed significantly. The Conservatives claimed with justice that the Act was their creation, which Labour had inherited, and while agreement about the broad purposes of education continued, combined with effort and enthusiasm for the new spread of the service, arguments about school forms seemed less urgent. The Conservatives were determined to resist comprehensives in general, maintaining a considered detachment. Inside Labour, pleas for comprehensives, forced on the leadership by the 1951 conference, suffered from the real commitment to grammar schools inside the party and from confusion over the terms common school, multilateral, comprehensive and the like.

Labour was now caught within its own apparent achievement of one range of goals. Education remained a 'quiet' policy area through the cold war and the rising living standards of the 1950s, assuming its newly important place in an apparently immutable post-war order. Only the repeated failures of Labour in three general elections through the decade would demand the revision of Labour's central assumptions and so a new take-up of an educational agenda. It is to that very different construction of educational purposes that we turn next.

Meanwhile, we could suggest in a summary form what was distinctive to the educational politics of the 1940s. Most important was Labour's double-edged achievement: after the 1944 Act the conspicuous educational exclusions against which the party and movement had fought were done away with. Yet with Labour now in office as a (very) responsible government, this success around a politics of access (combined with the weight of administering the new system in often stringent circumstances) came to seem 'enough'. Other dimensions were lost. In particular, the class character of educational politics in the inter-war period had been displaced through the idea of 'citizenship' just as the notion of an alliance against capital had gone by the time Giles wrote his *New School Tie* (1946) which we examine in Chapter 4. In addition, the grass-roots demands and radical democratic campaigning within the forces and the domestic politics of the war itself were subsumed in the determined implementation and administration of Butler's legislation. The 1940s' settlement was thus overwhelmingly statist and effectively, despite dissenting voices (Giles's included), presented as 'non-political'.

4 Origins of the 1960s' settlement

This chapter is concerned with the genesis of the new educational settlement of the 1960s. We are interested, primarily, in the development of a framework of assumptions about 'education' which became the predominant element in public debate and which informed public policy. We omit, therefore, any detailed consideration of the administrative developments of the period: the Conservative administration of tripartitism, or the slow, local accretion of comprehensive school experiments.[1]

We suggest that the emergence of the 1960s' settlement is best analysed as the product of a distinctive alliance of three groups of forces: leading sections of the Labour Party, the organized teaching profession, and certain key intellectuals in the new education-related academic disciplines. These were the most active political agencies in the construction of the 1960s' settlement. We will also be concerned with another level of analysis: the social basis of the 1960s' alliance and the question of its popularity. Our main argument about the 1960s is summed up in the title of this book: a non-popular form of educational politics produced 'unpopular education'.

The post-war history of the Labour Party is the central strand in the story. The party was the political nucleus of the 1960s' alliance: it was Labour's social democratic repertoire which directly shaped state policy. Some features of this repertoire already had, as we have seen, a long history, traceable to Tawney's *Secondary Education for All:* the emphasis on education as state schooling, the absence of a more direct popular educative role and the stress on a politics of access at the expense of struggles over content, context or control. This kind of statist politics was reproduced, in an accentuated form, in the post-war decades.

Characteristic of the 1960s too was the close alliance between Labour and particular groups of intellectuals. We are especially interested in the role of the sociologists and economists of education and, more generally, with the place of the academic expert, as opposed to the political intellectual, in social democratic policy-making. Again, we will argue, the form of this relationship reinforced the non-popular character of expansionist policies.

The organized teaching profession was the third main element in the alliance. Teachers had played an important part in the inter-war politics of education and the association between teachers and the Labour Party remained close, secured, not least, by the numbers of teachers and lecturers who became Labour MPs.

But this relation too was reorganized, along with the internal dimensions of the profession itself. Labour's compact with the teachers assigned them to a particular, subordinate place in the alliance and tended also to distance the teachers from a popular and especially a working-class constituency.

The studies that follow (and they are studies, rather than a continuous history) are organized in part by 'agency' — Labour Party, experts and teachers, in that order — and in part by our preferred periodization of educational politics. We identify three crucial shifts. The first change was that from the bitter and defensive class politics of the 1920s and 1930s to the popular expectancy of the war and its immediate aftermath. The main product of this phase, the 1944 Act, had, as we have seen, a double impact: it realized Labour's traditional programme but disorganized the older forms of struggle. Modern evaluations of these years still reflect the same ambiguities.[2] Subsequent history was dominated by the struggle to recover a distinctive policy.

The second shift was from the frequently confused advocacy of the common school in the 1940s to the installing of educational 'equality' as a major party theme in the mid to late 1950s. The two periods had a common programmatic feature — comprehensive schooling. The common school was espoused, however, for different reasons and argued for in different terms. The left's advocacy of the 1940s was not in fact the same policy as the revisionist advocacy of the 1950s. The historical conditions were also very different: the version of the Labour left and of communist activists in the 1940s belonged to a moment of radical popular mobilization, while comprehensives became a central plank of the Labour right in a period of Conservative dominance. Although the more radical definitions of the common school continued to be upheld, notably by Marxist educationalists like Brian Simon, the modern idea of the comprehensive school was a product of the cold war era.

The third shift occurred in the early 1960s. *Signposts for the Sixties* (1961) and Harold Wilson's pre-1964 speeches summed up the main elements of the revisionist case, but joined them to newer themes, especially those of 'science'. This, the completion of the social democratic repertoire, came quite late. In what follows we look more closely, through particular writers and texts, at each of these formative moments.

Radical populism in the 1940s: science, democracy and the 'New School Tie'

The New School Tie was a short, popular, campaigning pamphlet written by G. C. T. Giles, the communist president of the National Union of Teachers (1944—5) and published in 1946.[3] It is the clearest expression we could find of the implications of war and immediately post-war radical populism for the school system and, more specifically, for the advocacy of the common school. It is useful to compare this left variant of popular educational politics with the main lines of social democratic policy-making, before and after the 1940s.

Giles was involved in official consultations around the Act and a huge programme of public meetings:

Everywhere I found general agreement that our country needs a modern scientific and democratic system of education. The old school tie tradition, which has dominated British, and especially English, education up to now, is out of date, inadequate for an epoch of rapid scientific advance, and unsuitable for the age of the common man. We need a new outlook — a *New School Tie*.[4]

Giles's pamphlet was an attempt both to express and to shape this new radical consciousness.

Giles's central goal was, in his words, 'equality of opportunity'. The inter-war injustices were described, measured and made real in terms of experience. The author's own story ('closed scholarship' to Eton and thence to Cambridge) was compared with the believable fortunes of fictional boys and girls blocked by family poverty or the intrinsic unfairness of the scholarship system. Despite 'brilliant exceptions', 85 per cent of children were confined to elementary schools, still, despite the efforts of teachers, schools for 'the lower orders'. Meanwhile the public schools continued to reproduce the prejudices and the privileges of a ruling caste.[5] The 1944 Act promised to change all this. All children would have the chance of a 'full and free education, under decent conditions' up to 16 at least. The Act provided 'the framework for a democratic and national system of education'.[6] Yet Giles explored the logic of access well beyond the limits of Tawney's or Labour's support for tripartitism. His radicalism lay in a stress on universal provision, his concern with content, and his emphasis upon popular struggle.

His starting point was basically popular: he adopted the standpoint of the average (male) parent.

The average parent is demanding for his children a better chance than he had himself, and as good a chance *as anybody else's children*. Primarily, it means the chance of a career, or at least of something better than an un-skilled, uncertain, blind-alley job.[7]

This demand suggested a popular critique of public schools, direct grant schools and, indeed, of all forms of selection. Selection only confirmed popular cynicism about the rhetoric of equality, especially the 'jargon' of 'parity of esteem'. Selection always appeared as a relatively arbitrary rationing of chances and was, indeed, a competition for limited prizes. Tripartitism, having no basis in nature, was incompatible with 'the democratic spirit of the Act' and 'the aspirations of the British people'.[8]

The new schools should, according to Giles, resemble the American or Russian models: taking all the children of an area, with a common curriculum for two years, followed by a core curriculum occupying 70 per cent of the child's time up to 16.[9] Unlike Tawney, Giles specified the broad outlines of such a schooling and the way it would differ from 'the old scholarly conception' of the grammar schools, the narrow vocationalism of the junior technical schools and the limitations of 'elementary education'. In particular it would include 'social studies', 'general science', music, art and handiwork. Specialization or streaming would be strictly limited until the age of 16, and more vocational paths thereafter would be linked to the expansion of higher education and the provision of non-vocational further education for all in county colleges. This broke decisively with any hidden retention of tripartitism within the walls of a single school. The curriculum was typical of radical versions of the 'citizen' discourse in its recognition of education's political content — the learning to be 'a conscious democrat'.[10]

Giles detected a popular fear, justified by the abandonment of Fisher's Act after the first world war, that the Act would be wrecked by inertia or vested interests. So he carefully scrutinized its compromises and evasions, especially the exemption of public schools and the retention of the dual system, for their reactionary potential. He supported the Act because of a very optimistic reading of post-war society and politics. Yet the outcome of the Act was seen to depend upon popular struggle in which the influence of parents could be decisive. After all, had not clause 76 of the Act insisted that authorities 'shall have regard to the general principle that . . . pupils are to be educated in accordance with the wishes of their parents'? In the light of later debates, Giles's interpretation of this clause is especially interesting: not 'parental choice' (which individualizes parents and reduces them to the position of consumers) but the right of all parents (and other citizens) to participate in deciding the general character of a national education system. Parents should have a say in the implementation of the Act 'not only through the councillors whom they elect, but *even more directly*'. [11] Only this could guarantee the success of the Act. Giles offered a (fictional) model of how local development plans, under the Act, should be discussed: in 'Barset' Colonel Blimp, Councillor Bumble and the headmaster of the local grammar school were publicly defeated in meetings of citizens all over the borough especially on the issues of cost and selection. Giles did not question the existing structure of educational administration; he stopped short at temporary mobilizations through association of parents and the local CEAs. But he certainly raised the question of popular control which was to disappear in the 1950s and 1960s. On matters of access, content and control, indeed, *The New School Tie* presented a clear-sighted and radical version of statist educational strategies.

Giles's conclusion on the relation between educational and other processes was more conservative. It anticipated, in several ways, the social democratic orthodoxies of the 1960s. Central to this view was a sharp contrast between the 1930s and the 1940s. The 'old' school tie belonged to a period of monopoly, unemployment, low wages and poverty — in short, to capitalist degeneracy. In such circumstances, educational reforms were easy to block and hard to argue for: the 1940s, by contrast, marked a change of almost epochal dimensions and certainly created entirely new terms for education debates.

The key features of the transformation were science and democracy. These two revolutions — of the scientists and of the people — were linked. Science promised an end to scarcity, but also changed attitudes to public education. Business needed trained scientists in order to compete internationally. Science also meant 'planning': a rational collectivization of national life in the interests of all. Science even heralded a period of international co-operation. It absolutely required an educational revolution of an egalitarian kind:

It [atomic research] proves too, that the application of science is not, and cannot be, the work of some solitary inventive genius, nor even of a selected and highly-trained few. It demands the willing co-operation of tens of thousands — scientists, administrators, technicians, workers. Science is the job of everyman. Its use or abuse will be decided by the common people. The common people must master science or be mastered by it.[12]

Giles's combination of democracy, science, planning and production was typical of English leftism in the 1930s and 1940s. The model of the Soviet Union and its ideologies of a technicist Marxism were clearly present in this scientific utopia. Yet we also find combinations that were typically social democratic: the notion that post-war society was the product of an imminent or already achieved transformation and therefore that popular needs and economic development could very easily be reconciled. The desires of 'citizens' and the requirements of the new economy could be expressed in education schemes which satisfied both. What was missing here was an adequate political economy, any knowledge of the actual nature of labour processes and therefore a more concrete account of the education—production relation. Similarly, huge divergences of experience, by class and sex especially, were hidden away in the key terms of an uncomplicated populism: 'the people', 'the common people', 'every*man*', 'the citizen'.

The almost-achieved revolution: the character and context of 'revisionism'

Giles's programme certainly represented a possible socialist strategy for education, but it was not to be realized in the 1950s. Popular support for the common school probably reached a peak in the early to mid 1940s, declining thereafter; a development linked to the terms of its advocacy.[13] Comprehensive school experiments in the 1950s were introduced by innovative local authorities, often on the prompting of the education officers and seldom with much parental involvement, the active opposition of defenders of grammar schools apart.[14] The public and direct grant schools were not swept away, as Giles had hoped, but remained, at best, a challenge to the integrity of the state system and, at worst, the basis for later reaction. The county colleges, by contrast, never materialized. Perhaps Margaret Cole rather understated the case in 1952, identifying 'a slight but perceptible recession since the hopes of 1944', but her incisive and unpompous essay presented the Labour Party as perpetually confused on these issues and still without a policy of any trenchancy.[15]

It mattered very much that the policies of the 1960s began to be developed, not in the optimistic end of the war, but during the crisis of the left that followed. This crisis can partly be understood in terms of the effects of the events of the

1950s on a radical tradition formed (or re-formed) in the 1930s. Each of the main features of this tradition — its Marxism, its conviction of Tory malevolence, its faith in 'the people' and its Soviet orientation — proved vulnerable to post-war conditions. The result was the marginalization of left thinking. Revisionism, a particular tendency in and around the Labour Party, was part of the same history, critical of Marxism for its failure to explain the present, yet with a brash iconoclasm of its own, as one-sided as the dogmas it attacked.

One feature of 1930s' Marxism was a conviction that economic crisis was insoluble in capitalist terms. Crisis heralded a socialist transformation or a fascist reaction. Thus, John Strachey, a leading Marxist theorist in the 1930s and a leading revisionist writer in the 1950s, in 1935 attacked the growing liberal consensus around 'planning' on the grounds that capitalist organization was incompatible with state intervention and high wages. This conclusion was reached, in Strachey's case at least, through an unproblematic *application* of Marx's accounts of capitalist crisis to inter-war Britain.[16] A more open view of the 1930s could have provided knowledge appropriate to the 1940s since many features of post-war conditions were already present — in politics, in the organization of opinion, and, outside the areas of the old industrial staples, in economic and social development too.[17] Yet in the absence of a development of Marxist analysis, the post-war boom, the achievement of full employment, the rise in real wages and the growth of domestic mass consumption were difficult to understand, and the initiative passed to more conservative analyses. One early response was to insist that capitalism had indeed been modified by the sheer growth of productive forces and by a change in the balance of class forces. As Strachey put it in 1952:

British capitalism *has* been compelled, by the sheer pressure of the British people, acting through our effective democratic political institutions, to do what we used to say it would never, by definition, do. It has been forced to devote its productive resources to raising the standard of life of the population as a whole . . . .[18]

But a more typical revisionist step, which reproduced the absolutism of the 1930s' judgements, was to declare that capitalism no longer existed and that Marxism had nothing to say about the new situation. This was the characteristic exaggeration of revisionism's central text, Anthony Crosland's *The Future of Socialism*.

A second 1930s' conviction concerned the fundamental malevolence of the Conservative Party. This again had origins in the experience of inter-war struggles and pre-war appeasement, but was reinforced by a version of Marxist theory that stressed the pre-given class character of the state and of ruling parties. This encouraged the belief that the Tories, once returned, would reinstate the policies of the 1930s. 'I have no doubt', wrote Strachey in 1952, 'that the instinctive *intentions* of the controlling forces of the Conservative Party are to reproduce as exactly as possible the social and economic pattern of the inter-war period'.[19] This prognostication was proved dramatically incorrect: the Conservatives invested politically in the 'more or less unlimited propensity to consume', celebrating, under

Macmillan, a veritable religion of affluence. One consequence was that the Labour Party lost its remaining claim to distinctiveness: a willingness to apply Keynesian solutions. Moreover, it now seemed plausible to argue (another fatal exaggeration) that 'the state' was in fact neutral, and that the post-war years had seen a transference of power not between classes but between 'industry' and 'the state'.[20]

A third feature of the radical tradition was what Raymond Williams has called its 'radical populism', [21] a strand already encountered in Giles. Any effective politics has, of course, to be popular, but radical populism put a special stress on great and irresistible groundswells of popular energy. Such a politics faced particular problems in periods, like the 1950s, when 'the people' seemed relatively content. In the face of such indifference, the politically active may become cynical and adopt more elitist political forms. It seems to us that this occured within the Labour Party in this period. There was certainly a tendency, most marked within the new revisionist current, to argue less from practical experiences and needs, and more from abstract ahistorical values ('equality', 'freedom' and 'democracy'), to stress central processes of policy-making, and to attempt to construct, 'top-downwards', a new constituency for the party.

As the case of Giles showed, the vision of an alternative Britain had owed much to the Soviet model. Once again, 1930s' commitments proved to be 1950s' liabilities. The battle of cold war affiliations once lost, Sovietism was easily stigmatized as treason. The actual deformations of Stalin's regime, the lack of democracy in the western parties, the Russian interventions in East Germany and Hungary added enormous internal stresses to the outside pressures. This was reinforced by the growing conservatism of English intellectuals and the influence of American social science that constructed a notion of 'society' around the very idea of consensus. Everywhere there was a pull towards the consensual middle ground. As Stuart Hall has put it, 'anything drifting left of centre seemed in imminent danger of falling off the edge of the world into the clutches of the Kremlin'.[22]

It was in this context, then, that Labour's educational programme was rethought. The revisionist tendency within the party, associated with the journal *Socialist Commentary*, the organization Socialist Union, the writings of Crosland, Strachey and Jenkins and, eventually, with Gaitskell's leadership of the party, was mainly responsible for this process.[23] Educational thinking was located within the broad revisionist analysis of Britain: a post- or mid-revolutionary society, so the argument went, only a society with the wrong people in charge.

Education and 'a more classless society'

Educational reform had a central place in revisionist politics. This was to be later demonstrated by Crosland's occupancy of the ministry of education and his feeling that 'many of my colleagues thought Education of the greatest importance'.[24] At the same time revisionist writings on education now seem very thin, narrow and unsatisfactory. Despite a pose of 'sensible' judgement, these texts are very doctrinaire: they develop some general principles about society then follow through some educational implications. As Crosland put it:

Our belief in comprehensive reorganization was a product of fundamental value-judgements about equity and equal opportunity and social division as well as about education.

In terms of the categories we have developed so far, this form of educational politics focused, very narrowly indeed, on *access*. Education was understood within the context of a 'social' politics, a politics, that is, that stressed the distribution of social benefits and privileges. As we shall see in more detail in discussing the sociologies, this involved a conception of 'class' that was fundamentally distributional, reduced to aspects of inequality. There were no necessary connections between these aspects, but in Britain, a peculiarly 'class-bound' society, the various criteria of class produced 'deep incisions' in 'the social body'.[26] Differences of educational opportunity were central to the perpetuation of privilege and social distance, reproducing the unfair chances for talent and the persistent differences in speech, manners, leisure and ways of life. Education, indeed, was 'the most divisive, unjust and wasteful of all the aspects of social inequality'.[27] It was also uniquely productive of 'resentment'. Education was not discussed as an end in itself, nor as a source of values of a humanistic kind nor as an element entering into economic productivity, the stress of the 1960s. It was discussed rather as a consumer good, a mark of status and a means to personal social mobility. The problem with education lay not so much in what it *was*, or what it *did*, but in *how it was distributed*. In this view, all sense of education as a lived process (occurring in and out of schools) was completely lost.

'Equality', the key term of 'social politics' was pursued in two rather different directions. Equality of opportunity was the first main aim, a more efficient and fair selection and reward of talent. The language and the distinctions of intelligence testers were, especially in the 1950s, retained at the heart of these discussions: 'pool of ability', 'untapped talent', 'the top 1 per cent', 'our beta resources' (Crosland) or 'the next 20 or 30 per cent' (Jenkins).[28] At this stage, however, this was more an argument about 'leadership' and (a kind of) social justice than about the 1960s' concern with economically useful skills.

Revisionism's *distinctive* argument, however, was that equality of opportunity was not enough. In a society like Britain, indeed, it would only serve to deepen class divisions. It must be accompanied by the pursuit of 'equality' — 'all that was enshrined in the age-old socialist dream of a more classless society'.[29] This involved some structural equalization, a lessening of social distance between classes, primarily through taxation and through social policies, and the promotion of 'growth' with its inherently equalizing effects.[30]

This was, of course, the most radical-sounding aspect of the programme. Radicalism was limited, however, in two main ways. It was limited, first, by the conception of class which we have already noted. If class was principally a question of distribution, then it could also be represented as a *matter of degree*. One really could refer to a 'more' or a 'less' classless society. The distinction was quantitative not qualitative. Class was not about social relations, or power, but about degrees of social difference or social distance, and the degrees of 'resentment' or contentment that followed. The *extent* to which social equality was desirable could become a matter of fine judgement, nicely measured, for example, in taxation policies. At this point, the second limitation often came into operation – the contradiction between 'equality' and 'equality of opportunity'. The argument about talent did indeed prescribe a degree of *in*equality. According to Crosland:

No socialist . . . has disputed the need for a degree of inequality here, both because superior talent deserves some rent of ability, and because otherwise certain kinds of work, or risk, or burdensome responsibility will not be shouldered.[31]

There may come a point when 'equality' reacts back on incentives, and it is important to identify this moment exactly. Social arrangements, therefore, should be equal enough but not *too* equal. What, then, was the (more or less) 'classless society'? Crosland's definition sums up the revisionist answer:

The second distinctive socialist ideal is social equality and 'the classless society'. The socialist seeks a distribution of rewards, status, and privileges egalitarian enough to minimise social resentment, to secure justice between individuals, and to equalise opportunities; and he seeks to weaken the existing deep-seated class stratification, with its concomitant feelings of envy and inferiority, and its barriers to uninhibited mingling between the classes. This belief in social equality, which has the strongest ethical inspiration of virtually every socialist doctrine, still remains the most characteristic feature of socialist thought today.[32]

There were three main implications of all this for educational policy. Labour should complete the programme of 1944, especially the raising of the school leaving age, the training of more teachers and the raising of educational standards in state schools. Labour must also 'tackle' the question of the public schools, not so much by abolition as by 'complete integration' within the state system. In this way the schools would retain their 'distinctive character', but the more socially mixed intake would break the old association with family and money.[33] Finally, Labour should encourage moves towards the abolition of selection at eleven and the growth of comprehensive schooling.

The resulting conception of the comprehensive school differed markedly however from Giles's. According to Jenkins, a comprehensive was a school which offered:

a wide range of studies from the age of eleven to eighteen and includes within its intake children now classified into the different types of grammar, technical and modern. It does not imply that those children will be taught in the same classes and all do the same work. They must be divided according to intelligence and aptitude . . . but the divisions will be less sharp and less final.[34]

Similarly for Crosland, 'division into streams according to ability' remained essential.[35] It was not the abolition of selection that was aimed at, but a 'softening' of it.[36] Comprehensives could not abolish all 'competition' or 'envy', but they could 'avoid the extreme social division caused by physical segregation into schools of widely divergent status'. They would lessen the 'extreme social resentment' caused by the failure to win a grammar school place, thought to be the only avenue to a middle-class occupation.

In Brian Simon's categorization of types of comprehensive school ideal, the revisionist version is clearly 'the sociological' or 'the socio-political'. It was the same conception that Simon was to find installed at the National Foundation of Educational Research during Crosland's ministry. As Simon has pointed out, the stress is not on an equal access to knowledge for all children (Giles's version) but on certain social-psychological principles: 'the need for children of different social classes to understand each other better'.[37] The problem here, as with revisionism generally, is that socialist-sounding words and phrases threaten, all the time, to tip over into something else: justice into legitimization, equality into pacification, social transformations into ideological effects, classlessness into 'rational' hierarchy and fraternity into 'social cohesion'. In this alchemy of socialist ideals and concepts, there is, as we have suggested, a deeply anti-popular trend. Popular experience is viewed from outside, from above, as a source of 'resentment' or 'contentment'. As we will argue more fully later, revisionism is best understood, not, indeed, as a form of socialism, but as an ideology of professional politicians.

The circle closed: education and economic growth

Revisionism formed a large part of the educational agenda of the 1960s, especially its *social* themes. Yet it belonged to a very specific phase of post-war development, a phase of conspicuous economic success and, on the left, of political defensiveness; of capitalist boom and Conservative hegemony. It looked to America and Sweden for its new social politics, bringing home the message of a more open society. The Marxists and radical populists of the period, still more heavily besieged, dug deeper into a national history but failed to produce a more adequate account of the post-war transitions. These conditions proved, however, to be quite transitory. The late 1950s and early 1960s saw the break-up of Conservative hegemony and the discrediting of the three ideological figures of 'affluence', 'consensus' and 'embourgeoisement'. Conservative management of the economy was shown to have failed and the underlying problem of profitability and capital accumulation took on more intractable forms. There was a revival, too, of middle-class dissent, the first phase of a 'new politics'. In a society assumed to have become middle-class, there were rediscoveries of distinctively working-class presences and challenges. The explosive emergence of 'youth', especially of male, working-class subcultures, became a focus for a host of more diffused social anxieties. These new social realities, especially the deepening of economic difficulties, now entered the discourse on education. The two main forms which they took were arguments about 'growth' and arguments about 'youth'.[38]

The earlier revisionism was weak on these themes. The main wobbles in revisionist writing, especially in the late 1950s, often came on questions concerning the new agenda. Here is Jenkins (admittedly the most banal and conservative of revisionist writers) on the relation of schooling, employment and 'youth', especially on abolishing the eleven plus:

There would be a softening of the process of selection because of a narrowing in the difference of prestige. There is no comparison between the effect of failure to get into a particular form and failure to get into a particular type of school. Of course, it can be argued that life is certain to bring its successes and failures and that there is no point in trying to disguise the harshness of human experience. This is so, but it is hardly a reason for wanting children to be branded into one category or the other from the age of ten.[39]

The dilemmas of equality in a class society are rather openly displayed here. They are resolved by what any hard-headed Tory would recognize as a sentimental gesture. 'Life' is still awkwardly at variance with humane educational aims. It was this gap which the new emphases of the 1960s were to close.

We might consider the new emphases through some representative and influential statements. One key figure was John (later Professor, later Lord) Vaizey. Vaizey was one of a group of economists and students of social policy who began, in the early 1950s, to apply the techniques of national income accounting to expenditure on the public services. From this 'dull, dry and statistical' beginning key issues arose, especially the reciprocal relations between economic development and the growth of the educational system. These themes were crisply stated in *The Costs of Education* as the search for 'an organic theory':

A rising national income requires a more skilled labour force to operate the economy, and therefore a rise in the educational attainments of that population, while at the same time releasing the resources for undertaking that education. This may be couched, in terms, especially, of trained manpower, to illustrate it forcefully.[40]

As an academic economist, Vaizey played a part in the development of bodies of knowledge (the economics of education, development and 'modernization') that provided the basis for the practical common sense of 1960s' educational policy-makers. As important was his conception of the economist's role in relation to policy and public opinion. The economist should be 'a craftsman', perhaps 'a critical commentator'. His contribution should lie less in 'highly theoretical' disputes, more in 'making pragmatic and helpful suggestions to statesmen and administrators'.[41] Vaizey certainly came to occupy a strategic position, of this kind, in 1960s' policy-making. He combined the worlds of professional economics, high university politics, and international organizations (especially the OECD and UNESCO) with those of social democratic politics, public inquiries and direct personal advice to leading politicians. He introduced the main general perspectives of the economics of education into official calculation and political discourse. This involved a deliberately 'practical' presentation of theory and a commitment to popularization. His Penguin Special, *Education for Tomorrow,* was published in 1962 and revised and reprinted throughout the 1960s.[42]

Vaizey's stance, however, was not uncontradictory. In professional debates, he was a sceptic, even an agnostic. He was doubtful of the main theories and technical findings of the field. One colleague, at an international conference of economists in 1963, commented on 'the systematic simplicity of Mr Vaizey's paper'.[43] Yet this did not inhibit advice to statesmen or prognostications about growth, affluence, the coming of a middle-class society or an educational new era. The ringing phrases read oddly today: 'It is quite true that by 1980 we shall be able to afford a lavish education service, a lavish health service, a lavish road system.'[44] Yet these writings of the 1960s are a prime source for the assumptions that underpinned policy and are second only to Sir Harold Wilson's speeches as a political statement of the importance of economic themes.

Vaizey's characteristic contribution was to offer a view of the necessary *convergence* of economic imperatives, egalitarian goals and human needs. It was not necessary to face the choices posed by Jenkins's vision of 'life' at all. All the arguments and most bodies of expertise, pointed inexorably to the same sets of conclusions. Contradictions (or the problematic character of the everyday social world) were granted only minor, technical appearances. The invariable form of resolution was the expansion of the education system in cost-effective and economically (that is, socially and humanly) appropriate ways. Typical of the optimistic sweep of the argument was his discussion of the convergences of 'manpower planning', the social ideals of Raymond Williams's early work, the criticism of grammar school education produced by the Crowther Report, the British Association's critique of premature specialization, and the findings of contemporary social scientists. It was:

heartening, for the cultural-cum-pedagogic argument for liberalisation, and non-selection, are reinforced by 'manpower studies'. When to this is added the over-whelming evidence, in report after report, of immense flows of talent leaving the education system at 15, 16 and 17, and of the potentialities for developing talent, a striking conclusion emerges. For the first time psychology, economics, sociology, and liberal opinion coincide exactly — more education is an indisputable basis of better education in every sense of that multi-faceted phrase.[45]

How, then, were these resolutions achieved?

The founding insight of the economics of education was that formal education could be treated not only as a form of consumption, but also as a type of invest-ment. Increases in national income made educational expansion possible in the form of the consumption of a surplus, but, so the argument went, 'education is also a major cause of the growth of output'.[46] It produced individual and social returns analogous to those accruing from 'physical investment': it was indeed an investment in 'human capital', in the intellectual and cultural quality of labour power.

If empirical tests of these principles remained vexatiously imprecise and tricky, their general validity or usefulness could still be held to stand:

When all these caveats have been entered, the evidence for two propositions seems to be overwhelming: the individual returns to investment in education are at least as high as the returns to investment in physical capital in a market economy like that of the United States; and the social returns, in all economies, are also extremely high. Furthermore, the changing requirements of the economy for skilled manpower should guide educators on the kinds of educational structure that is needed, and the content of the curriculum.[47]

The stress on education-as-investment already permitted the collapse of human needs into economic imperatives. Education was, after all, an 'investment in mankind'.[48] But these general perspectives did not necessarily prescribe egalitarian forms of educational expansion of the type that the 1960s' policies were represented as being. Indeed, Vaizey's own preferred perspective of 'manpower planning' could equally well point to a highly selective system, since it implied important discriminations between different types of 'manpower' and 'skill' — managerial, technical and manual for instance.[49] The economics of education certainly identified real relations between education and the economy, but it by no means followed that the dynamic of capital accumulation and the transformations of the hierarchies of labour pointed to the raising of the school leaving age or the abolition of the eleven plus. The recruitment of the economics of education to the side of social democracy required further assumptions and arguments.

Central here was the argument about skills and what may be termed the general thesis of 'upskilling'. At its most modest, this thesis merely pointed to specific shortages of 'skilled', even 'highly skilled' labour. These findings were usually based on comparisons between the formal educational systems of industrialized societies and their outputs of 'trained' people. The stress was usually on managerial and professional skills: 'We are short of nurses, architects, teachers, skilled clerical workers, social workers, engineers and scientists.'[50] We must note again, however, that the need for scientists, technicians and professional state servants did not necessarily point to egalitarian policies. Traditionally these occupations and the intermediate social strata had been catered for in general by the grammar and technical sectors of the tripartite system. An expansion of grammar and technical education and a reform of the curricula might have sufficed for economic requirements. Judged in its economic logic then, the argument for egalitarianism depended on a more global thesis about skill.

In Vaizey this tended to take two main forms. First, there was the assertion that all jobs everywhere in society were, nowadays, requiring greater stocks of ability and knowledge. This was allied to an equally general argument that knowledge itself had entered a period of geometrical expansion. There was just so much more knowledge to know. 'Resilience to change', 'flexibility' and 'adaptability' formed the second main strand in the argument. Employment demanded more than the 3 Rs: also the ability to calculate, drive vehicles, manage complicated equipment, 'meet the requirements of an increasingly complex social organization' and acquire 'a high level of emotional adjustment to situations of rapid change'.[51]

The argument was usually at the most general level. Specifically working-class resistances to 'the technological society' were rarely addressed. Vaizey often turned attention, indeed, to other targets: especially the inexpertise of civil-service mandarins (ignorant of econometrics and planning) and the old Etonians of Conservative cabinets. Leadership too should be meritocratic and 'flexible'. While the (class) levels of applicability of the argument were left unspecified, the full 'humanist' resolution was possible:

This (the manpower perspective) is not an anti-humanist point of view. On the contrary a high level of general culture — as well as being the ultimate end of educational activity — is necessary for the adaptation of the working force to the new economy. The place for the unskilled worker in modern economies is diminishing rapidly. As the economy develops it needs more, and more diverse, skills that rely upon a general background of education for their development. A growing economy also requires adaptable workers who can quickly and with ease leave one speciality and take up another.[52]

Again, very different real experiences are hidden here in a quite undiscriminating general thesis. Later in this book we will look more critically at these characteristic economic ideas of the 1960s, and especially at the completely unexamined category of 'skill'. It is however worth ending this section by noting the distance between the dominant 1960s' educational ideas and a popular or working-class perspective on education.

One revealing example is Vaizey's treatment of the question of youth, a treatment typical of this major contemporary preoccupation. Like 'skill' and 'growth' this was treated, in large part, as a general category: 'the apparent spread of delinquency and social breakdown among young people' and 'the growth of an autonomous adolescent culture'.[53] On the whole, liberal opinion in the 1960s was on the side of 'the young': Vaizey welcomed the more questioning, more scientific, more self-reliant attitudes of young people, defended them against moralists, and drew, himself, on a liberal reforming Anglicanism.[54] In so far as adolescent behaviour posed problems, he looked, of course, to educational solutions. At this point, however, the class character of the argument became more apparent: it was only certain kinds of 'youths' who posed problems: 'children of lesser ability from the working class':

They come from homes where parental concern with their achievements is not high and where frequently the most important factor for developing intelligence — the use of accurate English with a large vocabulary — is uncommon and from delinquent and semi-delinquent streets. If only to prevent delinquency, therefore, the schools must try to overcome these handicaps. The effort would lead to a substantial improvement in the achievements in school of the children of the working class.[55]

The identification of delinquency with educational 'failure' and with the family and neighbourhood culture of working people is a typical sociological truism of the period. More surprising is the completely explicit statement about the purposes of the whole schooling enterprise that follows:

This [improving the schooling of working-class children] would undoubtedly be the most effective way of eliminating the social problems of the so-called delinquent areas, a name which masks a much wider social problem – the failure to integrate the unskilled and semi-skilled working class into a society which is becoming predominantly governed by the values and standards of the professional middle class.[56]

This is surprising because it completely abandons the characteristic stance of most social democratic argument, a stance which, at one moment at least, is at the side of, or on behalf of, the working class. The stance here is explicitly on the side of the 'professional middle class' for whom other social groups constitute a problem. We find again that same professional middle-class Fabianism which begins to emerge as the 'hidden curriculum' of much social democratic thinking about education in the 1960s.

The 'old' sociology of education: features and phases

The close relation between Labour Party policy and the 'old' sociology of education has already been identified as a feature of the 1960s' alliance. In this section, we look more closely at this relation, focusing on the heyday of the old sociology, in the 1950s and 1960s.

Perhaps the most striking feature of the old sociology of education has been the continuity and consistency of its development. In the most recent work, based in the Oxford social mobility project at Nuffield College, A. H. Halsey and his co-workers construct a distinguished intellectual and political ancestry and insist on the continued relevance of a 'particular style of social research'. Its origins lie in the London School of Economics in the years before and immediately after the war, and especially in the social mobility studies directed by Professor D. V. Glass, but the ancestry is traced back to Charles Booth and the Webbs, and to a still longer tradition of 'political arithmetic'. According to Halsey, this tradition has always pursued a double intent: the accurate description of 'social conditions' and the advocacy of 'political reform'. 'It has been an attempt to marry a value-laden choice of issue with objective methods of data collection.'[57]

We shall return to the question of ancestry later, especially the extent to which the modern social research belongs to a lineage that can be traced back to the early nineteenth century in which 'statistics', investigation of the state of 'the poor' and state-related expertise have fuelled a non-popular form of politics. There is indeed a long Benthamite, Fabian, revisionist and social-reforming tradition to be traced here. What is missed, in all such pedigrees, is the precise post-war location of sociological expertise and the relations and dilemmas to which this gave rise. The most obvious feature was the location of expertise within the educational system itself. This was true for the sociologists themselves, each of whom traced their own paths through the educational system arriving at its university apex as professional academic researchers, but it was true, more structurally, for the academic character of the discipline or practice itself. The new education-related disciplines were an important source of public representations of schooling: their knowledges fed what we have called 'ideologies of schooling'. But they provided representations with a particular authority, backed by 'objective methods of data-collection' and by the professionalism of academic research. This power was used both to influence the higher reaches of the education system itself (through the introduction of a new sub-discipline) and to influence other sites of educational control, especially the public world of politics and policy.

As Halsey makes clear, the sociologists of education sought primarily to exercise the second kind of influence though they also influenced the main currents in teacher education. This was consistent with the Fabian origins of 'political arithmetic' and the policy-related traditions of the London School of Economics. As Bernstein has argued, it was from this source that the infant discipline, the creation of a handful of people, especially of A. H. Halsey and Jean Floud, gained its initial legitimacy.[58] What interests us in the tradition, from this perspective, is its characteristic duality: its drive towards disciplinary professionalism and academic self-reproduction (with the stress on autonomy and 'objectivity') and, on the other hand, the pull towards policy-making, especially within the social democratic connection. What influence did this connection — between professional research and professional politics — have on the possibilities of a popular politics of education in the 1960s?

The consistency of the main tradition of post-war educational research means that we can present and criticize it as a unity. Nonetheless, it is useful to sketch a history of the tradition before considering more long-term features.

We may distinguish three main periods, though we should not expect a tight or unified periodization. We may regard the first period, up to the mid or late 1950s, as a period of foundations in a very strong sense. The sociology of education developed at the London School of Economics under the influence of the demographic expertise of Professor D. V. Glass and the social philosophy of T. H. Marshall.[59] Most of the early sociologists were trained as researchers on the LSE social mobility project which, from the beginning, had a strong educational emphasis. Like J. W. B. Douglas's book on *The Home and the School* it had strong connections with Glass's work on the Population Investigation Committee and the Royal Commission on Population, which reported in 1949. Most of the intellectual and political features of the tradition derive from this period: the close connection with government agencies and state funding, the general sociology of 'class' and of 'status', the demographic or 'sociographic' character of the method, the commitment to long-term accumulative results, comparable across time and between countries, and the ambition, best seen in Glass's own quite militant political style, to influence state policy. Because this early work was paradigmatic for what followed, we will draw on it heavily in discussing the main features of the tradition as a whole.

The late 1950s and early 1960s were also distinctive, but in a somewhat looser way. If the sociology of education grew up under the study of demography and social mobility, it was in the mid to later 1950s that it began to be defined and promoted as a distinct academic sub-discipline, itself formative of more general sociological orientations. This involved several important moves: the identification of theoretical forbears, more concerned with a general sociology than empirical social research (especially Mannheim and Durkheim); the definition (and limitation) of the sphere of the new sub-discipline — now defined as 'a specialized field of study'; the demarcation from adjacent sub-specialism, especially psychology and anthropology; the internationalization of the field of intellectual debate, especially the reception of American influences; and the concern with the teaching of the sub-discipline and, especially, its introduction into teacher education. If the most important texts of the first phase were the reports on detailed empirical researches into educational inequality, the second phase was characterized, in part, by the authoritative reviews of the state of the field and by the production of 'textbooks' or 'readers'.[60]

It is not that the older concerns were dislodged, but they were certainly framed and understood in a new way. First, the particular province of the sociology of education was more precisely defined and thereby limited. A broader definition of 'education' in terms of cultural transmission or reproduction was rejected in favour of a stress on formal educational institutions. 'Education' in other words was closely identified with 'schooling'. Education was treated as a specialized set of institutions whose internal and external relations were to define the object of study.[61] This move in sociological definitions, already implicit in the approach via social mobility, committed educational researchers to the same 'statist' solution that we have already traced in the history of social democratic politics. Formal institutions were at the centre of the stage; they were regarded indeed as the characteristically modern educational form, appropriate to 'industrial society'. Less formal kinds of knowledge, produced in other social sites, were bound to be rendered marginal by this preoccupation, reappearing, however, as 'problems' for educators, as inhibitions on 'education'.

Second, the relation between education institutions and other social sites, though grasped as the central 'macroscopic' problem of the new discipline, tended to be formulated in structural-functionalist terms.[62] The sociology of status and class was overlaid by a more Americanized vision of the desirable integration of social institutions and by the large ahistorical abstraction of 'technological society' or industrialism. Lacking a macro-sociology of its own, the sociology of education tended to absorb these elements piecemeal, while arguing against certain 'function-alist' excesses, especially the neglect of conflict and change.[63]

Third, it was within this theoretical space, that the newer economic emphases of the 1960s were then thought.[64] To the older problematic of inequality was added the concern with the economic efficiency of education as a process of selection. This additive process reinforced — it certainly did not challenge — the fundamental social-democratic assumption of the 1960s: that egalitarian forms of educational expansion were entirely compatible with the needs of a modern technological economy. This connection, indeed, was seen as lying at the heart of the rationale of the new discipline itself. As Halsey and Floud put it in 1958: 'In short, industrialism gives rise to — or at least justifies — the sociology of education as a specialized field of study.'[65] The chief textbook of this phase, Halsey's, Floud's and Anderson's *Education, Economy and Society* (1961), comes near to celebrating this connection, adopting, in a quite uncritical form, the leading propositions of the most propagandist forms of the economics of education.[66]

The third period is even less easy to describe with any sense of coherence. Projects begun in the 1950s (like Douglas's for example) often came to fruition in the 1960s. We might think of the 1960s, however, as the decade in which the intellectual and especially the political project of the old sociology was partly realized. From this perspective, the history, up to the 1970s, was a real success-story. Within the education system, the new discipline was installed and its emphases disseminated with startling rapidity. Bernstein's judgement — that sociological expansion was aided by the institutional expansion of teacher education — is surely correct.[67] But the cementing of the policy connection was equally marked. In his interviews with Crosland and Boyle, Maurice Kogan points to the growth of a new educational establishment in which social scientists played a leading part, including professional academics like Halsey and Vaizey.[68] The connection was strengthened by Labour's return to office in 1964. Crosland tells how, as Minister of Education, he used the ideas of sociologists and economists, constituting his own informal consultative bodies. To such 'experts', indeed, he attributed the successful undermining of the practice of selection at eleven plus: 'It wasn't the Department, in fact, that cracked the Eleven Plus doctrine, but it was mainly such outsiders as Vaizey, Floud, Halsey and the rest.'[69] Crosland, himself an economist, was a key figure in linking post-war social science to the transformations of the post-war Labour Party, a project begun very early in *The Future of Socialism.* At the same time, sociological findings were increasingly mediated to a wider political public especially through the educational reports of the 1960s. Bodies like the Plowden Committee included on their membership not only a traditional membership of HMIs, teachers, local educational administrators, but also the chairman of the Social Science Research Council (Dr M. Young), the editor of *New Society* (a major popularizing organ of the new sociologies) and professors of economics and social administration. Such inquiries were often founded in part on the sociologists' problematic: in this case the close association of 'home and social circumstances and academic achieve- ment'.[70] Similarly, research on the ground followed the main themes announced by Glass and then by Halsey and Floud. The key moments were Douglas's *The Home and the School* (1967), Halsey's directorship of the experiment of the educational priority areas in the later 1960s, and a cluster of school-based studies deriving from the department of sociology at the University of Manchester.[71] Only by the end of the decade was the 1960s' sociology of education beginning to reach its limits, to be challenged by entirely new paradigms. The history of challenge or dissolution will be discussed in later parts of this book.

An anatomy of statist research

We want to stress four main features of the old sociology: the relation of two key concepts — 'class' and 'status'; the characteristic method; the main findings and explanations; and the relation to politics. This is intended more as an analytic description of key features of the tradition than a full-scale criticism.

An excellent starting point is Glass's introduction to *Social Mobility in Britain*, published in 1954:

The core of the general investigation is the study of social mobility in Britain — of the extent of movement in social status or social position by individuals of diverse social origins. Such a study assumes a hierarchy of social status — that society is arranged in a series of layers — and that there are criteria which may be used to indicate the status level, or position in the hierarchy, of an individual or a group.

Later in the same introduction he discussed the problem of method:

The studies in this volume are rather formal and quantitative; the subtleties of social relationships have not generally been examined. This limitation springs from the need to establish an order of priority in developing systematic research into problems which, as occurs so often in sociology, have hitherto been treated on an *ad hoc* basis.[72]

In comparing sociology with demography, Glass stressed the interdependence of research and government activity and the need for 'an overall picture' of a quantitative kind. It was necessary first to chart the actual movements within the population and 'the primary objective characteristics' with which mobility or immobility were associated. The tradition was to follow this programme with remarkable exactitude, including Glass's stress on statistical standardization and on comparable and accumulative results.

The first point to be drawn from the description is the distinction between status and class. Despite the centrality of both notions, their meanings and relations were to remain persistently unclear. We have traced three main sets of usages, the first characteristic of the earliest work, especially of *Social Mobility in Britain*, the second of the whole middle period of the later 1950s and 1960s, the third associated with the modern Oxford mobility studies and with theoretical clarifications which draw on the sociology of Max Weber. We might call these three versions: status over class; class as status; and class alongside status. All three versions share a tendency either to marginalize the classic conception of class or to redefine it in a relatively weak form.

In *Social Mobility in Britain*, 'status' and the associated notion 'citizenship' are promoted over class as the major categories of social difference. The studies conform, in this respect, to the sociology of T. M. Marshall (who, according to Glass, suggested the project in the first place)[73] and to the moment of 'citizenship' as described in Chapter 3 of this book. As Glass put it, 'the research is concerned with social status or social prestige, and not with social class in the classical sense of the term'.[74] Social mobility was defined as movement between status groups, not between classes; status was defined as groupings of occupations ranked according to the degrees of prestige awarded to them by the community as a whole.[75] The essays consistently use phrases like 'movements up and down the social scale', while terms like 'working class' and 'middle class' are conscientiously placed in inverted commas. Here, at least, the preference is clear, though Glass's argument that *Social Mobility* also throws light on social class remains cryptic and confusing.[76]

In the middle period, the same or similar social phenomena were simply renamed 'class'. The title of the main education study within the social mobility project was *Social Class and Educational Opportunity* (1956). The same or similar social grouping now appeared as classes. Some variant of a familiar scheme was used throughout the tradition with occasional changes of terminology: upper and lower professional, clerical, non-manual and supervisory, skilled and unskilled or 'upper' and 'lower' working class.[77] If class disappeared in the earliest work, in the middle period it was redefined *as* status, made to conform to a sociology of 'stratification'. It assumed a form required by the substantive concerns of the inquiry into social mobility — the form of 'origins' (usually fathers' occupation) and 'destinations' (usually sons' class position or status). As Anne-Marie Wolpe has argued, such categories systematically exclude women.[78] They also invite us to understand class as a form of distribution and social evaluation rather than a relation of power and exploitation. Moreover, the original implication of stratification theory, that 'lower' social status is, in all respects, evaluatively inferior, was retained. Individual social mobility was accordingly an entirely rational strategy; anything that militated against it — forms of collective struggle or alternative cultural preferences, for instance — might be seen as deviant or pathological. The whole sociological approach to working-class culture (in the shape of parental attitudes to schooling) was framed within these assumptions.

Finally, in the Oxford studies, class and status are systematically distinguished along neo-Weberian lines. Class is a feature of 'similar market and work situations'; 'status' retains its connection with subjective social evaluations, but tends to become an omnibus category embracing all significant social distinctions which are not rooted in 'class' (for example, gender, age and race).[79] In practice, classes still consist of occupational groupings and the category still sits rather inertly in the research as the basis of statistical calculation. Classes are seen as an outcome of the division of labour and class structure may be transformed by economic change, but classes are not a source of transformation. They may compete for educational resources (one of the most interesting themes of the old sociology) but do not engage in more collective forms of struggle.

The effect of these intellectual features is very similar to those we noted in the Croslandite politics of education. There is a sense in which the old sociology has never been concerned with a politics of class, but always with a politics of status. From Marshall and Glass to the later Halsey, the concerns have been with equality of opportunity and more social mobility and, beyond that, with a lessening of social divisions, an evening of conspicuous status distinctions and a greater social unity on the basis of 'fraternity' or 'citizenship'. According to Marshall, the welfare state must recognize the necessity of some inequality but was opposed to 'rigid class divisions' or 'sharply distinguished culture patterns'.[80] Glass stressed the importance of social mobility in lessening feelings of personal frustration and securing social harmony.[81] In Halsey's Reith lectures of 1978, he stressed a third route to 'social order': neither Soviet communism nor nineteenth-century liberalism, but 'fraternity as citizenship', a social ideal drawing on both Tawney and Marshall.[82] Again, the danger is that equality becomes, in these analyses too, less an end in itself and more a means to social order or cohesion, while fundamental social relations remain unmodified. We must return to this criticism in a more consolidated way later.

Turning to questions of method, we have already noted how Glass himself saw quantification as a relatively blunt tool for the analysis of 'social relationships'. The later history of the tradition exemplified his comment. The most effective radical cutting-edge of the research corresponded to its methodological strengths and the ability to map, over long periods and with comparable results, the main class-based inequalities of educational access. The tradition has produced a formidable documentation of this kind. Its persistent weakness, aside from the neglect of women which, in the most recent studies, is quite simply astonishing, lay in the explanations offered for the outcomes observed.

Some explanatory purchase was to be gained, initially, through statistical correlations of a relatively straightforward kind: especially with other demographic data (the size of families; the pressure of larger or smaller cohorts of school-age children on existing provision; obvious material aspects of housing and other resources). It was also possible to gauge, comparatively, the effects of changes in the overall organization of schooling, especially where these were of a radical kind — the inauguration of secondary education for all after 1944, for instance. It was also possible to show the somewhat differing movements of 'class chances' in education in different regional histories, as for example in the famous comparison of south west Hertfordshire and Middlesbrough. Especially after the later 1950s, however, research was committed to the twin hypotheses that educational outcomes were much influenced by the social and cultural background of school students and by the detailed character of school organization and selection. It was on this 'qualitative' ground that 'sociography' began to fail, for it required an understanding of 'experience' and of cultural process, for the investigation of which the 'administered' questionnaire, the random sample and the extensive survey were very blunt instruments indeed. Attempts to cut into the lived cultures of particular classes and social groups by treating them as measurable variables produced, at best, tautologies (working-class attitudes are those which inhibit individual success at school) or merely reinforced the social biases of the researchers. As Klein put it in 1965:

Even the most sympathetic writers on working-class ways of life remark on what appears as a stubborn determination not to develop — and not to allow others to develop — attitudes or behaviour that would make for a richer and more interior life.[83]

The categories used in this research were often obtuse to the point of sheer brutality. Homes were judged 'favourable' or 'unfavourable' to educational success on the basis of administered questionnaires in which answers like the following were 'each awarded one mark':

at least one visit to the primary school in the course of the year of the inquiry for reasons connected with education, including the discussion of the child's secondary education with the Head Teacher . . .; a stated preference for some form of selective secondary education; the intention of keeping the child at school at least to the age of 16; the wish that the child should undergo some form of further education or training on leaving school.[84]

Classification followed on a scale from 3 to 4 ('favourable') to 0, 1 or 2 ('unfavourable'). A similar exercise produced proportions of parents who could be said to be 'mildly frustrated' or 'strongly frustrated' in relation to their desires for their children's education.[85] The problem here, as in the early quantitative studies of adolescent attitudes, [86] is that, at best, complex attitudes are boiled down to points on a scale, ripped out of the context of surrounding beliefs and rendered trivial by divorcing them from the experiential conditions within which they make sense. Short of a long methodological treatise, perhaps the best response, for the moment, is 'parents 10; sociologists 0'!

More generally, the method conformed to the preferred theoretical and political framework. 'Sociography' was adequate only to a politics that focused on questions of educational access. If the concern was equality of opportunity, it was adequate to compare the class distribution of access to levels of the educational system with the class distribution of measured intelligence. A more radical measure, which was also adopted early in the tradition, concerned class inequalities of educational outcomes irrespective of 'ability'. This implied the drive to equalize the proportions of students from different social backgrounds reaching a given stage in the progress through the educational structure.[87] But neither calculation paid attention to the actual forms of educational content or to the connections between knowledge, power and popular control. The old sociology was complicit, therefore, in that narrowing of educational politics which had been a feature since the 1940s. Its detailed findings remain valuable, but its explanatory frameworks and limitations of scope remain positively disabling for a more developed socialist politics.

The political implications that *did* follow from the earlier research were, however, stated with great clarity and force, especially by Glass himself. He was drawing the main conclusions as early as 1954, at the end of the introduction to *Social Mobility*, and with a characteristic change of gear:

And at this point, I should like to step outside the frame of the studies contained in the present volume and put forward personal views which are explicitly 'loaded' in that they have a value basis.[88]

There followed a thorough lambasting of the public schools (for cutting across the line of social mobility) and of tripartitism (as deepening social divisions within the population). Comprehensive schooling was advocated as 'the background against which effective subsequent action might be developed'. It was left to Douglas and others to develop the other, compensatory side of the sociologist's repertoire, the deepening intervention into the conditions of cultural reproduction within the working-class family, though Glass wrote a militant introduction to Douglas's study too.[89] By the late 1950s and early 1960s the sociologists were developing the full range of policy prescriptions associated with this phase. As usual Glass's own version was among the most radical: the expansion of higher education to 18–20 per cent of the age group, the general adoption of comprehensives, the scrutiny of the contents of curricula (by teachers and educational experts), the adoption of discovery methods and the development of a more collaborative relation between teachers, parents and children.[90] There is no doubt that in all these respects, as in others, the sociology of education fuelled the 1960s' policies and especially the move away from tripartitism. Before we try to sum up its general political character, however, it is worth commenting on one further limitation.

It has often been argued that the most important contribution of the sociologists was the undermining of the notions of innate and measurable intelligence which provided the rationale of selection at eleven and the practice of intelligence testing.[91] There is some truth in this, but the argument needs to be qualified. The relation of the old sociology to intelligence testing was somewhat more ambiguous than this account suggests and it may be that it was Marxists and self-critical psychologists who were decisive in this more particular struggle.[92] Certainly the *results* of IQ testing were central to the method of the old sociology. Its first move, as we have seen, was to compare the social distribution of educational access (especially to the grammar school) with the social distribution of measured intelligence. On this basis, indeed, the Hertfordshire–Middlesbrough study suggested that among the most able groups, equality of opportunity of access to grammar school education had already been secured. It was only in the course of the second move in the argument — embracing a more expanded concept of equality — that the arguments against measured intelligence came into play. It was shown that, in terms of class chances, the 1944 Act had made little difference and that working-class children had actually suffered from a fiercer competition with middle-class children for grammar school places. Something of the practical legitimacy of measured intelligence was, however, preserved and the results of IQ testing have been used by Halsey and others to this day.[93]

The failure to break entirely with older notions of 'ability', and with the distinction between 'nature' and 'nurture' which underlay them, was to be important for future debates about equality. Sociologists had concentrated on 'environmental' determinants of 'educability', arguing that policy should first attempt to transform them. But what if such policies should then begin to falter as they did in the 1970s? Space was still left for recourse to genetically based arguments about natural abilities. There was, indeed, a deeper complicity between the stress on family background and the retention of notions of innate ability. Both explanations neglected the conscious activity of the child or adult learner and what were later to be explored as the specifically 'cultural' dimensions of schooling.

How then can we sum up on the politics of research in this tradition? These intellectuals were certainly not politically passive; their research was informed by a strong political sense. More problematic was the nature of the connection between two professionalized practices: the practice of formal politics and the practice of politically informed research. The connection was essentially of a high-political and statist kind. It operated through personal advice to potential governments, to persons with power within the educational apparatus and, especially, to Labour ministers of education. The social character of the relation, at its most intimate, is well caught in Crosland's descriptions of meetings 'in my house': 'People like John Vaizey, Michael Young, Noel Annan, Asa Briggs, David Donnison and so on' had very 'serious' and 'very unacademic' discussions there, always around 'matters where a decision was required'.[94]

This was a pattern of elite politics revolving more around the private salon than the party branch. It lacked contact with popular educational experiences and evaded some of the disciplines of popular politics. It is true that the sociologists addressed a wider audience too: through official reports, through the press, through the speeches of politicians and, sometimes, through their own more popular writings. But these activities were usually structured in a non-popular way, through academic journals and international symposia. More important, however, was the basic standpoint adopted in the research: the orientation towards reform via the state rather than to popular knowledge and agitation. This was paralleled by the fundamentally passive, external and often downright insulting images presented of working-class parents and children, images more likely to disorganize self-activity than to encourage it.

This is not the only standpoint available to researchers. The educational priority area (EPA) experiment was a more directly popular mode of research, though the relation between researchers and working-class communities was still structured through state agencies.[95] A better comparison may be with older political and intellectual styles. Intellectuals like Tawney or G. D. H. Cole had a more organic connection to a popular left tradition. Though both were university teachers, they were also active political intellectuals, polymathic in their concerns, heavily involved in working-class education. They wrote much history (their primary disciplinary commitment) but were also journalists, authors of political programmes, inveterate pamphleteers and even 'sociologists'.

This was harder to achieve in the post-war years, partly because of the academicization of research, partly because of the difficulties of an open intellectual leftism in the period of the cold war. The dilemmas can be seen among those groups which did struggle to continue popular traditions: especially communists or ex-communists and the groups around the New Left. Particularly interesting in education are Raymond Williams and Brian Simon, the latter very much the inheritor of the radical populism of G. C. T. Giles. Those who resisted the pressure of academicization longest were more often students of history or 'culture' than of 'social science'. Sometimes their work was seen as more innovative, even at that time, than the work of the sociologists. A. H. Stewart's verdict, at a conference called to consider the contribution of sociology to professional training, is an interesting one:

It is possible that sociologists are themselves the victims of the divisive society they describe and have become so engrossed in the sociological machinery that it is left to the literary gentlemen to discern the direction of the vehicle and consider where it should go.[96]

It is important, then, not to see the growth of an academic, professionalized intelligentsia as some inexorable secular tendency from which it is impossible, perhaps disreputable, to break. The high-political, statist orientation of the 1950s and 1960s was as much a creation of its own time and of conscious political preference as the possibilities of a more direct popular connection that may be opening up now.

Teachers as professionals

Teachers constituted the third main element in the 1960s alliance. More correctly, social democratic politicians made an alliance with the teachers, influencing them at the same time to become 'professionals'.

This discourse of educational professionalism, the usual form of address of teachers by politicians in the 1960s, involved positive and negative images, repressions as well as incitements. The most important negations were of the teacher as trade unionist and of the teacher as politician. The first was condemned for her materialism, for being over-concerned with the conditions and rewards of her labour; the second for failing to keep separate her politically neutral educational expertise and her recognized political role as a citizen. This period saw a deepening of these long-standing definitions, according to the main tendencies of a statist politics.

Here is one full and conscious statement of these themes, an address to the College of Preceptors at the height of a skirmish over the future of the Burnham Committee in 1962:

Education is perhaps the most important issue of domestic policy and it is essential that the public has its rightful say in what is done; it is certainly arguable that at university level the public has had too little say. On the other hand, if teachers are to have self-respect, they must have self-government. It seems to me that education is a national issue and the proper place for political debate is essentially at a national level as well as a local one; and this involves an open acknowledgement of the growing power and function of the Ministry of Education . . . . But at a different level — the level of day-to-day decisions — it seems to me the teachers ought to have far more say.

For, if anything is to be learnt from these last unhappy months, surely it is this. The teachers care passionately about their work; and to care passionately is in fact the better side of a claim to professional status. By this very caring they earn the right to responsibility. But by virtue of their exclusion from responsibility the teachers have been driven to irresponsibility; understandable if not excusable. They do not only want more pay — we all want that, and it is in my view only attainable by a real change in the place of the public sector in our economy — they want more acknowledgement as well.

I suggest that as a matter of urgency the teachers have the task ahead of them of seeking professional status; and of seeking a role in educational policy-making which is greater than that they play at present.

In my view other roads to advancement are barred to them . . . Involvement in decisions is what they can get, and what will do most good.[97]

Obviously this is an incitement to professional self-government. The model used elsewhere in the speech is that of the doctors. Self-government is closely linked to the acquisition of expertise which assumes an exaggeratedly technical even modernistic character. Teaching, like medicine, is on the verge of a Great Techno-logical Breakthrough:

As the driver speeds along the track we all know that the people in the factory are those who really matter; as the cosmonaut speeds to the stars we know that it is the people who designed the capsule who really count. This is what the educators now are, and are acknowledged to be — the back-room boys (*sic*) who really matter.[98]

Autonomy, however, is seen as circumscribed and conditional, limited by the claims of 'the public' and the necessities of public finance. Popular participation is assigned to the locality, to the immediate and the mundane; national public interests are readily identified with 'the ministry'. Teachers are to have a say in 'policy' but are to appear in the policy-making sphere as professionals with a definite and limited area of competence. Their strategies must certainly conform to the imperatives of economic planning, especially to the need to recruit more teachers in a period of expansion, and to the disciplines of the incomes policy. The pursuit of wage claims without reference to professional standing is the chief form of irresponsibility. This figure of the teacher as militant wage bargainer was calculated to trigger the most hostile reactions from politicians in the 1960s; witness the dire warnings of Edward Short and Harold Wilson in the wage battles of 1969.[99] It is important to remember the conditional character of this compact in a period when the emphasis has swung from 'autonomy' to control: self-government was always dependent on good behaviour and was always organized through the controlling hierarchies of the profession itself, of schools and of unions.

The stress on professionalism, however, was clearly associated with the removal of educational content outside the realm of political contention. At the dead centre of autonomy lay the 'secret garden' of the curriculum.[100] Politicians entered it at the risk of charges of totalitarianism (if in power) or subversion (if on the left). As Crosland put it: 'We are educational politicians and administrators, not professional educationalists'.[101] Technique and specialism were heavily stressed: 'Mr Chips has followed the Village Schoolmaster into the history books'.[102] One common image of the comprehensive school was of a college of specialists, providing a wealth of social and academic services and, by implication, having many opportunities for self-development and posts of special responsibility.[103] The favourite image was of the professional person – highly skilled, technically knowledgeable, flexible, self-reliant and mainly masculine: perhaps the new headteacher, impatient of technical obsolescence, buying in a computer for his timetabling; or a little team of expert curriculum planners ('a brilliant young mathematician, psychologists and teachers') collaboratively designing a new team-taught maths course. How much better than the alternative route to self-advancement: 'the more working-class, trade union path' that promoted pay over power! [104]

It is important not to confuse this favourite image with the realities of teachers' consciousness, struggles and strategies in the post-war period and before. Yet the professional strategy has had a long-standing appeal for teachers, not least because, up to the 1960s, the struggle for professional status was often waged *against* the state and had only limited successes.[105] The offer of professional status and 'say' in the 1960s was bound to make connections with a consciousness of this long history. The pursuit of professional status had been the dominant strand in teacher politics since the battle against the Revised Code in 1861, and the emergence of the National Union of Elementary Schoolteachers a few years later. Professionalism appeared as a coherent strategy for dealing with divisions among elementary school-teachers and within teaching as a whole. It was also one primary means of asserting a degree of self-respect and collective solidarity in the face of the enormous condescension of the Education Department and the middle-class world as a whole. Professional self-government was a way of equalizing conditions, while the call for a unified state education system, with rights of transfer between sectors, was part of the same project. Links between teacher strategies and the Labour movement's commitment to egalitarian expansion were made early. Between the wars there was a significant move of elementary teachers into the Labour Party. The National Association of Labour Teachers and left sections of the leadership of the National Union of Teachers consistently advocated some version of the common school, running well ahead of the Labour government after 1944.[106]

The curriculum was a key focus of the battles. The earliest encounters were against tight state control of the curriculum through payment by results and the successive 'codes' of the Education Department. By the inter-war period official control of the curriculum was much looser and operated mainly through competition for free places in secondary schools (which encouraged streaming) and the universities' control of examinations for secondary schools. This period also saw the development of child-centred methods, the significance of which was not exhausted by its connection with professionalism, but which certainly helped to enhance teacher control of the curriculum. It was not, however, until the Beloe Report of 1960 that teachers gained a measure of control over their own examination system (the Certificate of Secondary Education). It was not until 1963, after considerable controversy, that teachers gained control of the Schools Council on Examinations and Curriculum.

There has, then, been a long-term convergence between the demand for educational expansion and the main forms of teacher politics. This is not to say that professionalism and the relation to social democracy have been the only or even the main influences. The development of progressivism, for example, cannot be understood outside the main context of the teachers' practice, the classroom itself and the daily struggles — for order and control, for the consent of the pupils, and for the development of skills and confidence on both sides — which dominate experiences of school. One implication of child-centred methods, especially when applied to the secondary school, is to give some autonomy to the pupil, and therefore to lessen the direct forms of conflict. To regard such methods as an arbitrary importation of 'theory' (as the main critics of progressivism were to argue) is to miss a principal dynamic of the development of the whole education system: the daily guerrilla warfare of the school.[107]

Studies of contemporary teacher attitudes suggest that professional definitions remain strong within the informal culture of teaching. Perhaps their principal function, at this level, is to demarcate firmly the province of the teacher and the parent. This is the conservative face of professionalism most often encountered by parents and often strongly resented by them. As one headmaster put it:

I have quite a professional and dedicated staff . . . . I mean we often have to call on parents for assistance but there's no place for parents who want to tell us what to do and how to do it. After all my staff are professionals.[108]

The evidence also suggests, however, that 'professionalism' is variously understood, especially in its relation to trade unionism. Teachers struggle against and within the definitions offered of their role. They may, for instance, refuse the choice between 'professional' and 'trade unionist' altogether, as this teacher does:

I regard myself as a professional. I've got certificates and I have certain responsibilities which I feel very strongly that I must fulfil. That is the only way I regard myself as a professional. And I suppose that I set myself standards in these responsibilities which I try to maintain. But why I cannot be a trade union member — a strong trade union member and a fighter — I don't know.[109]

Other teacher strategies, important for our later story, may take professional definitions and push their logic further than the officially sanctioned version. Many teachers have taken seriously the offer of participation in educational policy-making. Some of them have appeared in the politics of policy-making, not merely as 'the experts' of the region, but as teachers who are *also* socialists, feminists or members of particular parties. The development of the common school is incomprehensible unless we recognize the active organizing energies of socialist and communist teachers and educationalists. Such people have used their positions of professional responsibility for what are, in fact, broad and entirely legitimate political ends. The history of such organizations as the Teachers' Labour League, the National Association of Labour Teachers and the main teachers' unions, especially the National Union of Teachers, is full of such examples.[110]

Another response is to push the autonomies of the classroom to its limits, a strategy associated historically, first with various kinds of progressivism, latterly with a more specifically socialist or feminist conception of educational content or pedagogy. The history of this practical radicalism within teaching is largely hidden, though well known through the personal experiences of many teachers. Minimally, teachers have simply insisted that there are reasons for educational activity which are not exhausted by the child's future occupation or class or gender destiny. This allowed a space for the development of non-capitalist elements in the curricula and some limited transformations of the authority-relations of teachers and taught. Less commonly, an alternative or oppositional conception of the content and modes of education came to be linked to an alternative social goal, or a view of what it was actually like to be working class in a capitalist society, or oppressed as a woman or a black person.

Though hidden, those developments were a marked feature of the 1960s and 1970s. Given the context of professionalism, they often produced highly contradictory situations, as the William Tyndale case was to show most graphically. Indeed, it was in these contradictory forms that radical teachers were to appear in the 1970s, along with the other folk-devils of the Conservative press: as 'long-haired hippie teachers', as educational experts out of touch with parents, as scatterbrained idealists losing sight of educational basics and as the 'minority' of the actively disaffected, using the schools for 'subversion'.[111] It may be that the violence of these campaigns and the extreme character of the imagery reflected the real inroads made into authoritarian practices and 'capitalist schooling' in the 1960s and early 1970s.

Conclusions: the social democratic repertoire

We return now to the questions posed at the beginning of this chapter. What *were* the assumptions within which educational goals were defined and pursued in this period? More generally, what has been the social democratic repertoire of ideas in education, in its longer continuities and its particular 1950s' and 1960s' forms? The main elements have remained surprisingly constant, but with changing emphases and different contemporary meanings. The other leading theme is the internal complexity of social democratic ideas, the coexistence of different and sometimes contradictory ideas, which acquire coherence only for the particular situation in which they arise. As Raymond Williams has put it, in criticism of an earlier version of our own account:

We are not dealing simply with a complete ideology, but with different tendencies, which at certain times, and particularly at times of crisis, precipitate more general, theoretical and intellectual constraints.[112]

In this section we will describe the internal complexity outlined by Williams; later we will look at these ideas more critically. We will concentrate on assumptions about educational goals and especially the connection between education, social equality and the economy.

The most obvious feature of the Labour Party's educational repertoire has been a persistent duality of goals. This duality has often been noted by writers within the tradition of 'British socialism' itself, especially by those somewhat to the left of the predominant Fabianism. Tawney's description of the difference between 'practical equality' and 'equality of opportunity' remains classic, cited in most subsequent debates.[113] He identified equality of opportunity as a fundamentally bourgeois creed, born in the battle against the *ancien régime* and adopted as a practical philosophy by the English middle class. As a social goal it had great strengths; a high degree of openness and social mobility remained, he argued, important in modern societies. But equality of opportunity was what Tawney called 'the Tadpole Philosophy', for it was supposed to reconcile some poor wriggling creatures, with no arms or legs, to an early death on the grounds that some of their friends could 'rise to be frogs'.[114] Opportunities to rise were no substitute for practical equality; on the contrary a high degree of social mobility depended on the absence of great disparities of position.

What matters to a nation is not merely the composition and origins of its different groups, but their opportunities and circumstances. It is the powers and advantages which different classes in practice enjoy, not the social antecedents of the varying individuals by whom they may happen, from time to time, to be acquired. Till such powers and advantages have been equalized in fact, not merely in form, by the extension of communal provision and collective control, the equality established by the removal of restrictions on property and enterprise resembles that produced by turning an elephant loose in the crowd. It offers everyone, except the beast and his rider, equal opportunities of being trampled to death. Caste is deposed, but class succeeds to the vacant throne.[115]

Elsewhere Tawney suggested that practical equality too had a specific social basis:

The idea of social solidarity which is the contribution of the working classes to the social conscience of our age has its educational as well as its economic implications. What it implies is not merely *la carrière ouverte aux talents,* indispensable though that is, but *égalité de fait,* not simply equality of opportunity but universality of provision.[116]

Similar distinctions recur: Crosland's 'equal opportunity' and 'social equality'; the more technical statistical definitions in the sociology of education — the difference between meritocracy and mobility and the equalization of 'class chances'; the return in Halsey's later, more philosophical accounts, to the problematic of liberty, equality and fraternity.[117] For Halsey, equality of opportunity in its 'liberal' forms was closely connected to the concern with technological progress, and the effective use of national resources. He traced this cluster of attitudes back to nineteenth-century political economy, illustrating its classical forms from the writings of the economist Alfred Marshall.[118] It was this 'liberal' tradition, according to Halsey, that failed in the 1970s. Equality, by contrast, presupposes a 'social basis in fraternity' and has its own historical pedigree in 'socialism as fellowship', an idea central to 'the native brand of political thought' running from William Morris, through Tawney to Richard Titmus.[119]

The distinction is serviceable enough as a starting point. Certainly Labour's educational ideas have, as Rodney Barker has stressed, persistently employed both sets of notion.[120] The demand for equality has been social and cultural in nature, a demand for some equalization of conditions in order to achieve 'fraternity', social harmony or 'a common culture'. Equality has been valued as a source of social cohesion; inequality opposed because of its divisiveness. Such notions have commonly been linked to a social organicism, shared with more conservative social philosophies. Both conservative and socialist versions have evolved, in the British case, through a long historical tussle with a succession of modernizing philosophies from late eighteenth-century utilitarianism onwards.[121]

Equality of opportunity has belonged, rather, to this enemy camp. Ethically, it has insisted on the priority of individual liberty, especially the liberty to realize talent. In later, democratic versions, the opportunity to realize talent becomes a right of citizenship. Whether in its 'sociological' forms or more philosophical variants, it assumes inequalities of condition; the problem is to secure a 'more open society' in which non-functional inequalities are eroded, but necessary inequalities remain.[122] These may be thought of morally, as the natural reward for talent, ability or 'enterprise'; or they may be thought of, more explicitly, in relation to economic or political activity, as a necessary division of labour or of functions, within economic organization or within government. The connection with economic ideologies and purposes has, historically, been peculiarly close. Equality of opportunity could be understood essentially as an economic goal, based upon generalization from the most apparent features of capitalist social relations: individualism, competition, the market. As we have seen, education has been regarded, within this framework, as either a consumption good or as a form of investment. The ultimate point of reference here has been the essentially liberal idea of society as a market, within which individuals compete. The point, according to this philosophy, is to enable them to compete more fairly.

For both traditions 'class' (variously defined) is a problem. For egalitarians it is a problem because it creates social conflict, envy, domination and is intrinsically oppressive. For those who stress opportunity, it represents a range of artificial inhibitions on the reward of ability and on a rational and efficient social organization. For both positions education is a very important means to reformation, but its effects are differently envisaged. Egalitarians stress education's human or cultural effects, often defining these *against* the forms of existing society. From the perspective of equality of opportunity, education is the prime instrument of social engineering since it provides the means by which inherited 'class' or 'status' can be detached from talent. The concern with the associations of 'status', 'social mobility' and education in the early sociology of education is the obvious case in point. Crucial differences on education have most often focused around selection. Among consistent egalitarians there has been pressure towards universal and common provision; equality of opportunity, by contrast, implies inclusions and exclusions, but favours forms of selection that are flexible and 'fair'. Egalitarians have tended to push for more or better education as of right; liberals have tended to view its distribution as qualified, subject, in the end, to calculations concerning the utility of egalitarian moves. They are likely to be extremely sensitive to the tension between equality and liberty, between 'individualism' and 'collectivism', and to what T. H. Marshall called 'the antithesis inherent in the principles and structure of the welfare state':

It is the problem of establishing equal opportunity without abolishing social and economic inequality. I say this is inherent in the nature of the Welfare State because it is my opinion . . . that the Welfare State, as we know it, must necessarily preserve a measure of economic inequality. This problem, therefore, is a permanent and not a transitory one.[123]

It is possible to cite relatively pure examples of both positions from different phases of the development of the repertoire. In his general moral stance, if not always in his detailed proposals, Tawney was a key figure in the definition of educational egalitarianism. Sidney Webb (to whom, with Beatrice, *Equality* was dedicated) personified Fabian 'capacity-catching' and a combination, of a rather modern kind, of meritocratic and 'national-efficiency' arguments.[124] If the sociology of education was founded within largely liberal terms, it moved in an egalitarian direction. Defenders of 'community schooling' or of destreamed comprehensives may certainly be counted as egalitarians;[125] defenders of streaming, of comprehensives as internally diverse and allowing many paths to success, or, in another sphere, supporters of the binary system and the 'new polytechnics', may be deemed out-and-out Fabians.[126] The association between Fabianism and the liberal end of the repertoire has been very close; the strongest egalitarian stresses have tended to arise on the left, and to the left of the Labour Party.

Much more commonly, these two strands have been combined. In both political and sociological writing, the common move, as we have seen, has been to start with equality of opportunity and move thence to equality, usually via an argument about the inadequacies of the former. Arguments about 'equality' appear, even in the most utilitarian of arguments about economic growth. For Crosland, comprehensives were necessary to remove the waste of talent revealed by Robbins and Crowther *and* 'to increase the sense of social cohesion in contemporary British society'.[127] Harold Wilson, however, supplies the most striking instances of Labour's dualism, especially in his speeches in the run-up to the 1964 election. These speeches combined predominantly Vaizeyite stresses with elements of the revisionist version of social equality and even, in the rhetoric at least, a more grass-roots egalitarianism:

I do not want to anticipate the debate on education, but it [the need for scientists] means that as a nation we cannot afford to force segregation on our children at the 11-plus stage. As Socialists, as democrats we oppose this system of educational apartheid, because we believe in equality of opportunity. But that is not all. We simply cannot as a nation afford to neglect the educational development of a single boy or girl. We cannot afford to cut off three-quarters or more of our children from virtually any chance of higher education. The Russians do not, the Germans do not, the Americans do not, and the Japanese do not, and we cannot afford to either.[128]

In these speeches, the starting point is often the need for scientists and the intrinsically democratizing role of science and technology as opposed to the inertia and stuffiness of existing status-ridden forms of management. There is a classically liberal, 'modernizing' framing of the whole argument: 'The Britain that is going to be forged in the white heat of this revolution will be no place for restrictive practices or for outdated methods on either side of industry.'[129] Yet note what follows: the 'gut' appeal to the party's egalitarianism ('segregation'; 'our children') and the extra emotional boost of 'educational apartheid'. This connection with the party's left traditions is reinforced by a generalized invocation of where we stand 'as socialists' or, in case this is a bit strong for some present, 'as democrats' too. But then back we go to the task that is really in hand – 'we simply cannot as a nation afford . . . '. The extract ends with the roll-call of capitalist competitors and the imperative of a British response. There is no doubt which elements of the repertoire are in dominance here but the heterogeneity of appeals and audience is also clear.

The *combination* was very important politically. The economic themes and, especially, the stress on the need for a generally better educated workforce, gave a thoroughly hard-headed and vulgar materialist justification for equalizing policies. As we have seen, the stress on the need for greater skill and 'flexibility' reconciled the tensions between humanistic ways of thinking about education and the kind of occupational determinacy against which Tawney had rebelled. Teachers could, in theory, concentrate on doing their best for the child with the assurance that it would benefit him or her in the most obvious material ways too. Educators were informed, after all, that there were plenty of skill-rich and interesting jobs for school-leavers whatever a direct experience might suggest.

Labour's ideological repertoire needs to be viewed, in the end, as a product of the party's particular place in British society and politics. The long-term dualism of educational ideas has expressed, quite directly, a double commitment. Labour's Fabianism or liberalism has been centrally concerned with the mission of managing and reforming a capitalist society, by removing, especially, the most important inhibitions to capitalism's progressive side – a more 'open' society. In the more technological or 'economic' part of the repertoire, the connection is plain enough: Labour's leadership has been concerned to establish the conditions for a faster rate of accumulation of national capital. But, as we noted earlier, the less direct ethical implications of 'equality of opportunity' also matched and helped to reproduce the visible character of capitalist social relations. The other side of Labour's ideas has revolved around the representation of popular interests in education. Egalitarianism is the elementary form of a popular educational politics, asserting on behalf of subordinate social groups, a greater degree of fairness. At this very general level of analysis, Labour's repertoire has been formed in the relation between popular interests and 'capitalist schooling'. Labour, especially Labour in power, has always served two masters in this way, usually by insisting on the identity of their interests. It has constructed working-class interests as national interests, very largely as the interests of capital. This project of the harmonization of class interests is what, in the end, warrants the term 'social democracy'.

The Labour Party, then, has been a site of struggle between popular educational interests and the stake which different sections of capital have in the educational system. This should not be thought of as a passive role of 'representation', but as part of the active conscious *construction* of popular needs and strategies of accumulation. This prompts two further sets of questions. The first concerns the character of the 'popular' in Labour's post-war alliances — what social groups did it best represent? What social groups were more objects of its policies? We have used the term popular, so far, with deliberate generality to include all non-capitalist stakes in education. But it will be important, in the process of our critique, to identify the social basis of Labour's policies more accurately. Second, it is important to ask, all the time, which elements of the repertoire are in dominance at particular historical moments. We want to end this more descriptive section by noting the dominance of the liberal or Fabian elements in the 1960s' variants.

This dominance was partly a matter of emphasis: the subordination of the more egalitarian themes under the heavily stressed 'national efficiency' arguments. Popular interests were to be served, mainly through capitalist economic growth; a changed education system was a means to this end. Characteristically, the argument did not take off from a definition of popular educational needs, except in the general, usually rhetorical invocation of equality. The combination as it appears, for example, in Vaizey's writing was certainly weighted in a different way than in Tawney's, where popular educational needs were promoted over capitalist imperatives. But we think that the post-war period, especially the 1950s and 1960s, saw a deeper transformation of egalitarianism in relation to the liberal emphases. The very character of the demand for equality was changed, politically and morally.

To see this clearly, we have to be more discriminating than the usual equality—equality of opportunity distinction allows us to be. We have to look more closely at the egalitarian side of the argument and note that there are different emphases there too. In particular, as we have seen from time to time throughout this chapter, 'practical equality' may be understood mainly as a *means* to other objectives, especially to 'social cohesion', the removal of 'resentment' or the securing of the conditions of 'social order'. This view of equality as a *means* has to be taken alongside the containment of egalitarian demands, sometimes in relation to other 'ideals', especially 'liberty', sometimes in relation to functional inequalities that are alleged to be necessary for economic activity or political rule. The shifts of emphasis here are subtle, but palpable and, we argue, of great significance, morally and politically. Morally, they make of the demand for fairness, justice and a common humanity, a mere instrument of control to be dispensed in appropriate quantities: in terms of Tawney's fable, this is to permit a few more tadpoles to grow up in order to satisfy the consciences and secure the privileges of those who are already frogs! It is simply untrue that the revisionist notion of 'social equality' is the same ideal that informs, say, William Morris's *News from Nowhere* or, for that matter, Tawney's *Equality*. In both the older socialist texts, revisionism's order of moral priorities is reversed: 'practical equality' (or what Morris called 'equality of condition')[130] is a good in itself, a more advanced social ideal than mere equality of opportunity; a more orderly society may follow from the achievement of greater equality, as one of many associated benefits. Socialism is more, in short, than an instrument of social engineering or pacification; it involves a moral critique and a practical transformation of the existing forms of 'civilization'. Revisionism fits William Morris's definition of 'the Whig frame of mind', not his definition of socialism:

Before the uprising of *modern* Socialism almost all intelligent people either were, or professed themselves to be, quite content with the civilization of this century. Again, almost all of these really were thus contented, and saw nothing to do but to perfect the said civilization by getting rid of a few ridiculous survivals of the barbarous ages. To be short, this was the *Whig* frame of mind, natural to the modern prosperous middle-class men, who, in fact, as far as mechanical progress is concerned, have nothing to ask for, if only Socialism would leave them alone to enjoy their plentiful style.[131]

There was, then, considerable sleight of hand or a degree of self-delusion in the identification of revisionism with socialism and, indeed, the tendency in the sociology of education to claim a socialist pedigree. This is clearer if we consider the political implications of the slides we have noted. For these involve a radical shift in terms of class standpoint: a vision of reform not from the side of the relatively poor, or oppressed, but from the side of the controllers, even if power is meant to benefit the sufferer. It is in this sense that Croslandite politics and the 'old' sociology of education belong to a long tradition of English middle-class reform and social investigation. The identification of Halsey and his colleagues with the Webbs or with Charles Booth (but *not* with Henry Mayhew) is extremely accurate: the parallel between the long-standing concern with popular morality and behaviour and the sociologist's interest in 'educability' is likewise very close. In the end, however, the proof of political standpoint is in its political effects, and it is to these and to a larger critique of 'social democracy' that we turn in Part Two.

Part Two
Social democracy: the limits

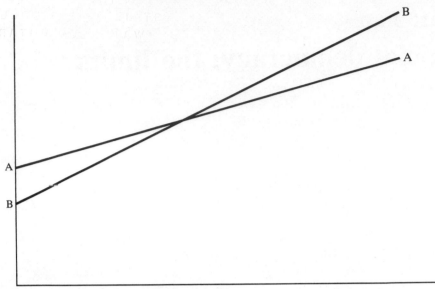

Hypothetical graph of standards of attainment
(line A) and individual's needs (line B)

Suppose that line A represents a steady increase over a period of time in the standards of school leavers' skills in any area one chooses: literacy, numeracy, speaking a foreign language, coping with family life. It would appear that all concerned are to be congratulated. If, however, line B represents the level of skill *actually needed* by an indivdual, then despite the laudable efforts of those involved the person concerned is ill-equipped.

Source: House of Commons Expenditure Committee Tenth Report, *Attainments of the School Leaver* (HMSO July 1977), p. xiv

Introduction

The purpose of this part of the book is to look more critically at the educational policies of the 1960s and at the bodies of knowledge which informed them. We conduct this assessment in three main ways. First, we seek to relate *policy* to *practice* by looking at changes in the educational system in this period. We turn from discourses, expectations, and strategies to outcomes, tracing these mainly through administrative conditions and the kind of result that appears in the official record itself. We are concerned to identify the points where, in their own terms, policies were realized and the points where they were not. What emerges is a significant pattern of differential realization, but we will also be concerned to mark, in a preliminary way, certain key absences in this record to which we shall return. This is the subject of Chapter 5.

Second, we evaluate the 1960s' policies more broadly — not just by these 'internal' criteria. If policies were differentially realized, they were also, in important aspects, not realizable at all, certainly not under the conditions that were accepted as necessary or natural. This was in part because the goals that were set were contradictory: the achievement of some involved the negation of others, a deepening, even, of their problematic character. But policy also rested on false or inadequate knowledge concerning the ground of intervention and, indeed, the means of intervention itself: about the character of social relations in the family—school—production complex and about the nature and limits of 'statist' solutions. These two aspects, the contradictoriness and 'utopianism' of the 1960s' policies, were closely related. 'Great expectations' involved envisaging and actively promoting imaginary solutions, to which the term 'ideological' properly applies.

In Chapter 6, we return to the assumptions that guided sociological research in this period, especially when it took as its problem the question of working-class 'failure' at school. We suggest that the main absence in the explanatory project of the old sociology was a critical appraisal of the effects of the social and sexual divisions of labour, and, behind that, of relations of patriarchy and of class.

In Chapter 7, we return to the more 'economic' assumptions of the period, especially those focusing on the question of 'skill'. In the course of criticizing skill as a category, we suggest elements of an alternative account of changes in the labour market and the social and sexual divisions of labour since the war. We stress the determinacy of the resulting structure of adult places on outcomes in the schools. Finally, we illustrate the importance of forms of popular knowledge and culture by looking at recent studies of the cultures of the school.

Our third mode of assessment is to look at the 1960s' policies from a specifically political standpoint. Why were the 1960s' policies so vulnerable in the decade that followed? Why, in a more narrowly political aspect, did a social democratic hegemony in education prove incapable of resisting a populist Conservative critique? Not all the answers to such a question can be given at this stage; the historical conditions of the 1970s actually precipitated this dissolution. But we *can* identify certain political vulnerabilities. Our analysis here is related to arguments already indicated about the social basis of the 1960s' settlement and about the limits of statism as a socialist or egalitarian strategy. We sum up and expand these arguments in the concluding section of Part Two.

A critique of this kind operates with considerable benefits of hindsight, though less securely than is possible with more distant historical periods. It can only be written with a knowledge of subsequent developments. There is a built-in danger here of historical and political arrogance. If the past is treated only as a site for the generation of modern conditions, what was specific about conditions, and therefore about political calculations and choices at that time, may be overlooked or simplified. The corollary of this is the adoption of a modern Olympianism which consigns not only past illusions, but also desires, energies and expectations to a dingy record of 'failure'.

There are, perhaps, two main correctives to this. The first is to recognize what is involved in the opposite standpoint. It is futile, we would argue, to treat the past, as some professional historians have always advocated, only 'in its own terms', to employ only the categories of the past to explore only the past itself. In the strict sense, this is an impossible procedure: there is no simple act of 'recovery' uninformed by the experiences, needs and concepts of today. We are inescapably historical beings: the object of history is not just the past; it is the past—present relationship. To pretend to historical contemplation is a form of delusion. We owe to the struggles of the past (and to ourselves) not only an archaeology of recovery or memory, but also the dignity of contemporary importance, and therefore the dignity of evaluation.[1]

The second corrective, then, is to recognize, explicitly, that histories are informed by contemporary needs. It is these that set the agenda, consciously or not, even if the history is quite distant. In our case the necessity of critique arises from the need to consider the conditions of a more adequate popular politics of education today, one that connects with popular experiences. Critiques of this kind should always have two sides: negative evaluations should form the basis of more creative thinking about today. In this part of the book we stress the negative side; later we will try to draw out the positive aspects. To put the matter more practically, modern strategies must draw on and learn from the struggles of the past, but must also innovate. It helps if the explanations adopted, of both past and present, are attentive to conditions and determinations, as well as to choices and to agency.

A project like this is in any case feasible not only because of hindsight, but also because the intermediate period has seen real advances in understanding. The critique will draw on the knowledges which were produced out of the circumstances we will describe in Part Three of this book.

We want to stress two particular intellectual debts. The first is to a deeper understanding of processes conventionally (and misleadingly) described as 'economic'. We refer, in particular, to modern debates on the nature of labour processes under modern capitalist social relations. The key work here has been a book by the American Marxist, Harry Braverman, *Labor and Monopoly Capital*.[2] This book has had a profound influence on the understanding of 'work' in modern societies, east and west. It is important to us less for its treatment of education and more for its account, drawn from Marx but historically extended, of the position of the labourer under modern conditions. Central here are the processes by which modern capitalist industry dispossesses labourers of control over their own conscious productive activity. Braverman's account of these processes throws into question many of the conceptions of skill and of science which informed the 1960s' debates. It also allows us to think more freshly about 'class' in a way that reasserts, through all the sociological confusions, some of Marx's primary insights. Braverman's work has been rightly criticized for its neglect of struggle or the labourer's strategies of *re*possession[3] but it has also stimulated much thinking and research on particular labour processes and industries, not least among those interested in women's work and especially clerical labour.[4] Within this post-Braverman debate, however, powerful critiques have been developed of the knowledges that informed 1960s' orthodoxies. This also has profound and largely undeveloped implications for educational studies. It points to 'work' and, in Marxist-feminist insights to the family too, as key sites of educative processes, of the production of knowledge and subjectivities. One implication, to be explored later, is the centrality of the social and sexual divisions of labour, as relations of power and dispossession, for the outcomes of formal educational processes in schools.

A second body of work on which we draw is the concern with 'culture' and with cultural production. We cannot review here the whole development of 'cultural studies' even from its more proximate origins in Britain from the late 1950s and early 1960s.[5] We wish merely to stress the complementarity between the study of culture and of education, especially where neither term succumbs to partial or trivializing definitions: 'high' literary or artistic production for instance, or 'what happens in schools'. We are then centrally concerned with the ways in which forms of consciousness arise, with the ways in which human beings understand and transform their social world. As we have already argued, 1960s' orthodoxies failed to grasp the significance of cultural processes even for the most intimate transactions in and around the school.

In our critique, we draw heavily on these bodies of work: the first to criticize the economic ideologies of the 1960s, the other to question the dominant sociological understandings.

5 Great expectations: the noise and practice of reform

The economic ideal of the intellectual wage earner is a national State controlling the industry of the country, in which each is rewarded according to a weird theory called 'the rent of ability' . . . as the capitalist uses capital as the test of remuneration . . . as the wage labourer demands the social organization and control of the products of labour, so the middle class intellectual desires ability to be the test of income.[1]

William Paul

Versions of 'the 1960s'

This chapter is concerned with the ways in which changes in education policy were advocated and carried out in the 1960s. The one did not follow from the other. A critique has to be undertaken on two levels: to interrogate the proposals themselves (uneasily adjacent, often incompatible and held loosely together by ambiguous key terms), and to contrast the ground of the reforms with their real outcomes. We shall argue that there were major discontinuities between a political and educational discourse of reform and the changes undertaken.

In that way, we hope to resist some influential retrospective interpretations of the decade. These have tended to emphasize, with enthusiasm or disapproval, a pattern of continuous development. Both Brian Simon and yet also Butler and Boyle in their conservative revisionist history have traced a steady evolution of the comprehensive school — for Simon the belated removal of hindrances, for Butler and Boyle the judicious tolerance of possibilities already present in the 1944 Act. In other versions, the decade has been characterized by its spectacular irruptions. Bernstein, in a famous sweeping summation, concluded that its reforms were misdirected because 'education cannot compensate for society'.[2] For the early *Black Papers* the reforms were intolerable because their destructive 'social engineering', carrying all before it, had to be reversed. All of these sketches found a strong congruence in the events of the 1960s; all of them concentrated on reforms in the terms in which reforms were proposed, as a steady opening up of access to all levels of education.

Our own account sees the changes as far more partial and uneven. We want to bring out the incomplete adoption of the social democratic policies; the extreme discontinuities and inequalities between various levels of policy; the movements

towards tighter educational management behind the back of declared objectives.
The key terms in 1960s' policy-making had then, and now, a treacherous obvious-
ness: in Laclau's words:

the meaning of the ideological elements identified . . . must be sought in the
structure of which they are a moment, and not in ideal paradigms . . . It is precisely
this background of shared meanings that enables antagonistic discourses to establish
their difference.[3]

We have to understand not a unitary bundle of aims and their attempted implementation but a constant jousting over the control and inflection of policies advertised as
the outcome of a consensus. We have also to see that later declarations that
educational reforms had 'failed' were made possible because of the great expectations
which had accompanied what was only ever a partial and incomplete implementation.
The later attempt at tighter controls on teachers and taught rested on the spurious
claim that liberal reforms had been tried and found wanting.

The decade has nevertheless acquired a summary retrospective coherence on a
number of counts. At its beginning was the Crowther Report, the first of the
magisterial reports produced under the aegis of the Central Advisory Council on
education.[4] At its end were the student protests of 1968, themselves taken by some
as evidence of rushed and botched changes ('more means worse') and then the first
of the *Black Papers*: an omen too easily derided. Between them came the 10/65
circular which tried to define, without controversy, the possibilities of comprehensive schooling. In Kogan's quasi-official account, Boyle's 'statist radicalism' converged
effortlessly with Crosland's rational pragmatism.[5] In that conjuncture it could be
boasted that education was a 'non-political' issue.

We could look briefly at other undoubtedly distinguishing features of the 1960s
before attempting to suggest contrary movements. To begin with, there was a
dramatic expansion of provision. Government spending on education did indeed
grow very significantly from the later 1950s, and the raw figures have often been
cited as one kind of account. Thus, between 1953 and 1972 public expenditure
increased by 82.9 per cent but educational expenditure by 242.9 per cent. Education
spending as a proportion of gross national product was 3.2 per cent in 1955 but 6
per cent in 1969. During the 1960s, education grew faster than any major national
enterprise except gas and electronics.[6] The figures, and the language of figures, are
themselves characteristic of a stress by experts of the 1960s upon measurable
'growth' and 'advance'. It is not easy to tell from them quite what is being measured
or how that might relate to any mutation of purpose within schools themselves.
Much of the increased spending was in any case a response to demographic movements. The National Plan of 1965 calculated that the primary school population,
which had risen by 160,000 in the last five years, would increase by 695,000 over
the next five. Class sizes were also lowered significantly during the decade. However,
one of the few explorations of the figures was Vaizey's comment that there had
been 'a switch away from the use of teachers to the use of other forms of labour,
and from labour to "things" '.[7] He also found that a greater proportion of the

increased money had been allocated to those staying beyond the leaving age: a shift of resources to higher income groups, of which we shall take the contrasting fates of the Robbins Report on higher education and the Plowden recommendations on educational priority areas as the most marked signal. In any case, Anne Corbett in 1972 could write that fewer than one child in fourteen received any nursery schooling; that one in seven primary classes (and one in three secondary) were over-size; that three in four primary schools (two in four secondary) were probably in sub-standard buildings, while adult education was the system's almost forgotten poor relation. There were persistent and sometimes extreme differences in provision between regions and between different groups, of which two came off 'consistently badly: working class children throughout the system, girls beyond school leaving age. They look like being joined by a third − the children of immigrants'.[8] Expansion, then, occurred but not straightforwardly 'for all' and with a partial brake on education spending (and a movement of resources towards housing) in the first Wilson government.

If more money was given to education, more also was asked of it. The other obvious feature of the decade was the increased political concentration on education as the site for the fulfilment of a huge variety of expectations. These expectations, it should be stressed, were inculcated and constructed with increasing force. The promises of education began to be worked as elaborately as those of consumer goods had been with the removal of post-war austerity. A mark of education's new centrality was Halsey's ability to claim that, after 1956, the Labour Party 'began to see the possibility of education as a serious alternative to nationalization in promoting a more just and efficient society'.[9] In the following years both party manifestoes, but also official reports and a strong body of educational studies for a general audience, suggested grounds for discontent with existing provision, and proposed reforms through which various larger social changes might be realized. Labour's main educational slogan, from the 1961 *Signposts for the Sixties* through to the 1964 manifesto was 'investment in people'. This was suggestively double-edged: it compounded human capital arguments for the growth benefits of educational spending, with a vague populism. By the National Plan of 1965, this had been further spelt out:

Education is both an important social service and an investment for the future. It helps to satisfy the needs of the economy for skilled manpower of all kinds, the needs of any civilized society for educated citizens who have been enabled to develop to the utmost their individual abilities, and the demands by individuals for education as a means both to improved economic prospects and to a richer and more constructive life.[10]

There was a rapid movement of ground over the meanings (and their discrepancies) of the expansion, with tangled but new and distinctive emphases upon ideas of educational equality. The dominant view had been that the system contained divided but complementary forms of provision: separate but equal, with movement

from one sector to another not wholly barred while different forms enjoyed a
'parity of esteem'. By the middle of the 1960s, that line was proving impossible
to hold in relation to the differences of provision for secondary schools, which
were foreseen to be strategically indefensible. Crosland's own advocacy of
comprehensives in 1956, as we have seen, had been largely negative, concerned to
avoid 'extreme' and obvious division. Quite rapidly, no position less than this
seemed tenable. Newsom, for example, had been a strong advocate for secondary
modern schools and his 1963 report caused considerable political inconvenience by
its failure to support comprehensives more openly.[11] But by 1964, Boyle reports,
'he too recognized the difficulty of any long-term attempt to defend the selective
pattern'.[12] The result was the bloodless retrospective DES gloss on comprehensive
development:

if children of different backgrounds were to share a common educational
environment, one aim of the 1943 White Paper could be achieved. . .
'social unity within the educational system . . . would open the way to a more
closely knit society'.[13]

This did not rule out the possibility of 'creamed' comprehensives which were
grammar schools in most respects except name, while some authorities maintained
grammar and comprehensives at one and the same time. Elsewhere the line was held:
public schools were scarcely challenged and direct grant schools held their position.
Or it was actively reformulated: it was the same Crosland who took a DES brief on
the need for a 'binary' system of higher education, again deploying the 'parity of
esteem' formula when different controls and purposes were intended for the two
sectors.

This partial, pragmatic, but extensively promoted removal of obvious inequality
served also to displace or pre-empt more ambitious arguments for an education
service promoting equality in positive ways. Kogan has described a move from one
definition of equality, concerned with equal access and equal opportunity, to
another which sought action in relation to the child's social background, and without
which formal equality would be bogus. One turning point here was Boyle's very
public statement, in the Newsom foreword, that 'all children should have an equal
opportunity of acquiring intelligence'.[14] Another was the Plowden Committee's
concentration on the ways in which parental attitudes could determine a child's
school behaviour before school was even reached. Later Halsey concluded that
the significant test of educational equality was, instead, equality of outcome in
attainments and in employment for those entering schools on an apparently equal
basis.[15]

The movement of discussion around these issues was very rapid. But it also
oscillated between extremely general claims and particular details which were
highly specific and formidably exact. The concern with 'equality' could become a
technical debate about access and outcomes, to be ratified by detailed research
findings of the kind appended to several of the reports. There was a similar contrast

between the demands for 'comprehensive' schooling and then the long typologies of modes of comprehensive provision, which were so complicated that professional expertise was required to understand them. At one end, the arguments, often because they were couched as 'non-political' appeals across party lines of support, were abstract or even vacuous. At the other, they were of administrative precision, needing minute and knowledgeable implementation.

So it was not surprising that there should have been real worries about public support for the new educational ideas. The uncertainty was articulated in the Newsom Report's introduction:

Our report is not simply addressed to those who have the power to take administrative action. They need the support, perhaps sometimes the incitement, of an informed public opinion. It is there for the asking. Never before has the cause of education had so much popular support. Why, then, worry?[16]

The report's own worry was that the 'relatively unspectacular' needs of the boys and girls with which it was concerned would be 'overlooked'. This itself suggested that the depth and direction of 'popular support' for the education of working-class children in secondary moderns was a highly uncertain quantity. Social democratic recommendations for educational reform were ever more caught in problems of political support (from parties but also from parents, children and teachers) as they were driven to address real tendencies towards divergences of educational interest. For example there were, throughout the 1960s, very different degrees and kinds of concern with the perceived requirements of the labour market: beyond the minimal certainty of the first Robbins objective for higher education, that it should offer 'instruction in skills suitable to play a part in the general division of labour', there was much disagreement about needs and aims.[17]

More urgent were the problems posed by the school disaffection of male working-class youth, and then by the anxieties of middle-class parents about qualifications and mobility; and these pointed in different directions. (Neither middle-class youth nor working-class parents were centrally inscribed as objects of policy until later.) ROSLA and Robbins were instances of specific ways out of particular difficulties, but the larger political necessity was to bind both the symptoms of school refusal and the signs of escalating parental demand into one argument about 'our' children, and to make the argument widely convincing. As the decade began, there was a large and eerie gap between the plethora of authoritative educational pronouncements and evidence of any general resonance of their concerns. In it was posed the major set of dilemmas for the politics of education during the 1960s.

Education's 'wide radical appeal'

We do not, then, want to take at face value the obvious 'themes' of the 1960s: expansion, expectation, equality; nor do we accept that social democratic thought spread evenly throughout the education system in the period. There was a distinctive social democratic 'moment' in the formulation of policy, but it was always caught within sharp limits. Social democratic thought, for a number of reasons, could only have a partial and uneven impact. This was sometimes because of the inadequacy or incoherence of the central proposals themselves, especially the attempt to reduce class to a remediable or removable variable. Often it came from a lack of means, and of political will, to implement proposals. There was an under-estimation of the power of the DES to delay, deflect or neuter policy initiatives. Local authorities retained initiative over the forms of secondary schooling as did teachers over the curriculum. Cultures within the classroom were not necessarily considered at all. However, the central problem lay in the political balance of forces in education as the reform period began. In 1960, Crosland argued that education was the chief issue that could make 'not a narrow class or sectional appeal, but a wide radical appeal to broad sections of the population'. Next to this we could set two alternative vignettes from the 1970s. In one of them, a DES witness to the Commons Committee reviewing educational expansion maintained that ' "the feel" is a very important bit of our trade' and did not conceal indifference to the views of the 'non-educational stage army'; while the writer of an authoritative review of the introduction of comprehensives argued that it might be necessary to introduce a measure:

whether by a local by-law or by the school with the support of the local authority, to compel parents to come to school at least once a year to discuss the school's report . . .'first catch your hare . . .'. [18]

These vignettes give glimpses of some difficulties of the 'wide radical appeal'.

At the time Crosland was writing, there were indeed few signs of distinctively working-class claims upon education since the 1944 settlement. He would have known, in relation to the forms of secondary schooling, of the strong Labour tradition in defence of grammar schools, understood as the chance for exceptional working-class children for whom public school privileges were unattainable. A Fabian poll of 1952 reported that most Labour authorities had no enthusiasm for comprehensives and valued chances in the grammars, while in 1958 Labour's own poll found only 10 per cent who thought selective schools undesirable.[19] The spirited arguments for comprehensives in party conferences year after year represented in part, as Labour leaders knew, movements in the composition of active party membership towards professional—managerial class strength of participation, and particularly the contribution in the party of teachers themselves. The leadership was unwilling to share such confidence in the popularity of the notion of comprehensive schooling, though adept in recognizing the extreme unpopularity of selective examination. The result was the notorious situation where the party's proposals for comprehensive reorganization in 1964 had the gall to argue that 'within the new system, grammar school education will be extended'. A later comment on this defence of grammar schools was Marsden's remark that some

Labour councillors were 'out of key with even the limited advances of central policy', and that this was due to a lack of information and 'the peculiar propensity of some natural conservatives to operate under a Labour banner'.[20] The remarks may have some truth in them. Yet suspicion of the new schemes, and of the rival definitions of tripartite, multilateral, and comprehensive schooling, may not only have stemmed from an understandable degree of confusion that the Boyle—Crosland consensus had partly encouraged. When the Nuffield surveys of the 1964 and 1966 elections found that education was not seen by voters as a major issue (despite controversy over Labour's intentions) this may have indicated, not just the degree to which the policies were being portrayed as all things to all voters, but, precisely, a low involvement in those ways of making a politics of education.[21]

Working-class involvement with schools since the war had not necessarily been different in kind from its relationship to other social services, after all. Elizabeth Wilson has written that the earlier history of the welfare state is characterized by a persistent 'thread of working class hostility for state provision' and this should be compared with Cockburn's argument that:

the working class has an interest in receiving services . . . capital has an interest in seeing them serviced . . . struggle takes place over levels of provision and over the amount of control of provision given to the consumer.[22]

During the period we are reviewing, many working-class families were to be more forcefully interpellated as 'clients', involved in the pathology of 'deprivation', and education moved towards closer links of this kind with the other social services. Working-class distance from the activities of schools was always latent: not only were the schools experienced indirectly and vicariously through children, but their demands and expectations in learning were hard or impossible to grasp as decent housing provision was not. The availability of a scatter of grammar school places had been double-edged. If the grammar school offered a way forward or a way out, it could also seal boundaries between working-class children and the parental culture. Hoggart's essay on the scholarship boy's experience, Jackson and Marsden's tracing of working-class children through a grammar school, were contemporaneous with Crosland.[23] Moreover the divisions they found between those in grammar schools and other working-class boys were being reproduced inside secondary moderns as, for reasons we shall look at, examinations were extended. Both Crowther and Newsom worried about these effects, including the danger that schools would have a 'seriously depressed class of pupils on their hands'.[24] The over-all picture which the early reports (and other evidence) gave of schooling and the working class connected with a longer history, from well before the 1944 Act. It showed a characteristic wariness and distance from school among working-class parents, much resentment and lack of involvement among children. The new strands were the attachment, at least in some constituency parties and by some parents, to the possibility of a grammar school chance; and a new level of unrest among teenagers caught up in the more visible youth cultures of the 1950s. The grammar school thread was never yielded by sections of the Labour Party, least of all by its

Prime Minister, and one result of this was the argument later, against the school reforms, that they had conceded the possibility of achievement by measurable standards, in open competition, to a set of informal tests whose results were less available. The enormous task confronting the reforms was thus to seek the involvement and consent of working-class parents who stood back from the schools, and of their children who were restless inside them. It was not surprising that the task was consistently approached through administrative reforms of one sort or another. Questions of more basic kinds — what differences would a working-class parent be likely to expect for a daughter or son from the experience of schooling? — were never considered within social democratic parameters. It was left to Halsey, many hard years and experiences later, to wonder whether the reforms might merely have streamlined a system in which a majority were taught, mainly by 'a huge hidden curriculum, a sense of their own relative incompetence and impotence — a modern, humane and even relatively enjoyed form of gentling the masses?'[25]

Quite opposite political problems stemmed from the growing concern with schools among parents attached to opportunity for their children. Boyle recalled silencing a Monday Club audience by asking how many of them knew personally a single professional parent who allowed his child to attend a secondary modern when he could buy him out of it. To him, it seemed obvious that it was 'the growth of a "middle income" society' which would make a bipartite system less politically viable and that it was in Conservative areas that the changes would have to be made.[26] One technical indication of shifts, to which a response would have to be issued, was the increasing percentage of the relevant age group achieving various qualifications, who then felt an entitlement to a further period of education. The Robbins team, despite its elaborate statistical work, considerably underestimated the accentuation of A-levels, and later felt uncertain of the causes. Our own view would expect that these were linked to the more general shifts in class composition since the war and the development of a 'new' middle class whose specific location has been understood in different ways, and on which no adequate work has yet been done. For Bellaby, the new middle class are:

a section of the labour force composed of non-manual workers in various positions of control in the process of production and distribution, or in the reproduction of the social conditions on which production depends . . . . Educational qualifications are seen as giving the holder credentials to exert symbolic control.[27]

For Poulantzas, the tendency to further the separation of mental from manual labour had encouraged a complex cultural identification with mental labour even where (as was not foreseen in the 1960s' expansion) advanced 'qualifications' lead only to subordinate places. His argument allowed for an 'objective' process of deskilling and loss of control in mental labour, developing alongside a lived distance from the manual working class and underscored by 'rituals, secrets and symbolisms' involved in the longer experience of education.[28]

To the Conservative Party, the new visibility of education as an issue caused some difficulties, but largely of a tactical kind. Boyle has written of concern that secondary policy 'was becoming altogether too egalitarian' and that comprehensive reorganization would not be the end of the process. The aim of the Tory leadership was to make concessions where they seemed inevitable, but of the most limited kind. 'Comprehensive' schemes could and would cover a number of quite restricted developments; the giving of priority to primary and nursery schooling would automatically restrict secondary energies and possibilities. All might be social democrats now, but not necessarily with much conviction. For Labour, the dilemmas were much more fundamental: tripartism had become indefensible but there remained deep uncertainties within the party about the nature of its replacement; nor was there an unequivocal welcome for or familiarity with 'progressive' teaching. Information and evidence from local authorities, the teaching unions and other bodies was formidably voluminous and detailed. It was perhaps partly a relief to Crosland on taking office to find so many levels of organization and of consultation standing between the government and the shape of a coherent new policy. The dwindling stature of the Education Ministry under the Wilson governments, the movement of spending away from education towards public housing, were probably connected with persistent unease and dissatisfaction about the new policies. In that sense, it would be wrong to identify social democratic ideas with the party under Wilson: attitudes both more 'traditional' (for example a strong concern to defend the 1944 grammar schools against ambiguous schemes by administrators) and much more radical lay uneasily next to the dominant consensus.

The social democratic passage, then, was caught acutely between different class claims and expectations of education and, in dissimilar ways, political suspicions and mistrust of the whole educational arena. Of all this the reports were the major test. It was these reports which insistently brought educational problems and new educational thinking to public notice. It was their recommendations for policy, backed by unprecedented detail of argument and depth of research, that underwent political surgery.

Examples of this included the three major changes of policy in the 1960s, of which one, ROSLA, was implemented at a much later date than Crowther and Newsom had demanded on detailed grounds. Another, the movement to comprehensive schooling, occurred in a way that did not meet the issues with which the reports dealt. A third, the 'binary' system of higher education, cut directly across the remit and intentions of the Robbins proposals. This is not to say that the reports were in any way sacrosanct, or that they were all social democratic in character: the Robbins Report was in many respects a different kind of operation. But Plowden was a set text of social democratic ideas, instantly attacked as such: and its implementation varied between the weak and the derisory.[29] The reports could not, of themselves, deliver legislation. As it proved, the change to comprehensives required the management of the Labour Party, with considerable difficulty. The work of schools in relation both to industrial training and to the needs of 'communities' required the belated realization of possible interventions under the management of the state. The significance of the reports, in our terms, is that they were heavily influenced by the work of the 1950s' experts — and made it generally known — but even more, that ideas from this source were steadily more unwelcome to the DES.

After Plowden, in fact, the Central Advisory Councils on education (made up of teachers and administrators with a sprinkling of industrialists and others) were never reappointed despite their legal requirement in the 1944 Act. Corbett, in the fourth edition of her invaluable study, regrets this because:

there has been no sign . . . that the committees' essential virtue has been replaced: their unique capacity to create a consensus for change . . . the most stable base for development that any government has.[30]

One of the strongest reasons for their disappearance seems to have been the chafing of the DES at the flow of ideas from a group relatively distanced from the state. Well-placed observers, Vaizey and Halsey, both concluded that, on the main questions in education since the war, policy had effectively been determined by the permanent civil servants of the department (who were by no means committed to sending their children to the state schools which they administered).[31] The contemptuous reference to the views of the 'non-educational stage army' has already been mentioned. A permanent secretary of the DES was to refer to the reports as 'an entire waste of words and waste of time', though complaining of a similar report that 'we had to write all the stuff for it'. Similarly, it was felt that the department itself could set up 'various committees to tackle various problems' and that this was a 'perfectly satisfactory way of working'.[32] This view was not shared by the OECD, whose critical report on the department, issued in the 1970s, was impatient with its tendency towards secretiveness and isolation from current educational thought.[33] The department's work appeared rather anachronistic, certainly in relation to the reforms of education across Europe which the OECD examiners were urging. But in the 1960s, the department preserved its traditional views and powers which had in no way been social democratic. It was yet another force standing between reformers' intentions and policy implementation, a spectre at the feast of the 'wide radical appeal'.

The framework of the reports

The needs of industry

The long row of thick reports and their supplementary volumes now looks forbidding and, from this distance, their tone can seem gratingly patronizing, and their commitment to reform equivocal. Even in 1959, a leader in *Education* found the Crowther Report 'a conservative, not a revolutionary document' that reaffirmed ideas current in 1944; while several politicians were disappointed by the lack of boldness in Newsom, to say nothing of his recommendation that 'general social problems, including education, in slum areas' should be dealt with by — an inter-departmental working party. . . .[34] But even in relation to school and work, where

Crowther was highly traditional, the arguments came to be located in a different conception of educational possibility; while in the handling of 'ability' in relation to 'environment' the reports made a break with received ideas of IQ that seemed decisive and still looks so, despite the strong revival of arguments about genetic heredity and intellectual potential. We shall look at both topics, with a note on the reports' attitudes towards gender.

Cockburn has said, writing of the welfare services in general, that 'not only does capital need efficient and appropriate labour, it also needs to disarm working class discontent'.[35] It was in just this double respect that the 'needs of industry' were consistently taken up in the reports. Crowther, appointed under and reporting to a Conservative minister in 1959, was completely explicit. 'Youth' (almost invariably male working-class youth) needed a preparation for industry which employers themselves could no longer adequately provide. It needed, also, help and support through a difficult period marked by a male juvenile delinquency 'at its worst in specific neighbourhoods . . . where the local climate of opinion is . . . not only defiant but deviant'. [36] (A year later the Albermarle Report spoke of 'a new climate of crime and delinquency . . . the crime problem is very much a youth problem'.)[37] The report's main argument was that the work and cost of training should be taken over from industry by the state, through a further year of school. It cited a predecessor of 1916:

Can it be assumed, then, that the conditions of juvenile employment are such as in themselves, and without the aid of formal schooling, as to establish the character and develop the industrial efficiency of young citizens? [38]

The raising of the school leaving age was proposed for its benefits to individuals, but it was noted, in any case, that should the demand for young labour fall off, it would be cheaper to provide for the age group through schooling, especially if this resulted in its being better 'equipped'. ROSLA would both secure an extension of the school's influence through 'the difficult and important period of adolescence' and allow for an initiation into work. Teachers should try experiments in the 'no man's land between school and work' and some would be 'difficult to carry out because they will not easily be kept within the bounds set by school regulations, trade union rules, labour legislation, insurance requirements . . .'.[39]

Recommendations of this sort and this dimension of the reports as a whole bore out Marx's argument that

because the necessary training . . . is more and more rapidly, easily, universally and cheaply reproduced with the progress of science and public education, the more the capitalist mode of production directs teaching methods etc towards practical purposes.

Others confirmed his prediction of pressures towards: 'the greatest possible reduction of labour in all spheres to simple labour; the elimination of all vocational prejudice among labourers . . .'.[40] That is, attention was concentrated on the majority who would need to be 'able to adjust' to rapid changes, the 'mobile' and 'highly adaptable' labour force of Plowden. There were only superficial contradictions between Crowther's 'reduced need in the future for "skill" ' and increased demand for 'general mechanical intelligence', and Newsom's 'the level of skill will tend to rise' or Plowden's workforce 'not only more skilled but better able to learn new skills'.[41] Either way the reports foresaw that jobs might be boring and worried that 'responsibility might fall into irresponsible hands' where in large unskilled groups 'difficult problems of human relations' arose.

This anxiety was linked to others about youth crime, youth spending and youth sexuality as part of the registration in the reports of a crisis of authority. They led outward to the demand that there should be a conscious effort, through education, to prepare both sexes for the family, if the family were to remain 'secure . . . and we can be content with nothing less'.[42] From here it was a matter of stages to Plowden's view that education involved 'the whole family'. In a savage passage Crowther complained that, for those not doing homework, and even despite some paid work for boys and some home help by girls, the gap between work and school hours was excessive. Many had 'too little to do' and their 'lack of ability and purpose' suggested that directed activities would be required outside school hours and terms.[43] It noted a new 'freedom of unsupervised association' and the youth service's failure to 'retain the bottom quarter or third of the population'.[44] In the Albermarle Report on the youth services, the cultural consequences of structural location were addressed directly. Young unskilled workers would be conscious of having been left behind by selection, and their work would leave them with a considerable surplus energy in addition to 'tensions and emotional problems'.[45] Youth workers were encouraged to provide chances for them to 'talk out their difficulties' and should counsel towards a better understanding of public affairs, employment, and preparation for homemaking.[46]

In the Crowther Report, then, supported by the Albermarle Report and by Newsom's request for firmer actions by magistrates against truants, the main themes were youth and work, youth and school, but also youth and the family and youth and the social services. By the time of the Plowden Report (1967) and the 1968 Seebohm Report on local authority services, the need was argued for co-ordination across all the social services, while attention broadened outwards to areas and to 'communities'.[47] Where comprehensives had been pragmatically commended by Crowther for areas where they could 'act as a socially unifying force', Plowden proposed criteria for 'deprived areas', as such, in which schools needed extra support and where 'community schools' should first be tried out. Earlier, the reports had advised the state to take greater responsibility through schools for appropriate work training and for the sensitive handling of transitions from school to work and from youth to parenthood. Now whole districts were solicited by Seebohm as state clients. The incidence of delinquency would be highest where there was little sense of community 'and hence little social control' or where

in a situation of strong social control the predominant community values are, in fact, criminal. Such ideas point to the need for the personal social services to engage in the extremely difficult and complex task of encouraging . . . community identity and mutual aid . . . .[48]

By this stage, at which the education reports were terminated, the boundary between the job of schools and of the social services was being eroded.

In these respects, the reports were very explicitly concerned with the reproduction of capital: with the provision of appropriate labour, with the disarming of discontent. Some of the quotations might seem to belong to the late 1970s. But there were several differences, as Laclau would suggest, in the whole 'structure of which they are a moment'.[49] Crowther typically argued against a single-minded concentration on the national income: industry did not exist for the teenager's sake, and going to work should be justified because it was 'the right thing' for the adolescent and not because of any 'reference to industry's need of juvenile labour'.[50](Albermarle commented that 'man's deepest needs are not satisfied by a mechanical participation in an economic process' though to those for whom work offered no chance for fulfilment society 'owes a special debt'.)[51] The reports were consistently benign in thinking that the needs of the economy and of the individual could, nevertheless, be matched. To some extent, their attempt was to protect school pupils against irrelevant demands, and to experiment (sometimes expensively, as Plowden was self-consciously aware) with new ways of teaching and learning. They were trusting that schools and teachers would adapt to new circumstances. Their stress was not on controls and sanctions, but on the release of talents and interests, particularly in the Plowden endorsement of progressive methods.

Together, the arguments and their implications remained Janus-faced. Although the forces party to school and social service reform, in these and allied reports, were neither strong nor agreed nor knowledgeable enough to form a clear strategy, their efforts in thinking about working-class youth, working-class life and working-class labour were not entirely pragmatic and directionless. The general manageability of labour could only be strengthened through a heightened manageability of and through education. Much of what the reports suggested prompted moves from hunches and rough guesswork to a drawing of lessons about educational management. This would later require some breaks with social democratic promises, now regarded as constraints.

The nature of ability

The second and more original theme of the reports was their handling of the distribution of 'ability', the incidence of 'failure' and the relation of both to 'home background'. Here, if anywhere, lay a classic occasion for the social democratic construction of a response to a political breakdown of confidence in the post-war settlement. Unease with 'tripartite' notions of type of mind had advanced to a formidable assault upon the bases of IQ testing. This had become linked with wider publicity for the uneven geographical distribution of grammar school provision and to anxiety, even panic, about the hurdle at 'eleven plus'. A senior ministry official, 'not himself by any means an out-and-out comprehensivist', asked Boyle in 1962 to

imagine similar families in a suburban street where as a result of a twenty mark
difference or less a girl at No. 2 would receive a grammar place where the majority
of teachers were graduates, a girl at No. 4 a non-selective place with few graduates.
'That is the problem entailed in defending a system based on selection.'[52]

The task of successive reports was to question precise notions of measurable
intelligence without falling into the abyss that might follow their abandonment.
Plowden came dangerously near to this in the wistful remark 'what we would like
to know is just how much more ability could be uncovered in the population if
everyone was given the most suitable home and educational environment.'[53] In this
sentence, many of the reports' key moves were caught. Intelligence was replaced by
the more flexible notion of ability, itself connected to interests and needs. There
was a strongly quantitative concern, nonetheless, with 'just how much more' could
be found by a dredge into, for example, the 'second quartile'. Behind this lay the
newly stressed importance of 'background', treated usually in an atomistic
concentration on the individual child's 'home'. Newsom's study of three ideal type
individual children, Brown, Jones and Robinson, at times read like a satire by
Swift — or perhaps more accurately a 'Robinsoniad' by Defoe himself, since
Robinson, a child 'in the bottom quarter of ability' just happened to come in nine
out of ten cases, from the 'homes of manual workers', though this left him still his
own inimitably individual self:

granted that a Robinson is more often an unsatisfactory pupil in these various ways
than a Brown is, the question still remains open whether it is these propensities
which help to make him Robinson, a boy bad at work, or whether he falls into
these bad habits because he is only and inescapably Robinson.[54]

Perhaps the most accurate comparison would be with Crompton's *Just William*.
For Plowden, as ever the most subtle and tortured of the reports, 'socio-economic
classes' were 'heterogeneous and artificial' and what mattered was not occupation
or income but 'the family's . . . whole cultural outlook', though the determinations
upon that cultural outlook were not examined.[55]

The exact movements of these arguments were important. This was not least
because, as Plowden pointed out, there was indeed a danger that a form of testing
whose objectivity now seemed spurious might be replaced by one whose
subjectivity was even less available for inspection:

the I.Q. scores are not so highly correlated with parental occupation as are the scores
in attainment tests or probably as are teachers' ratings . . . in the right circumstances
. . . the I.Q. test may serve to pick out a child of ability who would be passed over
by an attainment test or a teacher's rating . . . .[56]

In 1959 Crowther's attitude has been brusquely cavalier. Even though 'about
14 per cent' of those tested and classified at 11 would have been reclassified by
tests at 15 'this is what we should expect from the changes and chances of mortal
life . . . we cannot hope to avoid error by further refinements'.[57] So even if '40 per
cent' of national certificate students showed themselves 'equal in intelligence' to
university students when less verbal tests were used, the proposal was not to

reconsider either testing or higher education provision, but to be more aware of students allocated to technical colleges who 'though of comparable basic capacity' would need 'quite a different teaching approach'.[58] This acknowledged a certain rough justice but no fundamental harm in the use of testing to support existing and unequal divisions beyond secondary level.

By comparison, Newsom and Plowden used two increasingly tortuous 'explanations' of some now admitted social determinations upon 'intelligence'. Newsom conceded that, although there could be no denying 'the existence of a basic genetic endowment', this had so far proved 'impossible to isolate'.[59] In the safer Plowden formulation, 'environmental and hereditary factors interact inextricably'.[60] This allowed the reports' authors to suggest relationships between ability and class: 'the gap between the measured intelligence of the children of manual workers and of middle class parents begins to widen at a very early age'.[61] Newsom's research contrasted ideal types of children and their families. There was an above even chance that Newsom's achieving child, Brown, would have a skilled manual worker as father, and Browns 'congregate in London and the Home Counties': whereas in schools of 'the worst slum areas' over a third of the boys were 'of John Robinson's kind'.[62] Robinson, added Sir Alec Clegg (one of the report's authors) later, is 'now black',[63] and Plowden found that the 'less intelligent, less ambitious and more passive parent' would be found down the 'social scale'.[64] Facts about housing conditions, diet, and so on were said, again ambivalently, to show 'the progress, or lack of it, made towards equalizing even the simple circumstances of life between children of different social classes'.[65] The final knot in the argument was to follow this odd suggestion that different classes might have equal 'circumstances', by admitting that 'there must always be a great diversity of parental occupations'.[66] The conclusion was the attempt to soften or ameliorate the starker signs of class difference: 'the *grosser* deprivations arising from poverty can be removed' (our emphasis).[67]

All of this amounted to a rejection of the current sortings into forms of school as untenable, combined with a hope that money could be found to alleviate poverty. This was a clear movement away from the *status quo* of the 1950s. But there was no break with a paradigm of measurable qualities, even if the qualities measured were now more often 'curiosity' and 'involvement' than abstract 'intelligence' distributed over a 'curve'. To that extent, there were still differences of achievement by which children would be produced by schools, 'equipped' for different places in 'the general division of labour'. The reports suggested that the state should compensate for poverty, and that it should be more wary and flexible in its underscoring of educational difference: 'streaming can be wounding to children'.[68] Inequality itself was still approached elliptically, as an unfortunate by-product, residue or anachronism which, with the right kind of interventions, could be controlled, if not abolished. Again the reports could be read in two ways. The wish to provide better circumstances for a child's development was benign, and accelerated experiments in more open forms of teaching: but it was connected with batteries of examinations, though of a new kind. The attack on 'deprivation' provided spaces for new kinds of relationship between schools and their communities: but it was also part of the increasing monitoring, through the range of social services, of working-class areas. We want to look at these developments by contrasting the implementation of Robbins and of Plowden.

The needs of boys and girls

There was no discomfort at all in the reports about gender. The sexes were accepted unquestioningly as different, with correspondingly different 'needs', and it was around the notion of 'needs' that one aspect of the reports' rationale rested. Crowther commented, with fleeting concern, that only 8 per cent of girl school leavers in 1956 were receiving further education by comparison with almost a third of all boys under 18. For Crowther there could be no doubt that boys thought of 'a career' first and of marriage and the family second, and that with girls the reverse was true. Given this, it was only 'sound educational policy to take account of natural interests'. The curriculum should be one which 'respects the different roles they play'.[69] Boys would, said Newsom, 'need an element of adventure' (though 'stealing from a supermarket seems to put the matter in a different light'), while many girls, though apparently chiefly preoccupied:

with personal appearance and boy friends . . . are ready to respond to work relating to the wider aspects of homemaking and family life and the care and upbringing of children.[70]

Newsom had a section on 'housecraft', including 'realistic' conditions in which girls could practise running a flat, redecorating a room, thinking about mothering.[71] When it was argued that pupils should be led 'beyond their personal preoccupations . . . to some wider conception of their role in life', this actually entailed a work in which the school would construct 'natural' interests for the majority of girls towards an understanding of their responsibilities primarily as mothers and home managers, though Crowther's sixth-form girls might be attracted by some vocational skills: 'shorthand, typing, and in some schools, accounts are the core round which secretarial courses are developed'.[72] Views on girls and employment were limited to a few tips: the reports concentrated on the handling of future male labour.

   In commenting on girls and youth culture, Newsom's and Crowther's confident views gave way to an almost embarrassed coyness with mildly religious overtones. The key notions were respect and honour: Newsom suggested that the boy should honour the girl he loves. Nowhere was the text more distant, than here, from aspects of working-class culture, towards which its aversion was unconcealed. A strongly conservative attitude towards female dependence and vulnerability was underpinned by fears of declining moral standards and family breakdown. Typically, Newsom moved away from Crowther's more vigilant supervisory proposals towards expansionist policies with an emphasis on the school's caring role. This included support for the autonomy of schools from the needs of industry. Yet ironically in the case of girls, this 'space' from work which the school offered would bind the girl even closer to a traditional role in the home and kitchen, or what 'many, perhaps most of them, would regard as their most important vocational concern, marriage'.[73] It seemed that for Newsom social skills were a means of learning to cope with monotonous jobs; leisure the sphere of creative but restrained self-expression; the school curriculum a powerful agency in amplifying 'natural' differences even in their modernist forms — 'a new concept of partnership'.[74] The reports never suggested that gender differences carried any imbalance of power, let alone exploitation, inequality or oppression. In all these respects social democratic reformism stayed firmly masculine.

In sum, the reports developed a body of ideas on problems caused by male working-class school leavers, and these ideas were both partially benign, protective and optimistic and yet firmly posited on the need for a mobile, pliant — well-schooled — labour force. They broke the dominance of the concept of fixed and especially of hereditary intelligence, and replaced it by notions of ability, interests and needs which allowed more space for development to both child and teacher: yet preserved the notion of an ability *range*, linked to home background and perhaps even to class, whose bottom end could be encouraged and whose 'second quartile' should no longer be firmly separated from achievement above it, but whose curve — and the 'diversity' of parental occupations on which it depended and to which it then delivered children again — could (if unfortunately) not yet be challenged. On gender relations, in so far as the subject was treated at all, their views remained (if in modified ways) traditional, with some encouragement to the schools to seal girls further into their 'natural' interests.

We shall look next at the starkest of the contrasts in the political implementation of the reports' proposals; then at aspects of 1960s' developments which were articulated on social democratic hopes, though operating to some degree behind their backs; finally at the way in which Labour introduced the comprehensive schools, not directly addressed in the reports.

Policy proposals and the forms of their implementation

Responses to Robbins and Plowden

In neither case were the reports' authors satisfied with the consequences of their work. Crosland sanctioned a binary system in which universities and polytechnics were separately funded. This cut directly across the remit and intentions of the Robbins proposals. Lady Plowden complained that her committee's report had had little effect (though the angry response to it by opponents of 'progressivism', concentrated on paragraphs 504–7, had its own political significance in the later 1960s).[75] The Robbins Committee had been, in any event, a different sort of animal from the others. It was appointed directly by government, not under the Central Advisory Council, and never pretended to elaborate more than a few rather banal remarks about the nature of higher education. Its eyes were firmly set on the details of possible courses of development, and particularly on their cost (with Treasury representation on its team). Robbins's task was to cost and plan an idea, the moment of whose political necessity had come. The Macmillan goverment accepted its findings instantly in the run-up to an election, and neither party gainsaid its projections of demand and the political pressure consequent upon the demand. The two parties disagreed upon detail, and Labour — more accurately, it would seem, the DES — proceeded to erect a very different kind of system of higher education than Robbins had intended. In a manner classic of the political conjuncture, it did so by arguing that the polytechnics might become popular, civic, locally responsible institutions as against the universities' traditional elitism: shades of grammar school opportunity against the privileges of public schools! The other side of the coin, inevitably, was tighter controls on polytechnic spending and a firmer integration between their work and the needs of industry.

Yet the basic, simple contrast remained. Higher education proceeded immediately to a very substantial expansion indeed, and did so at a great pace and without the political infighting that accompanied so many other developments. It was quite otherwise with the Plowden Report's famous and innovative recommendation of educational priority area experiments. The recommendation was that

the gap between the educational opportunities of the most and least fortunate children should be closed, for economic and social reasons alike. . . .The programme should be phased to make schools in the deprived areas as good as the best in the country.[76]

It was always clear that the report's suggestions would be expensive — the gap to which Plowden pointed was never more than minutely pointed to in actual experiments. In his speech to the NUT shortly before his transfer from the department, Crosland said that 'we set up a special working group inside the department to go through all recommendations' and that 'certain parts of the report on the management of schools and things like that' had been accepted as had the 'principle' of the EPAs.[77] But Halsey, working inside the experiments, found little action on most of the Plowden recommendations and that the absence of national definition of the areas to be involved left it to local authorities to recommend certain of their own schools.[78] In the Birmingham conurbation, the authorities suggested 25 per cent of their schools, as would follow from Plowden's own criteria; the Department accepted 8 per cent. Despite the ensuing sophistication of mathematical indices (!) to quantify the criteria of deprivation, investment in the EPAs was made, as we shall see, in ways quite other than Plowden's. Neither resources nor political will were to be used to see 'just how much more ability could be uncovered in the population'. As in some modern version of the missions, research delegations from the expanding universities were sent to report on beleaguered, courageous, resource-starved pockets of experiment.

From CSE to the binary system: the rise and rise of qualifications

Crowther commented in 1959 on the general rise in demand for qualifications for jobs which had not previously required them and where no specific expertise was involved. It was claimed that, whether or not the qualifications were 'really necessary', they were 'here to stay': the particular influence on this tendency would be an increase of the supply of labour relative to demand for it, seen by the report as the entirely 'natural' result, in the conditions of a prosperous economy, of a demographic bulge. The argument showed clearly that tests would therefore not qualify for jobs, but serve as the objective pre-condition for competition, rationalizing a terrain on which selection could take place: but the report went on to suggest a further extension of secondary examinations. Ensuing discussions were never far removed from balancing carrot and stick.

As often in the Crowther Report, the argument that it would be wrong to 'stand in the way' of further examinations, with an implication of opportunities for individual development, lay thinly separated from the assessment of need for highly mobile and adaptable workers, available for labour processes as yet undesigned. The contribution of schooling to this availability would then not only be in the rationalization of local variations across the country (such as the age of transfer between schools, discussed by Plowden), but in the extension of 'objective' differentiation between groups entering the workforce, so as to produce actively, through schooling, a greater pliability of labour. In these cases, below the specialist skills of GCE, attainments beyond simple arithmetic and the 'capacity to understand written instructions' mattered less to employers than 'character and temperament'. Employers, said Newsom, 'do not always want clever people'. These qualifications would work within the school 'as a means of showing the pupils where they stand': schools told Newsom of experiments with character certificates which had proved to have an incentive value for school leavers.[79]

Two developments were already implicit in the Crowther—Newsom exploration of ways and means of extending new kinds of examination. One was the danger of creating 'a seriously depressed' grouping of those not taking examinations. The other stemmed from the realization that tests of this kind could only be based on strategic possibilities within particular schools, and so would have to be controlled by classroom teachers. The outcome of this, following the Beloe Report of 1960, was a settlement between the ministry and teachers in the Certificate of Secondary Education, allowing increased teacher control of the syllabus. Further down the road, in the next decade, it was then possible both for the media to be scandalized by examinations which could not be failed, and for protests to be mounted against the teachers' powers of self-determination — enjoying, for example, 'the right to disregard his client which no other professional worker enjoys . . . arbiter of ends as well as expert in means'.[80] At this early stage the effects of examinations upon school behaviour were only to be surmised. By 1970 a Schools Council Report, *Cross'd with Adversity,* noted the difficulties of encouraging inner city families to develop a 'normal' relationship with teachers when they could see little occupational value in school work.[81] If the 'scales' of opportunity were 'tilted' against them, the idea of effort as a means of upward mobility would be received with scepticism. Given this working-class indifference or resistance, the extension of examinations might require a more overt and problematic compulsion.

At the other end of the system, there was a decision to extend polytechnic education offering degrees validated by a new national body, the Council for National Academic Awards. This was a particular case, following a familiar DES pattern. As with the tripartite division of types of mind, to which the department had clung as long as possible, or as with the 'separate but equal' CSE–GCE relationship, polytechnics allowed flexible and very extensively monitored experiment in new types of degree qualification. The dangers (as in the United States) of overt stratification within a huge university system was avoided. The range of types of higher, as of secondary, qualification, was considerably stretched.

All these extensions of qualification were contradictory both in their feasibility and outcome. Innovative work was allowed in some CSE examinations, also under the deliberately 'high' standards of the CNAA. The growth of examinations produced a stress on 'character' and an increasing 'objective' differentiation between those entering the labour market. But it also threatened to lower the status, even the credibility, of 'achievements' central to political ideologies directed at aspirations to mobility in the name of opportunity for the 'ablest': 'working class children suffer when applying for jobs if they cannot bring forward proof of their worth achieved in authoritative examinations' *(Black Paper, 1975)*.

Halsey, in a study for the OECD, wrote that educational thresholds had been raised for every point in the 'occupational hierarchy' and that the general upgrading had been particularly marked for 'technicians, supervisors, higher grade service workers and some skilled manual workers'. In his commentary on the failure of some of the 'liberal' policies to which he had subscribed he argued that:

the typical history of educational expansion in the nineteen fifties and nineteen sixties can be represented by a graph of inequality of attainment . . . which has shifted markedly upwards without changing its slope.[82]

Educational priority areas and the tightening of state planning

The changes of the decade, not only those which were structural but also the swelling of teacher numbers and the programme of school building improvements, involved greater spending and thereby the necessity for increased planning, for which Crowther had argued in 1959. Such planning had not been familiar to the DES and, throughout the 1960s, there were complaints of the department's inability to supply basic statistical information. The promotion in 1965 of a National Plan under Labour further facilitated the establishment of a DES planning unit (1966) and so the possibility of resource allocations in detail in the projections of the next major White Paper in 1972.

The topic may seem arid, but it had reverberations of increasing significance. We shall look at one such 'technical' decision, the deferment of ROSLA, in a moment. Another was the emphasis, in the early 1970s, on primary building schemes, and the immediate result in a shortage of funds for ambitious comprehensive plans. In these and other cases there ran a narrative first, of more ambitious decision-taking on plans little available outside the DES (of which Hencke has explored one major instance in the reorganization of teacher training) and second, of 'managerial' or administrative implementation whose interventions in the consequences of policy were a subtext to the discourse of reform – or a great deal more than that.[83] Halsey's report on the EPAs recorded the ambition for widespread and thorough-going assaults on undemocratic local power structures and on the inadequacies or absence of locally available employment.[84] But nothing of this order was possible inside the accepted definitions of what EPAs might mean.

In one way, the EPA experiment was an early educational instance of Cockburn's demonstration that increased corporate management of state facilities, in the rationalization partly enforced by their cost, had necessitated finding new ways to 'involve' the state's neediest 'clients', both for its own information and its own protection.[85] The EPAs should be connected with other and more precise attempts at local intervention: through from the Home Office's Community Development Projects and Comprehensive Community Programmes to the Environment Department's frankly labelled area management trials. As in these cases (especially that of the CDPs) some of the workers who explored the social relations of the area came to draw their own political conclusions, so also could local and central state agencies.

The EPA intervention in the areas of toughest school problems was the educational case of an increased co-ordination of local and national state action. We have seen that Newsom, Plowden and Seebohm all pointed the need for greater integration across the social services. Some of the problems entailed were later discussed in meetings between chief education officers and their DES colleagues from 1971. *Management in Education Services*, issued by the Society of Education Officers in 1974, noted that the service was isolated by its problems in imposing standards. The Revised Code had left 'a legacy of resistance to any form of manage-ment'.[86] Areas around which the service would need to concentrate were positive discrimination, strategic planning linked with other social services, and the calculation of resource effectiveness. One authority, using a management consultancy, was interested in deviance, leisure and 'adjustment' as 'social indicators'.

More forceful and revealing was the 1969 Russell lecture (requiring a speaker with 'knowledge and ability to speak of working-class and delinquent boys and girls') given by the ex-DES civil servant Maurice Kogan. This concentrated on the frustration of social service administrators who lacked 'power and influence'. It was a 'far too admired creed that civil servants should avoid the entrepreneurial style and be bureaucrats ostensibly accountable to ministers'.[87] There should be a time when 'young turks' were 'given their chance'. He went on to argue, in tones reminiscent of Carlyle and the anxieties of a Victorian middle class, that clearer aims should be developed in the relations of social worker and client or teacher and child, so that discretion would operate within 'limits . . . known, understood and accepted by superior and subordinate'.[88] Cockburn's finding that there was a tendency towards greater separation in local authorities between the enhanced power of permanent professional administrators and the diminished powers of temporary political representatives was confirmed in Kogan's complaint of uncertainty, whether administrators were 'executive managers in their departments or staff officers to ministers'. But ideas for future planning should be tested against 'organizational models' such as the EPAs to bring about a growth in the 'perception and discretionary freedom' of administrators. It was against this background that the OECD was to complain of the lack of public participation in English educational planning: a complaint that seemed to be substantially resisted in the ensuing Commons inquiry. Firmer central intervention in the curriculum and in performance assessment were both imminent. In neither respect were the social democratic — or any other — ideas of the administrators available for public discussion; while no Central Advisory Council after Plowden was appointed.[89]

'Comprehensive' ideas and practice

We saw at the beginning of this chapter some of the reasons why pressures against the tripartite system had become overwhelming, and why it fell to the Labour Party to implement their introduction. They did so, as we have also suggested, in circumstances of division among those it attempted to represent: a strongly accumulated legacy of post-war working-class wariness of state education, a resilient minority tradition of working-class grammar school support, a push for wider avenues to mobility from middle-class groupings, nevertheless worried by the possible loss of grammar school standards. In the rhetoric of the party's leadership, the ensuing concerns were the avoidance of 'extreme social division' (Crosland) and the determination to stand by the grammar schools (Wilson). In the more diffused public discussion prompted by the party, Marsden has noted a swirling mixture of different kinds of argument: the meritocratic commitment to the economic harnessing of wasted talent and the provision of a broader ladder of qualification; a stress on community benefits in the promotion of unified neighbourhood schooling; an egalitarian theme of open, cross-class schooling — in Marsden's phrase, 'the best comprehensives we have — primary schools' — if only in the negative sense of reduced pressures for streaming and examination.[90]
That left social democrats had their backs to the wall was seen in the very ambiguous passages where Brian Simon and David Rubinstein, advocating comprehensive growth, adroitly summarized a whole range of reasons for the move that were *not* necessarily egalitarian in motivation: for instance what they called 'the fact' that the 'technological revolution' created new 'needs and opportunities'.[91]

Piecemeal local changes in the 1944 tripartite system were, in any case, extensively under way during Tory administrations in the 1950s. Comprehensives had been sanctioned particularly in cases where dual provision was too expensive or, as in new towns, for the kind of value which Crowther attached to them 'as an effective sign of that unity in society which our age covets'.[92] There had been innovative experiments, especially in Mason's Leicestershire plan. In 1964, the Conservative Bow Group's journal proclaimed that leading Conservatives were converted to comprehensives despite 'backwoods resistance'.[93]

Labour then took office, not only with a tiny majority and with an already imminent and serious financial crisis, but without its own view of comprehensives clearly established and with local and central state planning for comprehensives already well advanced. Under Crosland, the party which presented itself as responsible for the movement towards educational equality never sought to involve interests beyond those of the DES and of teachers. The declared pragmatism of the DES, with its task of presiding over the intricate complexities of local— central state relationships through 'listening' and 'counselling' then had a specific outcome: the department stood between the notional comprehensive ideal and the adjustments and deflections of its varied implementation. The October 1965 circular, though it aroused tactical howls of protest, did no more than offer, in familiar departmental style, an edited version of six types of change already being attempted by local authorities. Its implementation encouraged a national movement towards comprehensives, but the meaning of the movement was never in any way radical. When Labour left office in 1970, only 10 per cent of secondary children were in fully comprehensive schools. Rubinstein and Simon showed that the great bulk of the change at that stage consisted in the redesignation of secondary modern school as comprehensive.[94] And Labour was still allowing authorities with more than 10—15 per cent of its catchment in grammar schools to add O-level GCE work to secondary moderns, as had been recommended by the Conservative White Paper of 1958. Marsden's bitter conclusion in 1970 was that:

the resulting structure will be a super-selective tripartite system of independent/direct grant, grammar/unskimmed comprehensive and skimmed comprehensive/secondary modern . . . Tawney's maxim: 'Onions can be eaten leaf by leaf, but you cannot skin a live tiger paw by paw'.[95]

As Labour allowed a variety of schemes with no view of its own, lacking any popular base for a stronger line or party unity around it, so it disclaimed any concern with the curriculum in which Crosland declared himself and his officials not 'in the slightest degree competent'. The vacated ground could then be occupied by the teachers. Teachers had worked to publicize education as a cause, as in the campaign for education of 1963. The largest of the teaching unions, split to some extent between the different interests of groups of its members, moved from mildly requesting a period of secondary experiment in 1959 to cautious support for the full comprehensive model in its 1964 evidence to Plowden. By the early 1970s, it was opposed to Mrs Thatcher's retention of selection. The main change here was the achievement of greater control by teachers through demand for recognition as a profession. They secured dominance of the Schools Council, such that by 1976 it was said that the council was 'in very poor standing with the department'.[96] The pioneering of curriculum innovation by the council involved both some detailed working-out of the consequences of 'progressive' ideas and the subtle adjustment of forces between teacher and pupils. But initiative rested firmly with the 'professional' skills of teachers, away from the DES's watchdog function with which it was increasingly dissatisfied, as Kogan's remarks suggested. But either way no political direction of the comprehensive reform was attempted at the level of the schools' internal workings: it was not clear even what that would mean. Far less was there any attempt at public debate, rather some pressures towards dampening its potentially dangerous electoral consequences.

In these circumstances, it could later be reported that, within a policy concerned with greater equality of opportunity, the movement of expenditure had been towards higher and sixth-form education, with a proportionately greater improvement in conditions and facilities for 'non-manual' groups. Halsey wrote that, despite experiment, English education had 'remained predominantly an avenue for the stable transmission of status from one generation to another'.[97] Nor could it be otherwise because Labour policy had undercut the physical forms of segregation but challenged neither the existence of 'ability' distributed on a curve (and now assessed in streaming, banding and other tests which, Plowden had suggested, might correlate more highly with parental occupation than those of the IQ test itself) nor the dependence of pupils and parents upon teachers and experts whose authority had been greatly enhanced. On the content and purpose of knowledge no comment had been made. Overt channelling by 'types of mind' had (to some extent) been replaced by less visible differentiation. But in a fascinating detailed account of the arrival of some local comprehensive schools in different circumstances and areas, some of the main issues in the whole debate (social class, school outcomes, the problems of achieving greater 'equality') were scarcely mentioned.[98] In retrospect Butler suggested that it might be possible to speak of 'composite or comprehensive schemes of secondary organization', while for Boyle the problem had been 'to get it across that "secondary reorganisation" did not necessarily mean the large, "all-through" comprehensive school . . . there were other alternatives'.[99]

Glimpses of social democracy

In all respects, then, the partial implementation of social democratic ideas remained as ambivalent as the ideas themselves. Comprehensive schools did remove forms of separation, to some degree; they did allow a greater autonomy of teachers and pupils. Yet they were not encouraged even to begin to implement stronger definitions of equality, nor was public support for them secured. Even more ironic was the fate of the raising of the school leaving age. The delaying of its introduction until 1972 meant that its salience was caught in the strongly hostile attention given to schools in the media by that time: the highlighting of truancy, delinquency, unrest in schools put the innovation strongly on the defensive.

In summary, the decade was decisively not one in which reforms everywhere displaced the earlier settlement. Paradoxically it was true both that social democratic ideas had been tested and found inadequate — and that they had never been properly tried at all.

6   The sociology of education: a critique

In this chapter we look at the sociological understandings that underpinned 1960s' policies. As we noted in Chapter 4, the strength of the old sociology of education, from D. V. Glass's original conception onwards, was the mapping of educational inequalities. Throughout the 1960s and beyond, sociologists continued to monitor the effects of educational changes through the indices of inequality that had been established in the early surveys. We have already noted the main features of this mapping: the use of notions of class or status group to make inter-generational comparisons, usually of father's occupational group and son's educational achievements; the comparison of the class structure of educational access with the class distribution of 'ability' using the results of intelligence testing; the calculation of class chances of reaching particular levels within the education system.

We want to stress the very paradoxical nature of that project. The main paradox hinged upon the persuasiveness of this record of inequalities as, on the one hand, indicating the goals of policy and, on the other, the inadequacies of the forms of explanation that were adopted to account for these recurring phenomena. In so far as sociology influenced policy, this paradox progressively deepened. Research continued to show that policies, informed by sociological understandings, did not in fact remove inequalities. On the contrary, they seemed to produce, with monotonous regularity, the same or similar educational outcomes. There was a dynamic of self-destruction or, at least, of self-critique at the very heart of the tradition.

This paradox went deep. The very categories and methods of the research were implicated. The ideas and research techniques employed to monitor educational change were far from neutral when it came to the task of explanation. The reduction of 'class' to social stratification, the reduction of cultural process to discrete and apparently measurable variables, and the extreme difficulty of handling relations of gender, all derived from the attempt to produce standardized and comparable statistical results central to the monitoring process. These same categories and absences indeed proved positively disabling when it came to explanation. The most obvious merit of the tradition, the concern with accumulative results over long time spans, also encouraged a certain conservatism. Innovations risked losing the virtues of comparison. The most striking instance was the assignment of girls and women to the marginalia of the major statistical projects, a feature reinforced rather than amended in later work. Girls are systematically excluded, for example, in the recently published study by Halsey, Ridge and Heath, despite its sub-title, 'Family, class and education in modern Britain'.[1] As is common in books of this kind, what is specific to a masculine experience is treated as the general case, from which the experience of girls is bound to appear as a deviation. Terms like class, occupation, and adulthood are treated as neutral about gender when actually conceived in specifically masculine forms. Such studies invite, at best, parallel accounts of girls' experience in the same social democratic mould.[2] What is specific to gender relations may thus be obscured. The only form in which women appear in the 1980 study is as mothers of boys. Nor will upholders of women's domestic role find much satisfaction here. In their review of qualitative materials, drawn mainly from Jackson and Marsden, the authors systematically obscure the educative role of mothers:

We have ourselves directly compared our survey evidence with that of Jackson and Marsden who present a Hoggartian interpretation of the key role of the mother. But our data lent no support to this view. Either or both parents play their part in forming the educational fate of their children.[3]

The overwhelming impression given by this study is of the application of increasingly ingenious techniques to a narrowly conservative set of questions.

In this chapter, we conduct a critique of the main tendency in the sociology of education in three main stages. First, we review the evidence for educational inequalities which provided both the ground of explanation of the old sociology and the source of its own internal self-critique. Second, we look at the main forms of explanation for these recurrent observations, especially the emphasis on home background and on the operation of the schools. Third, we note the main absences in this paradigm, especially the absence of a critical assessment of what was typically called 'modern technological society'. We note the absence too of any adequate account of cultural forms and processes.

'The evidence': then and now

In 1961, Halsey, Floud and Anderson pointed out that 'widespread social amelioration since the second world war has not removed persistent class inequalities in the distribution of ability and attainment'.[4] Douglas concluded his cohort study of 1964 with the words that 'the evidence set out in this book gives strong reasons for believing that much potential ability is wasted during the primary school years and misdirected at the point of secondary selection'.[5] Four years later, in a continuation study that took the same cohort through to school leaving age, he noted that:

the social class differences in educational opportunity which were considerable at the primary school stage have increased at the secondary, and extend now even to pupils of highest ability. Thus nearly half the lower manual working class pupils of high ability have left school before they are sixteen-and-a-half years.[6]

Girls, despite achieving significantly higher scores at primary school, received fewer O-levels due to a steady decline in their measured ability in secondary school and their disproportionate failure to complete the examination course at all.

The official reports of the 1960s were also preoccupied, as we have seen, by the problem of 'failure'. Robbins was concerned about 'the large reservoirs of untapped ability in the population, especially amongst girls'.[7] This was highlighted by the close association between fathers' and children's education: 32 per cent of the children of fathers who had been educated beyond the age of 18 were attending degree courses, compared with 2 per cent of children whose fathers had left school at 16. Newsom was concerned about average and below average ability children: 'our children' who would become 'half the citizens of this country, half the workers, half the mothers and fathers and half the consumers'. This half of our future contained 'much unrealized talent': 'the country cannot afford this wastage humanly or economically speaking'.[8] The Plowden Report was based in part on 'a growing awareness . . . of the importance to the individual of his (*sic*) family and social background',[9] sponsoring research into the association of home, environment and academic achievement. This suggested:

that the most vital factor in a child's home is the attitude to school, and all that goes on there, of his mother and father. The interested parent has the interested child. In contrast, we have been conscious of the unfairness that dogs many boys and girls through life. The loss to them and the loss to the community that arises because of the inequality of educational opportunity, is avoidable and in consequence intolerable.[10]

If we compare these findings with similar results produced in the 1970s, it is apparent that little changed, despite the proliferation of certification, especially the introduction of the Certificate of Secondary Education, which provided qualifications for the majority of children. The percentage of boys and girls leaving school with no examination certificate fell from 51 per cent (both sexes) in 1965–6 to 16.4 per cent of boys and 14.6 per cent of girls in 1976–7,[11] but there was little change in the class patterns of further and higher education, with 65 per cent of 16–18-year-olds with professional fathers in full-time education in 1975 compared with only 14 per cent of children with fathers in unskilled manual occupations.[12] The Halsey, Heath and Ridge conclusions manage an optimistic gloss on similar results, largely by reposing hope in comprehensive reorganization, the effects of which were not yet fully reflected in their sample.[13] Nonetheless, their long view of forty years of educational change (as opposed to their predictions for the future) is fundamentally pessimistic:

In summary, school inequalities of opportunity have been remarkably stable over the forty years which our study covers. Throughout, the service class has had roughly three times the chance of the working class of getting some kind of selective secondary schooling. Only at 16 has there been any significant reduction in relative class chances, but even here the absolute gains have been greater for the service class. If the 'hereditary curse upon English education is its organization upon lines of social class', that would seem to be as true in the 1960s as it was in 1931 when Tawney wrote.[14]

In the 1970s, gender inequalities have come under closer scrutiny especially by feminist researchers.[15] Two recent studies are written from very different perspectives: Eileen Byrne's belongs to what has been described as 'the "equal rights" liberal reformist tradition',[16] the feminist equivalent, in many ways, to the social democratic tradition we have been exploring; Rosemary Deem's looks at inequalities from a Marxist-feminist perspective.[17] The two studies reach very similar conclusions about the position of girls in education, while differing profoundly in their explanations. Byrne concludes: 'It is disheartening to see that after 25 years the gap of achievement is as great as ever in higher and advanced technical education.'[18] Deem likewise stresses the persistence of 'discrimination and differentiation' in girls' education, especially in higher education.[19]

Dominant explanations

By the late 1950s and early 1960s, the class-related patterns of educational inequality under the 1944 Act were becoming very clear. The key problem was variously described: achieving 'equality of opportunity', 'differential educability', stopping up, in the usual plumbing metaphor, 'the leakage of talent'. Since all the statistical series showed that 'wastage' was heavily concentrated among children of 'the manual working class', the problem was how to explain and to prevent working-class educational 'failure'. If there was agreement about the problem, there was also convergence around certain broad structures of explanation. These were already being sketched by Halsey and Floud in 1958:

In principle, the sociologist's task is clear: to analyse the social factors which influence the educational process from two main sources. There are those, on the one hand, deriving from the family environment and general background of teachers and pupils . . . and, on the other hand, there are those deriving from the social organization, formal and informal, of schools, colleges and universities. In practice, the educability of an individual, given his personal endowment, and unique life-history, is a function of the interaction of all these *social* factors; . . . it represents his socially determined capacity to respond to the demands of the particular educational arrangements to which he is exposed.[20]

Those 'two main sources' — 'family background' (almost always, in practice, that of pupils) and the internal functioning of schools — were exhaustively explored in the years that followed. Though the foci and methods of studies differed, most research was contained within these limits. We can best illustrate this by comparing two very different phases of research, represented by Douglas's *The Home and the School* (published in 1964, but begun in the 1950s) and the Manchester based studies of Lacey and Hargeaves (published in 1970 and 1967 respectively, from a project begun in 1962–3).[21]

Both sets of studies present relatively sophisticated analyses within the broad problem of educational access. Douglas sought to go beyond the conspicuous exclusions represented by the limitation of grammar school places and their arbitrary regional distribution or the wastage involved in early school leaving. He sought to go 'still further back' to 'apathy at home', poor teaching in primary school and to the streaming of children under 11.[22] Lacey saw himself as laying bare 'the social mechanisms within the school in an attempt to explain the disappointing performance of working-class boys in grammar schools since the Education Act'.[23] Hargreaves set his study within the context of the move towards comprehensives and the Newsom Report's concern with children in secondary modern schools.[24]

The two sets of reports differed in method and focus. Douglas's large-scale survey involved the very problematic use of information collected by teachers, doctors and social workers about a random sample of children born in 1946.[25] It concentrated on the home–school relation, with the stress on the home. Douglas's primary explanations were in terms of the accumulative under-privileging of children in working-class homes, tendencies reinforced by the schools, but especially by streaming.

At first sight, the Manchester studies are very different. They are small-scale, intensive, observational and 'qualitative', focusing on the internal life of schools. Both authors, especially Lacey, stressed the relative independence of the school and its particular character as a site of social relations.[26] They were much more interested than previous researchers in Britain in the informal and cultural dimensions of schooling. Drawing on the sociology of deviance, they described the formation of sub-cultures within the school – Lacey's 'anti-group' and Hargreaves's 'delinquescent sub-culture'.[27] Despite the originality of this, it is surprising in retrospect how much these studies stay within the problematic of the home and the school and within the boundaries of a social democratic politics of access. In both cases the formation of school-based sub-cultures is seen as a reflex of failure (or, as Lacey put it, of 'defeat') at school, the product of frustration and blocked ambitions. The overall pattern is explained, in the end, in terms of the relative poverty of resources in (many) working-class homes and the complex processes by which teachers differentiate between children and consign them, formally or informally, to 'streams'. For Lacey the key is the 'relative failure in the competitive process' of family–pupil teams with genuine academic ambitions and energies.[28] Failure is followed by demoralization and the development of the 'anti-group' culture within the school 'which constantly erodes the competitive ability of a high proportion of the students'. The main implications of the research are some modifications of the streaming system (for example mixed ability teaching or 'setting') and the development of a new type of teacher, half educator, half social worker:

Their job would be to pick out, early on, cases that would require additional help and supervision, to encourage parents, and, where necessary, to supplement the parental role by providing an additional source of help and encouragement.[29]

Hargreaves similarly saw the solution in terms of preventing 'status deprivation' among the 'low stream boys' and of pre-empting the formation of distinct and opposed sub-cultures.[30] Ideally, the solution would be to abolish selection; more practically, more opportunities should be provided for the social interaction of pupils from different streams 'preferably in a co-operative enterprise'.[31] Teachers should become more aware of the informal level of their classrooms and actively woo boys 'of high informal status'. The book ends with an appeal to teachers to consider the major internal reforms of teaching practice necessary for greater equality.[32]

Both the studies also start to move towards concerns which were to be more typical of the 1970s and have a harder, more pessimistic edge than earlier publications. Lacey concluded that his study 'throws doubt upon the feasibility of "equality of opportunity" in a stratified society'.[33] Hargreaves described the relation between the school-based sub-cultures as 'class warfare' and stressed how, after initial individual rejection, the delinquescent culture acquired a collective character.[34] Despite the shift in method and concerns, however, these studies remain recognizably with the same problematic. A useful comparison is with Douglas's description of the main themes in *The Home and the School*:

These . . . considerations lead one to suspect that there are still both social and regional inequalities leading to waste at the time when children are being selected for secondary schools. And still further back, children who have to face apathy at home, poor teaching at school and the contempt of their class mates for the process of learning, are unlikely to succeed in their studies or to stand as good a chance in the 11+ examination as children of comparable ability, who have not had to contend with adverse circumstances such as these. It may be thought that this is a type of inequality which can be removed only by profound social changes that may take a generation or more to achieve. This is not necessarily a true conclusion. Perhaps deficiencies in the home or community can be offset, and social inequalities of opportunity reduced, by raising the standard of teaching in the primary schools or by altering the methods of streaming by ability.[35]

It is plain that Hargreaves and Lacey were asking very similar questions about the secondary school. Their main achievement, perhaps, was to show *how* certain associations between family background and school performance were secured and how they were lived through within the schools themselves.

Questions unasked

Schooling in society

We want to identify two sets of unasked or partially asked questions: those concerning the relation between the outcomes of schooling and the nature of the society as a whole, and those concerning the specifically cultural processes within and around the schools.

Although the old sociology was centrally concerned with inequalities of access, it was informed by a view of what we have called 'context' — a view of the place of schooling within society. In particular it worked, often implicitly, with a particular view of the relation between the family, the school and the structure of places in the adult world, a structure that was termed 'class' or 'status'. It is useful to start a critique by digging out this view and considering some of its implications.

The most obvious feature was the concentration on the family—school relation and the neglect, relatively, of the relation between the school and the adult society. This was reflected both in the direction of research and the objects of policy-making. Policy focused on a deepening regulation of family life and upon the reform of schools. The main bearers of problems, aside from pupils themselves, were seen to be parents, especially mothers, and teachers: the first because they were incapable of fully enriching the lives and the minds of their children and of encouraging them to do well at school; the second for their inveterate tendency to typify, label, grade and select their pupils, so creating or confirming the very patterns of ability which they sought, for technical pedagogic reasons, to define. The broader society was much less critically viewed. Indeed, in a curious way, it remained persistently off-stage. It was a source, certainly of demands and needs, but not exactly of causes. While the educational system ought certainly to move in harmony with 'an advanced industrial society', the determinacy of this context upon educational outcomes was not fully grasped.

This major absence can be gauged more clearly if we look at this matter from two main points of view. The first of these concerns the relative poverty of the general sociology to which the old sociology of education was attached. By 'general sociology' we mean the way in which the society as a whole was understood. Because of the strongly empirical policy-related nature of the tradition, this space tended to be filled rather arbitrarily according to more general sociological fashions. Most immediately, for the research itself, society was thought of as a system of social stratification, organized around groupings of paid occupations. More generally, especially in the 1960s, the space of a macro-sociology was filled by structural-functionalism and especially by the large ahistorical abstraction of 'the technological' or 'modern industrial' society.

This impoverishment took two main forms that are especially relevant to our own argument. Sociologists had very little to say about social relations that cut across or complicated occupational or status hierarchies. Sex—gender relations are the most obvious case. As Anne-Marie Wolpe has argued, the dual role of women

– as housewives and mothers and as at least 40 per cent of the waged labour force – cannot be adequately described, let alone explained, within the framework of stratification theory.[36]

The case of gender is illustrative, though, of a more general point: the need for a more developed and complex set of categories than those supplied by empirical traditions of social inquiry, or large-scale functionalist theory or, for that matter, a 'classical' Marxism.

The problem is not merely one of adequately complex description. Even if gender and other relations had been supplied and their relation to class understood, the old sociology of education would have remained inadequate. Its main categories were (and are) descriptive, even methodological: they are designed to enable certain calculations to be made; they do not deliver explanations. 'Class' is again the best example. Occupational groupings, defined as classes, provide the methodological basis for calculating educational inequalities. But the more class is defined in this way, the less value it has as an explanatory concept. This can be seen very clearly in Douglas's work. Here classes were *further* redefined for the purposes of exploring certain correlations. Douglas was especially interested in the relation between mothers' and fathers' educational experience and the performance of their children. To make this calculation, he redefined 'social class' to include, centrally, educational criteria.[37] This had the distinct advantage of including the education of the mother as well as the education and occupation of the father as a criterion of the social class location of the family of origin of the child. But it had important implications too for possible explanatory strategies. Educational performance was now *intrinsic* to the primary definition of social classes; it was an aspect of 'class-ness' itself. Unless we break out of this problematic altogether, it is difficult to avoid the resulting tautologies: working-class people are people who do badly at school; people who do badly at school are working-class. We have another useful (if by now familiar) finding – that educational advantage or disadvantage is reproduced generationally – but at the cost of the explanatory power of an already seriously impoverished major category. We are told, over and over again, that working-class people are more or less materially deprived, lack cultural 'resources' and do not encourage their children at school. But *why this is so* (in so far as it is so) remains perpetually obscure. As one sociologist put it:

Given the kind of educational system and kind of relationship between school and home which exists . . . differential educability is linked to social class background. But social class is just a shorthand way of referring to a complex of factors which correlate with occupation. It describes the distribution or incidence of a phenomenon but does not explain its occurrence in any causal sense.[38]

This quotation introduces the second way of looking at the first major absence in the tradition. In so far as 'class' determines educational outcomes, it is seen as operating mainly through 'social class background'. As part of a critique of tripartitism, of IQ testing and of selection at eleven plus, the stress on class background had considerable force. It was possible to show that testable abilities and performance at school were closely related to the social production of ability within the home. This early limitation of human capacity certainly remains one of the deeper, hidden injuries of class.

Yet the way in which this theme was handled limited its more radical implications. Among the sociologists of the 1960s, only Bernstein is a partial exception here.[39] Typically, there was a tendency for the argument to stick at the point where the injustice of selection had been revealed. The class character of educational backgrounds was not related to the class organization of the society as a whole and especially to processes of political and cultural domination. It was recognized that working-class children were systematically disadvantaged at school. It was also recognized that the wider society was deeply stratified. Yet the fuller connections between these two sets of observations were not made. They were not understood as aspects of a more unified process. The old sociology developed, in other words, no theory of the reproduction of social classes within which to place its more particular 'educational' findings. In the absence of such a theory, the stress on 'social class background' took on a much more conservative hue, akin to a long tradition of philanthropic commentary on the 'moral and physical condition of the poor'. At the worst, the stress on 'background' (or for that matter on the practices of teachers) displaced attention and blame away from an unequal society and on to the principal sufferers. It was not society that needed to be questioned and changed but working-class attitudes and behaviour on the one side and the practices of the schools on the other.

We can summarize our findings on the first major absence. Within the sociology of education, homes and schools rather than the society as a whole were seen as the sites of problems and pathologies. What was demanded of schools and of homes, what kind of society was in fact being reproduced, was not the subject of deep questioning. Direct social criticism was limited to a politics of 'status' and to the search for a fairer, more open society within existing social relations. Policy prescriptions were inattentive, therefore, to the limits of social reform. There was a tendency to believe, in Douglas's words, that problems could be solved without 'profound social changes'. In particular, the existing social and sexual divisions of labour were not thought of as problematic: the former was simply the necessary product of 'the technological society'. It produced 'demands' upon education to which education should 'respond', a difficult and sometimes conflictual process of adjustment.

It was thought especially important that the elements of class—cultural inheritance in the British (or especially English) educational system be modified to allow greater mobility and 'equality'. As we have seen, it was difficult within this framework to pose the possibility that 'the technological society' or its characteristic class formation and division of labour continued to limit the educational possibilities of working-class children. Had not the technological society been recruited to the side of egalitarian educational expansion? Was it not the somewhat archaic *persistence* of class practices which inhibited the development of a more open and more cohesive society? The main direction of social change, so it was assumed, was to erode class differences, not to maintain or recompose them. An expanded and reformed education system could help in this. But two sets of further inhibitions must be removed, and here we are returned to the characteristic terrain of an *educational* sociology. First, the still differentiated parental communities must be equipped to respond more fully to the new opportunities for their children; second, educators must learn to compensate for, rather than reinforce a pattern of inherited inequalities.

It is worth insisting again that this pattern of beliefs, aspirations and 'solutions' can only be fully understood in relation to the historical contexts out of which it was produced. In particular the underlying optimism can be traced to the radical expectancy and the 'citizenship' discourse of the 1940s, an optimism reflected in a similar way in Giles's belief in the combined effects of science and 'democracy'. The sociology of education bears too the stamp of the 1950s, especially the deep interment of all traces of a Marxist anatomy in favour of a widespread but not altogether uncritical reception of American sociological paradigms. Together with the evident successes of the post-war boom and of liberal conservatism (and also the collapse of the socialist 'alternative' in the USSR), structural-functionalism helped to provide a generalized social philosophy whose dominant trait was a determined optimism. This was further reinforced in the euphoric 1960s by the Labour Party's own version of social progress, scientific innovation and educational expansion.

One way of understanding the political and intellectual mutations of this period overall is in terms of a profound *liberalization* of socialist thought and practice. Socialist elements of thought and culture were modified to conform to radical liberal paradigms. As we have already suggested in discussing the Labour Party's repertoire in this period, radical liberalism differs from socialism in the way it identifies certain social features as 'problems'. If socialism, as an analytic political category, means anything, it must involve the critique of capitalism: social problems are traced, primarily, to the capitalist organization of society. Radical liberal analyses differ from this in insisting on the inherently progressive character of modern societies and identifying the sources of problems elsewhere, typically in archaic or residual social elements inherited from a feudalistic, militaristic or hierarchical past. It is these that must be modified, modernized, reformed. Problems are seen as inhibitions to progress rather than being intrinsic to the dynamic of 'progress' itself: hence the optimism about 'reform', about an expanded role for the state and, in this case, about progress through public education.

It is important to end by stressing the *political* reversals that are involved here. Sections of the dominant class certainly remain a problem within a radical liberal perspective, especially those sections that conspicuously reproduce their own unearned advantages by buying educational and other privileges. But popular practices are equally problematic, equally in need of 'modernization'. Popular attitudes and behaviour have to be conformed to the necessities of progress. Pushed to its logical resolution this sets radical liberal intellectuals in a position of outright opposition to many elements of working-class practice that have been developed to make the proletarian position in society inhabitable. For this reason, if for no other, radical liberal policies, in their characteristic statist forms, will be experienced by working people as an intrusion, if not as a further set of oppressions.

Education and culture

The second major absence in the old sociology was an adequate account of cultural processes. In the first chapter of this book, we defined culture as 'the shared principles of life characteristic of particular classes, groups or social *milieux*'. We stressed the connection between cultural forms and everyday life: culture as the process by which social groups 'make sense' of their social conditions of existence. Cultures, therefore, have a particular intimacy with practical activity. Although common sense is not at all immune to ideological resolutions, the problematic character of social life is likely to be expressed there more openly than in the more arbitrary constructions of academics which may not, in the same way, have to stand the daily test of serviceability.

These starting points imply some methodological imperatives. If cultural forms are produced in ordinary social intercourse they will not be properly understood if abstracted from this context. This renders a large range of sociological procedures extremely problematic: the abstraction of 'attitudes' as statistically measurable variables, the construction of individual life histories and the social psychologist's laboratory experiments. If cultural forms are a way of handling material circumstances and objective possibilities, they will only make sense if these too are grasped. We have to understand not only the 'rationality' of opinions but also their elements of realism. This injunction applies not only to 'working-class culture' but also to the common sense of middle-class groups and of 'intellectuals'. Finally, we have to treat cultural forms as elements of social life which are actively *produced*. They are produced, in fact, in much the same way as physical objects and commodities: by human activity on the basis of the materials and conditions of production that are already given. Cultural production, like material production, is a system of transformations of this kind. As we suggested in Chapter 1, all theories of culture or ideology that employ models of transmission and passive reception fail to grasp what is specific to the production of meaning.

The general character of a 'cultural' critique may now be clearer. The old sociology, especially in its quantifying forms, tended to abstract elements of cultural systems from their immediate lived context. This was especially the case in the treatment of parental opinion and pupil culture. Collective products were treated as aggregates of attitudes held by individuals in a way now very familiar from the public opinion survey. Moreover, since the full character of popular educational dilemmas was not grasped, popular attitudes were stripped of much of their good sense and realism.

In the handling of parental and pupil opinions, indeed, the old sociology stayed within two basic models which can be traced through the long history of middle-class social inquiry.[40] On the one hand, within a framework of environmentalist explanation, educational working-class opinion was treated in terms of deprivation. On the other, in a construction very like the moralism of much nineteenth-century social comment, working-class attitudes were understood in terms of deviancy from some rational norm. In either case, and even in the more developed analyses of Lacey and Hargreaves, working-class responses were seen as exceptional, as departures from adequate parentdom, as, at best, the product of 'failure'. This tendency was reinforced by the reception and residual persistence of cultural theories drawn from structural-functionalist sociology, in which popular attitudes were judged for adequacy against 'core' social values. Any discrepancy provided the explanatory ground for failure in terms of either psychic or cultural deficiencies or rationalizations for such deficiencies. This style of analysis evaded two major questions: whether there was something problematic about there being a working class (or even 'lower social strata') in the first place and how the real *logics* of parental opinion and of pupil culture were related to this structural position.

In the absence of either insight, working-class practices were judged according to their approximation to a social ideal which was in fact that of the ideal middle-class parent: familiarity with the school, relative ease with the teacher, an unambiguous recognition of the individual advantages of certification, a valuing also of education 'for its own sake' and hence a wholehearted encouragement of the child. As we suggested in Chapter 2, working-class orientations towards schooling have always been much more ambiguous. This distancing from school has been so persistent an historical feature that it can hardly be seen as pathological. It was, perhaps, the failure to recognize these class-specific features in a way that really made sense of them that was the deepest flaw of the old sociology. Certainly it was one most closely related to subsequent political disasters.

It is important to end this chapter by stressing the interdependence of the two main absences we have noted — in shorthand, of 'structure' and 'culture'. Taken together they made it very difficult to pose questions about the effect of the pattern of adult opportunities on the educational performance of working-class children and their parents' attitudes. Yet in retrospect these questions are the obvious ones to pose. It seems obvious enough that popular attitudes to schooling will be heavily influenced by the possibilities, quantitative and qualitative, of social betterment by this route. If schooling offers, in return for conformity and hard mental labour, only very slim and individualized chances of 'social mobility', we might expect, at best, a quite instrumental attachment. This is not so much evidence of parental or pupil failure, nor even of the failure of the schools. It indicates rather the nature of educational conditions and the limits of educational reform under capitalist and patriarchal relations. Therefore we now need to turn to the way in which these parameters were presented in the 1960s, especially through arguments about the structure and character of the adult labour force.

7 Schooling, skilling and social relations

In Chapter 1 we argued that 'the needs of capitalist industry do exercise a major influence on the character and the structure of the education system'.[1] We also stressed the importance of the family and of sex—gender relations more generally as a further set of powerful determinations on schooling.[2] We now look more closely at these influences. We are especially concerned with the questions posed at the end of the last chapter: what are the limits of educational reform under capitalist and patriarchal conditions? How in practice are these limits imposed?

There are perhaps two broad kinds of answer available to us. They centre on rather different kinds of phenomena. We may think of capitalist or patriarchal influences as working through state agencies, public policy and through politically organized pressure. If we attempt to trace the effects of such influence we are likely to find it in relatively formal aspects of the educational system: in features of school organization (for example tripartitism), in the formal content of curricula (for example sexual differentiation and discrimination against girls), or in the internal regimes of selection and the typification of pupils (for example public examinations, or streaming). Such features can be more easily related to the character of public debates, legislative innovation or administrative pressures: for this reason, if no other, there is a tendency to exaggerate their effectivity.

The most obvious case would be where industrial interests develop a distinctive strategy for influencing the general development of the schooling system. A good case could be made for the influence of business interests and of the Federation of British Industries in holding down educational ambitions in the 1920s and 1930s.[3] We shall discuss a similar case later in this book: the role of spokesmen of industry in discrediting 1960s' policies in the decade that followed.[4] Such explanations do not altogether convince. They do not, on their own, really account for the successes of industrial interests in either of these cases, for example.

The second type of answer centres not upon organized pressure and its effects, but upon the pervasiveness of capitalist and patriarchal relations which come to define what is normal, natural and therefore to be accepted in everyday life. These relations are relations of power in at least two senses: they confer on agents located within them unequal powers to achieve desires and satisfy needs; they also powerfully determine outcomes, especially in so far as they evade a fully conscious and collective politics. These influences — the sheer experiential weight of dominant social relations — operate at every level of determination. They influence government policy. They shape the forms and contents of schooling. They dominate the calculations of educational agents — pupils, teachers and parents alike.

They also shape the context in which some forms of organized pressure possess more power than others. All governments, for example, operate with some conception of a national interest and consider educational policy in relation to these criteria. Conservative and social democratic governments since the war have judged national interests primarily in terms of economic success and, latterly, of economic survival. This concern has been forced upon them by the deep exigencies of international competition and the long crisis of profitability and investment in Britain. In the absence of a socialist strategy for solving economic problems, national interests have been defined according to the character and needs of the existing system, according, that is, to the conditions for capitalist profitability. Public policy is structurally weighted, in other words, towards capitalist solutions. Whatever else educational policy has to deliver, it must certainly aid, or appear to aid, the pursuit of 'growth'. It follows that groups that speak from a knowledge of the dilemmas of capitalist management or from that perspective, have a particular weight, especially when they can present a global or collective view of management's problems.

This structural weighting of social life affects the whole terrain of politics. Socialist, feminist or, indeed, social democratic forces always operate on enemy territory. The relation of radical or reforming strategies to working-class culture is no exception here since capitalist and patriarchal conditions affect everyday perceptions and produce a common sense realism. It is radicals who always have to question everyday assumptions, 'raise' consciousness and make the familiar look strange. This produces a characteristic set of problems: the tendency for radical or reforming ideas to run ahead of popular knowledge, to become in fact 'utopian',[5] lacking a full sense of the realities of social life and of its problematic and contradictory character. This is most likely to happen where there is a large social distance between policy-makers and people, and where agitational activity is limited to parliamentarian and statist forms.

This, we would argue, is broadly what happened in the 1960s. At the level of the formal politics of schooling a dominant consensus was installed. Social democratic politicians and theorists sought to reconcile a traditional socialist commitment to educational equalization with a plausible analysis of capital's requirements. The central role, here, was played by certain economic ideas which centred around the notion of 'skill' and a view of the relation between schooling and employment. Politically, these conceptions and associated policies had major advantages, at least in the short term. They helped to neutralize the more direct forms of intervention in the education system by dominant economic interests, such as were normal in the inter-war period and were to become usual again in the 1970s. They justified a considerable autonomy in the development of schooling, which favoured the interests of those social groups (especially the professional middle class) with the greatest stake in its functioning. Some of the gains made in this period, the move towards comprehensive schooling, for example, did represent real popular advance.

These limited successes nonetheless involved huge costs. The harmonies that were constructed between capitalist imperatives and popular needs were, in large part, imaginary. Consent was won at the cost of ignoring fundamental social relations and processes. At the same time these relations continued to set limits to the achievement of policy goals, confounding them in fact in a plethora of anticipated results. We may say, indeed, that the main site of determinations on schooling was not state policy-making during this period. It was not here that the limits were mainly imposed. That was a realm, rather, of 'great expectations' and illusory freedoms. Determinations worked in altogether more diffused and subterranean ways, especially through popular experience of the existing structural organization of society.

The main site of determinations was the structure of places in the adult world or the social and sexual division of labour. It was the unequal structure of society that continued to produce unequal educational outcomes. Against the stresses of the sociology of education, however, it is important to insist on the role of popular knowledge in this process. Unequal outcomes were not secured mechanically through 'background' or even through selection within the schools. Determinations from the structure of society continued to work *through* popular understandings and through the elements of realism in common sense. This in turn increased the distance between social democratic policy-makers and the popular, especially the working-class constituencies: the idealism of the first was rebuked by the realism of the second. It was into this space that the levers of a popular Conservative 'realism' were to be inserted in the 1970s.

In Chapter 7 we explore this interpretation of the 1960s in more detail. We examine, first, the dominant 'economic' understandings of the 1960s, or those most relevant to educational policy. We look especially at the central notion of 'skill' and at the belief in a continuous and general post-war increase of 'skill' requirements. We set these constructions against what we see as a more adequate account of the social and sexual division of labour during this period. In the last part of the chapter we turn to some recent studies of the cultures of schooling as evidence of the forms of a popular realism. It is important to add that we remain primarily concerned with critique and with showing how the weaknesses of 1960s' policies contributed to the transformations of the 1970s. We are not primarily concerned, at this stage, with the development of a more adequate 'sociology' of education.

Skill: a critique of a category

We have already noted the centrality of assumptions about 'skill' in the social democratic repertoire of the 1960s, especially in its more liberal or Fabian variants. 'Skill' was the linchpin of a particular combination of arguments. On the one hand, it was used to pinpoint economic changes and needs. The expansion of employment in the white-collar occupations and in the service sector, increasing automation and the application of science to production and complaints about specific shortages of skilled labour all produced a situation, it was argued, in which a more skilled labour force was required. A more 'technological' society required more scientists and technicians and a higher general level of 'skill'. On the other side, skill was used as a kind of metaphor for educational expansion. It was axiomatic that schools and colleges were the main generators of skill and that the expansion and equalization of schooling could unlock human capacities that were currently 'wasted'. The relation between educational qualifications and economically useful skills was likewise seen to be very close. Qualifications were increasingly seen as a requirement for entry into the occupational structure. Throughout the reports, political speeches and the more technical researches of the 1960s, we find these persistent beliefs: that post-war society required, generally and not merely for its elites, a wider diffusion of skill and that a reformed and expanded educational system could supply it.

Assumptions about 'skill', moreover, were very important politically. They provided ready-made answers to the old Conservative retort against 'over-education'. No longer were there hewers of wood or drawers of water; the economy was to be peopled with knowledgeable and indispensable workers in white coats. That tension between the humanistic purposes and the determinacy of occupational destinies (which we noted in the case of Tawney) was similarly resolved. Educators and parents were informed (whatever their direct experience might suggest) that a freer and more 'relevant' curriculum would find an appreciative echo in the world of work. Educationally valued knowledges and dispositions would become, in turn, useful skills.

The category of 'skill' itself remained unexamined and uncriticized. It functioned as a sign which combined impressively neutral references to technique with some thoroughly positive moral connotations. Who could gainsay the value of 'skill' especially if the immediate point of reference was medicine, the conquest of space or the magic of the computer?

In fact the concept is extremely problematic. One symptom of this is its wide range of meanings; another is the way it elides qualitative distinctions. We saw how Vaizey used the argument from skill to cover certain technical abilities or specialized masteries, but also to include more general social disciplines and attitudes, including, for example, preparedness to 'face the risks inherent in the process of economic growth'. This extension is entirely typical of discussions of 'skill'; the 'social and life skills' of the Manpower Services Commission are a further case in point. Included here is a willingness to organize one's life according to the demands made by employers and to form an element in a mobile, flexible and malleable work force. Of course these *are*, under existing circumstances, among the most desirable features of labour; as we will argue in more detail in Chapter 11, on the Manpower Services Commission, they are certainly the features that employers most desire![6] The main problem (for the moment) is that these general characteristics of amenable labour are described as though they were purely technical concomitants of production divorced from broader issues of economic and social organization. 'Skills' are also qualitatively similar: we may speak of more or less 'skill' (or of 'skilled', 'semi-skilled' and 'unskilled') but these categories disguise essential features of social context and human effect. Social situations and human capacities are systematically technicized; arrangements are moved out of the realm of evaluation, choice and politics and into the realm of abstract necessity.

The effects of these reductions may be clearer if we look at the question of skill from two perspectives. The first perspective is one informed by the eye of the educator. (We might notice, in passing, this interesting contemporary reversal, since it is normally 'industrialists' who critically scrutinize schools.) What might be the educator's meditations on the subject of 'skill'?

She might start by noting that human capital theory invites her to consider 'skill' as a form of investment in children's capacities akin to investment in machinery and in 'plant'. She might consider the analogy deeply misleading; for it disguises the character of the human bearer of skill and the fact that skills develop by exercise. Skills are reproduced, or developed or modified through their practice. Jobs may therefore be judged by educational criteria too: how do they contribute, by exercise and by repeated activities, to the 'education' of the labourer? Do they extend and develop mental capacities, stimulate curiosity and muscular energies, produce practical and theoretical understandings? There is more involved here than in the psychologistic conception familiar from the science of management, of 'job satisfaction'. Our educator, believing that human beings produce themselves, educate themselves in their practical activity, would be as interested in the objective limitations of the job, as in the worker's ingenuity in humanizing them. What opportunities, she might ask, does the job provide for the development of interests, of knowledge and of self? Can the job be justified at all, indeed, on these educational grounds? Are not, indeed, many such jobs 'a scandal'!? The reflections of our educator (whom some may wish to stigmatize as an educational 'progressive') are of course completely imaginary, but they highlight, perhaps, some questions about jobs to which we will return.

The second perspective on skill is to stress the importance of social context. The point is now a familiar one from much recent writing on the labour process in modern societies. Skill is not merely shaped in relation to natural process and technology; it is formed in the social relations within which it is exercised. Indeed technical processes themselves bear the stamp of social relations. André Gorz, for example, has argued that social relations form and shape technical relations (relations with nature) to the extent that we cannot conceive of 'technique' outside of the social relations in which it is embedded.[7] Althusser makes a similar point in insisting that the acquisition of 'know-how' always involves preparation for a particular *social* position.[8] Braverman, following Marx, connects technical innovation with the need actively to control the labour force. There is, according to Braverman, a world of difference between machinery abstractly considered and machines as they are actually employed under capitalist social relations:

The control of humans over the labour process, thus far understood, is nothing more than an abstraction. This abstraction must acquire concrete form in the social setting in which machinery is being developed. And this social setting is . . . one in which humanity is sharply divided, and nowhere more sharply divided than in the labour process itself. The mass of humanity is subjected to the labour process for the purposes of those who control it rather than for any general purposes of 'humanity' as such. In thus acquiring concrete form, the control of humans over the labour process turns into its opposite and becomes the control of the labour process over the mass of humans. Machinery comes into the world not as the servant of 'humanity', but as the instrument of those to whom the accumulation of capital gives the *ownership* of the machines. The capacity of humans to control the labour process through machinery is seized upon by management from the beginning of capitalism as the *prime means whereby production may be controlled not by the direct producers but by the owners and representatives of capital.*[9]

Of course the social division of labour which Braverman describes acquires, in modern industry, an immensely elaborated form. We can no longer speak of a single person 'the capitalist' or of the simple archetypical 'labourer'. The management of social production has become a complex internal enterprise with its own divisions of control, knowledge and command. The labourer too has become a collective entity the social being of which is intricately fragmented and divided. Yet, as we shall see when we turn to the *historical* development of the social divisions of labour, the distinctions he draws between those who control and design the forms of human labour and those who work within these conditions remain as real today as in the early days of 'modern industry'.

Indeed the key division here, between the conception of tasks and their execution has, as Braverman argues, been extended and deepened. It now embraces whole areas of work outside the classical formations of early industrial capital and the industrial working class. Braverman takes clerical labour, in fact, as the classic modern site of this division:

In the beginning, the office was the site of mental labour and the shop the site of manual labour . . . Scientific management gave the office a monopoly over conception, planning, judgement, and the appraisal of results, while in the shop nothing was to take place other than the physical execution of all that was thought up in the office. Insofar as this was true, the identification of office work with thinking and educated labour, and of the production process proper with unthinking and educated labour, retained some validity. But once the office was itself subjected to the rationalization process, this contrast lost its force. The functions of thought and planning became concentrated in an ever smaller group within the office, and for the mass of those employed there the office became just as much a site of manual labour as the factory floor.[10]

The stress of Braverman and others on the social relations within which skills are exercised, and indeed composed, constitutes, in our view, a decisive rebuttal of the dominant 1960s' conceptions of skill. It may also lead us to question the historical account associated with this conception: the idea that modern technological societies have seen a progressive increase in the mental requirements of labour on an average or global scale. The undermining of this thesis has, in turn, immense educational implications, for it suggests that far from acting as a motor of educational advance, technological societies may actually work systematically against egalitarian forms of educational expansion, or at least constrain them within definite limits.

One common criticism of Braverman's work has been his relative neglect of the struggles of the class of labourers in modifying capital's drive to establish direct control.[11] As Braverman himself put it, he deliberately concentrated on 'the "objective" content of class', making no attempt 'to deal with the modern working class on the level of its consciousness, organization, or activities'.[12] It is important, however, to set 'skill' within this context too. It figures largely not only in 'management science' and in economic and educational literature, but also in the practical resistances of workers to management control of the workplace. Here again, however, 'skill' is revealed as something more than technical command: it is a stake in struggles over control.

This theme and many others are interestingly illustrated in Michael Mann's research on Peterborough.[13] Mann argues that in nine different organizations which he studied, the 1000 workers were deeply divided between those whose job attainment was the result of the collective power and organization of a 'craft' and those whose job attainment was the result of an 'internal' labour market under the direct control of the employer. He argues that the technical aspects of almost all the manual jobs, including those dubbed 'skilled', were within the capacities of most workers. 'Using technical notions of "skill" we find that almost all workers use less skill at work than they do, for example, in driving a car.'[14] What was, in practice, characteristic of skilled work was a combination of a relatively high level of interest and variety with a high degree of practical autonomy. One conclusion drawn from these findings is that 'skill' is not primarily a technical category at all: 'It is social not technical. The centre of the technique is not complexity, but autonomy and freedom.'[15] Skill, indeed, in its social and political aspects, is about power. Historically too the defence of skill, often involving real technical competences but never exhausted by them, has played a major part in working-class resistances.[16]

Qualifications, the labour market and the social division of labour

The second general criticism of the 1960s' assumptions concerns the relation between the structure of formal educational qualifications and the social division of labour. 1960s' arguments often assumed a very tight relation here: schools attested to the acquisition of skills. Certification was discussed as though it entitled the holders to appropriate and appropriately rewarded employment. But as Athar Hussain has convincingly argued in a critique of the economics of education, there is no necessary fit between the structure of educational qualifications and the social division of labour.[17] General educational qualifications (from CSEs to degrees) do not entitle their holders to a particular job, grade or income. They merely supply criteria which employers may ignore, evaluate in their own terms or use to rank applicants competitively. There is no necessary replication of the distribution of qualifications in the distribution of posts. This should not surprise us since the division of labour and the structure of certification are determined within different social sites and by different social processes. Systems of qualification, for example, may owe much to the professional struggles of teachers, to the internal needs of the schools in controlling their pupils, to current conceptions of pedagogy and to the demands of parental constituencies. In the 1960s in particular, these determinations often worked free from tighter articulations with occupational destinies. Employers, for their part, certainly require a differentiated workforce, but for the mass of general labour, their criteria by no means conform to those of educational 'ability'. What does mediate the relations between these sites is the market in labour on which individuals compete for employment. The level of qualification required for a particular post is, however, within the discretion of the employer who may indeed promote his own evaluations of 'the good worker' over the abilities attested in certificates. It is the individuals who seek posts who take the strains and costs of the arbitrariness of these relations — in terms of un-employment, under-employment and dis-employment — rather than employers who can adjust their requirements according to market situations. Once again, skill as a qualification for jobs is no simple technical matter: it rests on complex social evaluations and on the struggles of the market place.[18]

A parallel point can be made about the ways in which employers, in practice, evaluate the significance of qualifications. They serve mainly to establish competitive differences between applicants and to attest the presence of certain general dis-positions. In his research on American management's evaluation of qualifications, Berg points out:

The respondents assured us that diplomas and degrees were a good thing, that they were used as screening devices by which undesirable employment applicants could be identified and that credentials sought were indicators of personal commitment to 'good middle class values'; industriousness and seriousness of purpose, as well as salutary personal habits and styles.[19]

In terms of working-class employment in Britain in the 1960s, it is important to note that most school leavers possessed no formal qualifications at all. In any case, as the Blackburn and Mann study shows, even in the early 1970s, formal qualifica-tions or other tests of 'ability' played quite a minor part in employment decisions in Peterborough. From the worker's point of view, 'career processes are hazardous'. In particular, the establishment of 'exclusive educational qualifications' was 'against the trend, in manual work' in the early 1970s.[20]

If we look at a longer term history of certification and employment over the last twenty years, the results are hardly encouraging for the explanatory value of human capital theory. Between 1960 and 1975, the percentage of school leavers possessing some form of certificate rose from 27 per cent to 75 per cent.[21] This increase did little to deflect a substantial crisis of employment which directly affected school leavers and young workers. This crisis continues and has deepened, giving its own particular character to debates on education and training in the 1970s. At a simple but fundamental level, the secular tendency to youth unemployment undercuts many assumptions of the 1960s. Employment is not dependent indeed on the processes of certification: it rests on specifically capitalist dynamics of crisis, competition and the repulsion and attraction of labour.[22]   .

The increase of 'skills': an historical tendency?

Apart from the fallacious argument from the general rise in educational qualifications, the belief in a general process of the increase in 'skill' rested on inferences drawn from the application of science and technology to the labour process, and from the increasing employment of technicians, scientists and professional workers. In addition, it was noted that chronic shortages of skilled manual labour afflicted British industry through the cycle of booms and slumps. It was due to the failure of the supplies of skilled labour, so the argument went, that employers were unable to take advantage of upswings in demand.

Both serious commentators and science fiction writers drew particular attention to automation. They predicted the demise of manual labour as factories were converted to new continuous-flow production techniques and were operated by highly educated technicians. Here again, however, contemporary analysis, in the hot pursuit of 'skill', failed to distinguish between labour required for supervision, design and initial production where technical knowledge was important, and that required for manning the automotive processes, jobs, for the most part, stripped of elementary initiative or self-direction. It cannot be argued, logically or factually, that automation increases the *overall* demand for labour with a high mental content. Advanced technology does not necessarily require the creation of a highly skilled workforce: science-based, capital-intensive industries can maintain and increase productivity through the use of a workforce that is, indeed, systematically *deskilled*.

More precisely, the long-term development of modern forms of capitalist production seems to have involved a *polarization* of skill and of educational require-ments (if these are judged primarily in terms of mental powers). The vastly expanded apparatuses of the production of scientific knowledge, of medical and legal regulation, of technically based communication, of management and administration and of the educational system itself have come to depend on an elaborate structure of higher education for the production of professional specialists. The increase of this sector has itself had a marked effect upon the average length of school attendance. These occupations account, however, for only a small proportion of total employment. Moreover, as we have seen, access to these places has remained socially restricted. While, in the 1960s, schools, colleges and universities were exhorted to produce scientists, technicians and professionals, only a relatively small proportion of young people were affected.

At the same time, the application of science and technology and increasingly sophisticated forms of control, shaped the work-experience of the greater part of the workforce. As Braverman argues, the division between conception and execution associated with capitalist forms of the labour process implies a division between the few who produce and apply technical knowledge to production and those whose labour is calculated, standardized and specified in advance. The division is necessary because capital must aim at having labour tasks that are calculable, predictable and routine. Labour must be performed at maximum speed with a minimum of wasted time, with a workforce that is cheap and easily replaceable. The general impulse and long-term historical tendency is to separate labour into its most simple elements. Each step in the labour process is divorced, so far as it is possible, from special knowledge and reduced to simple, abstract, transferable human energy. The relatively few persons who need to acquire special knowledge and training are freed from the obligations of simple labour. Capital intensive industry therefore produces three main effects: it repels labourers from production back into the labour market where they may be unemployed; it produces a limited requirement for technically qualified labour; and it dispossesses manual labour of concrete skills and competences.

Braverman explicitly argues against the view that this process involves an averaging of skills:

The mass of workers gain nothing from the fact that the decline in their command over the labour process is more than compensated for by the increasing command on the part of managers and engineers. On the contrary, not only does their skill fall in an absolute sense (in that they lose craft and traditional abilities without gaining new abilities to compensate the loss), but it falls even more in a *relative* sense. The more science is incorporated in the labour process, the less the worker understands of the process; the more sophisticated an intellectual product the machine becomes, the less control and comprehension of the machine the worker has. In other words, the more the worker needs to know in order to remain a human being at work, the less does he or she know. This is the chasm which the notion of 'average skill' conceals.[23]

Some reservations have to be placed against Braverman's general thesis. We have to recognize the importance of worker resistance in maintaining a host of informal controls over the labour process, the very centre of the basic forms of shop-floor culture.[24] Similarly, management must continuously respond to what is, in effect, a shifting frontier of control. In these struggles the defence, destruction and creation of socially constituted skills may play a major part. Skilled status may be constituted through the active organization and struggles of groups of workers who have been able to colonize, to mould or indeed to invent forms of expertise, real or apparent. They may achieve control over their own labour and over entry to their 'trade'. Management may attack these advantages or may, in turn, seek to transform them or turn them to the purposes of control. Despite the general tendency to deskilling, management may wish to invest in certain groups of workers a degree of 'responsible autonomy'. This strategy, compared by Friedman with that of 'direct control',[25] has the advantage of harnessing the adaptability of the skilled worker and offsetting the tendency to create labour solidarities. Responsive or responsible labour power of this character, forgone when people are treated as automatons, may be important for more flexible and less predictable work in the plant.

What, then, of the chronic shortages of skilled manual labour accompanying booms and slumps? Such shortages are, in an important sense, self-imposed, they are part of capital's own responses to temporary crisis. In times of recession employers attempt to minimize costs by cutting back on their training of apprentices and by laying off sections of their workforce. Indeed, this latter process — the ejection of workers from a particular branch of production, unemployment, and their take-up in expanding sectors — is a key mechanism of deskilling. After redundancy and unemployment, the status and differentials won in the worker's original firm may well be jeopardized. If the new job is in a different industry, the worker's skills may be redundant. Daniel[26] and Hill [27] have found strong evidence of this deskilling via unemployment. In periods of contraction, then, skilled workers are lost to an industry and the future number of skilled workers is also reduced by the cut-backs in apprenticeships.

In periods of expansion, these shortages are felt and produce bottlenecks in production. This may, in itself, prompt the introduction of new machinery to evade the dependence on skill. Employers may attempt to 'poach' the skilled labour of their neighbours and this may produce upward movements in wage levels. In this way, sectoral shortages of skill that have little to do with educational supply may be experienced by business as an acute difficulty.

It is important to grasp the complexity of the historical tendency towards the deskilling of the larger part of the labour force. Nevertheless deskilling has been a feature of the post-war British economy, especially in manufacturing industry. It is extremely difficult to provide adequate statistical series using categories that take account of the processes and differences we have described. The official series is hardly conclusive but our argument would suggest *some* association between the census category 'skilled' and the types of autonomy we have been describing. 'Skilled manual workers' constituted 30 per cent of the workforce in 1911, just under 25 per cent in 1951 and now account for less than 20 per cent.[28] In the iron and steel industry, where over 100,000 jobs were lost between 1961 and 1971, over half the losses were of skilled status. In 1961 about 47 per cent of workers in metal manufacture were classified as skilled; 42 per cent ten years later. In engineering, the traditional location of skilled craft workers and an industry which was to make a particularly vociferous contribution to 'the Great Debate', skilled workers as a proportion of male workers declined from 44 to 40 per cent over the same period.[29]

Less ambiguous evidence can be provided by case studies of changes in particular labour processes.[30] Particularly revealing here is the increase in white-collar employment in industry and in the public services.[31] By 1970, these two categories accounted for more than 50 per cent of total employment and the shift was taken as unambiguous evidence of the increasing demands made on workers' skills. This celebration of 'mental' work, however, ascribed the status and conditions of (typically) the nineteenth-century male clerk to the modern female clerical worker and secretary. Like most of the arguments about 'upskilling', it was unsupported by even the most cursory of historical perspectives. It is the process of the deskilling of labour that is, in fact, most graphically portrayed in the history of 'the clerkly classes'.

The nineteenth-century male clerk had a relatively poorly paid but high-status employment. He worked in close contact with his employer, dealt with matters across the whole range of the enterprise and might hope to be taken in as a partner. With the introduction of the typewriter in the late nineteenth and early twentieth centuries the whole social character of the office began to change. Tasks were sub-divided, apprenticeship disappeared, women secretaries replaced male clerks. The class-structured dependency of the clerk was replaced by the particular combination of class and gender relations which characterize the modern office. The office is now poised on the edge of a second major transformation: that associated with micro-electronics and word-processing. Again, far from increasing the technical competences of workers, these developments are already rendering secretarial skills obsolescent and attaching workers as mere adjuncts to machines. The word-processor operator of the 1980s is a far cry from the black-coated clerk of the nineteenth century and is a much more typical product of modern industry.

Similar patterns can be seen in public services which are major employers of female clerical and secretarial labour. There was expansion too in branches like cleaning and catering which, like retail employment, drew on female labour. Training for most of these occupations was minimal, promotion ladders non-existent or very truncated, wages low and unemployment rates higher than average. As Braverman put it:

We see here the obverse face of the heralded 'service economy', which is supposed to free workers from the tyranny of industry, call into existence a 'higher order' of educated labour, and transform the condition of the average man. When this picture is drawn by enthusiastic publicists and press agents of capitalism (with or without advanced degrees in sociology and economics): it is given a semblance of reality by reference to professional occupations. When numbers are required to lend mass to the conception, the categories of clerical, sales and service workers are called upon. But these workers are not asked to show their diplomas, their pay stubs, or their labour processes.[32]

We have shown that the belief in an historical process of upskilling is at best a one-dimensional portrayal of some limited features of certain occupational group-ings. In fact it is only possible really to believe in the thesis if one concentrates exclusively on the fortunes of the professional and business classes. We have seen that the notion of skill, as used in 1960s' debates, was a deeply ideological construc-tion. There are, however, some further implications of the critique. To the extent that human capital theory and the upskilling thesis was believed by teachers and pupils in schools, it was likely to have extremely awkward effects. It may have encouraged too grand expectations in the future bearers of routine labour. Over-aspiring young people, in their turn, were likely to appear as very inappropriate employees to the average manager of personnel.

The educational implications of our argument do, indeed, reverse the 1960s' orthodoxies. Far from demanding a more skilled workforce and evoking an educational response, employers were tending to define skill more narrowly. The main evidence for this was to emerge in the 1970s, along with capital's loud and authentic educational voice. Already, in the training sub-theme of the 1960s, the ground of later complaints and strategies was beginning to be laid, especially the distinction between 'general' and 'specific' skills.[33] The latter, uniformly required, did not refer to knowledge or mental abilities, but to general social dispositions: flexibility, adaptability and willingness to accept discipline. The next stage, as we shall see, was to attempt to impose such conceptions on the colleges or the schools, or to develop new public agencies for this purpose.

At this point perhaps, we should return to our educator (who is still very angry at the educational state of jobs) and ask her what she thinks of an *education based upon such practices*. Being a teacher of history, and keen to illustrate a long succession of Conservative oppressions she draws our attention to a quotation from an eighteenth-century divine and critic of Jean-Jacques Rousseau:

Tis necessary, therefore, in order to form a good citizen to impress the infant with early habits; even to shackle the mind (if you so please to speak) with salutary prejudices, such as may create a conformity of thought and action with the established principles on which his native society is built.[34]

'I think', she says, 'that they are still trying to "shackle minds" today.'

Patriarchal relations and the sexual division of labour

The social division of labour and therefore the occupational destinies of pupils are not only shaped by class relations and by the mental—manual labour divide, they are also shaped by the relations of gender, race and age, which, like relations of class, confer unequal chances of satisfying needs and desires. In focusing on one of these sets of relations — those of gender — we also want to stress two further dimensions of critique, the 1960s' neglect of women's position apart. First, we want to stress that 1960s' orthodoxies almost always assumed conditions of full employment, and second, that social divisions within the adult population, far from disappearing magically when confronted with a couple of O-levels, are very deeply rooted indeed.

Unemployment is an integral part of capitalist economic organization. This unemployed or surplus labour force should not simply be confused with the officially tabulated statistics which appear from month to month. Rather, the relative surplus population or 'industrial reserve army' takes a variety of forms in our society, including the unemployed; the sporadically employed; the part-time employed; women who as house-workers form a reserve for the 'female' occupations; the black population; and the reserves of migrant labour overseas. These categories and groups can be brought into branches of production and expelled from them as changes in production dictate. They may also act as a competitive force on the labour market, depressing wage levels and forcing workers to accept changes in the intensity of exploitation at work.[35]

In post-war Britain, it proved difficult to sustain a reserve army in its classical form, at least until recently. The commitment to 'full employment' (for a male, white and adult labour force) and the effects of the post-war boom accentuated the value of two particular sources of surplus labour: women and immigrant labour. The labour shortages were reduced by black settlement in Britain and by women's entry on to the labour market.

The growth of waged work among women has been the most striking development in the composition of the labour force since the second world war. Between 1951 and 1971 the working population increased by just over 2.5 million, and, of this increase, 2.2 million were women. Women were 36.6 per cent of the total labour force in 1971. Most of this growth was among married women. The proportion of married women within the female labour force rose from 38.2 per cent in 1951 to 63.1 per cent in 1971.[36]

This increase did not, however, expand the range of jobs available to women, but compounded the tendency for women to work in particular sectors (for instance the service sector and connotatively 'feminine' professions) and in the lower paid, impermanently employed levels of trades and industries. Between 1971 and 1976, for example, manufacturing industry lost 800,000 jobs, while the service industries gained 1.2 million. Of this large increase 900,000 jobs were part-time and of these, no less than 800,000 were taken by women.[37] Most women's work, then, has something of the character of the reserve army, though this operates differently for different groups of women, depending both on class and on the stage of life: we might compare, for example, the position of young women employed full-time for a period before marriage or the birth of children as sales assistants, hairdressers, receptionists or typists with that of married women part-time employed in professions like teaching, nursing, or social work, or in factory work or the service industries.[38] In the marked sexual division of labour within production, women are invariably assigned to the lower paid and less prestigious levels, or to professions or trades with a predominantly feminine character.

This pattern cannot be explained by a specifically female structure of qualification, though it certainly acts back on the feminine experience of schooling. Girls perform as well as boys in the processes of certification, though there are important differences in the subjects studied and in the patterns of post-school education.[39] Instead, what we see here are the very powerful effects of patriarchal relations on the employment patterns of women, a specifically patriarchal structuring of features of capitalist employment.

As we argued in Chapter 1, the key site of the reproduction of patriarchal relations is in the family. It is because women occupy a particular place within the social relations of the family, in reality or prospectively, that their position outside it is marginal or conditional. Descriptively, women's dual role can be grasped through the theory of the reserve army: it is because women can be 'returned' to non-waged work within the family, that they provide so useful a resource for capital. Similarly women may perform useful functions for capital, as reproducers of labour power and as consumers, in their role as mothers and housewives. Their usefulness for capital, however, depends upon the relations of difference, power and delegacy that are established between the husband /father and the wife/mother. The position of women is thus doubly determined and constrained: by patriarchal relations and the sexual division of labour within the home and by their patriarchally structured position within waged labour outside. Working-class women suffer from both specifically capitalist forms of dispossession since they work, often, within sectors that have been massively deskilled, but are also oppressed within forms of the family characterized by the peculiar privileging of the husband/father as principal breadwinner.

It is not easy to locate the specifically patriarchal oppressions of women most relevant to educational (in the broadest sense) dimensions. There is no obvious equivalent, within the family, to the division of conception and execution within the capitalist factory. We need to know much more, for instance, about the manual—mental character of housework, its forms of dependency and self-direction, and the kinds of production of self and of environment that it involves. Two important points can however be made, if somewhat speculatively.

First, that it is the isolation of housework and childcare, an isolation which is often extreme, that is most often experienced by women as a form of mental oppression, especially in relation to the more public and social life of the man. This isolation may extend to the social life of married women more generally, especially in the abolition of 'leisure' or 'free time' and in the patriarchal 'policing' of social contacts and a more public life especially with men who are not kin.[42] Traditional patriarchal attitudes to the education of women certainly reflect a construction of the mother/wife as a 'private' person, whose appropriate skills are limited to the personal, the affective, the 'moral' and the domestic. Second, femininity is always constructed in a peculiarly tight and dependent relation to masculine requirements and definitions. In general, indeed, women are continually subject to urgent demands from others. This applies as much to children as to husbands. Families have complicated and variant forms of delegacy whose commonest outcome is to assign to women the care of children and to leave the father, outside the hours of 'work', free for 'other things'. Such responsibilities may be freely accepted, but they do involve inequalities and therefore relations of power. Perhaps the most important educational point is that women have very little subjective space 'to call their own', a condition that involves, but goes much deeper than, the dispensation of time. Theorists of cultural deprivation or of 'education for parenthood' would do well to concentrate less on the cultural inheritances of child-hood and to look instead at what we may term the educational economy of mothers.

Schooling, culture and destiny

We now return, via this detour through structural relations, to popular knowledge and the experience of school. It would be possible to show, in a number of different ways, how popular knowledge had a surer grasp of the structural constraints on education in the 1960s than had sociologists and economists. We could look, for example, at parental attitudes, placing them in a long history of working-class ambivalence towards schooling. What appear in the 1960s' (and earlier) researches as pathologies or deficiencies (such as the lack of parental encouragement at school) can be seen, instead, as a sensible (if pessimistic) assessment of the low value of formal education beyond the point where it is useful for manual labour or the destiny of housewife and mother. It makes little sense to start by seeking the reasons for this realism in 'social background' or in the structures of the school. The limited value of formal education is an obvious enough feature on the cultural landscape of the working class, and it takes as its raw material the direct educational implications of the structural relations we have described.

We want to illustrate these themes in more detail by reviewing recent work on the school experiences and culture of adolescent working-class boys and girls, especially the groups which, in conventional 1960s' terms, could be said to 'fail' at school and be a symptom of 'wastage'. We want to draw particularly on Paul Willis's work on white working-class boys, but also on the less developed (but rapidly growing) bodies of work, much of it from feminist ethnographers and action researchers, on the experience of adolescent girls.[43] In both cases our approach is not to attempt to summarize or do justice to this work in its own right, but to show how some of its main findings establish the force of explanations in terms of structure and culture.

Willis's *Learning to Labour* breaks with 1960s' sociology and especially with the view that the responses of working-class parents and pupils constitute cultural deficiencies or rationalizations for failure. Concentrating on those groups of pupils who actively resist school, Willis displays 'the lads'' culture as a creative response to their particular location, through which, in fact, they prepare themselves for a destiny as manual labourers. This involves a rejection of the bargain which the school and the teachers implicitly and sometimes explicitly offer: conform and we will do our best for you. It involves the rejection, in fact, of most of what the school (and, by extension, education and study) can offer: not only certification based on developed mental capacities of a bookish kind, but also all the more developed and abstract forms of mental labour in general.

It is clear that notions of 'failure', which reduce the matter to questions of 'educability' simply do not fit these observations at all. Boys like 'Joey' and the other lads with whom Willis worked actually choose not to get on at school. A real struggle is being described here, not some incidental feature of the educational scene. Equally interesting are the forms of the revolt, linked as they are to *adult* situations and requirements which are specifically masculine, specifically working-class and, in this case, specifically white: the parallel with and preparation for the cultural forms of shop-floor culture, the rejection of what passes for knowledge in the formal curriculum, the refusal of the semi-dependency of childhood, the preference for an active and subversive practice over book learning and, in general, the orientation out from the school towards an adult working-class destiny.

Any close qualitative study of this kind is open to the charge of unrepresentativeness. Paul Willis himself has good answers to this charge, but it is also clear that responses to his book and the researches of others are now suggesting that the forms of the school counter-culture are widespread and constitute one *typical* popular response to schooling. The personal experiences of teachers, encountered for example in discussions of *Learning to Labour* in the preparation of this book, often suggest the same conclusion. Among recently published studies, Paul Corrigan's account of a group of 14- and 15-year-olds in Sunderland parallels Willis's findings. Corrigan, indeed, uses the analogy of 'guerrilla warfare' to describe the daily subversions in and around the classrooms.[44] Angela McRobbie's work with teenage working-class girls shows a rejection of school similar in its resistance to authority, if characteristically feminine in its outcomes and forms. We need more studies of this kind, looking at different schooling situations: for comprehensive schools, for different age groups, for black pupils and, especially perhaps, for the (apparently) conformist groups — Willis's 'ear'oles'. But there is enough material already to constitute a practical critique of sociological orthodoxies and to reveal the intimate connections between culture, educational outcome and the structure of places in the adult world.

Characteristically, the cultural processes by which working-class girls come to take their place as dual labourers in production and in the reproduction of labour power has not been a focus of the same detailed attention as that of boys. The work of the 1960s tended either to ignore girls as a relevant half of the world, or to posit analysis on natural instincts or interests which directed girls to the home. Indeed, one major problem identified in the 1960s was that girls were, if anything, being diverted too effectively from academic work into the domestic sphere. In what follows we draw heavily on the work of Angela McRobbie and on other work in progress.

The first element of the culture of working-class girls which propels them towards domesticity is that of the age continuum. This serves to categorize adolescent girls into a series of stages, each of which has attached to it a definition of appropriate gender behaviour. For example, June, a 15-year-old girl interviewed by McRobbie, saw magazines in age stages:

Well I buy *Jackie* and *Fab* now, but my sister, she's seventeen, buys *Honey* and *Nineteen,* so I usually read them too. Once you go to work you start getting magazines with more on fashion than love stories.

Chris, a 16-year-old, expressed a similar perspective on music:

I used to like the Rollers more than anyone else. But I think I've changed. I mean, it don't get you anywhere. You spend all your money on them and you're lucky if you even get to see them. You can't get them, so what's the point? I still like Rod Stewart, but I don't go mad over him. You grow out of that.

Maxine, aged 15½, outlined this age-related development of relationships and its pathological case:

It's not so much that I mind, but I think it would make my mum happy if she saw me with a boyfriend, steady like, by the time I was 16–17. I think she worries I'll be left on the shelf. See, my sister — she's dead pretty — she's had a steady since she was 14½. There's a girl down our way and everyone feels sorry for her, she's 26 and she's never had a boyfriend yet.[45]

The stages of, and behaviour attached to, this continuum gain their full meaning from the perceived end-point of the development — winning a man and getting married. This end-point is defined both by a realistic sense of structural limitations and by ideologies of domesticity and romance. The massive centrality of the family and its division of labour generate an image of women, that defines success and the realization of natural instincts in terms of attracting a man, creating a home and caring for the children and the husband. This definition of being a woman is given a sharp material edge by the position of working-class women in the labour market. With economic opportunities limited largely to the lower end of certain sectors of the labour market, low-paid, insecure and, in all probability, impermanent, a man with access to better paid labouring opportunities is an economic necessity. The older, single working-class woman referred to by Maxine is a two-fold 'failure': she has failed to attract a man and therefore to become a full woman through motherhood; she has also failed to gain the full economic status and security that is given by the male wage.

The second cultural element directing working-class girls 'freely' to marriage, child-rearing and part-time labour, is that centred on notions of femininity and romance. These notions are not arbitrary beliefs imposed on working-class girls by ideological apparatuses (ideology as indoctrination); they provide resources for the girls' own creative negotiation of a contradictory ideological and material situation. The different sexual activities expected of working-class boys and girls place working-class girls in a double bind. Willis reports the lads as categorizing girls either as 'easy lays' to be pursued at dances and after, or as potential girl-friends who, although attractive are not sexually experienced and whose domestic qualities (those of the 'Mrs') are vitally important.[46] Boys can be sexually adventurous before finding a girl with whom to 'settle down'; girls are expected to attract boys while 'saving themselves' for marriage. As the distinction between an 'easy lay' and a potential 'Mrs' is private to boys, the girls are put in a contradictory situation: they have to be available enough to attract but not so available as to be seen as promiscuous. In this situation, where working-class girls must ensure that they are both successfully hunted and chaste, femininity and romance provide means for negotiating the contradictory demands of boys. Femininity allows the basis of sexual attraction to remain, while converting it from active proposition to a selectively submissive appeal. The culture of femininity can thus hold the marriage-able qualities of attractiveness, availability and fidelity in an uneasy balance with the dangers of being unattractive or unavailable or, conversely, far too available.

The ideology of romance plays a similar role in negotiating this fraught terrain.

It transforms the material dominance of the male into a necessary and desirable component or indicator of 'true love'. It allies this dominance to a feeling of self-realization: the loss of self in romance is transformed into the highest realization of the female self. Romance also links sexual submission to true love whose end-point is defined as the permanent relationship (or its tragic denial). The contradictory cultural expectations of women can thus partially be managed through the ideologies of femininity and romance.

These ideologies not only help deal with the double binding sexual expectations of girls, but they can also be used to win space for girls in a hostile environment. In school, femininity plays a central role in the anti-school activities of girls. In an institution which holds qualification-oriented activities in the highest esteem, which treats pupils as children and which is dominated by male pupils and teachers, femininity draws together strands of working-class female resistance. It takes the naturalized stereotypes of male and female, and by exaggerating the boundaries, it defines an area of territory within which males cannot tread. The best-friend relationship between girls which McRobbie describes carries a culture of exclusion, secrecy and resentment which helps girls negotiate the surrounding male culture. Femininity is similarly opposed to the dominance in schools of qualification-oriented activities and of the definition of pupils as children. By emphasizing femininity and romance, working-class girls define themselves as adult beings in the world of private relationships in contrast to the school definition of them as unsexed children who should be immediately concerned with their academic work.

Ironically the consequences of these solutions to immediate problems are to guide girls to the sphere of domestic labour, waged labour and dependence on the male wage. McRobbie suggests that boys and girls have differential access to part-time labour during their school years, with girls expected to contribute significantly to unpaid domestic labour, leaving boys free to take casual employment in the evenings and at weekends. This, combined with the high level of expenditure needed to maintain an acceptable feminine appearance and culture, leads to girls being financially dependent on boys from the beginning (as well as to the creation of a hugely profitable market).

The logics of the cultures of femininity and romance are such that they take the gender stereotypes and through exaggeration use them to negotiate or resist oppressive features of the surrounding environment. The obvious cost of this is that the basic stereotypes are strengthened. The acceptance by girls of their future as homemaker/child-rearer, directs them to the specific parts of the labour market structured for the female school leaver which involve few long-term commitments on their part. The 'lucky' female school leavers are those who find employment in the 'glamorous' jobs — secretarial and some retail work for example — which trade low pay and poor conditions against the appeal to the femininity of the labourers and the possibility of romance.

The general conditions and insecurity of this labour market are such that they tend to reproduce female dependency on other sources of material support, as wages are often not sufficient to cover the costs of reproduction of labour power.

This support can be provided by the family of origin, but this solution, with all its restrictions on the adolescent/adult woman, tend to be short-lived, giving way to marriage as the alternative source of support and dependence. As McRobbie notes:

She [the working-class girl] is denied that crucial space, the privilege of her middle-class peers, the few years at college and university where thoughts of marriage are at least temporarily suspended and where sexual experience outside marriage is quite permissible.[47]

The conditions of work, taken on the basis of being temporary until marriage, thus make marriage all the more necessary for economic reasons and for reasons of personal freedom. Girls have been prepared for this, not only through the definition of marriage and child-rearing as the end-point of development, but also through the ideology of romance. McRobbie suggests that the ideology of romance is not taken as an unproblematic picture of reality by girls, and she gives examples of this realism. Vicky, aged 15, is reported as saying:

He goes his way and I go mine. That's how most of my married cousins are. They go out together now and then. I mean, take the kids to their Nan's on Sundays. When I go round to babysit, he's always going one place and she's going somewhere else.

That romance is not taken as a picture of reality does not deny it a role in the preparation of girls for marriage and child-rearing. The loss of self by the female which is central to the ideology of romance, paves the way for a real loss of self in marriage and child-rearing. Dependence on the male wage leaves little scope for financial independence and strengthens male authority and dominance in non-financial matters. Demands of housework and child-rearing are such that little space is left for the woman to act free from the demands of others. This lack of room for manoeuvre on the part of the woman is often heightened by renewed participation in the labour market often on a part-time or outwork basis which serves, not to give independence, but simply to increase the weight of demands. We suggest that the idealized loss of self in romance provides a training ground, in the imagination, for the mundane loss of self by women as dual labourers and subordinated 'partners' in marriage.

The cultural forms which we have discussed in this section must affect the whole pattern of educational outcomes. There is a sense in which working-class boys and girls 'choose' to succeed or fail at school. But these 'choices' occur within strict limits that are delimited by the wider structural relations: it is a 'stony desert', which they have to make habitable by their own efforts. As an individual project, the approved strategy of mobility through educational qualification makes some sense; as a general or collective solution, for women as a whole or for working people as a class, *it makes no sense at all.* Whatever would the educationalists and manpower planners *do* with a host of ambitious individualized school leavers clutching their educational certificates?!

One response to this, typical of the newer orthodoxies of the 1970s, is to attempt to tie activities in schools, colleges and special programmes tightly to the requirements of (working-class) jobs. This is to concede, to the nature of the structural determinations we have described, all or most of what is normally thought of as 'education'. We have already argued that the specifically mental requirements of most working-class jobs are very limited; that these jobs are, indeed, anti-educational. The alternative is to recognize that the attainment of popular educational rights and needs involves *the transformation of capitalist and patriarchal forms of social organization*; that serious educators, in short, have good reason to become serious socialists and feminists.

Conclusion

We are now in a position to sum up our main criticisms of the 1960s' policies. We will do this, however, mainly in view of their political failures, anticipating the vulnerabilities of the 1970s. We want to concentrate on four main criticisms: the contradictoriness of Labour's repertoire; the absence of a direct educational relation to the working class; the non-popular character of the 1960s' alliance; and the limits of a narrowly statist politics, focusing almost exclusively on access.

The first two points may be recalled quite briefly since they have informed our whole account. Labour, in effect, attempted to serve two masters: popular interests and those of capital. It attempted, in a way that very much conforms to classic Marxist definitions of 'social democracy', to harmonize the needs and politics of antagonistic classes. This duality had long been represented in the politics of Labour: the capitalist side, and its liberal or Fabian elements of thought and organization, achieved dominance in the post-war years, partly as a response to the experience of government. One effect of this contradiction was to ensure that politically Labour could not succeed. Either it would be forced to concede to capital and enforce 'capitalist schooling' and so further jeopardize its popular support, or, in the pursuit of a popular egalitarianism, it would lose the support of dominant economic interests. In fact, in the late 1960s and 1970s, both these tendencies are discernible as part of the internal collapse of a repertoire held together by the peculiar historical circumstances of the 1960s.

Once its statist policies were threatened, the Labour Party was likely to find itself in a position of peculiar bankruptcy. For, as we have noted several times, Labour had no direct educative relation to the popular groups and classes. It was to prove difficult, therefore, to develop a new policy on the ruins of the old that was more in tune with popular experiences. That challenge, and the same objective difficulties in responding to it, still face the party in 1980.

The non-popular character of the alliance involves a lengthier discussion since, though implicit in the critique and in the arguments of Chapter 4, the theme has not been fully developed. It is useful to ask three questions: who were the most important agents in the 1960s' policies, who were its principal objects, and who were the main beneficiaries?

The most active agents were professionals of various kinds. Under Labour's compact with the teachers, questions of educational content were assigned to that profession. The curriculum and teaching methods of schools were matters for professional experts and not, as indeed they should be, for an open and contentious politics. Similarly, questions of the popular control of schooling were subordinated to more narrowly administrative considerations — the province of local and national administrators. This corresponded to a more general shift in the nature of Labour's politics: the relative marginalization of the working-class elements and the growth of professional middle-class membership and preoccupations. In his study of these evolutions in Liverpool in the 1960s, Barry Hindess shows how the very styles of politics were affected: away from a concern with day-to-day problems and with the grass-roots effects of administration, and towards an overriding stress on principles of national policy. [48] In this second, middle-class, style, administration is regarded as a relatively neutral activity and the problem of the bureaucratic or coercive character of local state agencies is ignored.

This description fits revisionism too with great accuracy. Revisionism's educational policy was, indeed, a policy *of* the professionals: of professional researchers who supplied the facts; of professionalized teachers who staffed 'the service'; of professional administrators more 'expert', in their way, than ministers; and last, and by no means least, of the professional practitioners of politics itself, who decided on questions of priorities and values. Crosland again epitomized this professional political universe: the whole of his interview with Kogan can be read as a discourse upon professionalism and on the divisions of labour between professionals themselves.

How, then, do working-class people figure in these conversations? As we have seen, they figure predominantly in the form of problems, of objects, of policy's 'target populations'. Sociological researchers, official reports and political pronouncements present working people mainly as the bearers of educationally disadvantageous behaviour. They also operated, as we have suggested, with a notion of 'equality' that was close, perhaps identical, to a notion of 'soft' forms of social control: the idea of equality-as-a-means-to-social-cohesion.

This picture of the largely middle-class character of Labour's 1960s' programmes helps to explain the failure of the popular push for comprehensivization in these years. Again, it was mainly the professional sections of the local middle classes that pushed for these changes. This is reinforced by what we know about the effects of educational expansion since the second world war and what we may suspect (but cannot yet show) about comprehensivization in the 1970s. The Halsey, Heath and Ridge study, for example, shows that the class chances of reaching university education have remained constant since the war, but that the 'absolute gains for the service (that is, middle) class were massive compared with those for the working class'. 'There is', as the authors put it, 'no universal law linking expansion to equality.' The first to benefit were those already in a relatively privileged position.[49]

When we speak, then, of the *'popular'* elements in Labour's social alliance and educational programme in the 1960s, it is important to clarify what this means. The popular elements themselves consisted of an alliance in which sections of the professional middle class were clearly in dominance. This gave to Labour's repertoire some elements of opposition to the purer forms of 'capitalist schooling' and training. In practice, it lent a particular salience to those aspects of social democratic policy (those most consistently pursued) that concerned the educational chances of the children of professionals and those who wished to become professionals. If Labour's policies were 'popular' in this qualitative sense, they were certainly not 'working-class' and, still more surely, neither socialist nor feminist in character.

Finally, we must note the limits of a politics of access, especially for a popular socialist—feminist politics. Labour has concentrated overwhelmingly on access and has faced dilemmas which are those of a narrow statism unsupported by independent forms of popular education. This form of strategy, for example, is exceedingly vulnerable to changes in the structure of the education system itself. We have already examined the case of 1944 and there is a sense in which left strategy has still not recovered from this victory. Much the same is true of the shift away from the conspicuous exclusions of tripartite organization towards variants of the comprehensive school.

It is still not possible to talk about a post-comprehensive phase of school organization as though this reform was irreversibly secured. But we can consider the effects of a movement towards the common school upon the possibilities of popular struggles around access. The more the ideal of the common school is approached (or believed to be approached), the more a politics based on access loses its clarity and its force. The common senses of 'education' now operate with a particular plausibility: when selection is minimized or hidden, it really *does* appear that educational outcomes are simply the result of individual abilities. In fact, outcomes that are *similar* to those secured under tripartitism by formal selection and exclusion seem to occur in more 'open' systems too, but by the more informal interactions of structure and culture. Certainly they are no longer plausibly thought of as *only* a product of 'home and school'. A politics of access, then, undercuts its own rationale without in fact affecting the most fundamental educational determinants. It is in this particular sense, that this politics is 'reformist' and incorporative.

If we take account of these various dimensions — the contradictoriness of policy, its middle-class character, the absence of a real popular and especially working-class connection, the failure to speak directly to women and the limits of a politics of access — the exhaustion and collapse of the whole repertoire in the 1970s is easier to understand. It is to this history that we now return.

Part Three
Social democracy: the breaking

8 Recession, protest and the absent defence

This chapter looks at the faltering of the social democratic construction of schooling during the particular circumstances of the early 1970s. It engages, inevitably, with the proclamation of 'crisis' prevalent in so many areas, from government statements to the popular dailies. But for education there were specific difficulties, which could not simply be reduced to the new, crude and monotonously reasserted 'logic' which connected a general social crisis to a need for 'cuts' throughout the social services.

At first, as for example in *Framework for Expansion* and the strong declaration of commitment to nursery education under the Thatcher ministry, rising expenditure and rising expectations seemed destined to continue.[1] Yet, just as the recent innovations (comprehensives, ROSLA, educational priority areas) most needed to be secured, negative inferences were beginning to be drawn from opposed perspectives. These amounted to a set of diverse but distinctive uncertainties about the value of the newly central and prominent educational hopes. It could seem that education was no longer a necessary solution: it became a specific work of the new educational right to try and fix it as part cause of a problem, even of the multifarious 'crisis' itself.

This chapter therefore tries to understand the erosion of *belief* in the social democratic educational settlement. It tries to analyse this in terms of many different developments proceeding at various speeds, but coming together to leave the reforms — neither fully established nor worked through, and often actively diverted — undefended. We concentrate on two areas: first, on the dominant anxiety, at times hysteria, about the 'handling' of the British economy and social order, and its implications for what had been presented as some of the main ambitions of the 1960s' reforms; second, on the absence of a defence of those reforms in the new situation. From a variety of sources an undermining of faith in the policies of the 1960s went alongside the right's drastic onslaught upon them.

The crisis of accumulation: education and 'growth'

Carried out properly, an account of Britain's economic difficulties (which were intermittently visible from the late 1950s but more damagingly so from the later 1960s) would need to go back to the country's international position since the nineteenth century. Nor would the language of much political and press discussion, around 'economics' and the lack of growth, be adequate. The discussion would concern a sustained crisis of capital accumulation arising from social and political relations of struggle. In the 'debates' of the 1960s and 1970s the problem was however usually taken up in terms of the increasing failure to meet four objectives broadly agreed, with differences of emphasis, by post-war governments. These were full employment; economic growth; a balance of payments surplus; and stable prices. An analysis of these factors showed the steady, and later severe, decline in British capitalism over the period.

Long-term unemployment, thought in the two post-war decades to be a thing of the past, with an average unemployment rate of 1.5 per cent, rose gradually to 3.8 per cent in 1972 and accelerated to 6.8 per cent in August 1977, with this or a far worse level accepted as the likely outlook. Particularly hard hit were young people, among whom blacks, invisible in the official statistics, constituted a disproportionate sector. In addition to these groups were married women whose special position in the labour market led to a considerable underestimate of their real unemployment.[2]

The growth rate in the 1960s had stubbornly trailed behind that of major competitors despite increases in productivity from an index of 2.7 (1955–60) to 3.9 (1967–71). The overall growth of the British gross domestic product was 2.8 per cent per annum, compared with 3.9 per cent for the USA, 5.5 per cent for France and 9.7 per cent for Japan. Since then the rate of growth had shown short spurts and longer drifting recessions: the index of gross domestic product taking the ten years to 1978 grew by a mere 15.2 points. [3]

Meanwhile Britain's share of the world market as divided among the top dozen manufacturing nations had fallen from 21.9 per cent in 1951 to 10.6 per cent in 1970. A sharp series of increases in the prices of primary products accentuated a balance of payments problem made worse by movements of capital in and out of London. The £3828 million deficit of 1974 led directly to the intervention of the International Monetary Fund, and to the contracting of very large loan repayments on conditions insisted upon as the prerequisites for more orderly capital growth.

Above all else, in the forefront of everyday awareness, was the constant rise in prices. During the 1950s, there had been a steady 2 per cent inflation rate each year, felt as a minor problem or even as a stimulus. During the ensuing years this grew to 8 per cent in 1971 and then to 12 per cent in 1974 with an annual figure of 27 per cent in 1975 and a June inflation figure of 48 per cent.[4]

Behind all these factors, though much less discussed in the most publicized accounts of the situation, lay a decline in profitability. Post-tax profits fell from 7.1 per cent in 1964 to 4.1 per cent in 1970. Investment fell from 10 per cent of gross domestic product in 1960 to 7.9 per cent in 1972.[5]

These were some of the transparent, much brandished figures of economic failure. Under the Heath government, in particular, economic policy was driven to try and stem the decline with quite inadequate means. Policy was forced to respond to events well outside its control: one example was the instability of the oil market, another that national governments were impeded in relation both to movements of international capital and decisions of multinational companies. Externally, economic strategies were bound up with the complexities of assessments of Britain's future relationship to the Common Market. Internally, as the miners' strike was to show forcibly, their political plausibility depended upon the forces of resistance to moves which would increase profitability. More important to us here is the disagreement among economists about what had caused the situation and how it should be remedied. The most widely publicized accounts all placed the restoration of profitability to industry as the overriding political necessity, and all offered an implicit view of basic decisions which needed to be taken quickly. We review them briefly to show how indifferent or negative each was towards education spending, which for economists a decade or so earlier had been of such central relevance.

'Cost push' and 'demand pull' hypotheses both concentrated on the situation of manufacturing industry. Demand pull theory held that rises in aggregate demand in situations of low unemployment caused price inflation, due to wage costs rising through competition for scarce labour. Cost push theory claimed that rising costs resulted from the power of unions to force wage increases far in excess of gains in productivity. Firms could not absorb the increases and were obliged to pass them on. As plausible in fact, at that level of debate, was a counter-thesis that firms enjoying a large or near-monopoly market share could raise prices with little fear of losing their market dominance. The characteristic media versions, however, stressed high pay claims and the dominance of the unions: 'high' wages and 'strong', selfish unions became part of a shorthand political demonology.

Monetarists argued, by contrast, that prices increased because the state allowed money supply to rise faster than output could justify. Inflation was caused by too much money in the economy chasing too few goods. The state, it was argued, should give its main energies to the reduction of money supply, otherwise allowing market forces to prevail. Wages should be permitted to fall as well as rise, unemployment might well be necessary due to the decline of old industries, while enforced mobility and the acquisition of new skills would be prerequisites for the growth of new industrial sectors. Unions would be faced with a choice between wage rises (in real money) on lower levels of employment, or wage reductions (in real terms). In the private sector this outcome would be determined by each firm's capacity to pay, in the state sector by cash limits on money available.

More influential than any of these views, in the mid 1970s, was the account popularized by Bacon and Eltis, above all in their proclaimed 'major investigation into our economic ills' of November 1975, to which the Chancellor took the extraordinary step of 'replying' four weeks later. They suggested that Britain was about to become an 'underdeveloped' country, not because of unions or productivity or money supply factors, but because of a structural revolution in the service sector. Local authorities and central government had expanded their activities by 53 per cent and 14 per cent respectively in the decade up to 1972 in order to maintain full employment, and they had increased the wage rates of their employees until state spending accounted for more than half of the gross national product. 'Armies of teachers, social workers and civil servants' were putting pressure on the productive sector, causing exports to fall and investment to be diverted.[6] The opportunities of the 'technological revolution' of the 1960s, according to Bacon and Eltis, had been wasted by the enormous political commitment to the public services. This had set up a cycle of increased government action, higher taxes, rising unemployment and falling profitability and investment.

None of these views prevailed in any coherent way under the governments of the early and mid decade, but their elements were in play throughout — especially the determination to curb union power and to ration spending in the public sector. It was a Labour chancellor who came most directly to accept the full 'logic' of the new economic views, under the sharp insistence of the International Monetary Fund. In November 1974, the previous 'Barber round' of cuts under Heath were far exceeded as the rate of growth of public expenditure (which had been an average 6.1 per cent a year from 1963–8, and 3.2 per cent 1968–73) was reduced to 2.75 per cent. Further cuts came in rapid succession thereafter. In general, public spending had been taken to be the most accessible, least resistant area of economic management.

Against these developments, 'the economy' could also become a standby explanation or thread behind educational policy changes. Hencke, in his book on teacher training college planning, quotes a senior civil servant justifying his insistence on contraction in 1974: 'I hardly need to emphasize the changing situation arising from the oil crisis and its effects on educational expenditure generally.'[7] The rationale was conveniently vague. More generally striking, though, was the absence of any convinced plea whatever for education's contribution to economic growth as cuts began to bite.

The social democratic settlement had clearly involved large economic ambitions which were now left looking incredible. In scarcely over a decade earlier assumptions had been reversed. When the economy had seemed relatively healthy and predictable, with only creeping inflation, minor unemployment and the confident dawn of a 'technological' revolution, particular and general economic benefits through education had been predicted. The relationship between qualifications and employment and income had looked to be a constant causal link which held out the promise of eradicating gross inequality and poverty through the upskilling of individuals. At a national level the expansion of education held a similar promise of economic advance through the development of science-based innovations. Education had been regarded as a prime mover of economic development in the 1965 National Plan. Now, the economic maelstroms of the 1970s seemed to have quickly demolished these notions with the 'return' on such investments looking palpably poor. Despite the increase in qualified labour power and the creation of new technologies the economy ran into deeper trouble. Income inequality remained stark, while unemployment soared with those particularly hard hit being the supposed beneficiaries of the educational revolution, young people.

This strand of the rationale for the earlier social democratic settlement thus appeared to have failed in its (impossible) task. The demise of the ideology was particularly poignant. Not only did the economy fail to grow but it fell into a second slump. Not only did many young people not get better jobs but they failed to get jobs at all. The cruellest cut of all was that education had not only failed within one set of social democratic terms but that it was also held by an assertive new school of economics to be significantly responsible, as part of the ever-growing public sector, for the decline of British capitalism. If cuts were to be the solution, then on this logic education had little room for special pleading and would have to 'take its share'. Rather, the armies of teachers needed to be reduced. Education could not be the saviour of the economy but with a vengeance might become one of its scapegoats.

The crisis of hegemony: education and 'youth'

Just as the educational settlement was put into jeopardy by the economic move-ments and economic ideologies of the late 1960s and early 1970s so it ran into danger from the breaking-up of the post-war hegemony. The overall political dialectic between the mid 1960s and the mid 1970s lay between government by involvement, persuasion and co-operation, in which public services were handled as part of the 'social wage', a consequence of and reward for better industrial productiv-ity and order; and the attempt to move towards government by much firmer management. Often the tensions lay inside the same party (as in the furore over Labour's late 1960s' proposals for reforming the unions, *In Place of Strife*). While Labour, as the party of reform, came under increasingly difficult pressures (especially on its return to office and an inheritance of appalling dilemmas in 1974) the Conservative Party experimented uneasily with different modes of 'strong' leadership: from the abrasions of Selsdon Man and the early years of Mr Heath to a mode seeking populist ratification under Mrs Thatcher.

The first post-war Conservative versions of consent, following a difficult economic, political and ideological stabilization under Attlee, had fostered a long period of consensus based on hostility to communism and on capitalism's ability to deliver a consumer goods boom: the politics and ideology of a 'classless' affluence. This conservative version was to meet its 'Macmillennium' between 1961 and 1964 with a balance of payments crisis, the failure to enter the EEC, a rise in unemploy-ment and inflation and a series of exposures of a non-glossy Britain. It was replaced in the early 1960s by a social democratic variant based upon a promise of 'modernization' and on voluntary 'restraint' in the 'national interest'. This 'remarkable social configuration' (as Hall and others have called it) and its 'new labourist gospel' was:

just efficacious enough, just vague enough to forge a temporary alliance between managers, technicians and the few fragmented constituencies for social change created by the rediscovery of poverty. It had no other logic or historical base . . . Once tested it revealed its true internal logic — the attempt to conserve British capitalism and manage the crisis by the construction of a disciplined form of consent, principally under the management of the corporate state.[8]

As John Harrison has remarked, social democratic credibility depends on the ability to grant reforms to the working class without endangering capital's reproduction. The tightrope is stretched too far in a major crisis, whose central requirement:

is an increase in the rate of exploitation to provide the resources and incentive for further accumulation. Any attempt to implement major reforms will deepen the crisis, failure to grant them . . . will lose the party its political basis.[9]

The social democratic mode in both parties was by 1970 under acute stress which bit even more deeply on the Labour government after 1974. As dissent proliferated during the 1960s, political attention moved from the attempt at a national, collaborative renewal to angry demands for stronger authority. The anguish of middle-class opinion over national decline, at first post-imperial, then post-affluent (each stage amplified through the media) gradually resonated with a law and order panic and moves towards authoritarian forms. As this happened, it became possible to discredit both schooling and higher education by a covert or open demonology.

In this respect '1968', though in Britain a relatively mild and localized set of student protests, rapidly took on an irreversible symbolic significance. 'Student power' became linked with hippies, anarchism, left extremism and even the Irish Republicans. Elsewhere, Powell sought to attach immigrants to a mythology of enemies within. Even on their own terms, the movements towards democracy in higher education seemed to exhibit a disastrous first generation of the educational revolution. The universities were producing not the bright young managers and technicians of a renovated capitalism, but a new disaffected, in whom the work ethic and self-discipline seemed to have been replaced by hedonism and a disdain for rationality. 'We struggled hard all our lives to get by' was being met by what looked like, and sometimes was, a turning away from familiar ambitions: marriage, savings, career. On a more organized level there was the spectacular efflorescence of radical groups aiming at personal transformation and at social change through extra-parliamentary means.

If the elite products of the education system were found worrying, there was little more comfort to be had from the mass of school leavers. Education had been looked to for an economic and also a social renewal: for the production of a more flexible workforce and the assimilation of the immigrant population.

The workforce in the early 1970s, including its youngest members, in no way behaved as had been hoped: that is, as the owners of skills, as the individual capitalists, that human capital theory had expected. Karabel and Halsey summarized the argument and its oddity: a direct appeal to capitalist ideology lay in the insistence that:

the worker is a *holder of capital* (as embodied in his skills and knowledge) and
that he has the *capacity to invest* (in himself) . . . the *wage-earner,* who holds no
property and controls neither the process nor the product of his labor, is
transformed into a *capitalist*. [Italics in original] [10]

Rather, large sections of the British workforce behaved, at this time, as dispossessed
wage labourers fighting to maintain or increase their share of the value produced.
The strike rate trebled between 1968 and 1972. There were few signs, either, of the
new 'flexibility' about the organization of the labour process.

Schooling also failed visibly to alleviate the tensions surrounding the black
English. With the importation of cheap and vulnerable labour from the Commonwealth, capital had resolved temporary problems (labour shortage and resistance to
low grade jobs) only to create longer term difficulties. Schools were charged with
the task of 'assimilation' but the great majority of black children found themselves
in the same school situation as the Newsom report's 'John Robinson' whom the
report, said Sir Alec Clegg:

had found to be both physically and socially deprived, and . . . John Robinson was
now black. . .what we have done is build up . . . a group that are conspicuous because
they are a minority that has been passed over. We should not wonder if this minority
sometimes shows signs of disturbance and delinquency.[11]

As they entered the gulf between the ambitions of assimilation and the situation
of the Robinsons, black children also encountered both casual and more entrenched
forms of racism. 'Multicultural education' lay further ahead in the long spaces
between the hoped-for 'equalization' of opportunities and the lived experience of
black pupils in their actual location in schools. The whole subject is symptomatically
beyond the reach of this book; but it was noticeable in the 1970s that young blacks
remained resistantly different and increasingly proud of it. When the moment of
'mugging' arrived in the full force of a law and order campaign, schools seemed to
have failed conspicuously either to assimilate or to integrate a young black
population.

Three instances could be briefly cited of what became construed as signs of a
general unrest. One, ironically, was the final and much delayed implementation of
the raising of the school leaving age, one of the chief planks in the earlier reforms.
Because this took effect in September 1973 it was monitored in a period of major
industrial and social turmoil, resulting in an increased visibility for the 'problem'
of the 'discontented' pupil. At the same time, the grievances of those at school
took on a more organized form through the establishment of the National Union of
School Students and the start of a movement around children's rights. Scenes in
which pupils marched or asked for rights of consultation were heavily publicized.
Third, some of the radical social critiques from the 1960s began to be applied, by
some younger teachers, to the curriculum and to the social relations of the
classroom. Now there were teachers willing to look at the school as an oppressive
institution and to argue legitimate causes of pupil discontent. The rich mushrooming

of the alternative educational press showed the strength of these critiques. Later, the William Tyndale teachers were vulnerable to their media prominence as proof of everyday radicalism in school life. 'Militant pupils' and 'trendy teachers' became woven, as we shall see, into the very fabric of educational reporting.

Economic recession and increasing lurches in its attempted political management thus brought social democratic measures to high visibility and to the possibility of adverse judgement. In the post-war years schools had been a main carrier of hopes for a new and fairer Britain. During the period of major reorganization, Newsom could typically report (in 1963) that 'never before has the cause of education had so much public support'. A decade later all was changed utterly. For employers and economists the links between educational spending and economic growth were now dubious. In the desperate search for political explanations of national recalcitrance, the educational expansion and reforms seemed not only to have failed in their ambitions, but to have helped bring about a deteriorating situation. The Janus-faced metaphor of youth as bearers of the future and as threat to the moral order now turned its right cheek. Youth was construed once more as predominantly a threat, the forms of whose malaise were varied and often contradictory but under-scored by one strong alleged cause: a loss of discipline leading to declining standards and social fragmentation.

As for popular support, its absence was now striking. Achieved as the outcome of wide public organization and struggle and with a broad popular base, the new settlement would have been strong despite the vulnerabilities noted. But the reforms had been constructed from above: the working class, in particular, were their object rather than their author. The brief experience of working-class pupils and parents of reforms which had promised greater progress and equality was not now able to generate support in a period of heightened conflict when schools remained a distant and divisive escalator, out of the class, for the few. The reality of the reproduction of class differentiation was unchanged. New qualifications which had promised upskilling and better employment were proving a debased currency. If anything, the production of new aspirations was as likely to achieve greater resentment at their disappointment.

None of these problems were in themselves sufficient to explain the lack of resistance on behalf of education as a social service. A comparison would be with the strength of the defensive alliance mounted against cuts in the 1920s and 1930s. Nor is the comparative retreat from educational expenditure at all the main point. Between the later 1960s and the middle of the 1970s, the purposes of education were coming to be redefined across the board, in a spirit of sustained hostility to the social democratic reforms and their intentions, by an initially isolated, but then increasingly confident, group of right-wing polemicists. The success of the redefini-tion is inexplicable without looking at the simultaneous scattering of the forces behind the earlier settlement. Here there was no one cause but a set of relatively autonomous trajectories with their own priorities and momentum. Indeed what they shared was an entrenchment within specific tasks and problems as part of the now formidable educational division of labour. Those party to the new settlement were working on detailed structural and political difficulties, while others were reinterpreting the whole strategy without allegiance to the reforms and their sudden vulnerability. To its own surprise, the new educational right found itself knocking at an open door.

The absent defence

Labour in and out of office

If there is in some ways little to say in the analysis of the Labour Party at this time, then that in itself is the point which should be noted. Amid the proliferation of memoirs and diaries from the Wilson governments of 1964–70, two facts stand out: first, the rapid switching of education ministers (repeated, almost farcically, in 1974–6) combined with a gradual downgrading of the ministry's importance in the cabinet's affairs as a whole; and second, the general subordination of any concern with education policy to the more imperative and newly interpreted problems of economic and industrial disturbance. In personal terms, Crosland's contribution proved to have been irreplaceable: ominously so for what this implied about education's visibility among the leadership. Structurally, the leadership remained doubly bound. On the one hand, comprehensives were being portrayed as all things to all comers, so that ambiguity and discretion were more prominent than convinced argument. On the other, the achievement of comprehensive schooling had become the sufficient limit of ambition, involving protracted legal and political sniping around particular cases and over, for instance, the status of direct grant schools. As a result, exhaustion and confusion were among the main products of the wars of attrition around the length and organization of secondary schooling. Comprehensives remained still the main focus, and Edward Short's Bill to make their introduction compulsory only narrowly preceded the lost election in 1970.

The ambition to compensate by extra spending for inequality of educational opportunity was in any case doubly set back during Labour's term in opposition. One research finding about the limits of such reform to alter structural 'disadvantage' came in 1972 in the translation of Raymond Boudon's *Education, Opportunity and Social Inequality*.[12] Better publicized in the same year was Jencks's exhaustive study of American compensatory programmes, *Inequality*. In fact, later research on the Headstart projects called Jencks's work, already criticized on technical grounds, into question. Its wide reception was symptomatic of new doubts. Tyrrell Burgess, in his foreword to the British edition, found the whole book 'an elaboration of the chilling sentence of J. W. B. Douglas' that 'middle class pupils have retained almost intact their historic advantage over the manual working class . . . all too often liberals jump straight from their view of a social problem to proposals for a solution, without ever testing whether the solution is having the desired effect'.[13] He also remarked, in the same kind of phrasing as that of the *Black Papers,* on the schools' failures as 'engines of social change'. Elsewhere Jencks was used as triumphant confirmation of right-wing lamentations over the futility of 'social engineering'.

For Halsey, as we suggested in Chapter 7, the problem with the educational priority areas was whether the experiment was, in any real terms, to be given a chance at all. He himself had been a crucial figure, earlier, in the gradual replacement of educational psychology by the concerns of the sociology of education. Now he had been put in charge of action research programmes into the EPA projects, linked with the parallel development for the social services through community development projects. He saw the EPA as trying to find 'a strategy for educational roads to equality' but the underlying question was 'whether and if so in what circumstances education can change society'.[14] His own trajectory now brought him face to face with structural questions. Earlier simple equality of opportunity arguments seemed naive about such factors as class and family. A stronger definition of equality of outcomes was now needed so that the 'disadvantaged' child might have an equal chance in the 'more or less inescapable function of selection for different occupational destinies'.[15]

It was from this position that the experiments set out, but Halsey commented that the researchers realized there were still unresolved issues. Were they to be concerned with internal justice inside the school, or could they:

assume a wide programme of social reform which would democratise local power structures and diversify local occupational opportunities so that society would look to its schools for a supply of young people educated for political responsibility and linked to their communities not by failure in the competition but by rich opportunities for work and life?[16]

This might require an alternative curriculum providing knowledge and skills to 'cope with, gain power over and in the end transform the conditions of' a local community.[17]

The priority areas did not produce the cogent, lucid analyses and pamphlets which flowed from the community development projects. Nor did those involved come to the absolute limits of the community projects, in which, as political parties and the state were themselves brought into question, grants were withdrawn. But Halsey has vigorously recorded the diminished support given the work; and his own conclusion in 1972 was that 'the limits of an approach to poverty . . . cannot be remoulded by any kind of e.p.a. policy'.[18] It followed that, instead, 'economic inequality has to be tackled by policies directly aimed at economic institutions'. Thus Halsey's own progress along the road to Balsall Heath provided a courageous case of social democratic policies taken to the edge.

It was towards comprehensives, compensatory spending and the priority areas that Labour energy had been committed. The party never resolved on taking action over the public schools. The Newsom Commission on them produced typically divided recommendations. Among them was Vaizey's comment that 'the main objection to the private schools is that they are socially divisive. Some of them happen to have beds. It therefore seems less revolutionary to change the bodies in the beds than eliminate the beds'. Anne Corbett has said that the report brought out the persistent difficulty of Labour with the private sector. Abolition would have required considerable political stamina and resources, not least when the media's interest was sustained in Labour ministers or their children who had themselves been to private schools: 'but integration has also been impossible in effect since the public schools are not dealing in any commodity which the state would like, other than prestige'.[19]

In higher education, as we saw, Crosland accepted the department's own preference for a binary system. Otherwise the main innovation was the successful piloting of the Open University. Here the chosen form of the new university was severed from the party's links with other forms of adult education, to which it immediately gave competition based on much stronger resources. Raymond Williams records Jennie Lee as saying she had 'decided to steer clear of the old types of adult education and set up what looked as much as possible like a conventional university, including the "trimmings" '.[20] Once again education was to be 'provided' as a neutral good, outside any traditions of learning beyond, or opposed to, certification by the state.

The party's return to power in 1974 followed a bruising few years for its policies of the 1960s. Comprehensives, which were far from fully implemented or adequately provided with buildings, had been dragged back to the centre of political controversy. The priority areas had withered almost before they had started. In particular, as we will go on to suggest, there was no longer a strong link between policy and the concerns of researchers, who now felt radical doubts about the whole direction of these reforms. The result was that the leadership felt most urgently a need to respond to the loudest voices in the arena — those of industrialists and of the new right.

Reorganization of the state administrative apparatus

The shadowy figure of the DES has always been crucial to an understanding of the formation and implementation of educational policy; but some relevant information is not available and the overall picture is hard to construct. For example, there was not much given away in the department's evidence to the major inquiry by the Commons Expenditure Committee.[21] Kogan, who had served on the Plowden Committee's staff, has written that 'the power, access and expectations of MPs are simply inadequate for the tasks that are set to them'.[22] Even less is to hand for researchers working outside central and local government. Nevertheless, a number of pressures and constraints on the department's work seems to have come to a head during the 1970s, and what follows is based on such evidence as there is available to us.

To begin with, the internal organization of the department seems to have gone through a period of instability during the late 1960s and early 1970s. This resulted partly from the huge growth of the system which was being supervised, and an absence of adequate data on what had been set in train. The Labour government had encouraged the formation of a specialist planning branch in 1967, but this was wound up in 1970. Planning was switched to the Departmental Planning Organization on the basis of three principles:

1 Planning must directly involve those who must administer the policies that have to be planned.
2 Specialist skills must be built into the machinery in such a way as to ensure that they make a creative contribution to policy formation without being able to determine it single handed.
3 The planning machinery must keep close to ministers, exploring among other options those that reflect their known views and seeking ministerial guidance and endorsement from time to time.[23]

The DPO was the title for a series of committees composed of administrative civil servants putting their 'thinking caps' on after 'a day at the counter'.[24] The demise of the specialist unit, and the contrast between the first principle's certainty and the ambivalence of the second suggests there may have been internal conflicts over planning responsibility. But either way, as the examiners in a later and major OECD inquiry reported:

the feeling exists strongly within the Department that when it comes to planning leading to policy decisions for which resources have to be secured and allocated . . . informal methods, utilized by sensitive and fair-minded government servants, are superior to highly structured formal procedures which invite half-baked and politically sectarian opinions, and encourage demagogy, confrontation and publicity battles, leading to a lot of waste of time.[25]

We cited earlier the department's claim that ' "the feel" is a very important bit of our trade' — though 'the feel' did not necessarily extend to the children of senior officials themselves going to state schools.

After the Conservative government's return in 1970, there was an attempt to introduce methods of administration more familiar to business enterprises: programme analysis and review methods were favoured. In this system, objectives had to be defined, policy alternatives costed and measured for relative efficiency. At the meetings between DES officials and chief education officers, inaugurated in 1971, a set of objectives for the system was produced, including the economic objective of a suitably prepared and motivated labour force and the cultural objective of the propagation of a common culture.[26] As suggested in Chapter 7, these meetings noted 'a legacy of resistance to every form of measurement' in education since the Revised Code, and stressed resource effectiveness (aided by management consultants) and the need for liaison with other social services. These changes remained tentative and it was later argued that 'the experience of the DPO has been that, instead of trying to work from the general to the particular, it is more productive to start with particular options and to evaluate them against such strategic aims as are current at the time'.[27] Movements to increase financial accountability could only unevenly challenge predominant administrative styles. Moreover the new stress on cost-effectiveness was itself largely technical, and in no way a challenge to administrative inwardness. Hencke's study of one of the department's major actions in this period, teacher training reorganization, concluded that:

The DES is no exception to the secret traditions of our society . . . . Failure to make information available prevented colleges from planning their future, academics from tackling urgent curriculum problems, and local authorities from understanding the full significance of the enormous changes that were required.[28]

This internal instability and ambivalence towards planning in the department was only one of several larger problems for its work. These included a weakness of political leadership; the traditional gap between central and local government; the demands for greater public involvement; and the rise of competing government agencies.

Labour ministers have established some formidably documented arguments about the power of the permanent civil service to deflect ministerial intentions. This was aggravated by the persistent flirtation with education's 'non-political' status which had kept it away from Commons debate and from strong ministerial advocacy. If it was Vaizey's judgement that the civil service view could keep other opinion at bay and that the 1945 decision on tripartites 'was not going to be easily overthrown by such wild-eyed men as R. H. Tawney', it was also his comment that ministers went in and out of the department 'like a revolving door' — at a fair speed under recent Labour prime ministers.[29] To some extent, the department was obliged by default to prepare and implement policy.

In addition there was the long-standing complaint about the difficulty of having a national system administered locally. A permanent secretary felt there was 'a discontinuity in this system between the intentions of the Government at the starting end of the process and the actual outcome of a series of aggregate decisions by . . . local education authorities at the other end'.[30] This discontinuity could both ensure an immense time between central initiatives and their local effectivity and allow possible defiance and rearguard action against central instructions.

Meanwhile the department was subjected, in the early 1970s, to two linked investigations, from the OECD and then from the Commons Expenditure Committee, which stressed the evident unwillingness to take wider public soundings or to debate out policy implications. Just as the Central Advisory Councils had been abandoned, though this appeared to be 'a plain default of duty' by ministers, so the Commons committee's suggested 'standing commission' on educational policy, made up of trade unions, employers and 'citizens', has never been heard of. In fact the department seems to have resented both the 1960s reports and the later powers of the Schools Council. One subsequent change has been the privileging of the department's inspectorate over the relatively accessible discussions of the council.

As if all this were not enough, the department found itself not just caught in different demands — for cost-effectiveness, for greater public accountability — but under pressure from new state agencies, particularly the Manpower Services Commission of the mid decade. Evidence to the Commons committee suggested that the Training Services Agency was 'making a takeover bid for a substantial part of the educational system' and was even trying to change the school curriculum.[31] NATFHE argued that the agency had posed 'fundamental issues of educational principle' and that 'the approach of the TSA to consultation has already been seen to be more positive and open' than the department's.[32] Officials of the DES were not so free to comment, except that training had traditionally been separated from education and that this was nonsensical: 'the desirable objective is to integrate education and training wherever possible'.[33] The committee's conclusion from the evidence was that the department 'and the Department of Employment are in a sense competing for resources and liable to be judged one against the other by result'. The DES was thought 'less nimble in a situation where objectives themselves are changing' and that the TSA had 'moved at a tempo which DES could not (and indeed should not try to) emulate'. The committee welcomed 'the initiative and enthusiasm displayed by the TSA'.[34]

Given these stresses, the investigations, and the loss of initiative to new agencies we must suspect that the central civil service was in some disarray. It was in no position to resist the cuts, and had its own reason for involvement in the enthusiastic mounting of the 'Great Debate' whose outcome might restore control more firmly to the department.

The educational apparatus of the local state had been through a similar phase of upheaval. The changes in the economy, Cockburn argues, had by 1974 brought into existence:

a radically new pattern of local authorities. They are different from the old in their boundaries, in the share out of function and in the way they go about their work. It was the *internal* management reforms of the local authorities that were called corporate management and planning. But the *external* reforms were based on the same principles . . . the system as a whole was being geared up to govern more intrusively and more effectively.[35]

Four reports studied the internal management of local authorities and agreed in aiming at 'integration, control from the top, more efficient use of money and labour, forward planning'.[36]

These reforms also had an impact on the power of elected members: but their immediate effect on educational administration was dramatic. Geographical reorganization meant that stable routines were shattered as new authorities were created. The introduction of corporate management techniques also changed the balance of power inside authorities. New systems of management by objectives exposed each area of an authority's work to detailed analysis in isolation, while enhancing the power of those with overall responsibility. The tendency was to place power in the hands of a chief executive and the meetings of chief officers. Education Officers were no longer in sole control of education, since the 1960s' expansion, followed by expenditure cuts and increased statutory duties for authorities, had combined to produce 'fierce problems' of resources.[37] Since education spending might account for between 50 per cent and 60 per cent of a local authority budget it must have been tempting to look to the area for significant savings. Brian Simon's conclusion on corporate management was that while it had been perhaps laudably intended to rationalize resources its significance had been to leave education:

especially vulnerable to further economies and cuts on the part of local Pecksniffs who have always wanted to cut the maintained system of education down to size . . . a deliberate objective and . . . seen as one of the means by which educational development could be curbed.[38]

The conclusion must be that, just when the reforms needed major support from administrators as they began to take hold, the local and central state were each bound by other necessities and in no position to offer a strong or effective defence.

From deschooling to missionary pessimism

Such changes remained relatively invisible and undebated. A much more public and explosive impact came, at the start of the decade, with the appearance of books on schooling from well outside the dominant consensus in educational thought, in particular those in the Penguin Education Library. We do not want here to examine their arguments in detail but to look at their general significance, in three respects. First, here was a body of work which, in the case of deschooling, was reaching a very wide readership well beyond the narrower audience of the research in educational sociology — and which opened up controversy about education as that work had not. Second, some of the arguments doubted in a fundamental way whether state schooling was a good thing at all — moving the argument completely off the ground of extended provision to more fundamental issues. Third, and perhaps most important to our concerns here, these books, despite their diversity, were united in that they had contradictory or *no* implications for policy — so severing the foundation of policy on expert research which had become crucial since the war. Where Jencks's findings for example had cast some doubt on the social democratic analysis, and the EPA experience on the state's willingness to take it up, the new ideas rejected the whole frame in which the reforms were set. We go on to look at three broad groups of studies: the deschooling essays; the 'new' sociology of education; a set of structural analyses derived from or in dialogue with Marxism.

Deschooling arguments arrived in England as a complicated transplant from very different experiences in Latin America and in the United States. In the first case, they drew on a moment in third world history when the rise of state school systems seemed imminent, and on resistances to this development both because of a lack of resources and because other modes of learning seemed preferable to the qualification obsession of the western school system. In the second case, they drew on a long tradition of suspicion of industrialized society, from Thoreau to Paul Goodman, whose *Growing Up Absurd* was influential on both sides of the Atlantic. The reception of these works in the aftermath of 1968 linked them into the existing suspicion of educational institutions already common in the counter-

culture, and into student challenges to war-related research and traditional
hierarchies of teaching and learning in higher education.

Both Illich and Reimer suggested that the nature of school systems converted
liberal and humane purposes into repressive outcomes. Schools played at the very
least a largely custodial role; at their worst they were directly coercive. The job of
the school was to naturalize, through overt labelling, teachers' different
expectations of pupils. Examinations and certificates, in themselves never neutral
or objective, legitimated disparate outcomes in the shape of a pyramid. School
pupils were socialized into the dominant ideology and into understanding their
own futures in individual and competitive terms. Obedience to teachers and the
lessons of the hidden curriculum of the school's own rules and organization
prepared pupils for different places of work with greater or lesser expectations of
their own capacity to alter or change the society. Schools arose out of the landscape to claim an educational monopoly and thereby devalue everyday and
other non-school forms of knowledge: they existed in a mandarin separation
from family and workplace which their own expansion continually reinforced.

The effect of these ideas, particularly outside the educational world as such,
was dramatic. They touched raw nerves since as Lister says 'in most countries
educationists had long since given up asking the kind of first order questions about
purposes raised'.[39] In a stinging (and stung) review Vaizey remarked: 'I not only
disagree with them I disapprove of them'.

The texts were also largely polemical, with scattered ideas to offer about
alternatives, ranging from endorsement of Freire's work among peasants to ideas
of information exchange networks in large American cities which would be
dependent on telephones and computers. In England the political bearings of
deschooling were ambiguous. They included support for alternative schools
financed outside the state and often seeking a more generous ratio of adults to
children than state schools could afford, but they also supported distinctively
working-class schooling based in traditions of working-class learning outside
and in part prior to state education. Yet the interest in parental voucher schemes
was similar to that shown by Rhodes Boyson. Particular ideas included an
emphasis on children's rights, and a drive to democratize school government.
As often, in fact, the analysis allowed not one but a great many possible
strategies and priorities. But the swirling arrival of these arguments, followed by a
long line of paperback successors, kicked up dust enough to leave the 1960s'
research tomes looking distant.

Above all, deschooling, in all its variety, aroused distrust of schooling as a
regulated work of the state. It then allowed a surprising prominence to (from an
entirely different political and theoretical source!) Althusser's essay on 'Ideology and
ideological state apparatuses':

I ask the pardon of those teachers who, in dreadful conditions, attempt to turn the
few weapons they can find in the history and learning they 'teach' against the
ideology, the system and the practices in which they are trapped . . . how many
(the majority) do not even begin to suspect . . . that their own devotion contributes

to the maintenance and nourishment of this ideological representation of the school . . . . [40]

From a Marxist-structuralist paradigm Althusser's work paralleled many deschooling arguments even down to the way in which schools had replaced the churches as the key mechanism of social control. Both pointed, also, to the ways in which the logic of the institution or apparatus itself negated the best reforming intentions of teachers, educationalists and politicians. This was particularly important to a generation of young teachers, some already politically committed but many others not, who entered the state system in its reforming moment.

If deschooling spread substantially through the growing radical network including bookshops and resource centres, the new sociology of education was transmitted rather through teacher training and particularly through the Open University, for which the collection *Knowledge and Control* became a reference point in the early education course *School and Society*.[41]

The emphasis of the new sociology was on questions of epistemology. Rooted in phenomenology, symbolic interactionism and the sociology of knowledge, it focused attention on the status and construction of the curriculum itself. Where deschooling had asked very general, doubting questions about school and everyday life, the new work in sociology made problematic the very concept of knowledge itself and its allegedly 'value-free' status. As Halsey and Karabel commented in response:

If the concerns of the traditional sociology of education, most notably selection and socialization, are not quite relegated to the historical dustbin, it is nevertheless clear that they are now to be considered marginal to a discipline that looks upon 'the management of knowledge' as its central problem.[42]

'Management' on an agenda for research could range from the historical construction of what came to be constituted as a 'discipline', or of the 'subjects' of a curriculum, through the school's informal procedures for handling and grading pupils differently, to the most intimate details of a teacher's perception and understanding of what constituted apt behaviour and adequate performance in a classroom. The argument suggested the diversity and even the relativity of notions of what was knowledge. To that extent, the lack of detailed case studies to fill out the new programme was of little importance. The main implication of the work was sufficiently disturbing: both politicians and social democratic sociologists had assumed that reforms would flow down from the top, implemented by the professional skills of teachers on which such emphasis had been laid by their unions. Now, as deschooling questioned the outcomes and social meanings of that process, the new sociology interrogated that which lay at the very centre of the teacher's expertise. And while much of this work stemmed from the prestigious Institute of Education at London University, its implications for policy were non-existent: it seemed to inculcate a scepticism which might be disabling unless some other way forward were taken on some other terrain. An argument of critique about school subjects was one thing when looking back-wards to the school's taken-for-granted sureness of what it had to offer. It was quite another thing as pressure swelled in, and on, the state to control the basic requirements of the school curriculum. As the argument about the common curriculum began to bite, employers' views were stated directly. On the left, apart from some remarks in Gramsci's work and Raymond Williams's strangely neglected case (1961), there was little to set in their place.[43] The new sociology of educational knowledge then stood — quizzically, equivocally — between them.

To put the whole set of changes in educational thought differently: attention now moved to processes happening 'behind the backs' of reformers' or teachers' intentions. Above all, this was true, by the mid-decade, in the work of Bernstein, Bourdieu, and Bowles and Gintis.[44] Each spoke more directly against the illusions of reform. Bernstein had already warned ambiguously that 'education cannot compensate for society' and, even as attention began to move towards preparation for parenthood (the deprivation almost of the foetus), his essays combined highly original and rigorous taxonomies with probings about the direction and class basis of the reforms. Typically, he implied that new 'progressive' forms of education were also new forms of social control, distinctive because much harder for child or parent to understand or penetrate. 'Invisible pedagogies' were the means by which fractions of the new middle class sought to secure their own children's position in and through education, in opposition to the more visible pedagogy of other fractions and the traditional working class. Here and elsewhere the ideas were highly suggestive but extremely equivocal. Bernstein's later work had in common with Bourdieu's and that of Bowles and Gintis a mixture of Marxism and functionalism. What distinguished it was its consistently suggestive ambivalence towards 'progressive' reforms.

Bourdieu's work, in its belated, partial and initially unsatisfactory English translation, was still harder to grasp. Just as Bernstein has systematically been read in different ways, especially in his views on the linguistic codes of different classes, so there have been very diverse accounts of Bourdieu's central arguments. Again, though, his ideas at the very least undercut some of the 'empirical' bases of the reforms. However 'cultural capital' was understood in his work, it lay between and outside the terms of any shift in school 'provision'. It referred at once to class culture and 'know-how' outside schools, and to both formal and informal knowledges inside schools which the schools variously, and in the guise of neutrality, rendered legitimate or illegitimate. In the most general formulation:

In any given social formation, the dominant ES (system of education) is able to set up the dominant PW (pedagogic work) as the WSg (work of schooling) without either those who exercise it or those who undergo it ever ceasing to misrecognize its dependence on the power relations making up the school formation in which it is carried on . . . .[45]

In its extreme abstraction, in its stance towards its audience, and, above all, in the notion of reproduction to which it was attached, Bourdieu's position was in no way our own. Nevertheless, even a common sense understanding of his handling of reproduction (perhaps particularly a common sense reading, given the difficulty of the original) suggested how small the power of schools or teachers was to alter the social conditions which were also the conditions of their own existence.

If Bourdieu's pessimism was aloof, almost magisterial, the impact of Bowles and Gintis's *Schooling in Capitalist America* came partly from its opening assumption that reformers were in retreat: 'in less than a decade, liberal pre-eminence in the field of educational theory and policy has been shattered'.[46] That this was so was based on an 'incomplete understanding of the economic system'.[47] For Bowles and Gintis, the central contradiction in capitalist industrial development lay between the dynamic of expansion and the need for stability and order in the face of a growing class of wage labourers and a growing reserve army of unemployed or only casually employed workers. 'We refer to this tension between growth and stability as the contradiction between the accumulation of capital and the reproduction of the capitalist relations of production.' The aim of the work, a history of reform movements in American education, was to show that each was preceded by 'the opening up of a significant divergence between the ever-changing social organization of production and the structure of education'. The attempt of the reforms was always to close this divergence, to restore a correspondence or fit between education and production:

the major aspects of educational organization replicate the relationships of dominance and subordinacy in the economic sphere. The correspondence between the social relation of schooling and work accounts for the ability of the education system to produce an amenable and fragmented labor force.[48]

Thus more generally

major aspects of the structure of schooling can be understood in terms of the systematic needs for producing reserve armies of skilled labor, legitimating the technocratic-meritocratic perspective, reinforcing the fragmentation of groups of workers into stratified status groups and accustoming youth to the social relations of dominance and subordinacy in the economic system.[49]

The optimism of the book's conclusion sat oddly, as the authors themselves noted, with their 'stress on the reproduction of consciousness and skills consistent with capitalist expansion'. The missionary zeal of the critique of reform was by now hard to distinguish in practice from a thoroughgoing pessimism.

Our concern in a brief section, then, has not been to examine the proliferation of theories of schooling during the 1970s in their own terms: very clear expositions are available elsewhere. Instead we have tried to note first, the completeness of the break with the established concerns of educational sociology and with their implications for policy; second, the shift of attention away from schools and the intentions of those in them, to a position in which schools seem to be more determined than determining; third, the movement from empirical research towards theoretical and (in good and bad senses) utopian commentary; fourth, the rapidity of the break from the radical libertarianism of deschooling towards the sense of near closure in Bourdieu and Bowles and Gintis, albeit with some limited attempts to get out from under the implications of the analysis. A negative comment might be to mention the difficulties caused by this work for teachers: the virtual impossibility of understanding its bearings on school situations. More positively, the radical educational journals began the labour of taking on these theories in relation to an educational politics. In this respect much richer work was available than in the attemptedly neutral implementation by state, parties and unions of agreed social democratic objectives. If one problem was the analysis of the changes and the possibilities implicit within them, another, nearer by, concerned the responses of school pupils and their lived experience in and out of class.

Teachers and pupils

Teachers had played an important part in the formation of social democratic policies but, in the early 1970s, other issues came to the fore. This happened even as the main teacher union was becoming more forceful in its support for comprehensive reform. The NUT's *Into the 70s* (1969) commented on a 'profligate waste of ability' and argued that non-selective comprehensive schooling was crucial. It was sharply hostile to the systematic delay in the approval of new schemes and the retention of selection in *What's Mrs. Thatcher Up To?* The more urgent issue however became the unprecedentedly militant campaign around salaries, including the divisions inside the school caused by the salary scales themselves.

Here the 'professionalism' to which teachers had appealed in the 1960s, gradually gaining more control over the curriculum and examinations, was for a moment turned against them. At the end of the 1960s, Labour politicians repeatedly warned teachers not to 'betray' their professional status by wage militancy. The strong sense of injustice built up as the teaching force expanded and was asked to deal with new difficulties in the classroom was not checked by this appeal: strike action of a new kind led up to the Houghton pay settlement of 1975 at which local authorities were aghast. The pressure was linked with arguments between teaching unions about the meaning of 'professional' status, and, within the NUT, with the formation of a rank-and-file grouping that linked salary questions to those of internal democracy inside schools, in particular the distance of heads and administrators from the position and experience of young classroom teachers.

Inevitably, too, the experience for many teachers of comprehensive reorganization was traumatic. The *ad hoc* nature of the changes, made worse by a lack of money for new secondary building schemes under the Conservatives, entailed huge organizational difficulties, including split sites and very large schools. For many the actual processes of teaching became more problematic, particularly in a period of heightened consciousness about youth unrest. These changes sometimes meant that teachers and pupils from vastly different traditions were thrown together. As a result, conflicts over discipline, curriculum and the handling of informal school cultures were engendered among teachers and pupils.

In addition, the raising of the school leaving age, in effect from September 1973, resulted in an increase in the scale of the discontented pupil 'problem' and some

new attempts to handle it, including special disciplinary units. The change not only
increased the number of 'non-academic' pupils but also the scale of their grievances
and the ability of pupils to present them. The formation of the National Union of
School Students, and the movements for children's rights, were symptoms of a new
attitude inside schools, duly handled and amplified in particular ways by the media.

Given the general re-emergence of the theme of youth and social unrest, schools
found problems of truancy and 'indiscipline' highlighted in a new way. While pupils
have resisted schooling since its inception, the popular dailies constructed something
of a panic, at which we look in Chapter 9, around school militancy. They connected
the militancy, also — despite evidence of the political conservatism of teachers as a
whole — with new intakes of radical teachers, especially in the front lines of the
toughest inner city comprehensives.

The growth of teacher radicalism was no simple figment of the media's
imagination — but this of course is not to endorse their particular construction of
it. Clearly many of those involved in the counter-culture and student movements of
the late 1960s entered teaching, and took there a concern with the curriculum, often
protesting its distance from their own or their pupils' experience, and a concern with
social relations inside the classroom and the school as a whole. Grace, in his study
of inner city teachers, has made some suggestive distinctions between different
political attitudes towards the specific necessities of the schools in which they
worked. He also found that the division between liberal and radical teachers inside
such schools was that liberal teachers believed themselves to be 'outside of social and
political structures and relatively autonomous in relation to them', attempting to
realize 'universal' principles such as relevance and interest, or cultural comprehensive-
ness. They did not regard themselves as linked with working-class pupils and parents
since any attempt at larger structural change was seen as inappropriately political
from the 'impartial' position of educators. They could believe this since:

they had experienced in their work situations very little overt control of their
activities . . . notions of . . . a 'controlling apparatus' and of the necessity for struggle
against it were insubstantial in their consciousness, whereas notions of autonomy
were real and actual.[50]

These comments were based on research between 1975 and 1977, before some of
the later pressures towards standards and controls began to bite. Even before then,
the vigorous development of radical teachers' journals showed other positions being
forcefully developed. Sometimes these were concentrated, as in *Teaching London
Kids,* on the specific problems of a school subject (English and media studies);
others *(Radical Education, Socialist Teacher, Teachers' Action)* developed a more
general political analysis. There were also direct results from the growing strength of
the women's movement on awareness of sexism in education: of the dramatic
under-representation of women, who make up over half the teaching force, in
senior posts and the inspectorate; of gender assumptions in the curriculum and in
the careers offered implicitly and explicitly in and beyond the school. Women
teachers began to make problematic many of the routine expectations about

knowledges and futures. Rebellious or discontented or 'under-achieving' pupils began, in all these ways, to be seen, by some of those responsible for their schooling, to have justifiable grievances.

As this happened, the whole weight inside some schools began to move towards the educational 'shop floor' of classroom cultures and the restiveness of some teachers and pupils. Between policy prescriptions and their translation into classroom practice, there now stood a new series of ideas and movements and conflicts which left the prescriptions remote from the internalities of schools and from increasingly hostile external perceptions of them.

Conclusion

Cumulatively, the reforms were, in all these ways, brought into jeopardy during the early 1970s. They had apparently failed to help in the achievement of economic growth or social order. Their proponents were less confident, given apparently intractable difficulties of early practice. In higher education, research concerns had moved on to a quite different terrain. Inside the schools, there were particular struggles of a new kind. The field was open for a rethinking of educational purposes across the board and it is to this that we now turn.

9   Turning the tables: the Conservative education offensive

Fight for Education: A Black Paper appeared in 1969 as a set of dissenting right-wing essays from the margins of the educational world, by which it was largely reviled and discounted. Only six years later, by 1975, the fourth such *Black Paper* was able to claim with satisfaction a wide realization that 'education had not delivered the goods . . . there was now a case that had to be answered'. In the 'Great Debate' of the following year many of the writers' assumptions had become indistinguishable from those of the Labour government itself. By 1979, the electorate could walk past a large Saatchi and Saatchi election poster for the Tories: *Educashun Isn't Wurking*. In the ensuing government an ex-minister of education took office as the most committedly right-wing premier since the war, and appointed a *Black Paper* editor and articulately aggressive right-wing ideologue as her minster with responsibility for higher education. It was not just that within a decade the trail had been blazed for a thoroughgoing restructuring of education, but that the debate around schooling and its purposes had been put at the political forefront in the attempted recasting of late British capitalism, as a chief site for the staking out of new parameters of consent. We begin by noting in broad outline some of the connections and divergences between this and earlier periods in Conservative educational strategy.

The offensive: shifts and conditions

Little could be said by way of characterizing the Conservative Party's educational 'thought' from the inter-war years into the early 1960s. The whole idea would be paradoxical. There was no right wing figure comparable to Tawney (Eliot's writing was remote from prescription, Bantock's never found much resonance), while little importance was attached to the whole area of social policy except as reluctantly found necessary. Control over the state system remained firmly in the hands of senior civil servants whose experience, mainly, if not wholly, of private schooling, was noted (again) by a Commons committee in 1976.[1] Within the Conservative Party complaints about the dangers and failures of schools occurred in a steady drip and, as circumstances allowed, muttered grievances became shouted fulminations, leaving perhaps a formidable residue of proverbial wisdom: 'discipline never did us any harm'.

The basic Conservative repertoire and concerns made for a conveniently short and clear list. The private schools and links between a few of the more important of them and the dominant universities were consistently buttressed — privilege secured in an effective and quiet way with a persistent absence of serious controversy. In the state 'sector' (containing the overwhelming majority of all children) there was a persistent and not always benign neglect. Spending was willingly cut, sometimes hard, but there was always a tactical readiness to make occasional but rapid concessions, so as to pre-empt or recoup opposing demands: the 1944 Act is the best example of this Conservative logic at work. The final element in the repertoire was the emphasis on a school ethic of loyalty to 'traditional' military and Christian values. Churchill, quoting Disraeli, said that a nation was ruled by force or by tradition, while Butler (in 1952) thought that pride in and allegiance to school could become linked to the nation's institutions and way of life.[2] In sum, priority was given to the education of a predominantly masculine elite, while there was much support for pruning the schooling of, in particular, working-class children.

In some substantial respects the resilience of these few grounding assumptions has never been abandoned in a 'basic' Tory educational repertoire. Mrs Thatcher, on taking office in the 1970s, was willing to be unpopular in the ministry to help ease the Treasury spending burden; but Florence Horsburgh (herself a lawyer with little educational experience, as was Mrs Thatcher's Conservative successor Mark Carlisle) cut 5 per cent from expenditure on taking office at the edge of a boom in 1951. Just as the 1944 Act was prepared in the certain anticipation that 'a major measure of educational reform will be demanded in quarters that will make the demand irresistible', so later educational certainties were rapidly abandoned, whatever the opposition from the party conference.[3] Such a willingness (say) to work with comprehensive schools was also however a determination to mould them to the party's own ends. To take a last example: Angus Maude, an ideological continuity in himself, was associated with panics over reading standards in the early 1950s and late 1960s. His observation in 1969 that employers' requirements necessarily determined the curriculum for the majority, and that at least 10 per cent of 'less able' children might learn more at work than by staying on at school could have been made years or even decades earlier.[4]

Boyle's charge of Conservative policy saw a marked new set of additional inflections. The convergence (noted by Kogan) of his 'statist radicalism' with Crosland's policies has entered into the demonology of the *Black Papers*, plausibly, as a break or betrayal.[5] The party moved, or if not wholeheartedly convinced was at least strongly led by the Bow Group caucus, into an interest both in educational reforms and in educational expansion. Policy was rapidly redefined for the parents to whom eleven plus and the scarcity of higher education places represented the real possibility of their children's exclusion. It was, according to the party leader in 1967, 'never a Conservative principle that children should be segregated in different institutions'.[6] There was also explicit debate about the need for school changes in the interests of a recomposed labour force — the beginnings of a determined involvement in educational manpower planning which would later return to haunt the party's commitment to freedom of choice. Policy-makers

more than flirted with notions of compensation for 'disadvantage' through selective
additional spending, echoes of which lingered in Mrs Thatcher's declarations on
nursery schooling in 1972. Although the extent of the changes made and the
convergences with Labour have both been tactically exaggerated, the new right
could raise its head after 1969 over an apparently endless horizon of progressive
managerial consensus.

The rapidity and scale of its impact, however active, vociferous and energetic its
proponents, could not have occurred without fertile conditions. While these included
all the various developments noted in Chapter 7, another indispensable
momentum came from the increasing disarray of the Conservative Party itself. It
was this which made space for the promotion, surprisingly around schooling, of
themes that were to be made central to a new agenda right across the political
board. The key change was that schooling suddenly became a focus for political
disagreement and so, against all the party's traditions, for high and controversial
visibility. It became the particular site for a distinctive general strategy: expectations
and 'caring' were replaced by the acceptance of failure, in strongly competitive
terms, combined with the offering of explanations, even scapegoats, for its
persistence.

The double election losses of 1964 and 1966 had entailed furious struggles within
the party, involving disagreements and differences of interest which a plausible
ideology for the party in any area of policy would need to weave together. As
leader, a landed aristocrat, unmercifully mocked by Labour, had been replaced by
a grammar school boy: the party attempted to break its identification with
traditional elites and to stress a cross-class modernizing purpose against an 'archaic'
and 'divisive' labour movement. The uneasy alliance representing competing interests
of different fractions of capital was constantly threatened with splits. There were
open tensions between large and small concerns, between finance and industrial
capitals inside Britain and between 'British' and multinational interests. One case
was the fight on behalf of small concerns against the abolition of resale price
maintenance; another was the acrimony about entry to the EEC. On top of the
problems of antagonisms internal to the power bloc, was the social dissent which
in the later 1960s was added to the fevered combination of low growth and
industrial conflict. Liberal legislation had spawned a variety of moral pressure groups
(for example around abortion and pornography); the student movement distanced
itself from the universities as did the counter-culture (outwardly) from middle-class
values; sects and splinter groups proliferated outside the main political parties;
demonstrations and sit-ins had become widespread. The problem of leadership was
therefore one of finding ways of handling class relations as increasingly stringent
shifts from post-war experience were demanded.

To these developments Mr Heath's leadership of the Conservatives presented a
coldly abrasive face. In the late 1960s the party was driven generally, by the
combination of economic difficulty and social dissent, to attempt a move away
from the reforming middle ground. It became a main strategy to identify Labour
rule with 'breakdown' at many levels from inflation and strikes, to permissiveness.

The party's Bow Group yielded to the Monday Club, one of whose members in 1969 characteristically thought 'modifying socialism not enough': there was a need for a 'superhuman labour of rescue and an end of consensus politics'.[7] After its victory the leadership was explicitly and toughly determined to re-establish firm control and take charge, not least against union 'might', in a general reshaping of the social and industrial order. The party's pro-European ideology was as yet markedly managerial and technocratic, narrow in appeal, raw-edged in its determination to up the GNP at almost any cost. To the new centrality of a management for streamlined growth was then added a determination to take on the miners in confrontation without, in the event, adequate political support. To the party's already suspicious right, this combination was confirmed as disastrous. The dominant political consensus of a decade, offering social reforms against attempted industrial rejuvenation, had failed to be productive and had now lost its cross-class support in the accentuated version of 'modernization'. The need was to construct a broader-based consensus of a wholly different kind. For this purpose Powellite nationalism, both divisive and anachronistic, never looked adequate: its insufficiency warranted the now extensive search for a new and 'popular' conservatism. The first need of such a politics would be to orchestrate the range of disturbances into a near-total dissent from the prevalent consensus and its typical ideas and ways of working, with which the failures (already, 'crisis') could come to be connected. The hour of Black Paperdom had struck.

In the meantime, between *Black Paper 3 (Goodbye Mr Short)* in 1970 and the reappearance of *Black Paper 4 (Fight for Education)* in 1975, now with Rhodes Boyson as co-editor, Mrs Thatcher presided over an uneasy interregnum in Conservative educational policy. A distinctively Tory ideology of schooling was not immediately to hand, even though in some important ways, as suggested earlier, the whole arena was coming to be vacated. Yet, through and beneath the various educational events of the early 1970s, a 'coherent' account, attack and remedy was under continuous construction, with a forceful spokesman. This chapter tries to show the gradual convergence between party policy and the new educational right.

Mrs Thatcher at the DES

The first action of the Heath government was the withdrawal of Crosland's October 1965 circular (just as the first action of the Thatcher government was to be the repeal of Labour's 1976 Education Act). *Crossbow* (the Bow Group journal) found this pointless, unnecessary and provocative; and indeed the number of schools designated as comprehensive continued to increase rapidly.[8] Still, the decision was almost symbolic of what was to follow: the declaration of an intended shift of educational ideology with, as yet, no confidence or means with which to take up a new position.

In the same way, the major White Paper of the period, titled (almost nostalgically) *A Framework for Expansion* (1972) retained the familiar definition of purposes:

The last ten years have seen a major expansion of the education service. The next ten will see expansion continue — as it must if education is to make its full contribution to the vitality of our society and our economy.[9]

There were two changes. No mention whatever was made of comprehensive schools, while new priorities were indicated to be the provision of nursery education and a concentration on the school building programme. In fact, spending cuts almost immediately swept away the nursery pledge, and, before long, school rebuilding (including that needed to make good comprehensive schools on old and divided sites) was also set back. The more obvious sign of the new willingness for financial stringency was the extremely unpopular decision to charge for school milk. Even the decision to implement the raising of the school leaving age, on the face of it a further expansion, was influenced by the full registering of youth unemployment as a now serious problem. As a contemporary review put it:

with modern technical advance it is inevitable that pupils will be obliged to stay on at school longer and longer, that is, unless we decide to take people off the labour market by having an earlier statutory age of retirement.[10]

Otherwise, as Conservative commentators noted, Mrs Thatcher's ministry was rather colourless. In part, this may have been the return to older, 'instinctive' ways of downplaying state education by Conservatives, in part it may have been due to a loss of direction inside the department: nor had an alternative educational agenda yet become fully visible. The important move was the shift in the whole stance, away from the statement of goals for expansion, aimed at the amelioration or abolition of social problems, towards a declared responsiveness to 'public anxiety' about the internal workings of schools.

The main event of the ministry was then not legal decisions or educational statements inside the minister's control, but the acceptance of an atmosphere in which two developments received specific forms of definition. The raising of the leaving age came to be connected with school violence and general indiscipline; while the Bullock Report on English teaching came to be connected with 'standards' and their alleged decline. Both these were importantly new. In these respects, at the end of the period, the William Tyndale school saga (as revealing in its way as that of Risinghill for the previous decade) became, at least in its press rehearsal, the central spectacle.[11] It offered 'progressive' teachers who were at best 'sincere but misguided' and at worst 'dangerous' and 'politically motivated', parents who were kept out of school decisions and managers and inspectors who were failing in their statutory duties. It was in the ensuing and powerful new myth of school anarchy that the real inheritance of the Conservative redefinition was to be seen.

The raising of the school leaving age had long been anticipated with some foreboding in educational discussion, though this had been little picked up by the popular dailies in the different climate of the 1960s. A Schools Council paper of 1965 had warned that, 'for many, vocational motivation will be weak; it will be difficult to engage their interest and sense of relevance. Some will actively resent having to stay longer in school'.[12] This prediction was not surprising, given

tensions between working-class boys (especially) and state schooling which were
at least a century old. A study of a working-class school in 1962 noted that
'hostility is the key feature'. If a teacher came to the school 'full of idealism and
energy', he might well try to treat the lads as equals, but unsuccessfully, because
he would then be played up. 'He is the chink in the armour of a system which
oppresses them.' After a year, if a teacher 'is not qualified to move, he is another
drill sergeant'.[13] In the same way, a Welsh discussion document of 1967 foresaw
the need for the removal of 'feelings of inadequacy, frustration and boredom', and
that an attention to those issues would have an effect on delinquency. On the other
hand, an extension of examinations to those 'who do not have an examination
incentive' might 'serve only to publicize their incompetence in qualities measured
by examinations'.[14] As late as May in 1971, a petition which called on the government to postpone the raising of the age was signed by four fifths of all Scottish
secondary teachers, while in October an administrator connected the bleak outlook
with an extrapolation of the American situation in a pattern now familiar from the
study of the 'mugging' panic: many headmasters might 'do what I believe has
become commonplace in New York — ask for the school to be patrolled by police
in order to protect the staff and pupils against violence' *(Guardian,* October 1971).
Against all this was set the stipulation of the DES circular of August 1970:

RSLA ought not to consist simply of tacking on an 'extra year' but should involve
a review of the curriculum as a whole, so that the years up to 16 represent a
coherent educational experience for all secondary pupils.

The main emphasis of such anticipatory reviews was on schooling and work, and
school discipline.

   Sir Alec Clegg, for instance, discussing the high cost that would be involved in
new special programmes for 'slow learners', cited a headmaster who sought a new
kind of building as:

a bridgehead between school and work. He calls it a 'Newsom Barn' and it is designed
as a cross between a school and a factory workshop. It would be a place where 15
and 16 year olds could take on some man-sized production jobs.[15]

In the same vein the Schools Council worked with the Confederation of British
Industry to organize three pilot 'introduction to industry' schemes. Aims included
a greater employer—teacher understanding in improving the value to young people
of their final school years and their willingness to pursue training in employment.
This involved legal anomalies which in 1973 were remedied by the Education (Work
Experience) Act: 'enactments relating to the prohibition or regulation of the
employment of children shall not apply to the employment of a child in his last
year of compulsory schooling', where local authority approval had been given.[16]
Experiments were also strongly aware of gender. Halsall, in her book on
comprehensives in 1973, wrote that:

it is not difficult to tap sexual incentives, which are always only just beneath the
surface. They can be tapped by any means from courses in sex education, linked to

a consideration of the family and its needs, homemaking, child-rearing in both its physical and psychological aspect, do-it-yourself, dressmaking and beauty-care courses with something of an accent on hygiene

to courses on literature.[17] The knot was perhaps tied closest of all in the NUT pamphlet, *Work Experience and Secondary Schools*, which suggested that work experience was the 'education of the young adult in the differences between one collective institution – the school . . . and another – the factory or firm'. The school possessed 'all the human and material supportive agencies that exist for the benefit of the pupils' where in the workplace 'personal development of the people involved (i.e. the workers) may be only a minor objective of the organization'. But all these aims necessarily involved severe problems of discipline.

There was some evidence that the early RSLA years were indeed a 'tacking on'. In Coventry, whose provisions were researched in 1973, it was found that only one in-service training course for RSLA had been arranged; only one school was setting aside special accommodation for the RSLA pupils, as called for by DES building bulletin no. 32; school equipment and materials were in short supply, a position which deteriorated following the 10 per cent cut in education spending of November, and pupil—teacher ratios were being maintained at pre-RSLA levels. The extent of curriculum change was, at the most, an attempt to get RSLA pupils to take one or two mode 3 CSE examinations, telling pupils to take part in linked courses with technical colleges, or, as in the majority of cases, asking pupils to do an afternoon's community work such as visiting old age pensioners. There were indications that many authorities had not found resources for much more than this. Coventry's truancy rate for RSLA pupils for the year 1973—4 was 'conservatively' estimated to have run at 30—40 per cent, rising to nearly 60 per cent in the summer term.[18] The president of the National Association of Education Welfare Officers said in 1974 that:

in my own town, there has been a 75% increase in juvenile delinquency and about 80% is caused by 15 to 16 year olds. There is 50% absenteeism from schools among 15 to 16 year olds, and there has been an increase in the number of disturbances in classrooms, and violence towards teachers.

The department's own report, *The First Year after RSLA* (April 1975) noted 'a strong impression that misbehaviour had increased'. The teaching unions issued a series of reports on discipline and authority in 1975 and 1976.

In these circumstances, it was apparent that the media might highlight, as news, problems which were in many respects extremely old. The following report of a speech at the NUT Conference asking for the change to be abandoned appeared in April 1974. Pupils reached their last year:

barely literate, in spite of the devoted attention of their teachers. 'These malcontents express their disapproval of their enforced incarceration . . . during lunch hour or break they roam the school or locality like the inhabitants of Dodge City on a Saturday night fling before the arrival of Wyatt Earp. These corridor cowboys . . . .'

Such was the account in the *Guardian*. In June the *Sunday People* wrote of 'In our schools . . . defiance, gang war and mugging'. This was something of the texture of education reporting that preceded the notorious *Panorama* film for the BBC, *The Best Years?*, broadcast in March 1977.

Meanwhile, allegations that reading standards had declined during the 1960s had become part of the *Black Papers'* repertoire since the first issue in 1969. Such a decline was taken to be symptomatic of a more general disorder, itself a consequence of the weakening of the social bonds inherent in the egalitarian direction of the reforms. Although allegations about the low levels of literacy of school leavers have been almost perennial features of educational discourse throughout the century, the argument had a specific purchase in the context of the turn of the decade. After a period of unprecedented educational growth, the idea that standards were actually lower than before was bound to provoke controversy, and did. *Black Paper 1* had cited the *Daily Mail*:

Read the numbers, published now and then, of illiterate school leavers each year. Notice at an open day, just how few seven year olds, and even eleven year olds, can actually write and spell correctly. Look at the standard of reading books. It is generally low. Sometimes very low . . . . Yet more money is spent each year on educating our children, more recommendations made and mulled over (and forgotten) on this subject than any other.[19]

In 1972, research was published by the National Foundation for Educational Research which suggested that in the late 1960s reading standards had declined among certain groups of children.[20] The ensuing furore enabled Mrs Thatcher to decide on an inquiry into the whole question of reading and its assessment, to be chaired by Sir Alan Bullock.[21] Given that the inquiry's work spanned the early years of RSLA it in fact came to condense a number of themes into the issue of reading, a range of social issues concentrated as one item. Its activities also raised, in a new way, the question of educational 'experts'.

The allegation that reading standards were falling struck a particularly exposed political nerve, perhaps because reading is not only a common sense rationale for schooling but also a yardstick which can be applied by virtually all who have been through school. The ability to read represents a basic judgement of success or failure by those outside it. As with no other educational theme, almost any adult could feel included in the process of informal judgement – a fact which accounted for the debate's emotive connotations and peculiar resonances. At the same time, there was a general tension under the Heath government between politicians and the 'experts' in various regions.

The clearest example came when the DES and DHSS jointly sponsored consultations to investigate parenthood education and preparation during 1972–3. The initiative was an attempt to break what Sir Keith Joseph referred to as the 'cycle of deprivation', in his eyes a transmitted 'condition' which resulted in the constant recreation of 'disadvantaged' groups. But Joseph found himself confronted by a fairly solid body of opposing opinion, challenging the idea that education for parenthood could contribute directly to the solution of a complex issue. Michael Rutter, for instance, argued that there was no evidence of deprivation transmitted in this way.[22] What was launched as a new initiative came to a halt with the 1974 election, but Joseph went on to argue a eugenicist case about the fecundity of social class 5 which was contributing to a downward spiral since those reproducing most rapidly were 'least fitted to bring children into the world . . . mothers who were first pregnant in adolescence'.[23] Joseph was roundly condemned for these views, but it was entirely typical of a movement of opinion about 'experts' that *The Sunday Times,* in an editorial scathing of his arguments, linked his criticism to a more pervasive concern about orthodoxies in social and educational services:

across the range of social policies, especially perhaps education, proponents of the conventional wisdom feel little need to defend their position. If they are forced to do so, which they should be, those who think like Sir Keith Joseph must develop something more politically coherent than a shriek of prophetic rage.[24]

In the event, the rage was directed against Bullock's own expert judgement: ' W H I T E W A S H spells whitewash. Sir Alan Bullock's report on the teaching of English shrouds the reality in trendy pieties' was the *Mail*'s comment.[25] Substantial press attention, as we shall see, was given to the report's one dissenting member, the *Black Paper* contributor.

Bullock was therefore concerned with a particularly public area of educational practice, and the report's instigation, work and subsequent reception were caught in an increasingly vociferous educational 'panic' and sustained campaigning as had never been the case for its predecessors. In addition, irrespective of its general subject matter, the committee's brief was quite clear in one direction which was to have major, if often unrecognized, ramifications. It was charged with the task of considering what method of monitoring and assessment should be used in relation to the various skills involved in language development. Inherent in that brief was the suggestion that closer control over the operations of schools was firmly on the political agenda. Similarly the orthodox view that the curriculum was the preserve of the teachers, a 'secret garden', was being opened to challenge.

The Bullock Report, published in 1975, was as symptomatic of the 1970s as Newsom was of the 1960s. Though retaining a commitment to the compensatory theories so generative in Plowden, the report also searched for accounts of why there had been so many shortfalls in realizing the ambitions of the 1960s. In this respect conceptual innovation was eschewed in favour of a harder set of recommendations to ensure the implementation of the old policies. These stressed the need for more intervention in the home to counteract sources of educational failure thought to reside there. As with Joseph, the particular target population was the family in the unskilled working class of the educational priority areas — a continuity from those programmes but with greater resources of 'counsellors' and home 'visitors'. In addition to this reassertion of the compensatory strategy, based on a deficit model of social learning, the report identified teachers as the crucial variable — but as a problem rather than a solution. It was suggested that, because of the predominance of 'progressive' methods, some considerable confusion existed about methods. While these could be remedied at the level of the individual school through the development of teaching schemes, it was argued that there should be a way of externally assessing progress made inside schools. The need for the regular, national monitoring of standards of attainment was endorsed. The obvious assumption was that the competence of teachers could no longer be relied on automatically: teaching was too important to be left to the teachers, despite their 'professional' status. A little later, the work of Neville Bennett and associates was represented as a full-scale scientific study of 'progressive' teaching methods in practice, which had proved that they did not succeed.[26] This work achieved extraordinary national publicity, despite many disclaimers and considerable technical criticism.

The Bullock Report in fact argued that reading standards had not fallen, but this was to have little bearing on the course of subsequent discussion. The longer term implications of the findings went strangely unremarked, with its expansionist dimensions welcomed by the *Teacher,* the paper of the NUT. From Reg Prentice's comments at the beginning of the report, it was already clear that the cost of implementation — £100 million according to the union — would be prohibitive. Nothing was heard of proposals for a working party on capitation allowances or for a national language centre. The report certainly stimulated the adult literacy campaign of 1975—7, but in general the report's recommendations for closer monitoring were turned towards the Assessment of Performance Unit which the department had already set up.

By this stage, too, the movement from the vague circlings of the first *Black Paper* (1969) to the crisp confidence and range of Boyson's *Crisis in Education* (1975) had been strikingly tenacious.[27] By the mid 1970s the suggestively ambiguous central concepts of the right ('standards') and their imprecise but sweeping demands (for more 'control') seemed to be ubiquitous and virtually uncontested.

Black Paperdom

The *Black Papers* and their progeny were quite exceptional in recent Conservative ideology in Britain: both in the scale of their enterprise (seeking to change the parameters of political debate across a broad front) and in their apparently successful resonance with widespread uncertainties about children's school futures. Their ideas came to be available in a pithy new 'common sense' version of the whole educational region.

The early association between these writers and the sharp revival of genetic claims about intelligence and race after 1969 was not damaging — the contrast between the arid severities of the renewed psychological arguments and the colloquiality of the *Black Paper* writers became wider. Sir Cyril Burt contributed to the second *Black Paper,* and its opening 'Letter to MPs' noted his claim that standards were lower than '55 years ago, just before the 1914—18 war'. [28] However the analysis was not grounded for long in appeals to experts, and in Britain the resuscitated IQ debate made no sustained impact. Jensen and Eysenck continued to be bitterly

opposed, and suspicions about Burt's work were later very amply backed up —
though discussion of the possibility of later, more adequate 'findings' about
inherited intelligence has never entirely vanished. Instead, the new educational
right came more often to represent its views as a valuable recall to common sense
against the aloof expertise of theorists and bureaucrats. Rhodes Boyson's book was
advertised as 'a distillation of the twenty-four years in which he was a schoolmaster'.

The new ideas moved in three directions. They sought to discredit the achievements, purposes and resource needs of schools as they had been fought for all
through the social democratic consensus. They suggested various constraints and
controls within which schools should now be required to operate, and they argued
for changed terms of reference, which a Labour government was to accept as its
own. St John Stevas boasted, justifiably, to a Conservative Party conference that
the 'Great Debate' was being conducted on Tory ground and that this must be
counted as a triumph.

It would however be a serious, rationalist illusion to think that the essays were
written or read in a systematic way. The preferred manner was polemical: 'children
are not naturally good' was the swaggeringly archaic and 'unfashionable' credo of
1975.[29] The preferred style rested on pithy assertions, appealing to a sediment of
'common sense' and not to the analysis and debate of evidence.

In a 'hard' mode, the suggestion was of awkward truths, fuddled by mealy-
mouthed academics. Alleged 'facts' of inequality were taken as demonstrably
established. The claim in *Black Paper 2* was that working-class children are on
average *innately* less intelligent and, according to Boyson, genetic differences
accounted for '70—80 per cent' of intellectual abilities. To deny such data, the
argument implied, was to be guilty of 'social engineering', in which the pursuit of
equal opportunity amounted to the manipulation of the credulous young for
ulterior motives. In the same way, it was argued (in a new version of social
Darwinism) that competition was as essential to learning as it was to Britain's
economic struggle. The intellectually able should climb on the backs of the weak.
This was a vigorous, healthy process which, on this view, had been stunted by
the rise to power of 'progressive' teachers — variously cranks, anarchists,
sentimentalists and in general permissives, who colluded in the weakening of
authority and in the decline of traditional Christian values. Arthur Pollard told
the National Council for Educational Standards that 'the crucial battle' would be
fought against locally determined 'teacher-controlled' examinations such as the
CSE which represented 'movement . . . to the deliberate breakdown of such unity
of values and knowledge that our society still possesses'.

Evidence of all this was seen in broadly painted brush strokes of school truancy,
anarchy and violence, and by repeated claims of decline in the levels of achievement
in basic skills. A blanket reiteration of key terms — standards, controls — served to
drive out the main social democratic concepts whose discrediting was suggested by
continual inference. 'Remedies' lay in firmer controls. From above, growth should
be curbed: 'it is no good educationalists clamouring for more money when
(education) increases problems, lowers standards and increases widespread

cynicism'.[30] Traditional examinations would provide a goal for learning and a focus of hope for 'clever' working-class children. From below, parents should be given more information and more contact with the school. There should be experiment with a voucher system allowing for parental choice, and the popularity of particular schools would become a 'test of their efficiency'.

In a 'softer' mode, the right revival was also presented in education as it had been (and was to be more) in the area of race relations. It offered itself as the occupation of a sensible middle ground: 'One does not need to be a follower of Ivan Illich or the Black Papers to realise that there is rising doubt about the effectiveness and the values of much modern education.'[31] This kind of sentence managed to define a new 'centre' position which was of course very sharply to the right of the preceding consensus. The suggestion was of an agreed area of normal opinion under threat from ideologues and decent but misguided humanitarians.

Nigel Wright has trenchantly analysed the contradictions and incoherence of the *Black Papers* – their *non sequiturs,* inconsistency and often careless or tendentious handling of evidence.[32] But his intellectual demolition of the essays, in a detached and quasi-legal analysis, seems to strike thin air. The new right's most potent version of its own legitimacy rested on a new educational populism: 'Wherever I go I am besieged by people . . . anxiously questioning the present state of British education', wrote Boyson. [33] Awareness of an educational 'crisis' required no books: 'One only needs to talk to pupils, parents, employers and the general public.' It followed that evidence or even consistency were beside the point. The analysis sought its authority first in an appeal to 'parents', second in a stress on aspirations to mobility which also suggested their actual or potential frustration. It was these two 'moves' in the arguments which preceded but also accounted for their astonishingly high visibility in the 'popular' mass dailies.

The key shift was undoubtedly the appeal to the figure of 'the parent'. This was a basic departure from previous Tory educational work. There was no longer an appeal to 'traditional values' of an ever more obviously partial and selective kind: Boyson's sense of the past was in the Lancashire cotton towns whose history he had researched. Instead the new attitudes were offered as those of parental worry and unspecified popular disquiet – as ratified by the unspoken (though now conveniently articulated) fears of a parental 'silent majority'. In a classic 'populist' manoeuvre, a version of 'ordinary parents' and of parental interests was set against the forces by whom they were scorned.

'The parent' as such could only be a misleading abstraction that overlaid and disguised differences. Yet its ideological reach was considerable. The 'ordinary' parent was particularly reassuring against the permissiveness and rejection of the family imputed to the counter-culture at the turn of the decade. As a reference point, 'the parent' was classless, without gender, and seeking a better life for the child – a generalizing focus for worries about 'the nation' and its children. It was thus a unifying concept, collapsing differences and neutralizing them in a 'classless' ideology. This could then be affirmed positively, as advocated by the party's ideologists, against the 'divisive' and 'anachronistic' concerns with class origin of Labour and the Labour movement which, it was implied, only sealed the working-class child's fate. Attention was turned to 'parent power' and to a version of the 'them' by which its interests were ignored.

The overarching and plausible reference point for the ideology was the exclusion of parents from the processes of schooling, their lack of knowledge about the institutions which their children were legally obliged to attend. To the undoubted lack of involvement was fixed the powerful suggestion of 'what has gone wrong', given the palpable failure of many schools to reach or satisfy children or their parents. In an offered version of 'popular memory', this became the falling from greatness: a weakness and loss of necessary discipline, a lack of attention to the necessary skills and stages of learning. A parental 'us' was rallied against the serried ranks of an indifferent 'them'. As one parent wrote self-consciously in response to *Black Paper 1*:

Please continue with your good work; we 'ordinary' parents are disdained by the powers that be. We are not even considered competent enough for the courtesy of Annual School Reports any more. No wonder the country is in such a mess . . . .

The 'them' could also be broken up and identified. As an essay in *The Conservative Opportunity* (1976) noted, changes in the forms and methods of schooling a decade ago:

led to a great divide in education policy. On one side . . . stood the new educational establishment — administrators, both local and national, leaders of the teachers' unions . . . educational journalists and progressive politicians. On the other . . . stood parents, doubtful and confused.[34]

In the most lurid versions, the parent was set against the dangerous egalitarian whose aim was 'levelling down the higher standards towards a uniform mediocrity', at times in a sweeping conspiracy theory:

Just as the Labour Party and the trades union movement have always acted as an umbrella to shelter crypto-communists and fellow-travellers of all kinds, so the comprehensive platform attracts the educational crank, anarchist, permissivist, sentimentalist as well as some really hard-faced politicians.[35]

In the same way, educational administrators were identified as meddling bureaucrats. The most precise image of the parents' enemy (and after the cartoonists', the most colourful) became the progressive teachers and thinkers whose results could be seen 'all round us, in the growth of anarchy . . . if adults withdraw . . . the result is a vacuum into which all the worst features of the pop and drug world can enter'. Even calmer versions of this view polemically exaggerated the extent of changed teaching methods in schools ('intelligent concern for new methods shades off quickly into the belief that children must . . . never be made to do anything') and collapsed them into a wild variety of vices.

The credibility of these accusations rested on easily invoked uncertainty about new methods of teaching — nor, they suggested, was it clear in whose interests the changes had been made. In reality, the new methods had spread only unevenly and in disparate directions: some of the work had ambitiously rethought the conditions and purposes of learning, while other alterations in the social relations of teachers and taught were little more than strategic ways of retaining control. The necessary condition for the anti-progressive rhetoric was past failure to attach to the innovations any recognizable overall purpose. The accusation then was that progressivism was a fanciful experiment, particularly inimical to working-class education. This could only feed on the uncertainties about the new comprehensives, and the loss of often admired grammar schools, in particular among some Labour voters.

One dramatic climax of the whole 'parental' campaign was carefully orchestrated by Conservative politicians at Tameside around the 'threat' to the grammar schools. The other arrived so conveniently as to avoid the necessity of inventing it. If the William Tyndale school fracas took up many of the *Black Paper* themes and put them in motion, it seemed in particular to show the distance between experiments and unorthodoxies in teaching and the parents, to whom no reference was made: the gap between working-class parents and some teacher versions of working-class education.[36] While the exclusion of 'parents' from educational reforms gave the *Black Paper* writers their general opening, their educational ideology was specifically and surprisingly developed in relation to class opportunity: more precisely, to class frustration.

For if the new right evoked parental bewilderment and anger, it also addressed the fear that avenues of advance through education were being closed off. The founding editors of the *Black Papers* were precisely the scholarship boys (scarcely any reference is made to girls) who had climbed, by hard struggle, the ladder of qualifications whose devaluation they now feared:

both . . . were born in working class areas, and they feel bitter and angry that the fine opportunities given to them in the Grammar Schools in the 1940s are from now on to be denied to children with similar backgrounds.

But it had been a much earlier calculation of the Bow Group, in the early 1960s, that the Conservative Party should seek to appeal to 'an army of young men and women . . . risen out of the working class . . . a parvenu elite picked for their brains'[37] and who would be anxious to distance themselves from 'failures who are left at the bottom because of their innate shortcomings and deficiencies'. Now the whole cast of Conservative ideology, with education as its spearhead, was coming to illustrate Poulantzas's observation that the dominant ideology 'is often permeated by elements stemming from the "way of life" of classes or fractions other than the dominant class or fraction'. *Petit bourgeois* aspirations were everywhere assumed to be central parental motivations. Boyson himself had written of self-organization among the Lancashire working class, and his own work, written as a member of parliament after a long route through teaching to a headmastership, approved of 'self-help and participation' and 'the release of energies these activities always bring'. The emphasis was thus on achievement, on getting on by your own boot-straps, on the determined effort which made such progress possible. Against a fantasy of decadence attributed to the counter-culture, especially its promotion of hedonism against the work ethic, were counterposed the values of individual exertion and struggle: discipline, will, results, measurable advance. Attainment and the recognition of standards of attainment became a key guarantee of mobility and of possible escape. The open appeal was to the chances of avoiding a manual working-class fate. It was always implicit that this could only involve a tiny fraction since the majority's schooling would still deny them a 'good' education. More bluntly it was asserted that, 'without selection the clever working-class child in a deprived area stands little chance of a real academic education' — but, as in gambling, there would at least always be a chance which Labour's 'levelling' would deny.

The *Black Papers* had begun in a series of disconnected pushes, but even these served to 'organize' some of the conventional axiomatic wisdom, the stock of grumbles, which had retained real purchase while social democratic ideas took hold elsewhere: 'up there' in the colleges, government and liberal media. The right's new commentary was inextricable from a version of what had gone wrong, and that version was offered as 'obvious', as common sense. The ideological case turned (more cuttingly amid the beleaguered early 1970s) on the importance of aspirations to a better life and on schools as the central site of their fulfilment; or their frustration. The repeated motif was the warning about the 'holding back' of the clever child — and whose child, for a parent, is not?

The opening stage in the right's advance was therefore to commence the percolation of a new 'common sense' about schools — however half-formed and contradictory. At this point the ideas had a confusing status, combining general arguments with the advocacy of implausible experiments such as a voucher system which an elder statesman such as Angus Maude, for example, thought impracticable in 1971. The party leadership, at first uncertain about the whole shift, became increasingly receptive. Here was not so much an ideology which would either ground or conceal the 'cuts', which were fairly remote from *Black Paper* concerns, but lines and modes of argument which began to justify an active restructuring of the whole educational system. They could prepare the ground for a thoroughgoing alternative settlement, as the consensus began to break up.

Towards a new right policy agenda

The starting point for new policy suggestions followed directly from the belief in the axiomatic importance of competition rather than communality — combined with the acceptance that the eleven plus was now politically irretrievable. As early as 1970, *Black Paper 3* foresaw a time:

when between (say) 5% and 8% of children will qualify for Direct Grant and grammar schools, and other secondary schools — mainly comprehensive — will become the *normal* mode of education, with no stigma attached . . . those who qualify for the Direct Grant and grammar schools will be such a minority, that no sense of failure will be possible for the rest.[38]

Inside the comprehensives, the new emphasis was to be on streaming and setting, in effect allowing for two or three separate kinds of schooling under one roof. Rhodes Boyson, in any case, anticipated the conversion of large comprehensive schools into smaller separate schools of a specialist kind. Equally, he opposed the development of polytechnics in higher education into institutions of university character and status, while proposing that postgraduate fees should be raised 'to discourage our economic rivals from training their manpower cheaply in Britain'.

Even more important was to be the attack on the non-accountability of the education service, particularly on the now extensive powers credited to the teachers. From the centre, monitoring would be increased by a movement towards a standard curriculum for the majority of the syllabus, and by more vigilant work by the government inspectorate. From the local neighbourhood, parents would be given more say through a voucher scheme (whose details were never explored) or through the publication of school results, allowing both for greater pressure on 'less successful' schools and for parental demand that their children should be transferred to schools of a higher standard. Rhodes Boyson, described in a *Times* profile as 'an early Victorian Whig' (his entry in *Who's Who* included 'inciting the millennialistic left in education and politics' under recreation) recalled the more straightforward competitive pressures of early capitalism, when grants depended on school standards. 'This "payment by results" was less unpopular with teachers then than the low standard of schooling now is with parents.' Whether local authorities could possibly deal with the consequences of this system, quite apart from the problems of comparability between schools with blatantly different kinds of problems and wholly unequal resources, was left unspecified. It seemed more likely that the DES, with its own internal reasons for wanting to ensure greater control from the top, would apply checks on teachers and taught from the centre.

Surprisingly, much less was said in the early 1970s about the requirements of employers. Bogdanor's 1976 essay in a collection of articles on conservative thought stressed a wide programme for 'the humanizing of work relationships'.[39] In general, the industrial connections were to be made not by the new right but in Labour's adaptation of the whole agenda.

In some ways, then, the prescriptions implicit in the right's analysis were, polemical rockets about vouchers and so on aside, simple and almost entirely traditional. Spending on the state system, for the vast majority of children, should be curbed, in favour of a concentration on basic skills and work disciplines, under tight central control. There would be strong support for a very small grouping of highly selective state and private schools (though the selection would be based substantially on private income and to a much smaller degree on exceptionally competitive examination). Universities, purged of irrelevant courses and subjects, would be restricted to excellence in conventional disciplines, while polytechnics would be more tightly geared to the needs of local vocational training. For many parents the offered outcome was not the hopeless chimera of equality (now abandoned, it was suggested, in the educational systems of Russia and China), but a return to a degree of order and of basic school achievement.

The originality of the agenda lay in its presentation as a new, campaigning and easily grasped radicalism against the jargon of the mandarins. Its translation into actual policy, already made easier in the ways we have examined, was then crucially facilitated by its passage from the *Black Papers* to the media: above all to both the 'quality' and 'popular' newspapers. For all the quite tireless writing and campaigning of Rhodes Boyson, in particular (to which there was never even faint parallel elsewhere), it was through the reporting of education in the newspapers that the new right was able to 'deliver' its bad news on teachers and schooling.

10 Labour's appropriation: the Great Debate and after

We have tried to show the various conditions for the heightened visibility of a new right assault on the edifice of social democratic assumptions. In this chapter, we examine the rapid accommodation of the Labour government to the right's critique, in its selective appropriation of certain themes as a basis for its own initiatives. Throughout this period, the role of the media, and particularly of the 'popular' press, was exceptionally important and we look at this first.

The media and schooling: general considerations

One crucial step remained before the new right offensive could be politically effective. This was accomplished through the construction of a major 'panic' about schools, which sought to harness widely varying anxieties and discontents about education, and to identify 1960s' policies as their common cause. The implicit proposed remedy then lay at hand in alternative agenda developed by the new right and by certain industrialists. The stages in this process need to be traced in more detail.

We want to draw a distinction here between *popular knowledge* of schools (drawn from experience) and *public opinion about schools* (views claimed as those of a majority of 'the public'). These two cannot always be sharply distinguished, but they certainly do not necessarily coincide: and both have particular political purchases.

Popular knowledge of schools is paradoxical. On the one hand, schools are among the organs of the state which penetrate most deeply into cultural life. They are present in every group of streets, with a large workforce and an even larger and involuntary audience. There can be few people who have not had some recent direct or indirect contact with schools. Given the twin ideologies of the importance of parental aspirations for children and of the role of schooling in opening avenues of social mobility, that contact is often invested with a deep concern for children's futures. On the other hand, popular knowledge of schooling has a peculiar structure. Direct contact between adults and schools tends to be restricted, both geographically and in the type of contact made: though middle-class parents may be less ambiguous in their attitude to schooling. Despite recent attempts at strengthening relations between home and school, the connections have remained infrequent and mainly formal. A teacher ideology of professionalism has often ensured that the day-to-day world of schools has remained a closed book for the majority of the 'lay' population. Few adults know directly what contemporary schools are actually like.

The same cannot be said of pupils, of whom attendance is required, and whose knowledge of schooling is intimate and sometimes painful. This knowledge is however only selectively communicated to adults and may itself be discounted because children are thought unreliable informants. It is in this context, of schools being close and emotionally charged, yet not open to direct adult knowledge, that the media have a powerful position. They provide their audiences with pictures of what schools are like; they may suggest how schools differ from adults' childhood memories; they can provide interpretations of what is happening inside schools. A typification of actors, actions and motives is thus on offer which can supplement or stand in for the limits of direct adult contemporary school experience. Media campaigns can exploit the gaps between situated knowledge and memory of particular experiences and an abstract knowledge of the school system as a whole: it is in the gap that the media's power to construct general explanations 'connecting' the one to the other can operate forcefully. This ideological work has crucial bearings on educational policy. At the most simple level the media can determine the visibility of education as 'news'.

In normal circumstances, when it is not operating as a more general metaphor of social crisis, schooling is given only routine coverage in the media. It is not usually a subject of news at all for the popular press, while in the 'quality' press, coverage has been restricted to reports by accredited correspondents and comment from accredited experts. Such coverage is often in sections of a newspaper specifically designated as of interest only to readers already informed about the area. At times of major policy debate or controversy, the visibility and volume of 'education news' rise sharply and the emphases of its presentation change. Schooling ceases to be the province of specialist writers and readers and becomes general news on which all may comment. In such periods, its connections with other troubling social issues and themes become more pronounced: schooling may condense other 'crisis' themes and become a displaced metaphor for them. The structuring of education as a news topic can then have effects on school politics and policies through the operation of specific mechanisms.

Debates about 'specialist' areas are often first generated by pressure groups such as the *Black Paper* authors who make an impact in the media because of the 'controversial' views they hold. At an early stage, the media take-up of such arguments may be quite independent of popular concerns or any interest in those concerns. In a 'panic' of any substance or duration, it is the media's work to claim connections between the two, to try and ground the one in the other. Here, it is the specific activity of the media to 'find' public discontent which can be aligned or identified with the emerging agenda, to suggest that what is being said in the councils of specialist writers is in fact echoing and echoed by the experience of the lay public. Once this connection has been forged the topic has ceased to be marginal. The popular media have a special role to play in this process since they represent themselves as the voice of the ordinary readers – as merely voicing a 'public opinion' which they then invoke as the basis for a widening campaign, including calls for action. While in mass democracies, the views of a small group may be dismissed as of minority interest only, suggestions that these minority views have been substantiated in the experience of the general public can become a 'fact' which politicians can scarcely afford to ignore. Once the connection has been constructed between a minority's agenda and the force of a majority, but silent public opinion, which the media claims to 'articulate' on its behalf, a basis for a longer running campaign has been set up. The invoking of 'public opinion' provides platform and legitimacy for the newspaper's policy recommendations: 'the people' want something to be done. The weight of opinion thus conjured can then be used to give the topic an added urgency, enabling the stigmatization or exclusion of those taking a different view who are now 'out of touch' with public feeling or complacent about problems which 'everyone' recognizes. In these ways, a new set of assumptions may be given a populist character or inflexion. Definitions of the problem become self-evident and self-fulfilling. The gaps and uncertainties of popular knowledge have attained the confident coherence of 'public opinion'. The power of the media is, by this stage, such that it can force problems structured in a particular way on to the policy agenda and demand their resolution through policy changes.

The 'Daily Mail' and the 'Daily Mirror'

It is from this perspective that we can better understand the media's role during the 1970s. A full history of the ideological work preparatory to the 'Great Debate' would need to connect together a range of government and research reports, the activities of the new right propagandists, and the various branches of the media. Such a project lies outside our limits here, but we can outline some of the key processes through an analysis of two newspapers, the *Daily Mail* and the *Daily Mirror*, between 1975 and 1977.[1]

We chose to look at the *Daily Mail* and *Daily Mirror* because they represented the 'opposite' ends of the political spectrum on offer in the popular newspapers. Moreover, they both had specialist education correspondents, while their combined readership between July and December 1977 has been estimated at over 17 million. We took a rolling sample of these papers which gave us 312 editions of each, representing one third of all editions published in 1975, 1976 and 1977. During these years a *Daily Mirror* reader would on average find a seventh of a page every other day given to education items, the *Daily Mail* reader on average a quarter of a page, daily. This averaging out conceals the regular 'big splash' effect of special features, but in any case what is more important is the ways in which educational topics were structured.

Despite some important differences, there was a shared structure of assumptions and definitions informing the contributions of the two papers to the newly prominent controversies around schooling. What was presented as a 'debate' was in effect a monologue concentrating on items concerning teachers' lack of professional competence or the negative aspects of pupil behaviour. These two categories, only two out of the thirty-four in our coding system, accounted for about one fifth of the *Daily Mail*'s total coverage and approximately a third of the *Daily Mirror*'s Altogether we could find only two items on nursery education, three on class size, one each on the NUSS and on sexism in the curriculum, whereas 60 per cent of the 595 items in the sample concentrated on unfavourable accounts of school developments.

The weight of negative reporting is impressive but it is important to examine the logic behind such a push. We were tempted to look at the institutional positions of the various highlighted spokesmen, and then to ask whether a 'balanced' view was being presented. The severe limitations of this notion of balance were here in any case matched by its unhelpfulness: no discernible pattern emerged. Instead the key to understanding the selection of spokesmen lay with the fit between their message and an already established agenda (and we should emphasize that most commentators concerned were men). In effect, the message itself largely defined the propriety of the spokesmen. How else could we understand the highlighting in the *Daily Mail* of complaints by the light entertainment personality Hughie Greene that the IRA Marylebone siege and the standard of applicants to his television programme shared common roots in the schooling system *(Daily Mail*, 10 February 1975)? An apparently random collection of speakers were united only by their message to whose continuities we now turn.

Central to the reporting were pictures of the current state of British schooling. Images of incompetence, slovenly, subversive or just trendy teachers who had failed to teach or control the undisciplined pupils in their charge became too familiar to need elaboration. Background actors — wild-eyed theorists, out-of-touch bureaucrats and the complacent self-interested leaders of some unions — were as often sketched. Counterposed to these were some dedicated teachers, particular union leaders and the occasional bureaucrat who had been forced to face up to reality. The lay actors in the drama were seen as those imbued with common sense who were worried about falling standards — industrialists and parents fearful of reprisals about their children:

Protests to headmasters or governors usually meet with hostility. Protests to the bureaucrats at County Hall are even more hopeless. Anyway, most parents are frightened that if they make too much fuss, their children will suffer. [*Daily Mail*, 18 January 1955]

As for the new right, they were typified in the figures of Rhodes Boyson and the *Black Paper* authors who 'care passionately about standards' and are 'the real radicals' (*Daily Mail*, 2 April 1975) who 'in spite of a hail of abuse . . . refused to be silenced' (*Daily Mail*, 27 October 1975). Their opponents on the other hand were 'political fanatics' who had 'brought education into politics and condemned thousands of children to live below the best' (*Daily Mail*, 10 November 1976). These actors were then presented in dramatic extremes through the coverage of the William Tyndale dispute, while the BBC's *Panorama* film on Faraday High School confirmed some of the images.[2]

These pictures crystallized the matter into a specific cluster of issues and of suggested solutions. The reforms of the 1960s, especially the introduction of progressive methods and of comprehensives, were held responsible for an alleged decline in general standards and basic skills, for a lack of social discipline and the incongruence between the worlds of school and of work. The themes were broadened next to fears that 'British society as we have always known it is about to end' (*Daily Mail*, 8 January 1976), that industry was no longer competitive, delinquency increasing ('the infant muggers' – *Daily Mail* headline, 3 April 1975) and a lurid American future in sight. They were further unified by the proposed solutions – a greater control of schooling by non-teachers and a return to the traditional competitive education system. Although the means to these ends were various, parents were singled out as the group who would ensure that a traditional approach and its standards were maintained. Actual mechanisms for introducing 'parent power' involved the retention of selection and private schools as counter to the state system's imputed follies, the introduction of vouchers and the reform of governing bodies to give parents greater constitutional power. It was suggested that greater control would be achieved through the introduction of minimum standards which would be nationally applied and regularly tested. Industrialists, with their inside 'evidence' of decline would gain power, while that of the teacher unions would be diminished, so fostering closer links between schooling and the labour process.

Such was an outline of the agenda in our sample, and we now want to show how it was forced into policy considerations. One simple but effective means was the constant reiteration of themes to the exclusion of competing themes, so that specific interpretations sponsored by the agenda became axioms within the arena.

Readers learned, for instance, that 'the brutal truth is that standards have fallen' (*Daily Mail*, 4 November 1976), that 'literacy in Britain is marching backwards' (*Daily Mirror*, 7 February 1975) and that a *Daily Mirror* reporter had not 'the slightest doubt that general educational standards have slipped alarmingly in the past decade or so' (April 1976). By the time the Prime Minister opened the 'Great Debate' the *Daily Mirror*'s front page splash was 'Crisis in the classroom', while the *Daily Mail* could introduce its own 'great national debate into what has gone wrong with our schools' (14 October 1976). Once these themes had been repeated so often as to make them self-evident, the papers could employ previous reports (from their own paper or others) as evidence for further reports about, for example, the 'mounting backlash against progressive methods' (*Daily Mirror*, 26 April 1976) or the 'fact' that 'most parents and many teachers believe that children are less literate and numerate than they were 20 years ago' (*Daily Mail*, 9 July 1976). Lest readers suspected a touch of sensationalism, the *Daily Mail* assured them that 'the individual acts of classroom violence that you read about – frequently you may think – do not, even so, represent the real scale of the problem' (*Daily Mail*, 24 October 1975). This was a process of circular validation that enabled the new right and others to adduce the press discussion as 'evidence' of 'concern' when demanding the admission of the new agenda into parliamentary debate. Rhodes Boyson found it 'very difficult to obtain comparative figures over a period of years. Accordingly, we have to rely on indications gleaned from speeches, reports and researches'.

This raises the question of the sources of assertions which were cross-referenced to each other between the press, *Black Papers* and the speeches and writings of Boyson himself. Certainly, we could not find even one example which took up any of the powerful critiques of the assertions. Wright's *Progress in Education* (1977)[3] was a rigorous review of evidence relevant to the new arguments, though its conclusions pointed in a quite different direction. He claimed to find 300 errors of fact in Boyson's 160 page *Crisis in Education* alone.[4] No mention of this was found in our sample. Similarly, the severe criticisms made of Bennett's Lancaster study of *Teaching Styles and Pupil Progress,* [5] interpreted in the popular dailies as an indictment of progressive teachers, went unmentioned.

Indeed the treatment of counter evidence was revealing. The *Daily Mail* (24 March 1977) reported a press conference at which the accuracy of Boyson's figures was challenged. The challenge received a three word reference ('allegedly suspect figures'), the reply some 25 column centimetres. This included a justification of the need to 'toss hand grenades and lay land mines to trap the opposition' and to 'smoke out the local education authorities and force them to publish exactly how the comprehensives were doing', as well as the need for externally audited results and not internal figures 'that could be fudged'. The rest of the article restated the agenda, with particular emphasis on comprehensives and standards. Similarly the Bullock Committee's arguments[6] on standards and testing did not fit the agenda and were promptly condemned by the *Daily Mail* (19 February 1975) as 'W H I T E W A S H spells whitewash'. Sir Alan Bullock's Report on the teaching of English 'shrouds the reality in trendy pieties', while the *Daily Mirror* referred to it as 'the Bullock Report on Illiteracy' (19 February 1975).

Not only was the space given to the different perspectives important, but so also was the status ascribed to these positions. The agenda was presented as directly deriving from the natural order of things, so relegating any challenge to that agenda to the status of unreality. As the agenda was represented as being fundamentally connected to themes of natural rights and justice, the *Daily Mail* could greet the dockworkers (castigated a few years previously) as the 'voice of reason': 'dockers who earn good money defend their right to spend it on bingo or booze or educating their children at direct grant schools if they so choose' (24 October 1975). This theme of freedom and the right to choose served also as a basis for the defence of selection, its abolition representing 'a brand of unfairness — the denial of a strict formal education to children who would have liked one' and a denial of the natural order since 'we know how much our children vary . . . no one system is going to be perfect for all of them' (*Daily Mail*, 21 April 1975). The portrayal of standards proceeded in a similar vein as if there were, or could be, no debate about what 'standards' were or whether they were the self-evident goal of education — 'you see it's not educational standards that concern these politicians it's political theory. And the two don't make a healthy mix' (*Daily Mail*, 11 November 1976).

As for teachers, the *Daily Mail* argued that 'many schools are refusing the blandishments of the progressives and as a result are maintaining good standards' (13 January 1975), while the pronouncements of the National Association of Schoolmasters 'had the ring of sturdy common sense in stark contrast to the platitudes of the politicians and the starry eyed idealists who put them into the mess' (5 April 1975). One axis of the press's operation was just this representation of the agenda as rooted in a sturdy common sense – the 'reality' to which 'theory bears very little relationship' (*Daily Mail*, 19 July 1976), the 'simple truths' to which 'extraordinary as it may seem' many staffrooms would need to be converted by a 'big crusade' (*Daily Mail*, 5 April 1975). Inequalities were thereby naturalized, authoritarian pedagogies buttressed and any signs of the agenda's adoption in policy greeted as a 'sign of a return to sanity' (*Daily Mirror*, 14 October 1976).

The other, related strategy involved the construction of an image of the popular voice speaking through the press's mouthpiece. There were confident assertions that 'millions of parents are desperately worried about the education their children are receiving' (*Daily Mail*, 27 April 1976) and that 'parents throughout the country are becoming increasingly frustrated by the lack of discipline and the low standards of state schools' (*Daily Mail*, 18 January 1975). Even more potent was the version of a child's voice, desperately appealing for fair treatment: 'please sir don't be trendy' (*Daily Mirror*, 26 April 1976). Although indiscipline in schools was freely linked to industrial disruption and social delinquency, the majority of children were 'decent hard working individuals who want nothing more than to get on with their studies in peace' (*Daily Mail*, 3 April 1975), while – in an exceptional moment – even violence was accorded a rationality caused by 'the impotence and frustration of children who realised that they had been cheated by progressive schools and had not reached a good standard' (*Daily Mail*, 13 January 1975). What were exponents of a child-centred pedagogy to do if even children were demanding a return to more formal methods?

Finally, newspaper reports consistently displayed elements of self-fulfilling prophecies. If teachers defended the 'progressive orthodoxy', it was because they were 'sloppy in their own teaching . . . hopeless in keeping order. So it is very convenient for them to find a philosophy which justifies the freedom of children to do what they want' (*Daily Mail*, 18 December 1975). Such teachers 'dare not admit how low standards have actually sunk' (*Daily Mail*, 19 February 1975), while apparently clinching reports such as the media's version of the Bennett research were only the tip of an iceberg because of a 'conspiracy of silence' among teachers (*Daily Mail*, 24 October 1975). In the same way, theorists and administrators had suppressed the evidence: the *Daily Mail* wrote of the 'fanatical idealism of the bureaucrats and lecturers who refused to see what was happening even when it was pointed out to them' (2 October 1976). Thus the paper was finally able to write off its antagonists in a tone of 'mission accomplished': 'the conclusion cannot be ducked. It isn't that the experts couldn't see what was happening. It is that they didn't want to' (*Daily Mail*, 22 July 1977).

The disintegration of social democratic assumptions then came together with the new agenda and the weight of press polemic to allow its grateful and agile adoption by the Labour leadership. Shirley Williams adopted the argument that 'there is no greater betrayal of a child than to fail to provide him or her with the basic skills for work and life' (*Daily Mirror*, 8 January 1977). The same report noted the convergence of Williams, Callaghan and Boyson, just as the 1977 Green Paper accounted for Callaghan's Ruskin speech on education, as Prime Minister, as being 'made against a background of strongly critical comments in the press and elsewhere on education and educational standards'.[7]

It would be wrong to suggest that the *Daily Mail* and the *Daily Mirror* were one and the same creature. The residual character of the *Daily Mirror*'s commitment to a social democratic morality of provision was evidenced in occasional responses to the course of the 'Great Debate' and in the writings of such correspondents as John Pilger who challenged the debate's assumptions as though they were the emperor's clothes (18 October 1976). But it was through the largely shared language of crisis in the press and the mainly agreed agenda for action that governmental response was triggered. The *Daily Mirror* praised the Green Paper authors for having done their homework, while the *Daily Mail* was forgivably triumphant:

The penny has dropped. The government has finally made it official: our schools are not wonderful. Mrs Shirley Williams, the Education Secretary, has published a Green Paper which puts forward ideas to be discussed not decisions to be taken. But it reads strangely like another Black Paper . . . eight years later behind the usual bureaucratic bromides the educational establishment has at long last admitted that the Black Paper's criticisms of school standards were largely justified . . . The *Daily Mail* is delighted that things we have been saying for years are finally beginning to trickle through. [22 July 1977]

The employers' critique

The need for some new strategy towards education was, meanwhile, emphasized in increasingly vocal terms by a section of employers' representatives, as well as other industrial interests. Their concerns echoed many of those of the *Black Papers* especially the theme of teacher accountability. In addition they stressed their own theme: the need to restructure the relationship between schooling and industry. This was not in itself particularly novel. What was significant was their appropriation of the right's critique at a time of rising youth unemployment. Schools were therefore held responsible, at least in part, for the scale − if not the fact − of youth unemployment.

In early 1976, an article by Arnold Weinstock, managing director of the General Electric Company, was published in *The Times Educational Supplement*. Entitled 'I blame the teachers', it suggested that the shortage of skilled workers, especially in engineering, could be attributed to the anti-industry attitudes of many teachers. Weinstock alleged that such teachers usually lacked any direct experience of industry, yet were left free to propagate views based on that inexperience. Such freedom to operate, without any external control over what was taught and without accountability to the wider community was, for Weinstock, the source of the problem. The malaise, he argued, could be remedied in some practical ways, and his prescriptions in this respect were to be characteristic of much subsequent discussion:

Experience indicates that tightly administered organisations, in which you get on if you are good and get out if you are bad, have higher morale and provide more job satisfaction than their opposites. So perhaps a re-look at this side of the education system would be in the interests of teachers as well as the community. [*The Times Educational Supplement*, 23 January 1976]

This focus on the shortcomings of schools, mainly the accusation of failure to prepare young people for work because of casual attitudes among teachers, also involved other dimensions. John Methven, Director General of the CBI, stressed a line of demarcation between the responsibilities of schools and those of employers while resisting attempts to persuade employers to increase their numbers of young workers:

Employers are firmly of the view that shortcomings in the vocational preparation of young people are basically an educational problem which cannot be passed on to employers under the guise of training and induction. [*The Times Educational Supplement*, 29 October 1976]

As the argument that schooling should be concerned with the deliberate and selective preparation of the future labour force was being established, another rationale had been introduced into discussions, that of social justice. The failure of schools to respond to the pressing needs of the economy, could be represented as both reducing prospects of economic recovery and failing the children concerned because their education would be irrelevant to their future working situations. For example, Joe Rogaly of *The Financial Times* offered a typical summary and suggested that the question of curriculum content was of central importance, since:

industry is suffering from an undereducated workforce, while many working class children are being given the added disadvantage of a non-education on top of all their other burdens. [*The Financial Times*, 3 January 1976]

As we have shown in our discussion of the media campaigns, criticisms of education and the specific failure of schools became well-established features of a wider political discourse. The added voice of employers, with their concern at allegedly declining standards of literacy and numeracy, served to clinch the political climate in which new forms of intervention became possible. It was on this basis that plans for the Great Debate were laid.

The Yellow Book

Shortly after becoming Prime Minister in the spring of 1976, Mr Callaghan instituted a series of meetings with ministers, the first of which was held with Fred Mulley, the Secretary of State for Education. Following this meeting the Prime Minister called for a paper to be prepared on four aspects of the educational scene. These areas — primary education and the '3 Rs', the later years of compulsory education, examinations, and the education of 16–19-year-olds — were discussed in what came to be known within the DES as the Yellow Book. The report, prepared by the inspectorate, offered both a critique of schooling and a series of proposals which the government could incorporate as policy.

The Yellow Book illustrated the general cast of thinking which went into the making of the Great Debate, at least on the part of the inspectorate: mainly that it was to be an exercise in persuasion and the construction of consent. The required object, an increased centralization of control over the actual practices of schooling, would be sought through a political campaign rather than through administrative dictates.

The formal, legal approach, had, in the case of the rebellious Tameside local authority, generated a great deal of political criticism for the Labour Party. By forcing, or attempting to force Tameside to adopt a comprehensive policy during the summer of 1976, the government had avoided a political argument over comprehensivization *per se* by using a recourse to law as the sole level of struggle. The subsequent Education Act, which took up more time than the entire 1944 Act, was primarily intended to drive through that change, yet in achieving that aim, it left the real political initiatives with the right. Recalcitrant local authorities were still able to buy time in their struggle against comprehensivization, thereby protracting the issue and giving renewed weight to criticisms of the government as authoritarian.

The lead-up to the formal announcement of the 'Great Debate' was featured by a series of leaks to the press, the *Guardian* in particular, which hinted at some draconian move on the part of the government and the DES against teacher autonomy, through the imposition of some kind of national curriculum. This enabled the initiative to remain with the side of the DES, while the teachers' organizations, in particular, gave vent to their anger in anticipating of the worst. In the event, the main line of development which the Yellow Book proposed was the extension of the work undertaken by the Assessment of Performance Unit (APU), which would be charged with identification and definition of standards which children might be expected to attain. But here the situation of teachers was of critical importance since their representation on the Schools Council, given its existing constitution, could effectively block any significant changes in curricula innovation. Thus it was the Schools Council, and teacher representation on it, which was challenged by the Yellow Book. It proposed that the workings of the Schools Council should be examined, and that every effort should be made to increase the relations between schools and the world of work. The document therefore served as a briefing and a guide to the themes which Mr Callaghan was to take up in his speech at Ruskin College in October 1976.

Ruskin

The speech which Callaghan delivered at Ruskin College, Oxford, a well-prepared media event, proved to be slightly more sober in tone than some commentators had anticipated, and feared. Rather than confronting an expectant nation with a simple programme, Callaghan proposed a debate around the themes he was to outline. However it was also clear that the entire exercise was to be undertaken within the limits of a 'reality' imposed by a pressing set of economic factors:

There is a challenge to us all in these days and a challenge in education is to examine its priorities and to secure as high efficiency as you can by the skilful use of the £6 billion of existing resources. Let me repeat some of the fields that need study because they cause concern. There are the methods and aims of informal instruction. The strong case for so-called core curriculum of basic knowledge. What is the proper way of monitoring the use of resources in order to maintain a proper national standard of performance? What is the role of the inspectorate in relation to national standards and their maintenance? And there is a need to improve relations between industry and education.[8]

These leading questions, posed by a Labour Prime Minister, signalled a fundamental shift in the debate about educational means and ends. It marked, at the highest political level, the formal end of the long post-war phase of educational expansion which had been largely promoted by the party of which he was leader. The speech was therefore a declaration — a public redefinition of educational objectives — as well as a response to the more immediate events of economic crisis, cuts in public expenditure and the polemical weight of the Tory critique of Labour's educational past. Callaghan's speech crystallized many aspects of the contemporary situation.

The change in formal stance towards the teachers was an important shift for the leader of the Labour Party to register. By arguing the necessity for external controls on teaching and teachers, he both signalled an 'open season' on educational issues, in which teachers would fare badly, but also assumed a position — in popular terms — which was difficult to distinguish from that of the *Black Paper* authors. This is not to suggest that the sentiments expressed were wholly original for Labour leaders. During 1969, for example, suggestions that tighter controls on teachers might be forthcoming had been made in order to curb an increasingly militant teaching force. Edward Short, then Secretary of State for Education, addressing the 1969 NAS Conference, had pointed out that for teachers to act as other groups of workers could lead to unpalatable consequences. Militant trade unionism was incompatible with the job of teaching:

Do we really want a rule book which will lay down the minutiae of how the teacher is to do his job? Let me assure you that you are within weeks of considerable pressure to introduce one . . . once begun the process might be difficult to halt and impossible to reverse.[9]

Callaghan's inauguration of the Great Debate at Ruskin College was, as we have noted, a carefully staged media event. The speech secured maximum publicity being the main news item of the day, indeed of the immediate period surrounding its delivery. Although more conciliatory in tone than had been anticipated, it clearly set in process that movement which Short had observed might be 'impossible to reverse' at least in the short term.

The suggestions contained in the Yellow Book and taken up by Callaghan, in particular those about a core curriculum, were rightly recognized as being at the crux of the relationship between the state and education. As the *Guardian* editorial commented, before the Ruskin speech, on the existence of the Yellow Book, 'shudders will be seismically recorded in many teachers' common rooms today'. But in the case of the *Guardian,* some rearrangement in the patterns of control was regarded as clearly necessary:

Only the naive believe teachers can be left to teach, administrators to administer and managers to manage. Anyone who believes this should be led gently to the report of the William Tyndale inquiry, which demonstrates the difficulties of drawing clear boundaries of accountability in education.[10]

It went on to paraphrase the Yellow Book which had argued that:

A further weakness, as we may now perceive it, is that some teachers and some schools may have overemphasized the importance of preparing boys and girls for their roles in society compared with the need to prepare them for their economic role.[11]

Whatever the nice distinctions which can be made between an exclusively 'economic' role as opposed to one which is concerned with one's place 'in society', the tone of the Yellow Book and the Callaghan speech made for an unambiguous reading in some places. Rhodes Boyson offered the response that:

For ten years I have been advocating a return to standards. There will be a great sigh of relief among parents and Black Paper writers everywhere. Let me say we don't mind which government does this and I welcome Mr Callaghan's initiative.[12]

If Boyson's comments represent anything they show that Callaghan's intervention was at least successful in one immediate respect, mainly that of securing an initiative and gaining short-term political consent. At that moment the opposing political forces appeared to have been reconciled, with other positions marginalized from the debate, including those recently occupied by the Labour Party itself.

While the Great Debate was concerned with the wider cultivation of political consent, through a series of eight regional conferences which would discuss a prepared agenda (set out in *Educating our Children* (1977) published by the DES), there were obvious limits to the number of active participants involved. Initial expectations, that there might be an exercise in some kind of participatory democracy in the discussion of issues, were quickly shattered when it became clear that only 200 invited guests and the press would be invited to the different legs of the debate. Likewise the conference agendas, concerned as they were with the curriculum, assessment, teacher training and the relationship between school and life, addressed issues which had been constructed as being of concern to parents, but which did not necessitate parental involvement to resolve them. Rather, as Callaghan had proposed at Ruskin, 'what a wise parent would wish for their children, so the state must wish for all its children'. In the context, parental 'interests' were to be represented through the rational organization, by the state, of the school to work transition, and the matching of the appropriate skills and aptitudes to the needs of the labour market. Schooling and its social purposes were therefore to be politically subordinated to the perceived needs of a capitalist economy in the throes of crisis. A restructuring was required because of the failure of schools to fulfil the older social democratic equation that investment in education would produce economic benefits.

The political calculation involved then was the extent to which a new set of requirements could be introduced without actual confrontation. Shirley Williams, in an ambiguity characteristic of the period, argued that there was of course no intention to interfere at the level of the classroom: 'among the splendours of the English system are its flexibility, its imagination and the freedom of the teacher in the classroom'. Yet irrespective of disputes about standards, 'requirements are constantly rising . . . an increasingly complex industrial society demands better educated and trained young people'.[13]

In early 1977, the *Guardian* printed a confidential memorandum, prepared jointly in the Treasury and the Departments of Industry, Education and Employment, which identified the relationship between the government's economic strategy and the educational debate. The strategy, grandly, would need to be developed 'in a way which can provide a confident vision of the future and awaken a sense of national pride which we have not seen since the last war was won and the Empire was lost'.[14] The preference was for an approach based on the informal pressure of public opinion combined with national monitoring, which 'should provide a psychological impetus for the teaching profession', and this, added to 'greater stability in the profession now that posts are more difficult to find may help to raise standards more than any amount of overt exhortation'. The 'Great Debate' thus operated primarily as the final stage of legitimation for administrative and policy changes already prepared — perhaps the most overtly cynical example of Labour's preference for changes administered downwards with a brief show of token consultation. As *The Times Educational Supplement* pointed out in summary, 'the trappings . . . are unimportant alongside the climatic changes in received opinions which (the debate) was intended to proclaim'.[15] Basic problems about the relation of national government to local authorities remained unresolved: the formal imposition of new controls would have generated resistances which otherwise found no specific targets when faced with a more general and less visible 'public' redefinition of the field.

In the immediate wake of the Ruskin speech, local initiatives were at once apparent. In Liverpool a committee was set up to establish the possibility of a core curriculum and of methods of assessing attainment at 11, 13 and 16.[16] Elsewhere the school—work relation was taken up between schools and local authorities. The national response appeared as the government's July 1977 Green Paper *Education in Schools,* offered as a judicious summary of the 'debate' and approvingly greeted, as we have seen, in the press. The text of the paper has been analysed in some detail and with a certain sophistication by James Donald.[17] However we will look at the four main topics taken up in the document in order to examine some more general developments.

Themes

Curriculum and standards

The problem of defining what should constitute the school curriculum was all the greater because an advisory body, the Schools Council, already existed for that purpose, while the local take-up of curriculum innovation depended on the decisions of the headteachers. These difficulties lay behind the text's blandness:

The Secretaries of State will therefore seek to establish a broad agreement with their partners in the education service on a framework for the curriculum, and, particularly, on whether, because there are aims common to all schools and to all pupils at certain stages, there should be a 'core' or 'protected part'.[18]

Apart from the assumption of communality of interests shared by all pupils (which would lead us to consider the place of the private sector) there is only an allusion to the Schools Council's role, though it must have represented the primary inhibition to action. When Sir David Eccles had made a similar proposal in 1962, through the device of the ministry-based Curriculum Study Group, he had met the united resistance both of the National Union of Teachers and of the Association of Education Committees. The result of that encounter was, precisely, the Schools Council which, under the influence of strong teacher representation in the 1960s, had become identified with the introduction of progressive theory and practice, endorsing teacher professionalism and freedom of operation. Under considerable pressure the council was thus influenced to reform its constitutions, reducing teacher representation, during 1977.

Equally, the notion of a common core, a specific list of subjects and of attainment levels for every state school, was again strongly resisted by teachers, especially by the National Union of Teachers, as an encroachment on professional work against pupils' best interests. Yet some kind of core batch of subjects was required for any comparative testing. This was a problem besetting the department's Assessment of Performance Unit in its task of monitoring performance in such basic skills as literacy and mathematical competence, and of defining assessment criteria. Again, the paper only alluded to the difficulties.

A further obliquity characterized the claim that 'young people need to be equipped with a basic understanding of the functioning of our democratic political system, of the mixed economy and the industrial activities, especially manufacturing, which create our national wealth'. Contemporary political events included controversy over the National Front and its activities, but on questions of race and politics little was said. It was pointed out at the Bradford 'Great Debate' that no black faces were present and the question of racism was not confronted. The paper's own mention of race was brief:

It would be short sighted to think of the establishment in this country of communities of overseas origin only in terms of the problems they present. We should welcome the enrichment of our culture which these communities can provide if only we have the imagination to accept it.[19]

It was the combining of the hidden theme of race with concern about the consequences of youth unemployment which gave edge to proposals for more deliberate political penetration. In the later part of 1977, following events at Lewisham and National Front campaigns involving school children, there was strong press comment about extremist politics in schools. Proposals (such as those sponsored by the Hansard Society)[20] towards the development of organized political education in schools proliferated. For Shirley Williams it was important to 'try to edge young people away from the margins of politics and into the main-stream because, apart from the intrinsic dangers of extremes, those who spend their energies at the margins will find that they have wasted them, as so many found after the 1930s'. The concern for remedial action around political education sat uneasily next to the limited definition of the core curriculum and the issues remained unresolved.

Teachers

The sheer size of the teaching force, and the readiness of teacher unions to contemplate withdrawal of labour, meant that teachers needed to be approached with caution:

It is on the supply of good teachers in adequate numbers that the strength of the education system must rest. There is no hope of implementing the proposals in this paper without the full understanding and support of the teaching profession.[21]

The winning of teacher consent was, however, no simple task. Arguments that the qualifications of new teachers must be improved were uncontentious — indeed the teacher unions had argued for many years that this was important. The idea, for example, of an all graduate teaching force was seen as enhancing teacher status and was already a component of the professional ideology so enthusiastically pursued by teacher unions. But suggestions that greater control should be exerted over the actual teaching situation — at the 'chalk face' — directly contradicted the entire ethos of professionalism, the central premises of which involved the concept of autonomy. Faced with the possibility of the state prescribing a curriculum, or at least specifying a central 'core' of subjects, the teacher unions — especially the NUT — made their disagreement apparent. The work of the Assessment of

Performance Unit at the DES was an additional cause of concern, being identified as the tool by which the state could directly encroach on the autonomy of the teacher in the classroom. The Green Paper's announcement that the APU would embark on a programme of national assessment of the school system reinforced the pressure on teachers, despite disclaimers that the state had no intention of imposing a national curriculum: the testing syndrome was clearly concerned with the testing of teachers as much as it was with measuring the attainment of pupils.

That the state strategy incorporated the concept of consent as opposed to any direct coercion in relation to teachers, well indicated the entrenched nature of professionalism as an occupational ideology. But it would be wrong to assign too great a power to it. With a declining job market, and a surplus of trained teachers — newly qualified ones in particular — the teaching situation had become one in which resources and security were scarce assets. The constant tension between support for a 'professional' stance which eschewed militant action and the need for united trade union response was therefore particularly evident.

In some respects teacher unions were directly involved in supporting those proposals for the control of teachers which emerged during the Great Debate, at least in the sense of 'weeding out' the 'politically motivated' so beloved of press demonology. This position characterized the responses of the NAS/UWT for whom a teaching force purged of the politically suspect could only further the long-term cause of the profession. The opprobrium of the supporters of a 'professional' attitude was, for example, directed at those trainee teachers whose behaviour at the Bradford leg of the Great Debate brought the conference to a premature end. Students from a nearby college effectively disrupted the spectacle of the regional conference by protesting at college closures and the scale of teacher unemployment, thereby dramatically capturing the contradiction between the alternative modes of teacher response to the Great Debate — compliant acquiescence or a more vigorous mode of resistance.[22]

The control of teachers as an objective of policy remained abstract unless considered in the context of the individual school. At that level, the real holder of teacher 'autonomy' was the headteacher, since it was the head who was the effective watchdog over the activities of the teachers in the school. That the head-teacher required a separate scrutiny was argued in the course of the regional conferences during the Great Debate, and resonances of those arguments appeared in the Green Paper. But the Green Paper's call for care in the appointment of heads was moderate when compared to the injunctions from other quarters. The House of Commons Expenditure Committee in its report, *The Attainments of the School Leaver,* proposed the more radical solution: 'the DES should seek by all means possible to promote the concept of limited tenure for Headteachers on the understanding that there would be previously agreed criteria for evaluation'.[23] The control strategy was therefore given a single point of purchase, the most conspicuous representative of the individual school and the one who was best placed to ensure an adequate 'policing' operation. Thus a contemporary form of payment by results could be enacted. Although the proposals were not yet incorporated into any legislation, the political consequences could be easily anticipated as inducing a sense of caution and wariness into the actions of head-teachers. Who in those circumstances would so readily dispute the current orthodoxy, or resist the wider definitions imposed on the conduct of individual schools? As with teachers more generally, the desired effects appeared to be as much concerned with inhibiting the activity of the headteacher in favour of the dominant orthodoxy, rather than actual prescription.

During the Great Debate and the construction of the political climate surrounding it, we have noted that the role of the 'parent' and that of the wider 'community' were frequently counterposed to the domain of the teacher. Parents were seen as the embodiment of that 'common sense' required in the teaching situation, and a necessary redress to the influence of the unrestrained expert or pedagogue. But the actual extent of parental involvement in the process of schooling was problematic when displaced from the merely rhetorical level. These limitations became apparent when the issue of school government was directly addressed.

Schools and the community

During the regional conference, which constituted the participatory element of the Great Debate, parents were formally represented, but more often invoked as an absent but interested party. In effect, parents were spectators to the professional and political deliberations rather than active agents in an experiment in mass democracy. The distance of parentdom from the debate was as real as their exclusion from everyday schooling. Unsurprisingly therefore the Green Paper had little to say about the role which parents should have in the government of schools, postponing the issue until the Taylor Report on school government was published later in 1977.[24] Instead endorsement was given to the uncontroversial principle of keeping parents informed about what schools were doing so that they would be aware of what 'the education system and individual schools are trying to achieve'. In advancing a concept of the community which was constituted by parents, industry and commerce, the Green Paper did however signal the range of forces which might be considered the interested parties in school government. This was borne out by the subsequent recommendations of the Taylor Report, the reception of which illustrated the extent of divisions around any extension of popular control over schooling.

The Taylor Report, *A New Partnership for Our Schools,* proposed that the school governing body should be comprised of representatives from teachers, parents, employers and representatives of the local community. In addition it was recommended that older pupils should become members of the governing body where possible, and if permitted by law.

The report met a less than enthusiastic response from the government and over-whelming hostility from teacher organizations, the latter's attitude being effectively summarized by the NUT's argument that:

Lay people are not equipped to instruct teachers in the conduct of their work ...
the translation of society's expectations into specific educational aims, teaching
methods, curriculum content and syllabus design must remain the professional
responsibility of teachers.[25]

The reassertion of the professional autonomy position, designed to maintain the
distance of teachers from external constraints was, of course, characteristic.
Reluctance to contemplate any widening of the base of school government was
not the exclusive preserve of teachers, since it was shared by both educational
administrators and representatives of local authorities. One administrator offered
a typical response:

A warning that 'there are some peculiar elements lurking in the community' who
might attempt to get on post-Taylor governing bodies was issued at the weekend
by Mr L. J. Kail, senior assistant education officer, East Sussex.[26]

Thus, confronted with the possibility that new forms of control could, at least
theoretically, result in a loss of control, local government representatives in
particular were vocal in their opposition to the report. A dissentient on the
committee produced his own minority report which advanced just such a view,
arguing for an increased role in government by the local authority rather than a
ceding of control to another tier of administration.

   The argument for greater local authority influence was also supported by one
Conservative MP who coupled it with a support for teacher professionalism:

the reduction in direct local authority control over the schools may paradoxically
also help to reduce the say of the professionals. Lay councillors may count for
less – but so may their officers who have at least normally stemmed from the
teaching profession, and who normally manage to look through professional
eyes.[27]

In the event, the Taylor recommendations did not constitute an urgent priority for
government, and faced with the considerable antipathy outlined above, they were
effectively shelved. The rhetorical level remained paramount in the case of wider
control, over the school situation, both within the Labour Party and the new right.
Although unimplemented, the Taylor Report did reinforce the principle that the
world of work should be firmly represented within the school. This major principle
of the Great Debate, that the world of school and that of work should be brought
into a tighter harmony was the organizing theme of the discussions throughout the
period. The need for an effective state strategy was therefore a recurrent issue and
one which was clearly addressed.

The school and working life

The Green Paper formally set the seal on the school–work bond as the rationale
for schooling: the subordination of schooling to the requirements of industry was
complete. Gone were the references to any egalitarian ambitions for schooling –

instead the definition of education's effectivity was the extent to which schools
were able to match the stipulated requirements of industry. It is here that the
response was given to the complaints of industrialists endorsing the need to involve
industry in the planning of curricula as well as in the direct government of schooling.

The object of the school—work link, which was seen to involve schools directly
with individual firms, was equally concerned with developing a new ideology
among school children:

Young people need to reach maturity with a basic understanding of the economy
and its activities, especially manufacturing industry, which are necessary for the
creation of Britain's economic wealth.[28]

Such an argument had no place for the development of any critical purchase on the
structure of the world of work: the problem was seen as one of inculcating right
attitudes. The paper was concerned with the development of a remedial strategy
in the preparation of future labour power, against the deeper problems of youth
unemployment and of demands posed by restructuring in labour processes. The
focus remained on the generally couched and unproblematic preparation of 'young
people' for a conception of 'working life', without tight definition.

Such reticence was not a feature of the Expenditure Committee's report on the
Attainments of the School Leaver. The committee, which decided on its subject for
inquiry on the day of Callaghan's Ruskin speech, argued the case for a very intimate
relationship between the preparation of pupils in secondary schools and the
workplace, especially for those likely to enter unskilled or semi-skilled work. To
this end, it proposed a range of recommendations aimed at strengthening the
institutional connections between the two areas, through changes in teacher training
and in service courses as well as through exchange schemes sponsored by the CBI
and the TUC. Such schemes were not in themselves original having already operated
on a small scale by the Schools Council and the CBI. The shift was more in the
direction of a full cementing of the relationship.

As a strategy for the containment of youth unemployment, and as a policy for
restructuring educational priorities and utilities the proposals of the Commons
committee reproduced those which were to be found in the Green Paper. However,
while the lines of strategy could be set out, the question of which agencies should
be responsible for overseeing the process was more vexed. The Commons
committee noted that the DES was not the only agency concerned with securing
educational provision for the pupils in the period of transition from school to
work:

We are greatly concerned . . . at the contrast between the intensive activity over
provision for the 16 to 19 age group by the Department of Employment, through
its agencies like MSC and TSA, and the lower level of DES activity.[29]

The conclusions offered by the select committee was that some restructuring
of responsibility for the education of the 16 to 19 age group was essential.

That the DES should be quietly rebuked is not surprising, since its capacity for intervention in schools was limited by those factors which we have already discussed. The problems for central direction posed by teacher professionalism and local control necessarily inhibited the scope for DES intervention. But the DES itself was also strongly associated with the 'progressive' orthodoxies and strategic thinking which typified the 1960s. To ask it simply to accede to a new set of demands for the redefinition of objectives was too much to expect, and too great a political task to impose. Greater collaboration between industry and schools could clearly influence the character of the later stages of schooling, and even command the support of the department, but the area of post-school education and training was not one which could remain the province of the DES alone.

So it was that during this period the responsibility for the orchestration of post-school education was passed to the Manpower Services Commission. Direct schooling for industry required new agencies of control — unimpeded by any residual commitment to progressivism, by the restricting interests of teacher professionalism, or by the limitations inherent in local authority control. The commission, placed at the interface of schools and working life, was free to organize, train and direct in ways impossible within the existing school system. It is to the commission's activities and the ideology associated with its inception and practice that we turn in Chapter 11.

11 The rise of the Manpower Services Commission

Although we have so far been concerned with the school system, we want to argue that it was in the activities of the MSC that the best single condensation of Labour's educational politics in the 1970s was to be found. In its work we see the themes discussed in this part of the book reorganized into a powerful new whole.

The commission took up a by now jaded social democratic theme, the relation between schooling and employment, and translated it into a new language of training. It tried to transform areas in which earlier reforms had foundered, and in particular it sought to reshape cultural processes involved in the school—work transition. It took up some Great Debate themes, especially the demands of employers, and inscribed them into its own distinctive ideology. Beyond this, it broke new ground in exploring forms of organization and provision beyond the reach of the education service as such. Thus it became one paradigm — Labour's paradigm in chief — for a new educational settlement.

We will first locate the MSC in a history of manpower policy and give an account of its structure, activities and ideology. We then look at ways in which the MSC interpreted processes in the labour market which were increasing youth unemployment, and at its provision to ameliorate fundamental problems encountered by capitalism in crisis. Finally, we assess its role in shifting the entire ground of educational politics.

The MSC and manpower policy

Earlier we have noted some of the difficulties capital faces in trying to secure the stable reproduction of the labour force, accentuated by its continuous recomposition. We argued that while the 'logical' needs of capital could be defined with some certainty, concrete needs at a particular time were more complex: the dominance of one particular definition of needs was achieved through political and ideological processes and was not simply a response to one-dimensional 'economic' imperatives. We also argued that 'good' worker attitudes were more important to employers than particular skill competences. Both were in short supply in the 1970s — the one because of antagonisms inherent in the social relations of capitalist production and schooling, the other because of the anarchy of the market in which it was not found profitable to train 'skilled' workers during recessions. There was thus an increasing demand for state intervention to make provision rational and to control the training of young workers.

Until the 1960s, state involvement in training was minimal and consisted largely in supplementing industry's own programmes. Direct involvement was restricted to less profitable groups in whom industry had no interest, such as the physically handicapped. In the early 1960s, pressure increased for a more active state role, against a setting of near-full employment, skill shortages and a fear of overseas competition. The Industrial Training Act established Industrial Training Boards to supervise training in each sector and make levies to spread training costs and rationalize training 'quality' and content. By the end of the decade it was clear that the boards were not fulfilling their function: provision by 27 different boards was chaotic, apprenticeships were falling in number and new issues were posed by the growing unemployed. Thus a review of the 1964 Act led in 1974 to the creation of the MSC, whose initial concern was to rationalize and restructure all training and employment services provided by the Department of Employment. Soon it extended its reach to the adequacy and relevance of all forms of education and training received by young workers prior to or on entering work.

The MSC's structure made it semi-autonomous of mainstream government departments. Although its chairman was accountable to the Secretary of State for Employment, the commission had the responsibility to intervene freely and directly both in the labour market and in the further education sector (FE). This enabled it to proceed at a pace and in a manner alike unthinkable to the DES. Against a background of growing unemployment the MSC increased its staff from 12 to over 22,000 and its budget from £125 million to £630 million between 1974 and 1978.

Structurally the commission was split into three main divisions (formerly agencies): employment services (ESD), training services (TSD) and special programmes (SPD). The ESD was responsible for administering job centres and various mobility, recruitment and placement programmes, but it was the other two divisions which sponsored a bewildering array of projects that illustrated the flexibility of response allowed by the MSC's organization. We can briefly outline some of the more important initiatives.

The Youth Opportunities Programme (YOP), designed in 1977, rationalized all the *ad hoc* and temporary responses since 1974 to youth unemployment.[1] Described by Labour's Employment Secretary as 'a better deal for Britain's youth' the programme was to provide 234,000–260,000 places for all 16–18-year-olds confronted by unemployment.

Work preparation courses ranged from two week induction schemes, to help participants improve self-presentation and 'choose' an occupation, to three month short courses of training to operator/semi-skilled level. Work experience courses consisted of either six months in employers' premises or one year in training workshops provided by local authorities or similar agencies.

Other initiatives made their main impact on FE provision, especially the Training Opportunities Scheme (TOPS). Courses here provided intensive short training in skills in demand in local labour markets and, particularly in manual jobs, replaced certain forms of 'on the job' craft training. They also sought to find a common ground of generic skills, which could be examinable, beneath a diversity of local trades.

Additionally, there were direct measures of a new kind in the labour market. Jobs were subsidized or created through such schemes as the Special Temporary Employment Programme (STEP), Job Creation Programme (JCP) and Small Firms Employment Subsidy. Between them in 1977–8 these covered almost a quarter of a million workers. Finally, we might mention the MSC's sponsoring (at the prompting of criticism from the OECD and EEC) of a 'debate' on vocational preparation intended to provide a qualitatively new form of work induction for the majority of working-class youth.[2] This led in 1979 to detailed proposals for unified vocational preparation, a 3–6 month traineeship available to those excluded from apprenticeships.

Overriding this bewildering wealth of schemes and acronyms was the commission's particular take-up of ideas of skilling in the wake of the educational furore. There was now a distinct break with social democratic conceptions and with the largely negative complaints of the Great Debate. At one end, the repertoire of concern for justice and efficiency was replaced by emphasis on the need for 'employability' to which school provision was held often inadequate and irrelevant. At the other end, particular skills were to be replaced by (examinable) generic skills while the word expanded to encompass the Orwellian sounding 'social and life skills'. These terms were a response to conditions of new kinds of difficulty in the school–work disjunctu

Working-class youth's changing position in the labour market

The model of a 'mismatch' between school leavers and the needs of employers lay at the heart of MSC ideology. The employer critique of educational standards had been not just a view of the 'poor quality' of young workers but a perception of a more general breakdown of schools' licensing legitimacy – the validity of their assessment, through qualifications, of young workers' potential. In a survey of the attitudes and performance of 200 young workers at GEC, Rugby, personnel managers were acutely aware that academic and school-based qualifications did not guarantee successful job performance; that a good school record could well give young people 'aspirations' and a sense of choice which made them unwilling to persevere in even a skilled job.[3] Similarly, in a major survey of employers' reactions to young workers, alongside evidence from a wide variety of bodies, including the CBI and the Institute of Careers Officers, the National Youth Employment Council had found that employers placed increasing emphasis on 'motivation', coupled 'with the fact that a large minority of unemployed young people seem to have attitudes which, whatever their cause or justification, are not acceptable to employers and act as a hindrance to young people in securing jobs'.[4]

The employers' reluctance to employ school leavers then reflected, in part, their judgement that the qualities they wanted in their labour force, the qualities associated with work experience, were not those produced by schooling.

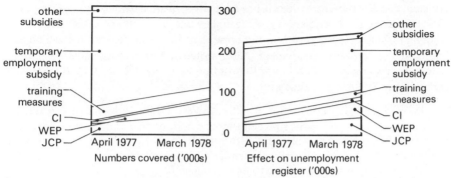

Special employment measures, 1977–8

CI - Community Industry   WEP - Work Experience Programme   JCP - Job Creation Programme

The 'other subsidies' are the Youth Employment Subsidy, Small Firms Employment Subsidy and Job Release Scheme. The training measures are MSC special courses for young people and training places in industry supported by the MSC. Numbers covered by all of these are based on statistics published by the Department of Employment, but allowing for 20% under-occupancy of places made available through the Job Creation Programme. The effect of the unemployment register is assumed to be 100% of numbers covered in the case of special programmes, about 70% in the case of training measures and the Temporary Employment Subsidy, and an average of about 50% for other subsidies.

Source: Manpower Services Commission Review and Plan 1978
Reproduced by permission of MSC

Irrespective of academic standards and examination passes, employers were increasingly unwilling to accept that school success guaranteed work achievement.

It seemed, also, that the reforms of school processes had exacerbated these problems. The development of different forms of learning and of different relationships between staff and pupils in the 1960s and 1970s, while helping to secure the necessary consent of pupils, had fostered dispositions out of balance with those needed at work. A TSD document (1975) argued that:

In recent years the social environment in a number of schools, with more emphasis on personal development and less on formal instruction, has been diverging from that still encountered in most work situations, where the need to achieve results in conformity with defined standards and to do so within fixed time-limits call for different patterns of behaviour. The contrast is more marked where changes in industrial processes have reduced the scope for individual action and initiative.[5]

Not only had schools changed in the 1960s and 1970s but so had the position of the working-class young in the labour market. The most obvious change was in unemployment which for the total population had risen by 45 per cent between January 1972 and January 1977, while it had risen by 120 per cent for those under twenty in the same period. This was caused by a combination of the vulnerability of young workers in an economic recession, a rise of nearly 1 million in the number of people in the labour market between 1970 and 1981 (estimated) and a disproportionate decline in jobs thought suitable for young people.

Historically, youth unemployment has always been a matter of political concern, and in different periods it has brought forward a variety of state responses. These range from the strictures of W. Temple,[6] who in 1770 advocated workhouse training for unemployed youths in the hope that 'the rising generations will be so habituated to constant employment that it would at length prove agreeable and entertaining to them', to the Junior Instruction Centres established by the Ministry of Labour in 1934, which aimed to:

give the boys and girls a real interest in life, to keep their minds and fingers active and alert, and their bodies fit, to teach them something that will be of real use to them whether at home or work, and without training them for specific occupations to give them the type of mental and manual instruction which will help them to become absorbed or re-absorbed into employment.[7]

Nevertheless, in previous recessions the problem had not been specific to young people nor had it been connected to a critique of schooling. The young workless had appeared to be a normal proportion of total unemployed. Solutions to the problem had been seen to lie in a restoration of employment levels as a whole. In the 1970s, in contrast, it was clear that youth unemployment was a specific problem and a permanent one, likely to remain whatever the recovery in the economy.

Equally 'bulges' in birth rates had occurred before. The early 1960s had seen a panic about youth unemployment as the post-war baby boom started to enter the labour market (the number of 15-year-olds increased between 1956 and 1962 from 613,000 to 919,000). Haunted by the spectre of a trade depression and the ending of National Service, the Crowther Report had pointed out that 'there could be a million young people on the streets with no work, nowhere to go and nothing to do'.[8]

That a comparable youth unemployment crisis had not developed earlier (though there were severe effects in some regions) was due to two factors. First, the expansion of the service and public sectors had increased employment for young workers, mitigating the worst effects of the accelerating 'shake-out' taking place in the manufacturing sector. Despite this, between 1961 and 1971 the number of jobs held by young people had fallen by almost 400,000.[9] The second and key factor had been the massive expansion in the numbers of young people staying on in full-time education — from 30 per cent of 15–17-year-olds in 1961 to over 50 per cent in 1971.

By the early 1970s, it was clear not only that total unemployment and youth unemployment were rising dramatically but that specific groups in the population were being hit disproportionately hard. The increase in unemployment served to reinforce the unequal prospects of young women and young people from ethnic minorities. A 1978 survey, for example, which compared the job-seeking experiences of West Indian and white school leavers in Lewisham found that black school leavers were three times as likely to be unemployed and concluded:

It is difficult to escape the conclusion that discrimination — be it intentional or unintentional — was an important factor in accounting for the difficulties faced by the black sample in the search for work. The young blacks we interviewed were looking for jobs just as hard and as efficiently as their white peers but were still being much less successful.[10]

In the early 1970s this phenomenon of a glut of juvenile labour was deflected by withholding the ROSLA age group from the labour market, but with the consequence of a move from scarcity to glut within two years.

By July 1976, there were 615,000 unemployed people under 25, including 199,000 school leavers. Youth unemployment as a percentage of all unemployment had increased from 19 per cent to 36 per cent for males and from 40 per cent to 65 per cent for females between 1966 and 1976. The *rate* of unemployment (that is, the number unemployed in a particular category compared with the total labour force in that category) for males under 19 had risen from 6.5 per cent in 1971 to a staggering 21.9 per cent in 1976.

While in the 1960s a youth unemployment crisis had been avoided by the expansion of the service and public sectors and the education system, no such countervailing tendencies were forthcoming in the 1970s. Public expenditure cuts restricted recruitment to the public sector and particularly hit the construction industry which had previously taken 15 per cent of male school leavers. Employment in agriculture and distribution, both traditional sectors for young people, declined in the same period and between 1966 and 1971 25 per cent of the jobs 'for' young males disappeared as did 23 per cent of the jobs 'for' young females.[11]

The 1970s also saw, beyond an absolute decline in the number of jobs available for young people, a change in employers' demands for young workers. Traditionally, as Frith argues, [12] young workers have always been typified as irresponsible, poorly motivated and quick to change jobs. They have been thought to lack the 'steadiness' of older workers committed by family and domestic responsibilities to long-term submission to the labour process. Young workers typified in this way had usually found work in the casual trades where control depended on direct discipline and supervision, but in the 1970s this 'solution' became untenable. Not only did the number of young worker jobs decline but there was also a concomitant reorganization of the labour process in those jobs which remained.

The general level of unemployment in the 1970s meant that for the first time in years, 'steady' adult workers were available for what had been jobs 'for' young people. An emphasis on direct control and supervision necessitated by the 'irresponsibility' of young workers was costly in terms both of supervisory labour and of potential disruption. The availability of 'steady' adult labour meant that the balance of costs could tilt towards them. This mode of control counted on the self-discipline and reliability of the adult worker and so it cut the financial and disruptive costs of direct control. The 1970s thus saw a recomposition of areas of 'casual labour' into 'semi-skilled' labour, and a shift in recruitment away from school leavers towards workers aged 22 and above. Frith concluded in 1978 that:

what is involved is not just a change in the type of job available but also a change in the type of worker demanded. In the past the 'casual' intermittent employment pattern of young workers was possible because there were plenty of jobs to be done by such workers . . . But employers are increasingly looking for a quality of 'steadiness' that is not the same thing as skill but may be achieved by a similar process of 'training'. There has always been evidence that jobs with training made for more stable workers than jobs without and it now seems employers are 'skilling' jobs, adding 'training programmes', as a form of work discipline.

What is being demanded is a 'responsible' attitude to work as much as a specific task skill . . . .[13]

The MSC and cultural intervention in the reproduction of labour power

These changes in the position of young people in the 1970s' labour market high-lighted two persistent problems for capitalism: the transition from childhood to adulthood and the ambivalent reliance of capital on the subjectivity of workers. It is in the context of these problems that we understand the MSC as a new stage in state efforts to restructure the working class — since:

there has never been a working class generation in this country that did not feel, for good or ill, the effects of State policies and practices which had the cumulative effect of structuring *in* certain skills, abilities, aptitudes and so on. . . and structuring *out* (marginalising, making difficult or illegal, or ridiculous) other qualities and powers.[14]

The transition between childhood and adulthood involves a critical transformation in which the young person moves away from largely dependent social relations within schooling and the family towards an active role within production and reproduction. The dynamics of this transition underwent a fundamental change after the second world war.

In the pre-war period, working-class youth had to leave school and take on the role of auxiliary breadwinners as soon as possible. Adult responsibility and work came early, but adult freedoms (particularly those of spending power) did not. Full employment in the 1950s dramatically altered youth's location in the economy of the family. With increased financial security, families could allow their children both a later entry into work and greater freedom to spend their earnings. While the experience of this change was gender specific, a new role for *all* young people as consumers and as a distinctive cultural group was created.

It was out of these cultural and economic processes, and their appropriation and ideological presentation by various apparatuses (the connection with delinquency, 'irresponsible' sexuality, and so on) that 'youth' as a social category was constructed in the 1950s and 1960s to carry a deeper message about the state of society and the social and political changes taking place. Youth became a 'thermometer' category, its dress and lifestyles a moral threat, acting as a powerful but concealed metaphor for social change. Moreover with the fading of National Service as a political option, real and imagined changes inside schools, and the increasing replacement of prospective work disciplines by unemployment, the MSC's work acquired real urgency. As the British Youth Council argued in 1977:

The MSC has indeed declared its fear that the failure of young people to get a job may permanently alienate them from the world of work and from society. Not only does this bode ill for the future productivity of the country's potential labour force, but it is also likely to cause high levels of crime and social unrest.[15]

The need for an orderly induction of young workers into production, combined with the persistent ambivalence of worker subjectivity, ran right through the myriad of MSC interventions.

For the young unemployed the MSC took initiatives either to replace the discipline of work directly or to encourage capital itself to supply it once more. Examples of direct training in the work ethic were the Coventry 'lightbox' assembly line and the core 'social and life skills' course. The 'lightbox' assembly line was part of an imitation company set up in a college so that young unemployed could learn about the world of work. The lesson proceeded thus:

In the 'lightbox' assembly workshop, a similar pattern of work has been established. Here trainees construct, wire, and test equipment, then package it and write the accompanying advice notes. The organisation is tight and efficient, and a convincing assembly regime is produced. When the light boxes reach their destination in the main College building they are dismantled, and their components fed back for re-assembly.[16]

The 'social and life skills' with which the MSC equipped its trainees derived from aims such as those 'to adjust trainees to normal working conditions, giving attention to such matters as time-keeping, discipline and the maintenance of satisfactory relations with (a) other trainees and (b) their supervisors'.[17] The social relations of production were thus taken for granted ('adjust'), the problem being to fit young people to such relations.

The MSC encouraged existing employers to undertake this work socialization in the 'real' situation by offering attractive financial packages through programmes such as WEEP (Work Experience on Employers' Premises). The Paper Products Training Board outlined the advantages for employers in Manchester:

a. No wages to pay — trainees received £19.50 per week MSC allowance.
b. No increase to total workforce.
c. Chance to assess over a long period the trainee's capability, aptitude and potential for future vacancies in the organisation.
d. Even if permanent employment cannot be offered the trainee is likely to regard the employer favourably for giving him/her work experience.
e. Similarly, the employers' local prestige and reputation should be enhanced because it has done something practical to help some of the young people in the area.[18]

The benefits in moulding the subjectivity of the new worker to the demands of responsible autonomy were held out in another paper from the same board. The scheme would:

improve the individual's motivation and commitment to work and the employing organisation by developing:

a. understanding and performance in specific and related jobs.
b. basic communication skills.
c. awareness of the demands, discipline and satisfactions of working life as an adult outside work.
d. ability to work as individual or as member of group.
e. ability to recognise personal capabilities and potential and to learn how to develop them more fully.[19]

And, said another section of the document, it would create:

d. employees who are more likely to respond to the need for changing jobs in the future and to flexible employment now.
e. employees who if allowed and properly encouraged will wish to contribute to a more participative environment in the future.
f. reduction in high cost manpower wastage in early years.
g. valuable source of manpower which may be developed for more responsible employment in due course.[20]

Even those aspects of the MSC's activity which seemed most concerned with technical competences were, on closer inspection, similarly wedded to the importance of moulding and controlling the subjectivity of the young worker. Concern for cultural aspects of production lay close to the surface.

The recomposition of skills was an early concern of the MSC and it set up a programme to investigate the groupings of skills and how such groupings affected one labour market in Derby. The aim of the skill grouping was:

to build up in specific areas, banks of statements or descriptors of skills and knowledge and, when applicable, of physical attributes, temperament factors and personal characteristics which will give a consistent and systematic way of describing what is required of a worker to do a job successfully.[21]

This approach to training drew a distinction between 'job oriented' and 'worker oriented' elements of each task. The 'job oriented' elements were the technical competences necessary for a task, 'worker oriented' elements those concerned with the subjectivity of the worker. In practice the grouping of skills concentrated not on technical competences but on the moulding of worker subjectivity. As Pirie emphasized: 'for the purpose of comparing the requirements of a range of jobs across different technologies research into worker oriented elements seems to offer the better chance of establishing communalities'.[22]

The logic of MSC activity in providing the wide-ranging cultural interventions of which capital was individually incapable was displayed most clearly in the vocational preparation debate which the commission initiated in 1975. This identified the preparation of school children for production as a primary concern of manpower policy and it pinpointed the failure of schools to do this adequately. The commission coined a new set of terms around vocational preparation and by

1979 these had been taken over by the DES:

the terms 'training' and 'education' have been commonly used as a rough and ready means of distinguishing between learning to perform specific vocational tasks (training) and the general development of knowledge, moral values and understanding required in all walks of life (education). But such definitions have obvious shortcomings. The majority of 16–18s are in the course of acquiring, whether systematically or not, knowledge and skills which will enable them to perform particular jobs, manage their private affairs, develop their leisure interests, and so on. The concept of vocational preparation treats the entire process of learning, on and off the job, as a single entity, combining elements of training and education to be conceived and planned as a whole.

This carried two important features – an overt concern to contest elements of working-class youth culture and an implicit argument that only the free-ranging activities of a body such as the MSC could undertake such interventions. Vocational preparation was not to be restricted to preparation for production alone as 'most schemes aim to use the participants' experience and horizons, and to use vocational needs and interests as a vehicle for the achievement of objectives relevant to their present and future activities as adults and in society generally'.[24]

The MSC took as its co-ordinates an already established 'world of work'. Certainly the MSC re-presented this world ideologically, making it, for example, more 'open' to young workers than it was and making unemployment appear as a product of individual inadequacies rather than as an endemic consequence of the capitalist mode of production. But this re-presentation did not mean that the MSC lacked, in practice, an accurate assessment of some needs of capitalism. The MSC took existing divisions between employers and workers, between different 'types' of worker and between workers with different 'interests' (particularly male and female workers) for granted. Where the MSC broke new ground was in the tightness of the link which it established between the needs of employers (both logical and perceived) and state provision.

The commission took the differentiation already achieved by schooling as its datum line, and concentrated its attention on those who left school at 16. The young worker, or worker to be, was taken as an already constituted category and, within this, the MSC fostered further differentiation. At the most passive this was by allowing 'interests' to run their 'natural' course so that, for example, adult male workers received 75 per cent of places on TOPS schemes concentrated in skill centres and employers' establishments, while female workers were concentrated in FE colleges.[25] This reproduced the division between engineering, construction and automotive occupations and clerical, commercial and hairdressing work. Clerical and commercial 'skills' were in any case being subjected to rapid 'deskilling'. The MSC provision similarly reproduced hierarchies of 'ability' ranging from workers equipped only with 'social and life skills', through workers trained to operator/semi-skilled level, to workers trained with similar technical competences as apprenticed 'craftsmen'. This differentiation carried with it another key concern

— the need to discourage many people from acquiring conceptual and critical skills. The MSC both provided work socialization for many young people who would not otherwise have received it and fostered the attitudes conducive to 'responsible autonomy' — the cheapest and most efficient mode of labour discipline.

This brings us to a last aspect of MSC activities — an attack on working-class organization. 'Crafts' represent, among other things, the success of certain sections of the working class in 'capturing' an area of competence—knowledge and thus in imposing conditions on capital for access to such competences and knowledges. The MSC attacked these divisions in two main ways. It undercut craft training on the job by providing intensive, off the job training in certain skills. More significant was the attack on craft barriers — the attempt, reflecting the deskilling process, to find the 'generic' skills (of responsibility, flexibility and so on) running across existing crafts and to base training upon them. Once such 'generic' skills were secured, then rapid changes of technical competence demanded by accumulation could be achieved free from the impedance of 'old' knowledges and working-class organization based around them.

The commission did not see its activity as limited to young workers, indeed it saw its job as concerned with influencing general attitudes by 'involving and interesting' other bodies:

It would . . . be wrong to suppose that there is some magic list of extra manpower measures . . . . The task is rather to create a new attitude to manpower. Manpower . . . should be in the forefront of government, industry and company strategy and policy, and not treated as a residual factor . . . . It is part of the Commission's job to make this clear in every possible way.[26]

Thus the commission outflanked the DES, demanding co-operation between educational and training apparatuses but arguing that the 'natural focal point' for their development was the various training boards and bodies. At a local level the commission became involved in the planning structures of local education authorities and produced 'guides' by which curricula could be made more 'relevant'.

The MSC and capitalist training: Labour's paradigm?

It would be wrong to overemphasize the direct impact of the MSC on schooling in this period: resistances and lags were formidable. Nevertheless a quite new model of capitalist training was visibly on offer — biting deeply into FE, spreading a new vocabulary of work preparation. Whether the commission was, or is, a paradigm of one move in a new educational settlement — or a transitional agency — lies unresolved, although its expansion by the Conservatives in late 1980, in response to 2 million unemployed, emphasized its structural position and increasing permanence.

Certainly the MSC showed Labour's particular appropriation of a part of the new right's agenda. It belonged to a pattern under the Labour government of

1974—9 whereby the state attempted to transfer industrial conflict into another arena where a practical harmonization of interests could be achieved. Representatives of industry and unions were invited as interest groups into tripartite negotiations, chaired by the state, designed to reach agreements in the 'national interest'. Such bodies as the Arbitration and Conciliation Service or the National Enterprise Board enabled the state to take a more direct command over the conditions for capitalist accumulation. The MSC exemplified this mode of politics in its structure and practices. The commission's various boards and committees displayed this tripartite partnership as it sought the consent of unions and employers to its training vocabulary and strategy. As it argued itself:

The Commission can be successful in its endeavours only by taking people along with it. In a free society, much the most effective way of securing the commitment of organizations and people to a course of action is to involve them in decisions, and we therefore consider it essential for there to be participation of the major interests concerned, and particularly employers organizations and trade unions, in the work of the central manpower authority and at many other levels.[27]

But under the Conservative government, the state has been drawn back from such corporate interventions. The MSC under Labour was an expensive and labour-intensive apparatus, very much a part of the public expenditure which the Conservatives now sought to reduce drastically. Nor were the MSC's themes, combining a concern for economic efficiency and an attention to the redress of gross economic injustice, likely to carry as much resonance with a radical right government as they did under the avuncular centrism of Mr Callaghan.

Nevertheless, the involvement of Labour with the MSC stood as a nadir, in the late 1970s, in this history of the party's educational hopes. Except for the claim that money was being spent to aid the 'underprivileged' unemployed, any attack on inequality had been abandoned: rather, the given inequalities produced by the social and sexual division of labour were underpinned. Training schemes would graft the unattached young into labour market disciplines. Any notion of a critical knowledge, of helping adolescents to understand their situation, was absent. The criterion by which schooling would be judged, by which it would be bypassed if its concerns were other or irrelevant to the new mission, was — 'employability'.

Meanwhile how and whether the commission would survive the new Conservative government remained in the balance, caught in larger political turmoils of the new Tory management of the economy during a severe recession. What is already clear is that in making savings, and in the implicit restructuring that goes with them, priority has been given to programmes aimed at moulding worker subjectivity. While, on the one hand, the Tories have signalled a withdrawal from employers' direct training programmes with their proposal to end state funding of the Industrial Training Boards, on the other, their determination to cut expenditure on YOP, the major programme of work socialization and cultural intervention, in fact had to give way in response to the ever increasing numbers of the young workless. In fact, the new measures announced in December 1980[28] represent an extension of the schemes to remove effectively from the labour market those of the 16—18 age group not in full-time education or work. At the same time the Confederation of British Industries roundly rejected MSC proposals for a sophisticated unified vocational preparation programme to ease the school—work divide — not because the work of cultural intervention was thought unimportant, but because it was a 'one-sided approach to a problem which had its roots in schools' and employers felt they were being 'asked to make up for the deficiencies in the school system'.

To schools, therefore, the problems were returned. The MSC stood as Labour's paradigm for capitalist training, supervised by a new apparatus of the state. There were signs that under Mrs Thatcher, the problems would be handled differently, with the state less outwardly visible — although the Conservatives' room for manoeuvre, particularly around the young workless, was to be sharply constrained by the unemployment being created by its own policies. Nevertheless, we should still note that Labour's attempt to pre-empt Conservative campaigns in the later 1970s had only delivered the debate firmly on the ground already occupied by the right. It is to the prospects of an educational politics under a radical Conservative government that we move in the book's final section.

By no means concluded

Must we then, if we are honest, admit that it is not possible to make the Act work efficiently in the next few years? . . . It *can* be made to work, and work soon. What is more, I believe it *will* be made to work. I base my confidence on the new spirit of the common people of Britain. I am convinced that, as a people, we have made up our minds to put an end to 1939 and all that — an end to poverty and insecurity, to privilege and vested interest, to war and threats of war. We understand something of what this involves. A new democratic consciousness is arising. Already it has found practical expression in the surge of feeling which swept Labour into power at the General Election. As the municipal elections have shown, the tide is still flowing. In March it will almost certainly engulf many of the County Councils. It is sweeping away the political obstacles in the path of social, including educational advance.

The first Labour Minister of Education is a woman graduate of Manchester University, who has no claim to any old school tie . . . We, the common people of Britain — parents and teachers, administrators and officials — share with her a tremendous task and a grand opportunity. It is up to us. 'The old is dead. We shall die with it unless we can give birth to the new.'[1]

Introduction

With this rallying cry G. C. T. Giles concluded his analysis of the possibilities of the 1944 Act. His book was intended as an intervention into the still fluid field of educational politics, and this was nowhere clearer than in his conclusion, which contained, among other things, a fable. The fable took readers to the town of Barset, and into its Education Office. The Education Officer, a man combining vision and pragmatism, had drawn up the draft plan as required of each local authority by the 1944 Act. The 'very sensible and realistic proposal of the education officer'[2] was eventually approved by the relevant committees 'in spite of remarks about blank cheques from Mr Councillor Bumble'[3] and a defence of vested interests by the chairman of the Technical Sub-Committee. The plan was publicized with the help of the local Council for Educational Advance, the local paper and the local teacher association, and more than half the borough's parents attended a parents' meeting to discuss it.

The meeting at the county school was the centrepiece of Giles's fable. The

headmaster, a keen and progressive educationalist, denounced the kernel of the plan
– multilateralism:

'Multilateralism', he declared, 'as interpreted by the London County Council, is a
totalitarian monstrosity. The Multilateral school of 2,000 pupils will be more like
a barracks or a factory than a school. It will destroy individual initiative in teachers
and pupils. It will sacrifice the able pupil to the less able, and so lower the high
standards of scholarship, which the secondary schools have built up in the last
forty years. The poor scholar will no longer have a chance to compete successfully
with the wearer of the old school tie'.[4]

The Education Officer thus faced a highly critical audience, 'but he was equal to
the occasion', [5] making an eloquent speech which defended the plan by appealing
to experience, justice, modernization, efficiency and to an educational and social
philosophy 'sound, democratic and in tune with our time'.[6] Thus, Giles tells us,
from the meeting at the county school the discussion spread to other parents'
meetings, into the local press and to the homes of the people. Education had
become 'a live issue in the borough'.[7]

From one perspective, the world of the 1980s seems to be an inversion of
Giles's world. In 1946 the obsolete social and economic system of Mr Councillor
Bumble, of the die-hard Colonel Blimp (with two sons at Eton and a feeling that
the country was going to the dogs) and of the 'economaniacs' (the careful
custodians of the rates)[8] had been given notice to quit. A progressive alliance
was organizing to press for mass meetings to discuss schooling, for increased
expenditure and for multilateralism. Today we see this world turned upside down:
Mr Bumble, Colonel Blimp and the economaniac are firmly installed in power,
while educationalists, teacher associations and egalitarians are in the wilderness.
The 'people' are having their say, not at local meetings, but through the depopulated
ventriloquism of the mass media. Their interests in schooling are defined, not in
terms of political citizenship and democratic participation, but according to a
mean and self-regarding version of 'parental choice'.

We have been concerned, in this book, to see how such an inversion was
achieved through the weaknesses of social democratic politics and the 1960s'
alliance; through the accurate exploitation of these weaknesses by a new populist
Toryism; and through the more subterranean determinations of economic failure and
of the sustained reproduction of class and gender relations. The case of Giles himself,
however, highlights some of the responsibilities that attend such an analysis. Giles's
fable may look innocent to modern eyes (and is certainly not the basis for a contemporary politics) but it poses very sharply the need for a popular socialist politics for
today. How can writers of a book such as this actively contribute to that end?

One option would be simply to leave the analysis as it stands, so that readers can
make their own judgements. This seems to us unsatisfactory: we feel an obligation
to try, to some extent, to close the gap between intellectual analysis and political
practice: we want, at least, to make the implications of the analysis clear enough for
people to see what, politically, we are saying. At the same time, such an exercise is

personally important, since writing this book at this time is also a kind of political education for those involved. However a project of this kind contains perils of its own. There *is* a distance fixed between research and politics, even where an attempt is made to research for grass-roots constituencies. We do not have, for example, the close experience of day-to-day school or teacher politics, or local politics to suggest detailed strategies. It is significant that, when we tried to write that sort of conclusion, it degenerated into the kind of moral exhortation that is a sure sign of making prescriptions for someone *else* to follow! All this suggests an explicitly political conclusion, but one which is tentative, suggestive and provisional – a 'conclusion' which is, like the situation it presents, 'by no means concluded'.

In what follows we deal with five main issues. The first two are closest to home and to our own competences – they concern the political role of educational researchers. First, we draw together our recurrent discussions of the position of educational research in relation to politics, drawing out some implications for this practice today. Second, we recapitulate some of the main features of the general theoretical standpoint which we advocated in Chapter 1, and which have guided our historical accounts and critiques.

One difficulty that attends the writing of contemporary history is that historical events necessarily overtake the researchers. We started writing this book before the general election of 1979 and our main stress has been on understanding the events of the 1970s in terms of a previous history. One consequence is that, although we have studied the forms of Conservative populism in opposition – as an effective practical critique of social democracy – we have not attended to the forms of Conservative populism in office. Yet it is 'Thatcherism' as government that is the immediate antagonist against which a popular socialist strategy will have to be defined. Third, therefore we need to understand more completely the main dimensions, strengths and vulnerabilities of this enemy, for 'enemy' it is. Modern Conservatism is even more inimical to popular education than its social democratic rival. In this part of the conclusion, then, we sketch our understanding of some of the main features of Thatcherism, especially in the educational domain. It is a sketch however which is incomplete, since the main lines of Conservative policy in education still remain only partially revealed.

In the final sections we turn to the problems of developing an adequate socialist response. The broad problem here is the construction of a popular educational alliance capable both of resisting the anti-educational and inegalitarian tendencies of Conservative policy, as well as providing the basis of a new socialist alternative. We consider the nature and the possible dispositions of the main elements in such an alliance, before moving to questions of strategy. As we noted earlier, we will be concerned here less with the details of strategy and more with the broader implications drawn from our analysis.

Finally, we turn to questions of agency. Much of our analysis, recapitulated here, has been concerned with a critique of the Labour Party and social democratic politics. It is important to pose the question: under what circumstances, and with what transformations, could the main party of the left in Britain become an adequate agency for achieving socialism and the educative work which that involves? We discuss this issue mainly by noting the inadequacies of current official Labour Party responses to the crisis in its own traditions.

Intellectuals and the politics of research

A concern for the relationship between 'intellectuals' and the politics of education has been one important sub-theme in this book. The main model of this relationship offered in recent history may be termed 'the social democratic connection'. Within the social democratic alliance, 'intellectuals', in this case defined by their academic location and expertise, played a crucial role. A few selected 'experts' gained privileged access to powerful personnel in the Labour Party and in the state, and were thus able to influence considerably the politics of schooling, from the top downwards. This served to align the Labour Party, in the 1960s, to a very particular formulation of the issues in schooling: attention was given to working-class 'failure' and, overwhelmingly, to the formal structures of schooling. The weaknesses of the model of 'intellectual' as academic adviser were similar to those of social democracy as a whole: in the end, it represented a non-popular, statist and anti-educational form of the relationship between intellectual work and politics.

More recently the new right has presented a different model of 'intellectual' involvement in politics. Intellectuals such as Cox, Dyson and Boyson served as 'range riders' for the new right in the late 1960s and 1970s, though their contribution was not to give policy advice to mandarins, but to create and publicize a new set of terms for thinking about schooling. The intellectual or 'scientific' value of the new right's critique was secondary to its construction of an appeal to popular attitudes. This initial ideological work accomplished, other intellectuals took up the same terms of reference and used them (consciously or unconsciously) as guides to work which unquestionably occupied the new terrain. The Gadarene rush to evidence 'the crisis' was on, and there was a spate of research reports, starting in the mid 1970s, concerned with progressivism, 'lower standards',[9] subversive teachers[10] or disruption in schools.[11] The predominantly Conservative media, as we have seen, were quick to pick up such reports and exploit them for immediate political advantage. Reports which took the new right seriously but produced contrary evidence were ignored, presented as confirming the new right position in any case, or dismissed as 'whitewash'.[12] The effective burying of the older expertise under the propaganda avalanche of the 1970s was a practical demonstration of its deep vulnerabilities.

A simple return to a Fabian model of expertise is not possible however for reasons other than those outlined above. The relationship of many younger intellectuals to 'left of centre' politics has undergone a transformation during the past decade. The breaks came with the new sociology and deschooling, closely followed by the first reappropriations of Marxism and the emergence of new forms of feminism. The 'policy' model of politics was rejected as neither possible nor desirable. After all, if schooling was inherently oppressive or conservative, what business had intellectuals of the left in fuelling its growth? And were schools suddenly to become non-sexist?

The rejection of Fabianism, however, left a huge political vacuum. If not to government, the Labour Party or a professional educational public, to whom should work on education be addressed? This dilemma (not confined to the British situation) is often writ large in the theoretical works of the 1970s. In contrast to the many pages demonstrating the nature of the connections between knowledge and power, or between schooling and capital's reproduction, a few closing paragraphs often appealed to loosely specified total changes as the prerequisite for a viable politics. Having witnessed ourselves the dilemmas of this kind of inorganic radicalism, in common with large parts of our own intellectual generation, we record this with a wry self-encompassing discomfort, not with any sense of arrogance or of problems neatly solved!

One solution, of course, was to turn to a radical or potentially radical educational public, especially to teachers trained during the 1960s and 1970s, who went through courses in the sociology, psychology and philosophy of education. The distinctive combination in some such courses of high abstraction and crushing detail, as well as a distance from (if not assumed superiority to) the everyday world of schools, all served, we suspect, to inoculate many teachers against 'experts'. The newer forms of socio-educational analysis were often no more attractive or accessible to practising teachers.

In the meantime, a second set of changes had made a return to policy-related modes of research even more difficult. The tighter control by the state of research facilities, not just in terms of money but even of access to the schools themselves, with some consequent attempts to define the permissible limits of research, served to block this path. One symptom of this has been the reception of state-funded research which produced unwanted results. The fate of the Community Development Projects is the best example, but there have been similar examples at the level of the local state. To draw from the 'wrong' (non-positivist) intellectual traditions; to ask the 'wrong' questions (how are the poor produced?) of the wrong people (the poor themselves) and to draw the wrong conclusions (that the state is not a benevolent, neutral agency) was to call down wrath on researchers' heads. The question of 'whose side are we on?' was sometimes posed dramatically.

More recent structural changes in the organization of state research have served to confirm this pattern. There have been significant shifts in the way in which the state organizes its own research operations — a move towards a flourishing of internal research departments in preference to independent research. Such departments have many advantages for the state in that the processes of research can be closely controlled. The questions asked and the methods used can both be defined in ways which structure results of particular kinds. All of this occurs under the considerable powers of the state as a direct employer and at times indeed within the Official Secrets Acts.

Such a low risk policy of internal research has been paralleled by changes in the control of 'independent' research in other institutions. Indirect research funding, over which the state has relatively little control, has been cut and what is left is being redirected to specific areas such as management science. Concomitant with this diminution of indirect funding has been the growth of direct fixed term contract research either in institutions of higher education or in private research firms. Such research is usually tied tightly to policy initiatives with the 'contractor-client' relationship to check steps outside a narrowly defined range of questions.

The final blow to state oriented research of a leftish character, has, however, been administered by the victory and the character of contemporary Conservatism. One feature of Thatcherism is its marked independence from social research as such, its conviction that the 'answers' are already available within its own practical counsels and programmes. As Conservative policy meets its own obstinate contradictions, this situation may well change. At the time of writing, however, the ruling party of our society has not time for even an opportunist sociology.

One aspect of our history, then, is the crisis of social democratic intellectuals and the deep dilemmas which it has produced. The dilemmas are especially profound because they come at the end of a longer history of two divergent tendencies: on the one hand, a considerable radicalization of certain intellectual strata; on the other, a long-term erosion in Britain of a popular socialism. We face a deeply contradictory situation: a strong but 'internal' growth of radical intellectual work and groupings, with their own developing networks spanning older parties of the left, the women's movement and informal agencies of collective education and support, but lacking, for the most part, a strongly popular educational role and connection. The securing of such a connection is, from this perspective, the principal task for the 1980s, but it can only be considered within a wider sense of appropriate educational agencies and strategies. But at least we should have no illusions about the alternatives; there is, for the foreseeable future, no possible return to the 1960s' forms of alliance, or none with any chance of political success.

Theoretical developments: innocence, realism and the possibility of progress

The theoretical arguments of the book have involved a double movement: the critique of social democracy and also, we hope, a practical demonstration that Marxist forms of analysis, drawing also on a whole range of 1970s' insights, need not slip into ahistorical abstraction and mechanical 'functionalism' balanced only by a hopeful rhetoric. The social reforming optimism of the period from the 1940s to the mid 1960s — from Giles's 'revolution' of science and democracy to Harold Wilson's mid 1960s' rhetoric — *was* 'innocent' compared with the pessimistic force of later analysis. Although the pessimism of the 1970s led to criticism of social democratic and liberal reforms, it offered little scope, theoretical or political, for struggles in and over education. We understand Marxism to be an intellectual tradition of analysing particular situations by uncovering the conditions on which they rest and, along with that, the conditions under which they can, politically, be transformed.

The differences between our understandings in 1980 and those of Giles in 1945 should by now be clear. No longer, for example, can the state be regarded as a neutral organ to be 'won' by any side in an electoral battle. The failure of social democratic reforms to make much impact on the power structure of Britain makes a view of elections as 'giving notice' to vested interests no longer tenable. Power does not simply lie in Parliament and town halls, waiting to be used for democratically decided ends. Similarly, the heroic progressivism of the Education Officer in Giles's fable would be more likely to be replaced today by the presumption that the administrative apparatuses of the state are self-interested, duplicit, and secretive. The key problems now posed concern ways in which political demands are refused or defused, or how, once conceded, they are turned against their own purposes. Socialist change necessarily involves transformation of state agencies themselves.

The main lessons learned in the 1970s however have concerned the possibility of achieving equality by educational reform in a society still structured by unequal relations of class, gender and race. As we argued in Chapter 7, the capitalist and patriarchal structuring of the social and sexual division of labour, allied to the necessary 'realism' of lived experience will continue to produce grossly unequal educational outcomes, so long as these structures themselves remain untransformed. That is why we believe that a genuine commitment to education, in its proper broader and honourable sense — to the real development and sharing of human knowledge, capacities and energies — leads, theoretically and practically, to socialist and feminist conclusions. In one sense, this is a pessimistic conclusion: it does undercut the easy identification of capitalist growth and egalitarian progress that has been characteristic, especially since the war, of British progressivism. But it remains pessimistic (as opposed to realistic) only if the possibility of a socialist adaptation, of education and also of economic and social life, is ruled theoretically out of court and is politically unimaginable.

Thus we feel a distance from Giles (the achievement of reform through good-tempered rational argument) but also from the faith in equality (planned by experts in education) characteristic of the 1960s. The shortcomings of these positions were the target of much of the reappropriated Marxism of the 1970s, but, while recognizing the advances made by 'functionalist' forms of Marxist analysis, we have tried to break out of its stronger versions. The suggested pliability of schooling to the 'needs' of capitalism undercut utopian reforms, but at heavy theoretical and political cost: all aspects of social life tended to be portrayed as the reflex of one primary aspect, most often treated as a 'correspondence'. Such a reduction was only possible by resolving the vast complexity of the particular into a rather static equivalence. Readers often had their actions converted, before their very eyes, into those of agents fulfilling, in inevitable ways, particular capitalist functions.

The more historical perspective adopted here questions some aspects of functionalist analysis. The development of schooling is no simple extrapolation from the changing needs of capital. The history of schooling is, we have suggested, one of discontinuities — a series of breaks and reversals, stagnations and advances, crises and settlements. We have suggested that political struggles were crucial to an understanding of such developments and that these struggles should alert us to the wide variations of futures possible on the basis of the present.

In trying to move away from a one dimensional argument we suggested that the cultural processes of schooling, while drawing specific repertoires from class and gender, to some degree represented partial solutions to the problems which schooling poses for adolescents. This concern to see the cultural processes of schooling as an integral part of any analysis carries significant political implications. It brings the guerrilla war experienced daily by many teachers and pupils into the centre of the stage rather than dismissing it as epiphenomenal. Similarly, it converts the 'pathologies' of truancy and class culture (seen as bad 'attitudes') into normal events with their own processes and rationality, which reproduce working-class boys as male wage labourers and working-class girls as dual labourers at home and in production. The nature of the common sense generated from these processes is also complex and contradictory. It contains the potential for developments ranging from a class and gender based socialist politics right through to elements of a racist and sexist nationalism. A future socialist politics will not succeed until it takes these forms of popular knowledge both as an object of study and a basis for political transformation.

We would still maintain that schooling is more determined than determining; that schooling plays a role in winning the consent necessary to run a divided society; and that schooling *plays a part* in the reproduction of labour power. The problematic of reproduction commits us to holding that the capitalist mode of production has certain requirements which, if not met, would entail its transformation. We have tried to look at ways in which schooling contributed to these deeper exigencies. One kind of answer suggested that schooling emerged when the site of production was separated from the major site of reproduction (the family). Schooling provided a link between these two crucial sites — it articulated the family to the now separate sphere of production. The teaching of 'skills' in schools rather than in the process of family production is a prime example: but the need of the capitalist mode of production for a continually self-renewing labour force is not limited to the question of 'skills'. In a real sense the 'skills' demanded of the majority of people by advanced capitalism are diminishing. More important are values and attitudes appropriate to the antagonistic relations of production and patriarchy. Schooling plays a significant role in attaching the 'unacceptable' elements of pupil cultures and in generating different class and gender based destinies.

To analyse this further we relied on the Gramscian concept of hegemony, understood as ' the spontaneous consent given by the great mass of the population to the general direction imposed on social life by the dominant fundamental group'.[13] Such consent is essential for the daily working of the capitalist mode of production. It involves matters both of overt consent and of the seen (but not noticed) acceptance of specific ideologies and relationships. Without this routine daily acceptance it would prove impossible to maintain the mode of production.

The concept of reproduction, posed next to the question of hegemony, points to the instability of the capitalist mode of production and the need for its constant change and renewal. Reproduction is only secured after considerable ideological work and is thus susceptible to educational work of an oppositional or counterhegemonic kind. The discrediting of the old social democratic terms and the development of a new policy by the right shows how new definitions can be constructed and put to work to realize changes in state action. These changes were no simple reading off from the changing 'needs' of capital but sophisticated ideological and political responses to a particular situation, which sought to construct a new common sense. The point here is that, whatever the 'needs' of the capitalist mode of production, a vast amount of ideological work remains to be done before coherent policy can be formulated, consent won and real change initiated. Such work will encounter resistances and involve miscalculations; its success can by no means be guaranteed.

It is also clear that feminism's insistence on the centrality of gender differentiation and relations is amongst the major legacies of the upheavals of the late 1960s, and that their impacts on intellectual and political work have been many and varied. We have come to see schooling as being closely related to the subordination of women, constructed historically and ideologically upon patriarchal forms of the care and bringing up of children. Child-rearing exhibits some of the most important articulations of patriarchy and capitalism as played out in schooling. We have done no more than trace the absence of gender questions, or their ideological construction, in educational policy. For example, we noted the absence of women from the political arithmetic of social democracy, and the ideological construction of natural differences in the reports of the 1960s and the new right's educational texts.

The assertion of the importance and determinacy of gender relations in educational processes has profound implications for educational politics today. It means that older forms of socialist populism which conflated the particular experiences of girls, young women and mothers with those of an undifferentiated populace, or working class, will no longer suffice as a political starting point. There is no simple, whole 'popular will' to which we can appeal. Nor should we accept versions of a 'public opinion' to which we are powerfully exposed after radical changes in cultural apparatuses over the past thirty years. We have learnt that the media can create an image of 'public opinion' at a distance from the variety of the actual, popular knowledges of their readers on whom, nevertheless, such an image may be influential. The 'popular' cannot be read off from its proclaimed manifestations. And a new politics of education will have to attend closely to the specific situation of women, and to the way patriarchal relations, in the family, in schools and in the domain of waged work, limit and profoundly shape individual opportunities for education. That is why we have insisted throughout that the forms of analysis and of politics that are needed will be both socialist and feminist.

The new right

The new right represents, we would argue, a bold attempt to 'resolve' the structural problems of British capitalism and to harness the social forces generated by this attempt to shift the whole frame of politics and public debate.[14] It thus represents a 'total politics' attempting to restructure all aspects of social and economic life. It is important to stress the strength of this political and ideological project before considering its more contradictory features.

The new right is often accurate in its identification of contradictions in British society. Most obviously, it has played effectively on the economic crisis which simmered in the 1960s and boiled in the 1970s, a crisis to which it offers a solution. But this is by no means the only contradiction upon which it has worked. It has identified the crucial discrepancy in social democracy between the claim to represent the working class and the wish to manage capitalism efficiently. Similarly, it has identified the gap between social democracy and any powerful popular base, and has made at least partially successful attempts to colonize this space. Particularly important here has been the reworking of existing themes in working-class experience, especially those of the oppressive nature of state bureaucracies and of the breakdown of the consensus and technical efficiency once claimed by social democracy.

This politics has taken existing ideological motifs (some of them very old) and some original themes, combining them into a distinctive new whole. Ideologically, it is best understood as consisting of two main elements, whose power derives from their interaction. One element is a series of class-specific doctrines which construct a social reality which is then naturalized. We constantly find 'laws' of economics and of human nature, 'differences' of race, gender and ability, and 'impulses' of competitiveness or acquisitiveness which are clearly defined and rendered natural. This is 'the way things are' (as 'every housewife knows') and this is the way they must be. Counterposed to these doctrines is another constellation — the familiar 'ethical' tenets of radical individualism. These propose the individual as the basic unit of social and political analysis with certain supra-individual bodies presented either as aggregates of individuals (the nation, the economy) or as the enablers of individual freedom — the state. Ethical precepts of self-reliance, initiative and good housekeeping complete this 'moral' constellation.

The power of the new right drama lies in the collision between the two elements: the individual confronts an obstinate reality which exists independently of human volition and is fundamentally fixed. The fate of society and the specific fate of individuals depends upon the accuracy with which they can adapt themselves to the 'truths' of this 'objective' world. To ensure the highest conformity of human action to reality, individuals must be cast loose to take responsibility for their own actions. The sum of these individual confrontations will add up to the greatest good for the greatest number. This drama pivots on the opposition between individual freedom and state interference. Such an ideological condensation is remarkably agile. It connects with real contractions (such as the failure of neo-Keynesian management and the experience of the state as oppressive) and with a technical politics (monetarism). It also enables the right to place itself (and the state under its power) on the side of 'the individual' and 'the people' against over-taxation, waste, sapping of initiative and lack of freedom fostered by central-ization. This agility enables the generation of a more authoritarian state form – 'slimmer', less visible, more intensively concerned with the policing of waste, the management of disturbance, and the clearing away of inhibitions to 'enterprise' and profit. This is the real content of Thatcherite politics: the throwing of the full weight of the state and of the apparatuses of persuasion on to the side of capital and the decisive levelling of all resistances, including those of working-class organization, to its renewed self-expansion.

If we look at the structure of the new right's ideology of schooling, we find the twin themes of naturalization and individualism reappearing. The ideology gives a strong definition to the natural, self-evident purpose of schooling – it is concerned with the competitive differentiation of pupils and with a provision of a service to industry. The content of schooling is similarly self-evident (a return to 'the basics') while competitive differentiation only serves to reveal, of course, 'natural' differences in ability, application and interests. The individualism of the ideology stresses schooling's importance for individual mobility and makes education subject to the individualism of the market place.

At one end of the repertoire the concern is both 'freedom' and the crucial argument is around 'parental choice'. This perfectly expresses, in a succinct form, all the main themes of Conservative policy: negatively, the opposition to Labour's statism and professionalism; positively, the (illusory) belief that market principles in education will serve a greater measure of justice to individuals than will collectivist interventions. Under the slogan of 'parental choice', it is possible to justify the whole range of structural changes – towards the reintroduction of selection, the competitive setting of school against school, the re-enhancement of private education, the reduction of public expenditure on elementary state services – currently being introduced or considered. What the 'tax payer' or 'the economy' (that is the middle-class parent and capitalist businessman) can no longer afford, every 'good' parent should now endeavour to provide 'voluntarily'. Ideologically, the effect of this is to homogenize the parental community and therefore disguise the grossly unequal social costs of policy. Practically, it means that every single source of educational inequality analysed throughout this book, and indeed by social democratic expertise, will be immeasurably deepened. The continuance by the Tory government of some elements of Labour's late educational programme – much of the work, for instance, of the MSC in relation to the young unemployed – is the only sign to date that this stress on the education of the wealthier, more privileged sections of the community will be modified by fears of its social consequences. This, however, serves mainly to confirm our own analysis of the MSC's significance and the specifically capitalist character of its interventions.

In a more general sense, the stress on 'parental choice' is profoundly undemo-cratic. It is undemocratic in much the same way as the system of economic organization whose principles it expresses within the field of education. Parents are reduced to the status of consumers – but on behalf of their children –

shopping around in the school supermarkets. They are to have as little or as much control over what is 'offered' (or what they can 'afford') as their current resources permit. We are invited to choose from the range of goods available, but this is a very different form of 'choice' to that available to the citizen (parent or non-parent) in a properly democratic polity. The 'main lines' in the supermarket are to be determined indeed, not by an active, participating politics of schooling but by measures of 'necessary' scarcity. The main escape from these constraints, and the direction in which Conservatism impels the middle-class parent especially, is to shop elsewhere, in the luxury markets of private education and a purchased privilege. The logic of parental choice, indeed, pursued to its ultimate conclusion leads to the radical deconstruction of a system of public schooling (in the proper sense).

More than this, 'parental choice', by sanctifying parenthood as the ownership of children, treats children not as present or future citizens, with equal rights to education, but as adjuncts to families which, in their real social existences, have markedly unequal resources and powers. The 'rights' of children exist, therefore, only to the extent that the social and economic location of their parents permits them. Such a picture is certainly gloomy for anyone with liberal leanings, but there are strong reasons to suppose that the victory of the right's definitions is far from complete. We now turn to look at some of the significant weaknesses of the configuration. We discuss the limitations of the 'mandate' as a political base, and point to some of the contradictions of the formation now that it is in power.

It is on the dual issues of winning consent and securing economic success that the new politics will be made or broken. So far an old ideological repertoire has been broken up and another propounded. This does not represent a stable acquisition of consent. If any simple return to the faiths of the 1960s has been prohibited, future progress is far from clear.

Although the repertoire of the new right has been powerfully propagated and has had effects at the formal level of ideology, little is known in any systematic way about its deeper effects at the cultural level. As we have argued earlier, it is tempting, but illegitimate, to extrapolate from formal ideology to lived meaning. One vote in May 1979 certainly does not, unless we fall under the spell of the 'mandate' arguments, represent popular enthusiasm. It represents more plausibly, a sense of the weakness of social democratic solutions and a willingness, highly contingent on ultimate success, to try another way. The central contradiction here is the conflict between the electoral advantages won and the perceived effects of subsequent policies. If recession continues and deepens, consent sought on the promise of prosperity will rapidly dissipate. Similarly, the appeal to national unity stands in contrast to the deepening social inequalities, in terms of class, gender, race and region, produced by state action, or measured inaction. The rhetoric of freedom looks thin next to policies in which the state steps aside to allow further subjugation to 'natural' laws — actually to capitalist imperatives.

The 'cuts' provide the most immediate problem in relation to schooling. The disparity between a commitment to improve standards and to cut expenditure requires considerable negotiation. The fiction of the 'non-educational' nature of the cuts has already been punctured, and the cuts are of course redistributive They take away from the state schools while giving to the independent sector: they move resources from rural and inner city areas, from working-class families and from the unemployed, to the schooling of elite and suburban groups. Such movements stand in the grossest contrast to the appeal to 'parents' as an undifferentiated unity, on behalf of 'our' children.

The populist appeal presents a further series of problems. A more authoritarian form of state is masked by a populist politics − the state becomes increasingly active in social life as ideology declares its withdrawal in favour of entrepreneurial initiatives. This lies in direct contrast to the continuing need of capital for active intervention to secure the conditions for renewed accumulation. Part of an attempted resolution of this contradiction is the ceding, in rhetoric at least, of limited forms of 'consumer control' in certain areas − particularly schooling. Propounded as a search for means by which (wayward) teachers can be held responsible by the 'public' for their actions, the real results have less to do with the involvement of 'non-professionals' in schooling than a considerable tightening of forms of direct control − again a greater authoritarianism masked by a populism. Yet this tendency, the very appeal to parental control, could provide a greater impetus for a genuinely popular politics *opposed* to the general direction of state policy than did social democracy's reliance on professionalism and expertise.

Thatcherism, then, is deeply contradictory and will continue so, even if its economic strategies secure some long-term successes. Its failures, however, will be no matter for rejoicing on the left. In the absence of a new and developed socialist alternative with a similar global reach, we will simply be returned to the dilemmas of the 1970s with fewer real resources and less hope.

Dilemmas of the Labour leadership

The immediate problem for socialists is to develop an adequate response to the real, though qualified, Conservative success. Our own conclusion from the analysis presented here is that such a response necessarily involves a fundamental remaking of the main patterns of post-war social-democratic politics. The choice which is sometimes posed for Labour Party activists between 'fighting the Tories' and longer term, potentially divisive debates is, in our view, an unreal one. Effective opposition at this time, demands transformations of the dominant pattern of left politics.

In the course of these struggles the question of whether the Labour Party will continue to be the main socialist agency in Britain will be posed. We will certainly not try to resolve this question here, but it is important to gain a realistic sense of the magnitude of the changes required. One way of doing this is to consider Labour Party reactions to the crisis in educational policy since May 1979.

We shall be looking at particular responses in more detail, but they have been, in general, disappointing. The full challenge of the new right and the inadequacies of previous policies have not been recognized. Comparing the present dispositions of left and right in educational politics, it is clear where the initiative lies. The superiority of the right rests on features we have already identified. The new right is in possession of a global vision of the kind of society, and of the kind of education system within it, which its policies are intended to secure. The vision expresses itself in a whole social morality which is capable of becoming the 'cement' of a particular social order. The new right recognizes that debates about education have a strategic location in this project — they have a particular power to define one possible future, while defining out others. In contrast to Labour's concern with the institutional scaffolding of state education, modern Conservative politicians, especially of the type represented by the Prime Minister herself, understand the wider 'educative' role of political parties and the importance of the day-to-day definition of the terms of debate. The new right uses a structural and inherited connection with the media of communication to disseminate its own social vision and to exclude others.

The more formed responses which have come from the Labour Party have been piecemeal and conservative. This has been true even where, as on the left of the party, the policies of the Labour government, from the period of the Great Debate onwards, have been disavowed. The most common reflex has been to urge a defensive operation either by protecting past gains (for example comprehensi-vization) or by threatening the initiatives of the new right (for example the promise in the 'draft manifesto' to abolish the assisted places scheme and to prevent local authorities from paying for pupils, selected on the basis of attainment, to attend private schools). In addition to this defensive posture, the manifesto and other recent statements propose new or refurbished elements of policy very much on the model of the old. The proposal to extend nursery school provision, the completion of the framework of comprehensive schooling and the extension of opportunities for post school education, however valuable in themselves, stay within the terms of the 1960s' policies: a statist politics of access.

We do not wish to be misunderstood on this point. We are *not* denying the independent validity and importance of such reforms. There are features of the 1960s' policies which it is vital to defend and which have, indeed, been inadequately defended. Comprehensive schooling (leaving aside the vital question of its forms and the terms of its advocacy) has been a real advance. Nursery provision (though again the form matters) will be an important item in a more adequate politics informed by feminist emphases; while we are now patently paying the price for earlier failures to deal with private schooling, which is evidently no mere residual enclave. Post school and continuing education remain an absolutely crucial arena for future struggles. Yet however important these elements of policy may be, the process by which they have emerged has been merely reactive (to oppose Tory policy) or additive (the revival of forgotten issues and promises never fulfilled). They have tended to emerge within the same pattern of elite politics, in the same 'top-downwards' way. What guarantee can there be that these policies will be any more realizable or any more popular than the old? At worst, they create the illusion that Labour has an adequate response by satisfying tests of political adequacy which are obsolete.

These general points are, in our view, so important that they demand exemplification. It is worth analysing more clearly one recent statement of some broad lines of future Labour policy. The following passages are from a speech by Labour's shadow spokesman on education to the Socialist Education Association in October 1979.

. . . . and we must plan and accomplish assaults on four fronts.

1   The National Executive Committee of the Party, together with members of the Parliamentary Labour Party and all those with local government experience, professional expertise and principled commitment must establish our education policy as a cogent set of proposals, related to each other, related to public demands and expectations and related to the economic, social, technological and cultural needs of our society. That set of proposals should be assembled into a Charter for Educational Development from which we can draw major new legislation that will reassert our educational values, recreate the aspiration of genuine universal opportunities, prescribe new provision to meet new needs and safeguard rights of participation in the government of education for teachers, parents and the public.

2   There has to be a major effort through every means possible to inform the Labour movement about policy, to stimulate understanding of and confidence in that policy and to mobilise activity in pursuit of that policy.

3   Building on that, we have to carry that policy to the public, destroying the myths about education which confuse and prejudice public attitudes to standards of educational provision and performance, generating public comprehension of and enthusiasm for our policies and building demand for qualitative and quantitative improvement in education.

4   As an essential element in both of these other activities, to conduct a relentless offensive against the conception, implementation and short and long term effects of Tory policies.

We have to use this period of opposition to make Education a central issue of political debate and public demand. It has to be a finger in the fist of progress in the next Labour Government. We must ensure that it gains the importance of economic, industrial and energy policy. That is an elementary necessity if we are to make our society more harmonious, more articulate, more reasoning, more tolerant, more democratic. That is a fundamental priority if we are to survive economically. Restriction of education, whether by financial parsimony or social disadvantage or by the waste and suppression of talent that results from incompetent and unjust systems of selection is wilful destruction of our very means of life.

This statement certainly has strengths, particularly the stress on the centrality of educational issues and a recognition of the importance of socialist educational values of 'universal opportunity' and of democratic 'rights of participation'. We will return to these strengths but we must first recognize that most of the questions which must be raised here (and sooner or later fought through) are either begged or closed. The agents of educational policy are defined very much in terms of the 1960s alliance — leadership sections of the party, professional educationalists and administrators and, that interesting category, those with 'principled commitment'. Vagueness aside (commitment to what?), our previous arguments would suggest that the category is, in practice, a socially exclusive one as, to most people, state schooling is far too ambiguous an experience to warrant 'principled commitment'. How, according to Kinnock, are these agencies to proceed? Not, it seems certain, by considering the experiences and structural positions of the excluded majority, not by recognizing the elements of realism in popular knowledges, not by *working up* these practical insights but by *passing down* policies devised from 'professional expertise' and 'experience'. There is, indeed, a strong suggestion that the more popular constituencies are not to be trusted, that values will have to be recreated, understanding stimulated, myths and prejudices dissipated and confidence created from the outside. The (undifferentiated) 'public' is once more the object of (professional) policy and not in any sense policy's agent. To criticize this by now familiar mode of politics is not to fall into a belief in popular spontaneity, nor to underestimate the power of 'myth'. It is to insist that the popular experiences of schooling (and of other sites and relations) are once more absent from this scenario instead of being the very ground and material of political transformation.

In order to begin to consider this dimension seriously, we have to break decisively from the ideological homogenization of popular constituencies. Kinnock's term 'public' is an ideological construction in the strongest sense. It disguises different needs, experiences and interests in education which are, sometimes, antagonistic. There is no evidence in the speech of even elementary distinctions between, for example, middle-class and working-class 'publics', or between 'publics' constituted in relations of gender or race, or indeed between capitalist and popular interests. 'Public demands and expectations' achieve, once again, their characteristically social-democratic resolutions in the magical alchemy of harmonization. There would seem to be, for Kinnock, no conflicts between 'the economic, social, technological and cultural needs of *our* society'. Who *we* are and the precise nature of 'our needs' are left unspecified, but they seem to be identified with the technological and economic momentum of a capitalist society. Is this a *socialist* position? Similar questions arise about the promise of education to make society more harmonious. Can education do this? Should it do this? Should it do this in the short term and without changes in other social arrangements? Against the obstinate recurrence of such questions the 'Charter for Educational Development' represents a paper politics and we are left with little more of substance than the anger and determination to oppose Conservative inegalitarianism.

The main strengths of the statement lie in the continued commitment to 'universal opportunities' and democratic control. Together these elements distinguish socialist reflexes both from the Fabian elements of Labour's own inheritance and, most sharply, from modern Conservatism. These features cannot, however, be left inertly as a passive source of assumed rectitude. Unless they are actively cultivated, intelligently thought about and, above all, practically specified, principles of this kind may lose their force or even change their very character. We have given examples of these almost imperceptible shifts and mutations from the long history of the terms 'equality' and 'equality of opportunity'. To combat such shifts we have to be able to define what we mean by being democratic and egalitarian, to recreate the conditions, impulses and arguments that led us there and to specify the practical consequences. In the process of this practical definition, we must expect to lose some previous political allies.

The phrase 'the aspiration of genuine universal opportunities' is a case in point. Such phrases may 'sound right' morally but they are susceptible to radically different appropriations. If the 'aspiration' part is stressed the politics may topple backwards, as Labour's 1950s 'revisionism' constantly threatened, into a politics of the softening of social divisions and of what we termed a politics of status. Where class and other structural inequalities remain, we are no further forward than a conservative liberalism. If the 'opportunities' aspect is stressed, the politics balances around a social democratic centre; it ambivalently acknowledges necessary divisions of function and of reward in the hope that no one will notice that these divisions also confer differential powers, shape subjectivities and divide the world, once more, into tadpoles and frogs. Such a politics may even confirm the main lines of Conservative educational policy by acknowledging a pre-given natural basis for such differences while, of course, avoiding the meritocratic extremes.

Moving on: some paradoxes

The truth is that the Labour leadership — for some very good reasons and by no means the leadership alone — is caught within what is, by now, a very 'traditional' view of educational politics. We feel the need to start moving beyond these limiting constructions of what needs to be done and by whom. A series of socially constructed divisions has come to stand in the way of new developments. These constraints are complex, involving genuine difficulties around which ideological elements have clustered. They have become effective both in constructing our experience of 'what the world is like' and in inhibiting the forms of political practice: their negotiation demands careful analysis.

Take, to begin with, the carefully sustained separations between 'adults' and 'children'. Capitalist schooling is certainly, among other things, a form of state intervention into the reproduction of labour power. It emphasizes, through the supervised translation of children from the privacy of home to the noise of production, the selection of a few and the frustration of the many. It differentiates sharply between the sexes and defines knowledge as that useful to the capitalist mode of production. In this historically specific form of education, children are treated as essentially passive — subject to adult authority. Schooling thus provides for real conflicts between adults and children. These power relations have a particular basis: the dependence of the newly born and the socialization of the young into existing relations bo*th* render children subject to adult power. On top of this, there is a vast cultural overlay: the treatment of the child as a separate type of person with various lacks (for example, a lack of sexuality, a lack of judgement, a lack of politics) and therefore subordinate to adults. Against this, specific child and youth cultures come to be defined in opposition to adult authority and in defiance (part real, part fantasized) of it. The processes here are deeply contradictory, partly acting for capitalism and patriarchy while partly opposing their demands. Children asked to be 'obedient' are then often found to have withdrawn to their own sub-cultures in the face of the demand. The existing adult—child power relations can then render even well-thought political interventions into such cultures merely another adult interference. Almost the only competing public image of childhood in England today is in the media fantasy of, and symptomatic outrage at, 'pupil power'. One immediate, straightforward (though largely unspoken) need is for experiments around, and versions of, 'children' as active participants in, not objects or recipients of, an educational politics.

In the same way, education has become too quickly and specifically the concern of professionals and parents — not of the excluded non-parents for whom the language has not even a word. Capitalist schooling has defined children as its objects, parents as those ultimately 'responsible'. This has been a consequence of the functioning of schools to reproduce labour power for social relations of production which the majority of parents themselves experience as dissatisfying, oppressive, or more recently unavailable in any case. In these circumstances, only a minimum of ideological work is needed to turn this into the hope of parents for a less burdensome future for the young. There develops an individualism of 'my' child, her or his 'chances', and for those in a position to calculate the odds, a judgement of the qualifications required and how to win them. The politics of the specific forms of the reproduction of labour power are transformed into the concern of parents for the individual mobility of 'their' children. Indeed, other questions and definitions of schools may even be rejected as 'politically' motivated. Schools and schooling are treated almost exclusively as the site of parental worry over individual children, while administered and controlled by professional teachers and state experts and administrators.

Yet, in the full sense, education and learning are altogether more general concepts than schooling: tied neither to specific age ranks nor to particular institutional forms. They refer to general features of human sociality: becoming aware of, competent within, able to change, the definite social relations of a particular society.

The starting point of critical elaboration is the consciousness of what one really is, and is 'knowing thyself' as a product of the historical process to date which has deposited in you an infinity of traces, without leaving an inventory.[15]

Gramsci saw the received relationship between 'intellectuals' and 'the simple' (without formal academic training) as transformed by a process in which the present is rendered as a contradictory product of the past with the potential for a different future. Education, in this larger sense, denaturalizes hierarchies of age: both 'old' and 'young' or 'new' are new members of the present if the present is understood as a process, rather than a given structure or set of tasks. Education crosses the division between parents and non-parents and spans particular ages: the narrowing-down to parents, professionals and schools becomes an overt object of an educational politics not its entire and sufficient starting point.

To say this is to be as yet nowhere near the concerns of the 'official party spokesperson': deliberately so. The issues have been grossly narrowed in recent decades, and not only in terms of agents (adults not children, teachers and parents not others). A politics of schooling involves a politics of what lies far outside schooling; and capitalist schooling (between the desire and the shadow . . .) is education only intermittently if at all. The former requires a detailed knowledge of the powerful and active constraints; the latter necessitates an imagination of quite other horizons.

We have stressed throughout, in opposition to social democratic policies, that schools are more determined than determining. This might imply that action in or around schools is limited to the point of futility, that changes must begin somewhere else. We reject this. The problem is to develop a politics of schooling which, while aware of its limits, tackles serious issues. At the beginning of the book we argued that, as a site of political work, the school is doubly peculiar: it involves people acting vicariously 'on behalf' of 'the young' presumed to be relatively helpless, and it involves a strongly emotional commitment to a better future. For a worker in the social services (in probation, say) or an employee in a factory, only limited gains are normally to be expected in the circumstances: the social relations of their work involve stress and damage as a matter of course. For a teacher or parent, expectations are inevitably far greater and far more laden. We want nevertheless to suggest that our analysis implies a politics of schooling on two fronts.

The first arena is identified by our modified understanding of a Marxist functionalism. We have argued that schooling does perform various tasks for the capitalist mode of production and for patriarchal relations, but that this is in no way guaranteed. For instance schools may not meet the particular needs of employers. To challenge, in any case, the attempt at an ever tighter functioning for capital is one type of politics of schooling. This is not because production is unimportant but precisely because of the inability of capitalist forms of production to realize the abilities of producers, who are themselves produced in stunted forms. The contestation ranges from struggles over the formal organization of schooling (such as the constantly divisive structures of certification) to those around more informal aspects (the reproduction of 'correct' attitudes and 'desires' through cultural processes). The fundamental issue is why should, and how do, schools serve to ease new generations into the antagonistic relations of production and of patriarchy? This is, in that form, a very general question: it can point to the most detailed particular issues — how and what and from whom will children 'learn about industry' in a school?

Second, we have emphasized that the politics of schooling is part of a wider process of bidding for consent. A counter-politics of schooling tries to discredit and stand outside the specific class and gender nature of the processes currently presented as natural and eternal. The immensity of this task is formidable. The starting points lie in the huge space between the current functions of schooling and education in the fullest sense, in its socialist and feminist definition. Of course this does not simply exist waiting to be 'realized': it will not be easy to form, its shape can only be known at later stages in a long process. Nevertheless previous working-class struggles and present critiques of capitalist schooling from feminists, socialists and children themselves suggest definite directions.

Most generally, a feminist and socialist understanding of education clearly opposes processes of schooling which are patriarchal and capitalist. Rather than mystifying or strengthening determinations upon schooling from the requirements of production or of 'woman's place', those connections will be examined as a central object of educational knowledge: how is the labour process organized, and experienced? What has been defined as the world of women? Such an education would try to redefine knowledge in terms of its ability to enable the subordinate to understand the social processes to which they are presently subjected. Open access to the definition and use of existing knowledge and to the creation and use of new knowledge are equally important: education should attempt to socialize the division of intellectual labour so that divisions of educational labour are defined in terms not of material reward, authority or status but of different kinds of task in a common cause. Education in this way becomes an active and co-operative attempt to gain control of the material and social world through analysis and action. Such attempts may be made equally by adult or child. If age hierarchies recede as the organizing principle of education so class and gender emerge more strongly. A unitary notion of 'citizens' with their 'common culture' is no longer tenable in an education structured by the attempt to understand and control a contradictory social world.

Looking for education, looking for the educators

Where then do we start to find attempts to close this gap between education and capitalist schooling? We give here, briefly, two negative and two more positive examples.

Despite the brave and usually isolated efforts of some teachers, and despite the major advance of the journals and networks (some of which are to be found in the end pages), the weight of state schooling stays stubbornly on the side of capital. Innovative and radical education has sometimes emerged in state schools, but only sporadically and briefly. The odds against individual teachers, or small groups of teachers, who lack firm external support are very considerable. This is starting to move in some ways, but could anyone deny that the change is slow? In addition, the notion of 'professional' work continues to define the teacher *within* the school: connections outside the school are difficult.

Further, the Labour Party has done little to assist socialist teachers: not so much because it has failed to pursue socialist practices of teaching inside the renamed comprehensives (say), but because it has almost abandoned its own educative function. It has restricted rather than fostered popular aspirations — the idea of a thirst for knowledge being quenched or slaked by the party! — and, to some extent, it has adopted anti-educational forms of organization. If the party is to perform an educative role, the emphasis must move away from the concern with state and parliamentary politics towards the grass-roots work of branches, away from the shifting around of already constituted blocks of influence (the card vote) towards a local agitational politics which discovers as it acts.

Meanwhile there is a growing prominence, outside state provision, of other educational movements seeking to retain an older socialist and develop a newer feminist commitment. In these groups, knowledge is produced and shared in quite different and new ways, dominated neither by the qualification nor by the committee. Membership is often drawn from those who have experienced further and higher education, especially if their histories have coincided with some phase of the new politics, ranging from the new left to the women's movement and often with a passage in and out of one or more of the smaller socialist parties. Such groups have not yet had but are beginning to develop popular connections; while other specific interest or community or cultural groups organize and, in many true senses, educate with, as yet, few firm links into directly political questions and organizations.

This returns us to a subterranean theme in this book: the development, given the shape of the post-war economy and the expansion of higher educational provision, of significant numbers of people obtaining first and higher degree qualifications — more numerous recruits for professional and managerial positions, or to put it with crude emphasis, the proliferating supervisors. There could be no simple movement from Gramsci's reflections in Italy in the 1930s on the links between the 'intellectuals' and 'the simple' to these developments, but *The Philosophy of Praxis* is brilliantly stimulating on some of the major questions here. In particular:

one could only have had . . . an organic quality of thought if there had existed the same unity between the intellectuals and the simple as there should be between theory and practice. That is, if the intellectuals had been organically the intellectuals of those masses, and if they had worked out and made coherent the principles and the problems raised by the masses in their practical activity, thus constituting a cultural and social bloc . . . . It is a philosophical movement properly so called when it is devoted to creating a specialised culture among restricted intellectual groups or when . . . it never forgets to remain in contact with the 'simple' and indeed finds in this contact the source of the problems it sets out to study and to resolve? Only by this contact does a philosophy become 'historical', purify itself of intellectualistic elements of an individual character and become 'life'.[16]

Many doubts could be raised here (around leadership, perhaps, or questions of gender) and much needs to be developed, particularly around the meaning of the 'philosophy' — 'of praxis'.

We use this essay, though, to make here only one small and one larger point. While education and schooling are conflated it is possible to equate educators with professionally certified and employed teachers — damagingly. More significant is Gramsci's tackling of the development of new intellectuals, allied with the subordinate rather than the dominant classes. The function defining these new intellectuals is their organizing, constructing and persuading (and at the same time learning) role. The ground for education in the Gramscian sense is the coexistence in subordinate groups of two conceptions of the world. One, the imposed conception, helps hold these groups in their subordinated place. The other, a shadowy conception emerging occasionally through practical action, provides the raw material for transformation into a politics of self-knowledge and also of opposition. It is with the critical elaboration of this immanent philosophy that Gramsci's new intellectuals are concerned.

This seems very important at a time when some of the new intellectuals in Britain have powerfully developed their own journals, organizations and often sophisticated forms of writing. The connections and groupings such people make in the next few years could have challenging consequences. Here we only note that forms of joint work are already emerging (between researchers and trade unions, in resource centres for local areas) where some divisions — of researchers and researched, but also of teachers and taught — are beginning to break down.

The Labour Party and a policy for education

We expect the 1980s to see a rich development of distinctively local activities. This will take place both through the parties of the left as they are altered and strengthened, and through the huge variety of groups around community politics, sexual politics, black politics and many other questions: the 'fragments' whose life and stamina and commitment to new kinds of political campaigning and conviviality far outrun most routinized forms of party politics. Nevertheless a national educational policy still needs to be formulated for the main parties of the left: fed by, but not just a response to, particular forms of local politics.

For the Labour Party, we want to argue, a new start is needed at this level. While a lot of work will be needed to stem and reverse Conservative inroads into educational provision, and more to try, even at a late stage, to make good — make real, and find socialist meaning in — the ambiguous pledges of the 1960s, the whole field needs to be rethought: partly, at least, in a spirit of 'what has gone wrong?' We want to repeat, in a very summary way, some of the issues that will need to be on that agenda: to list the areas where the old mould must be broken in new forms of politics.

Serving two masters

The problems here were fully discussed at the end of Chapter 4 and in the conclusion to Part Two. The party has attempted to serve at the same time popular interests and those of capital: to 'harmonize' opposing needs. In practice, the liberal Fabian version of planning has assumed complete domination (during the party's long periods in government) over its radical campaigning energies: many have abandoned Labour for that reason. In education, the tension between practical equality or social equality (the full commitment to sisterhood and brotherhood) and equal opportunity or equality of opportunity (the modernizing capitalist commitment to the career open to the talents, the attempted supercession of 'archaic' class differences by those grounded in 'objectively' certified 'ability') has always been uneven: the latter version has won out. The representation of 'the people' has moved steadily towards the representation of the professional managerial classes. There is no going back to the tenuous 'harmony', based on economic expansion; there is no going back, either, to simple notions of working class and middle class with (somewhere else, or uneasily fitted in) women and blacks. Different experiences and needs of education will have to be understood. For this reason . . .

Access is not enough

More is involved than changes in provision to allow subordinate groups access to or a given length of time within a specific level of formal education. The content of schooling is not neutral, but infused by elements of sexism and racism, and responsive to the conceptions of the world of different social groups. For Gramsci it was, 'not a question of introducing from scratch a scientific form of thought into everyone's individual life, but of renovating and making 'critical' an already existing activity'.[17] This is also to start thinking about a socialist and feminist philosophy of praxis (not just curriculum), socialist and feminist ways of learning and teaching (not just pedagogies), socialist and feminist ways of running a school and of thinking about its relation to its local area (not just control). This will, too, involve learning from and thinking about . . .

Non-state education

Increasingly there are equivocal feelings about present forms of state education, and a determination to meet needs of which it is unaware. Past instances included the various attempts (such as the movement for independent working-class education set up by the Plebs League) to assert a trade unionist and working-class view of the world against that offered in the Workers' Educational Association (sometimes) or university extension classes (more often).[18] A contemporary list might begin with women's groups of many kinds, forms of community education, black classes at weekends. There is already an enormous amount to be learnt in these alternatives. In the next few years, feminists and many others will face serious choices between attempts at changing state provision and at elaborating and innovating educational provision outside it. This will involve relating needs of schools to other needs and values arising from experience before, outside and beyond them: in contrast to the present domination of discussion by the needs of 'industry'. Yet here feminists, politicians and industrialists find themselves alike concerned with that which lies beyond and outside education . . .

Educational politics aren't sufficient

What *is* the secret of the obstinacy or reluctance or stroppiness of the worker or school pupil that requires so mighty an apparatus of education and management? Is it possible, if the social conditions of labour were changed, not to give token autonomies in the service of more flexible management and higher productivity, but to give real collective responsibility and among equals, that equivalent educational changes would be not only possible but essential? It is indeed not education that should conform to industry, but industry that should conform to the needs of human development. We need educational critiques of work, in factories and in homes, of the kind that some researchers, attentive to workers' experiences, are now beginning to supply. The longer (but not *that* much longer) term aim is not to meet the needs of capitalist industry as currently constituted in Britain in a weak and dependent form but to develop a form of social organization, linked to changes in the relations of sexes, which would actually produce more real wealth than a capitalist and patriarchal social order. In the meantime, English schooling is not accidentally 'at its best' among primary and infant classes: before competition and qualification become inevitable. Yet there are no educational enclaves which can be held for very long in this way. To think about educational reform is to think about changing the lived relations of sexes, the structuring of forms of production, the condition of women. Anything less than this is bound to fail. To think about it is only 'wildly utopian' in the impoverished terms of the irrecoverable circumstances of a brief period (the 1950s and 1960s) in one western capitalist country. Children seem to think about it already, much of the time. But none of this leaves education as comfortably non-political; and in reverse, it raises the question of . . .

A political education

The last shift concerns the character of the Labour Party itself, and the way its leadership especially conceives of 'education'. From the inter-war years on, the party's direct educative functions have become steadily narrower and more limited, while more and more trust has been placed in the reform of the state education system. The effects are now being reaped with a vengeance. The party has no independent educational ideals or vision of its own, no conception of what it is important to understand politically in order to transform the world in a socialist direction. It has no or very few organic links to the popular constituencies which it has historically claimed to represent. Its active working-class membership was mainly recruited in an earlier radical phase, especially in the 1940s. It still suffers from what Marx called 'parliamentary cretinism'. It is parasitic on its activists, even to the point of policing them, rather than enabling them to develop their own knowledge and political effectivity.

Nor is this just a question of 'fighting Tory myths' (in the deadest of clichés) or of 'carrying the policy to the electorate'. It involves *learning*, too. It requires research, preferably at the level of local branches, into the conditions and circumstances of local struggles — and how they are often determined a long way outside the locality. It involves making links with other agencies — black groups, women's groups, community activists, radical groups in the professions, researchers — to learn from and with them. It involves creating a real branch *life* which is eagerly looked forward to, which energizes rather than tires, which involves risk and challenge and new socialist understandings. Above all it involves a more extended educational activity well beyond the local membership, with its aim, less a direct party recruitment, than a movement of large groups of people back to an informed commitment to non-statist forms of socialist practice. At the moment (and with over 2 million unemployed officially as this book is finished) socialism is only rarely present in a fully public and articulate and moving way.

In these senses the contest between social democracy's unpopular education and Conservatism's capitalist schooling has been lost. The contest between capitalism and discipline, and socialism and education, has not even been attempted.

Notes and references

Preface

1   See Dan Finn, Neil Grant and Richard Johnson, 'Social democracy, education and the crisis' in *On Ideology* (CCCS 1977; Hutchinson 1978). A revised version of this article is available from CCCS: Education Group, *Social Democracy, Education and The Crisis* (CCCS Stencilled Paper No. 52 1978).

1   Perspectives on schooling and politics

1   For more complete maps of theoretical tendencies in educational research see the long introductory chapter in J. Karabel and A. H. Halsey (eds.), *Power and Ideology in Education* (Oxford University Press 1977) and Stuart Hall, *A Review of the Course,* Open University Course E202, Unit 32 (Open University Press 1977).

2   For an interesting review from the standpoint of a more social history of education see Harold Silver, 'Aspects of neglect: the strange case of Victorian popular education', *Oxford Review of Education,* vol. 3, no. 1 (1977), pp. 57-69. But the situation has been changing very fast in the last few years.

3   We include here many texts on the history of social policy and 'the rise of the welfare state', studies of particular government departments, biographies of policy-making politicians or public servants and many more theoretical studies of 'government'. An interesting example, germane to our themes, is I. G. K. Fenwick, *The Comprehensive School 1944-1970: The Politics of Secondary School Reorganization* (Methuen 1976).

4   ibid., p. 3.

5   See, for example, the stress on the evaluation of the roles of individual politician—authors in Gillian Sutherland, *Policy-Making in Elementary Education 1870-1895* (Oxford University Press 1973), and in J. S. Hurt, *Education in Evolution* (Hart-Davis 1971).

6   Fenwick, *The Comprehensive School,* pp. 3-4.

7   It is important to stress this against the tendency to overrate the novelty of later analyses of 'discourse'.

8   Especially interesting in relation to our own concerns are Foucault's *Discipline and Punish: The Birth of the Prison* (Allen Lane 1977); *The Birth*

of the Clinic: An Archaeology of Medical Perception (Tavistock 1973); *Madness and Civilisation* (Tavistock 1971); *I, Pierre Rivière . . .* (Peregrine Books 1979); *History of Sexuality,* vol. 1 (Pantheon Books 1978).

9   See, for example, the discussion of the educational technique of monitorialism and of military models of discipline in *Discipline and Punish,* pp. 135-69. Later in the same book, there is an interesting discussion of radical working-class attitudes to crime and of the inversions of dominant definitions that occur there. Even in these sections, however, Foucault's account remains ambiguous. On the whole, we agree with Michael Ignatieff that Foucault's conclusion appears to be that regulative sciences 'exclusively define the modes of public perception'. Certainly Ignatieff's own account of the rise of the penitentiary lays much more stress on the determinacy of social struggles, including struggles within the prisons themselves. See Michael Ignatieff, A *Just Measure of Pain: The Penitentiary in the Industrial Revolution 1750-1850* (Macmillan 1979), especially p. 220.

10   For example, much of the discussion of Foucault's ideas in the journals *Ideology and Consciousness* and *M/F.* On educational and allied themes, see especially Nikolas Rose, 'The psychological complex: mental measurement and social administration', *Ideology and Consciousness,* no. 5 (Spring 1979) and Karen Jones and Kevin Williamson, 'The birth of the schoolroom', ibid., no. 6 (Autumn 1979). More relevant to our period (and more aware of the limitations of the approach) is James Donald, 'Green Paper: noise of crisis', *Screen Education,* no. 30 (Spring 1979), pp. 13-49. This article also contains useful criticisms of our own earlier formulations (ibid., pp. 16-17).

11   For accounts of these traditions see Raphael Samuel, 'British Marxist historians, 1880-1980: part one', *New Left Review,* no. 120 (March-April 1980), pp. 21-96, and Richard Johnson, 'Culture and the historians', in John Clarke, Chas Critcher and Richard Johnson (eds.), *Working Class Culture: Studies in History and Theory* (Hutchinson 1979), pp. 41-71. Recent developments may be followed especially in *History Workshop Journal.*

12   See especially E. P. Thompson, *The Making of the English Working Class* (Gollancz 1963) and the more political and polemical pieces recently issued as *The Poverty of Theory and Other Essays* (Merlin Press 1978). The essay 'The peculiarities of the English' contains especially interesting passages in which Thompson's general stress on popular struggle, worked through in great detail in *The Making,* is applied to other historical periods.

13   Brian Simon's work in the history of education is important for combining a stress on 'policy' (including the high-political level) with a concern for the educational strategies of 'the Labour movement'. Later we draw on Brian Simon, *Education and the Labour Movement 1870-1920* (Lawrence & Wishart 1965) and *The Politics of Educational Reform 1920-1940* (Lawrence & Wishart 1974).

14   Louis Althusser, 'Ideology and ideological state apparatuses', in his *Lenin and Philosophy and Other Essays* (New Left Books 1971).

15   Samuel Bowles and Herbert Gintis, *Schooling in Capitalist America: Educational Reform and the Contradictions of Economic Life* (Routledge & Kegan Paul 1976).

16   Pierre Bourdieu and Jean-Claude Passeron, *Reproduction in Education, Society and Culture,* trans. R. Nice (Sage 1977). See also the many other works on these themes from the Centre for European Sociology, ibid., pp. 237-41.

17   B. Bernstein, *Class, Codes and Control,* vol. 3, rev. ed. (Routledge & Kegan Paul 1977).

18   Anne-Marie Wolpe, 'Education and the sexual division of labour', in Annette Kuhn and Anne-Marie Wolpe (eds.), *Feminism and Materialism: Women and Modes of Production* (Routledge & Kegan Paul 1978); Eileen Byrne, *Women and Education* (Tavistock 1978); Rosemary Deem, *Women and Schooling* (Routledge & Kegan Paul 1978); Sue Sharpe, *Just Like a Girl* (Penguin 1976); and, as a useful review, Mica Nava, 'Gender and education', *Feminist Review,* no. 5, pp. 69-78.

19   Research on labour processes in Britain and America was greatly stimulated by the publication of Harry Braverman, *Labor and Monopoly Capital: The Degradation of Work in the Twentieth Century* (Monthly Review Press 1974). For the state, welfarism, etc. see N. Poulantzas, *Political Power and Social Classes* (New Left Books 1975); J. Holloway and S. Picciotto (eds.), *State and Capital* (Edward Arnold 1978); Elizabeth Wilson, *Women and the Welfare State* (Tavistock 1977); Mary McIntosh, 'The state and the oppression of women' in Kuhn and Wolpe (eds.), *Feminism and Materialism;* Philip Corrigan (ed.), *Capitalism, State Formation and Marxist Theory: Historical Investigations* (Quartet 1980). This is only a small fraction of the relevant work: there is an excellent bibliography in Corrigan, *State Formation.*

20   Or, in subsequent self-criticisms, for example, *Lenin and Philosophy,* postscript to the essay on ideological state apparatuses; Bernstein, *Class, Codes and Control,* vol. 3, p. 174; Herbert Gintis and Samuel Bowles, 'Contradiction and reproduction in educational theory', in R. Date, G. Esland, R. Ferguson and M. MacDonald (eds.), *Education and the State: Schooling and the National Interest* (Open University Course Reader for E353, Society, Education and the State, Open University/Falmer Press 1981).

21   Some parts of the arguments that follow are developed in more detail in Richard Johnson, *Education and Popular Politics,* Open University Unit, Course E353, Unit 1 (Open University Press 1981). The sections on Marx's view of 'conditions' and on function and cause were written before we had read the excellent discussion in G. A. Cohen, *Karl Marx's Theory of History: A Defence* (Oxford University Press 1978).

22   The simplest form of the argument is to be found in the chapter on 'Simple reproduction' in *Capital,* vol. 1 (Penguin 1976), pp. 711-24. It is useful in this edition to turn next to Appendix, 'Results of the immediate process of production', pp. 1060-5, but there is a sense in which the whole of *Capital* is an elaboration of the simple model of reproduction found in vol. 1, ch. 23.

23   Marx, *Capital,* vol. 1, p. 719.
24   ibid., p. 724.
25   For the 1960s' images see Chapter 4; for the Manpower Services Commission see Chapter 11.
26   Marx, *Capital,* vol. 1, chs. 26-32.
27   Marx, *Capital,* vol. 1, ch. 10 and ch. 15.
28   For a particularly polemical version of this argument, by which 'Althusserianism' is identified with 'bourgeois social science', see Simon Clarke, 'Althusserian Marxism', in Simon Clarke *et al., One-Dimensional Marxism: Althusser and the Politics of Culture* (Allison & Busby 1980). For a more careful evaluation of the question of Marxist 'functionalism', see Cohen, *Karl Marx's Theory of History.*
29   This has been one of the issues raised by Thompson's 'Poverty of theory' and the debate on history and theory in *History Workshop Journal.* Our own position is similar to that developed very clearly in Perry Anderson, *Arguments within English Marxism* (New Left Books 1980).
30   See especially Paul Willis, *Learning to Labour: How Working-Class Kids Get Working-Class Jobs* (Saxon House 1977).
31   There is an increasing recognition among Marxist and feminist writers of the importance of consumption as an arena of the creation and satisfaction of needs and therefore as an important site of struggles. In this, as is quite often the case, they lag behind more conservative social theorists and well behind the practical consciousness of businessmen and advertisers.
32   Anna Davin, 'Imperialism and motherhood', *History Workshop Journal,* no. 5 (Spring 1978), pp. 9-65; Lucy Bland *et al.,* 'Women "inside" and "outside" the relations of production', in CCCS Women's Studies Group, *Women Take Issue: Aspects of Women's Subordination* (Hutchinson 1978). For an excellent discussion of one circuit of effects between capitalist forms of production, consumption and reproduction and specific forms of femininity, see Janice Winship, 'A woman's world: *woman* – an ideology of femininity', ibid., pp. 133-54.
33   Compare the argument in Althusser, 'Ideological state apparatuses'.
34   In the case of 'the capital-relation' between labourer and employer, for example, in the actual circuit of production and consumption which reaffirms the labourer's dependence on the wage and on employment. See Marx, *Capital,* vol. 1, pp. 161-4.
35   For a more elaborate definition of particular sites see Gintis and Bowles, 'Contradiction and reproduction'.
36   Our formulations here owe much to positions developed within the Women's Studies Group in CCCS, to the work of individual women in the Centre and to discussions in the Family–School Group.
37   We see the family as the main site of the reproduction of existing forms of relations between the sexes, agreeing in this respect with the feminist materialism developed by Christine Delphy. But we also agree with those feminist and Marxist-feminist historians and theorists who argue that concrete

forms of family relations are also constructed in relation to capitalist social organization and have differed significantly by class. Similarly, we agree with Delphy that the exploitation of women's labour within the terms of the marriage contract is a key source of the subordination of women, but would add that accounts of patriarchy must also grasp the conditions and relations in which human life itself is reproduced. Christine Delphy, 'The main enemy: a materialist analysis of women's oppression' (WRRC Publication 1977) and compare CCCS Women's Studies Group, *Women Take Issue,* especially Rachel Harrison, *'Shirley*: relations of reproduction and the ideology of romance', ibid., pp.176-96.

38 Richard Johnson, 'Educational policy and social control in early Victorian England', *Past and Present,* no. 49 (November 1970), p. 112.

39 For a full discussion of this relation see Jenny Shaw, 'In loco parentis: a relationship between parent, state and child', *Journal of Moral Education,* vol. 6, no. 3 (1977), pp. 181-90.

40 Jenny Shaw, 'School attendance — some notes on a further feature of sexual division' (paper given at a Conference on Patriarchy, Capitalism and Educational Policy, Institute of Education, University of London 1978). We are grateful to the author for making available a copy of this paper.

41 For chartings of this circle, see Sue Sharpe, *Just Like a Girl;* Angela McRobbie, 'Working class girls and the culture of femininity' and Dorothy Hobson, 'Housewives: isolation as oppression', both in CCCS Women's Studies Group, *Women Take Issue.*

42 See especially Paul Willis, *Learning to Labour* and Angela McRobbie, 'Working class girls'.

43 For the best example of this form of radical populist address in the 1940s, see the discussion of G. C. T. Giles, Chapter 4.

44 Alfred Schutz, 'The stranger — an essay in social psychology' in *Collected Papers of Alfred Schutz,* vol. 2 (Martinus Nijhoff 1971), p. 93. There are striking similarities between Schutz's description of common sense and that of Gramsci.

45 Raymond Williams, *Culture and Society, 1780-1950* (Penguin 1961); Richard Hoggart, *The Uses of Literacy* (Penguin 1958); Thompson, *The Making.*

46 Quintin Hoare and Geoffrey Nowell-Smith (eds.), *Selections from the Prison Notebooks of Antonio Gramsci* (Lawrence & Wishart 1971), p. 323.

47 In previous versions of this argument, the distinction we make here between representations and culture was identified with the distinction ideology and culture. This involves a very expanded use of the term 'ideology' to include all more formal discourses and systems of representation. It also implies that there is nothing 'ideological' in 'common sense'. In this version, we prefer a more limited and specific definition of the ideological (see page 272, note 51), a term which may apply both to elements in the field of public representations and to practical common sense views. See also the discussion of public opinion and popular knowledge pp. 208-9. Compare Richard Johnson, 'Cultural studies and educational practice', *Screen Education,* no. 34 (Spring 1980), pp. 5-16.

48   Karl Marx and Frederick Engels, *The German Ideology,* ed. C. J. Arthur
(Lawrence & Wishart 1970), p. 65.

49   This is because Gramsci makes a distinction between intellectual activity
(which all share in) and intellectual functions (which only some perform under
a specific social organization). Intellectual functions are also thought of,
however, in an expanded way — not as the production of knowledge or ideas
alone, but as directing activity: hence industrial managers are 'organic
intellectuals' for capital (*Prison Notebooks,* pp. 5-14).

50   Such analyses, however, do not exhaust the significance of productive
activities which, from another point of view, may transform elements of
nature, sustain material life, reproduce or modify social relations, etc., etc.
The omnipresence of signifying activity is not a warrant for the reduction of
all social activity to discourse, signification or language.

51   This view is argued (against more expanded uses following Althusser) in Jorge
Larrain, *The Concept of Ideology* (Hutchinson 1979). We are also grateful
for discussions with the author which have helped greatly to clarify our own
thinking. As Larrain puts it: 'For ideology to be present, the two conditions
which Marx laid down should be satisfied: the objective concealment of
contradictions, and the interests of the dominant class. Ideology is not a
simple error. It is a *particular kind* [our emphasis] of distortion, dependent
upon real contradictions, which demand their solution in practice before it
can be overcome' (ibid., p. 210).

52   See especially the discussion of teaching paradigms in Willis, *Learning to
Labour,* pp. 62-85.

53   This difference of class 'orientation' to schooling is a persistent finding of
educational research over several decades. For the finding (and the absence of
adequate explanations) see Chapter 6.

54   This applies especially to social democratic politics in its most middle-class
forms. See the analysis of class-based styles in local Labour politics in B.
Hindess, *The Decline of Working Class Politics* (MacGibbon & Kee 1971).

55   See pp. 41-2.

56   This is not to say that it is only in 'education' (that is, in systems of schooling)
that intellectual capacities are developed. In relation to working-class needs,
it may well be the case that they are best developed in what we later call
'substitutional' activity which may take a counter-educational form, opposed
to the dominant schooling system.

57   For valuable discussions of the particular position of such groups in relation
to the education system see Pierre Bourdieu, 'Cultural reproduction and social
reproduction' in R. Brown (ed.), *Knowledge, Education and Social Change*
(Tavistock 1973); Nicos Poulantzas, *Classes in Contemporary Capitalism* (New
Left Books 1975), part 3; Magali Larson, *The Rise of Professionalism* (University
of California Press 1977).

58   Hoare and Nowell-Smith (eds.), *Prison Notebooks, passim,* but especially
pp. 242-76.

Chapter 2   Popular dilemmas, radical strategies and the inter-war Labour Party

1   The portrayal of this dilemma is based, in the first instance, on a close study
of working-class radicalism in the period 1790-1850, but it can be traced
through the whole tradition of working-class radical education. See Richard
Johnson, ' "Really useful knowledge" : radical education and working-class
culture 1790-1848' in John Clarke, Chas Critcher and Richard Johnson,
Working Class Culture: Studies in History and Theory (Hutchinson 1979),
especially pp. 77-9, and for the later forms of this dilemma, Richard Johnson,
Education and Popular Politics, especially sections 7.1-7.3.

2   Johnson, 'Really useful knowledge', pp. 78-9 and 84-8.

3   Johnson, *Education and Popular Politics,* sections 7.1-7.2.

4   The educational attitudes of radical women are much less well documented
than those of socialist men, especially within the working class. But there are
rich materials to be found in J. Liddington and J. Norris, *One Hand Tied
Behind Us* (Virago 1978), a superb account of local working-class feminist
movements and activism.

5   The cultural politics of early nineteenth-century radicalism is much better
documented, by historians, than that of the later phase, thanks largely to the
scope and density of Edward Thompson's recoveries in *The Making of the
English Working Class* (Gollancz 1963). Indispensable sources include:
A. E. Dobbs, *Education and Social Movements, 1700-1850* (Longman 1919);
Brian Simon, *Studies in the History of Education, 1780-1870* (Lawrence &
Wishart 1960) and his two subsequent volumes on *1870-1920* and *1920-1940*
already cited; J. F. C. Harrison, *Learning and Living 1790-1960* (Routledge &
Kegan Paul 1961); Harold Silver, *The Concept of Popular Education*
(MacGibbon & Kee 1965); Patricia Hollis, *The Pauper Press* (Oxford University
Press 1970); Eileen Yeo, 'Robert Owen and radical culture' in S. Pollard and
J. Salt (eds.), *Robert Owen: Prophet of the Poor* (Macmillan 1971); and for
the later phases, Stephen Yeo, 'The new life: the religion of socialism in
Britain, 1883-1896', *History Workshop Journal,* no. 4 (Autumn 1977);
E. P. Thompson, 'Homage to Tom Macquire' in Asa Briggs and John Saville
(eds.), *Essays in Labour History,* vol. 1 (Macmillan 1960); P. McCann, 'Trade
unionist, co-operative and socialist organizations in relation to popular
education, 1870-1902' (unpublished Ph.D thesis, University of Manchester
1960); Raphael Samuel, 'British Marxist historians, 1880-1980: part one', *New
Left Review,* no. 120 (March–April 1980); J. P. Millar, *The Labour College
Movement* (National Council of Labour Colleges 1979); W. W. Craik, *The
Central Labour College* (Lawrence & Wishart 1964); Ann Phillips and Tim
Putnam, 'Education for emancipation: the movement for independent working
class education 1908-1928', *Capital and Class,* no. 10 (Spring 1980), pp.
18-42.

6   Studies of early nineteenth-century radicalism, of Owenism and the closely
associated secularist and spiritualist movements, of the socialist societies of the

1890s, and, indeed, of the popular liberal politics of the mid Victorian period suggest a popular cross-class social composition.

7   For more on the repertoire of popular educational strategies see Johnson, 'Education and popular politics', sections 7.1-7.9.

8   For evidence of intra-class differences in school use see J. S. Hurt, *Elementary Schooling and the Working Classes 1860-1918* (Routledge & Kegan Paul 1979).

9   J. M. Bynner, *Parents' Attitudes to Education* (HMSO 1972), pp. 39-40.

10   Johnson, *Education and Popular Politics,* sections 5.1-5.11, which relates historical evidence of resistance in schools to the findings of modern ethnographic studies.

11   Especially, in the period after 1870, on the issue of compulsory attendance.

12   Johnson, 'Really useful knowledge', p. 98; Yeo, 'Religion of socialism', pp. 21-3.

13   Johnson, 'Really useful knowledge', pp. 100-2.

14   Schooling in this phase was 'public' in only a rather special nineteenth-century bourgeois sense — organized by philanthropic and ecclesiastical agencies rather than by secular state authorities.

15   For his fullest account of this distinction see *Political Register,* 7 December 1833, especially pp. 581-3.

16   Johnson, 'Really useful knowledge', pp. 84-8.

17   ibid., p. 86.

18   For an outline account see Brian Simon, *Education and the Labour Movement, 1870-1920* (Lawrence & Wishart 1965), ch. 9.

19   In what follows we draw heavily on Simon's account cited above.

20   ibid., ch. 7.

21   ibid., pp. 176-86.

22   Annie Davison, quoted in Jean McCrindle and Sheila Rowbotham (eds.), *Dutiful Daughters* (Penguin 1979), pp. 62-5.

23   Annie Powell, quoted in Jeremy Seabrook, *What Went Wrong? Working People and the Ideals of the Labour Movement* (Gollancz 1978), p. 53.

24   On the popular Liberal alliance generally, see John Vincent, *The Formation of the Liberal Party* (Penguin 1972). On liberalism and education see D. K. Jones, *The Making of the Education System 1851-81* (Routledge & Kegan Paul 1977). On working-class politics and the Education Act of 1870 see P. McCann, 'Trade unionists, artisans and the 1870 Act', *British Journal of Educational Studies,* vol. 18, no. 2 (June 1970), pp. 134-50.

25   Simon, *Education and the Labour Movement,* chs. 8 and 10.

26   R. H. Tawney, *Secondary Education for All* (Allen & Unwin 1922), p. 12.

27   See especially his articles in the *Manchester Guardian* and 'Keep the worker's children in their place' in R. H. Tawney, *The Radical Tradition* (Penguin 1966), originally published as 'Prussianism in the school', *Daily News,* 14 February 1918 (an attack on the federation as 'the Bourbons of industry' concerned only with 'the cannon-fodder of capitalist industry').

28 Brian Simon, *The Politics of Educational Reform 1920-1940* (Lawrence & Wishart 1974), especially chs. 2 and 4.

29 The Geddes Committee (1921) consisted entirely of businessmen (ibid., p. 37); the May Committee (1931) included many prominent industrialists and financiers (ibid., p. 168).

30 R. H. Tawney, *The New Children's Charter* (Workers' Educational Assocation, n.d. [1932]), p. 9.

31 D. Reeder, 'A recurring debate: education and industry' in Gerald Bernbaum (ed.), *Schooling in Decline* (Macmillan 1979), pp. 123-8.

32 For a more detailed justification of the choice of this text see Finn, Grant and Johnson, 'Social democracy, education and the crisis', p. 155.

33 Rodney Barker, *Education and Politics 1900-51: A Study of the Labour Party* (Oxford University Press 1972), p. 37.

34 R. H. Tawney, *An Experiment in Democratic Education* (Workers' Educational Association, n.d. [reprinted from *Political Quarterly,* May 1914]), pp. 6-7.

35 R. H. Tawney, *Secondary Education for All*, pp. 25-7.

36 R. H. Tawney, *Equality* (Allen & Unwin 1964, first published in 1931 with several subsequent revisions).

37 ibid., p. 71.

38 ibid., pp. 71-2.

39 For which, see our analysis of the sociologies pp. 83-4.

40 In *Secondary Education for All* Tawney wrote of 'the vulgar irrelevances of class inequality and economic pressure' (p. 19), of 'the vulgarities of the class system' (p. 64) and, in general, of 'class' as an illegitimate 'intrusion' into educational matters.

41 ibid., p. 64.

42 ibid., p. 26.

43 ibid., p. 29.

44 ibid., p. 111.

45 See the espousal of teacher autonomy in *Secondary Education for All*: 'The aim should be to make our educational system an organic unity, alive in every part, served by teachers united, self-governing, and free' (p. 123), and of educational progressivism, see especially 'Presidential Address to the English Section of the New Education Fellowship', *New Era*, vol. 15, no. 2 (February 1934). (We are grateful to Kevin Brehony for this reference.)

46 Barker, *Education and Politics,* pp. 17-18.

47 For the classic Marxist definitions see Marx, 'The Eighteenth Brumaire of Louis Bonaparte' in D. Fernbach (ed.), *Surveys from Exile* (Penguin 1973), pp. 176-80.

48 *Equality,* pp. 100-1.

49 For the idea of 'spearhead knowledge' in early English radicalism see Johnson, 'Really useful knowledge', pp. 86-8.

50 For the Teachers' Labour League see Simon, *The Politics of Educational*

Reform, pp. 72, 113, 132 and 156.

51   For the details of this adaptation see Ross McKibbin, *The Evolution of the Labour Party* (Oxford University Press 1974).

52   Tawney, *Equality,* p. 207.

53   The larger process is well described in R. Miliband, *Parliamentary Socialism* (Merlin 1972).

Chapter 3   Conservatism, citizenship and the 1944 settlement

1   Conservative and Unionist Party, *To All Engaged in the Work of Education* (Conservative and Unionist Party 1928).

2   C. Norwood, *The English Tradition in Education* (John Murray 1929), pp. 172-3.

3   See A. Marwick's 'Middle opinion in the 1930s' in the *English Historical Review,* vol. 79, no. 311 (1964).

4   *The Economist,* 28 July 1934.

5   K. Lindsay, 'The early days of PEP' in *Contemporary Review,* vol. 222, no. 1285 (February 1973).

6   Liberty and Democratic Leadership Group, *The Next Five Years* (Macmillan 1935), p. 2.

7   ibid., p. 5.

8   A. L. Rowse, *Mr. Keynes and the Labour Movement* (Macmillan 1936), p. 68.

9   Liberty and Democratic Leadership Group, *The Next Five Years,* p. 39.

10   ibid., p. 310.

11   F. A. Cavanagh, 'The development of educational thought in the UK', in *A Review of Educational Thought* (University of London Institute of Education 1937), p. 37.

12   The National Union of Teachers, *The Struggle for Education* (NUT 1970), p. 9.

13   The Association for Education in Citizenship, *Education for Citizenship in Secondary Schools* (Oxford University Press 1936).

14   ibid.

15   *The Times Educational Supplement* (6 June 1934).

16   E. Laclau, *Politics and Ideology in Marxist Theory* (New Left Books 1977), p. 195.

17   G. D. H. Cole, *The People's Front* (Gollancz 1937), p. 15.

18   Lord Hailsham, *The Conservative Case* (Penguin 1959), p. 115.

19   'Cato', *Guilty Men* (Gollancz 1940).

20   'Gracchus', *Your MP* (Gollancz 1944).

21   W. K. Richmond, *Education in England* (Pelican 1945), p. 144.

22   H. C. Dent, *Education in Transition* (Kegan Paul 1944), p. 220.

23   Quoted in G. C. T. Giles, *The New School Tie* (Pilot Press 1946), p. 42.

24   Dent, *Education in Transition,* p. 221.

25   A. Calder, *The People's War* (Panther 1971), p. 290.

26 See D. N. Pritt, *The Autobiography of D. N. Pritt, Part 2* (Lawrence & Wishart 1966), pp. 111-26.
27 The Association for Education in Citizenship, *Roads to Citizenship* (Oxford University Press 1940).
28 R. A. Butler, *The Art of the Possible* (Hamish Hamilton 1971), p. 129.
29 Quoted in Cultural History Group, 'Out of the people: the politics of containment 1939-45' in *Working Papers in Cultural Studies 9* (CCCS 1976).
30 See S. Hall, 'The social eye of Picture Post' in *Working Papers in Cultural Studies 2* (CCCS 1972).
31 R. A. Butler, *The Art of the Possible.*
32 P. H. J. H. Gosden, *Education in the Second World War* (Methuen 1976), p. 239.
33 Quoted in P. Addison, *The Road to 1945* (Quartet 1977), p. 173.
34 *Report of the Committee of the Secondary Schools Examination Council on Curriculum and Examinations in the Secondary School* (The Norwood Report) (HMSO 1943).
35 *Report of the Committee on Public Schools appointed by the President of the Board of Education* (The Fleming Report) (HMSO 1944).
36 Workers' Educational Association, *The Public Schools and the Education System* (WEA 1943), p. 16.
37 R. A. Butler, *The Art of the Possible,* p. 120.
38 R. Barker, *Education and Politics 1900-51* (Oxford University Press 1972), p. 74.
39 Ministry of Education, *The Nation's Schools,* pamphlet no. 1 (HMSO 1945).
40 E. Green, 'Education for citizenship' in Herbert Tracey (ed.), *The British Labour Party,* vol. 2 (Caxton 1948), p. 161.
41 Giles, *The New School Tie,* p. 102.
42 Louise Morgan, for Birmingham and District Council for Educational Advance, pamphlet for Birmingham Education Week, 6-15 March 1947.
43 See Barker, *Education and Politics.*
44 Ministry of Education, Central Advisory Council for Education (England) *School and Life* (HMSO 1947), p. 49.
45 ibid., p. 55.
46 *The Times,* 20 December 1948.
47 *The Times,* 30 December 1948.
48 *The Times,* 29 December 1948.
49 *The Times Educational Supplement,* 30 June 1950.
50 Conservative Political Centre, *One Nation* (Conservative Political Centre 1950), p. 39.
51 ibid., p. 46.
52 See M. M. Lewis, *The Importance of Illiteracy* (Harrap 1953).
53 Conservative Political Centre, *One Nation,* p. 46.

Chapter 4   Origins of the 1960s' settlement

1   For which see J. G. K. Fenwick, *The Comprehensive School 1944-1970: The Politics of Secondary School Reorganization* (Methuen 1976); R. Pedley, *Comprehensive Schools Today; An Interim Survey* (Councils and Education Press 1955); David Rubinstein and Brian Simon, *The Evolution of the Comprehensive School, 1926-66* (Routledge & Kegan Paul 1966); Michael Parkinson, *The Labour Party and the Organisation of Secondary Education* (Routledge & Kegan Paul 1970). For an important local study of an innovating authority see P. H. J. H. Gosden and P. R. Sharp, *The Development of an Educational Service: The West Riding 1889-1974* (Martin Robertson 1978).

2   See, for example, the exchange between David Rubinstein and Billy Hughes on the role of Ellen Wilkinson, *History Workshop Journal,* no. 7 (Spring 1979), pp. 157-69.

3   G. C. T. Giles, *The New School Tie* (Pilot Press 1946).

4   ibid., introduction, p. vii.

5   ibid., pp. 9-11.

6   ibid., p. 25.

7   ibid., p. 70.

8   ibid., ch. 9.

9   ibid., pp. 77-83.

10   ibid., p. 82.

11   ibid., p. 102 (emphasis supplied).

12   ibid., p. 65.

13   This, at any rate, is Fenwick's judgement (p. 36). See also Rubinstein, 'Ellen Wilkinson reconsidered', *History Workshop Journal,* no. 7, p. 164.

14   See, for example, Fenwick, *The Comprehensive School*, pp. 45-52 and 94-103.

15   Margaret Cole, 'Education and social democracy', in R. H. S. Crossman (ed.), *New Fabian Essays* (Dent 1970; first published 1952), pp. 91-120.

16   See John Strachey, *The Nature of Capitalist Crisis* (Gollancz 1935). See particularly Strachey's bitter and dismissive assault on Cole's argument that a high-wage adaptation of capitalism was possible (pp. 333-51).

17   This is now generally recognized by social and economic historians of the inter-war period, sometimes indeed to the neglect of the real bases of older more 'pessimistic' accounts. See, for example, John Stevenson and Chris Cook, *The Slump: Society and Politics During the Depression* (Cape 1977).

18   Strachey, 'Tasks and achievement of British labour' in *New Fabian Essays,* p. 188.

19   ibid., p. 195.

20   C. A. R. Crosland, *The Future of Socialism* (Cape 1964, first published in 1956), pp. 7-10.

21   Raymond Williams, *Marxism and Literature* (Oxford University Press 1977), p. 2.

22   Stuart Hall *et al., Policing the Crisis: Mugging, the State, and Law and Order* (Macmillan 1978), p. 228.

23   For an (extremely partisan) account of the development of 'revisionism' see Stephen Haseler, *The Gaitskellites* (Macmillan 1969).

24   Maurice Kogan (ed.), *The Politics of Education: Edward Boyle and Anthony Crosland in conversation with Maurice Kogan* (Penguin 1971), p. 161.

25   ibid., p. 190.

26   For Crosland's discussion of class, especially class in Britain, see *The Future of Socialism,* pp. 118-22.

27   ibid., p. 188.

28   For example, 'We cannot be content with correctly distributing all the (as it were) alpha material, but must make the best use of our beta resources also.' (Crosland, *The Future of Socialism,* p. 147) and see also Roy Jenkins, *The Labour Case* (Penguin 1959), p. 86. These texts are also scattered with plentiful references to what Crosland called 'the tiny minority of brilliant geniuses'.

29   Crosland, *Socialism Now and Other Essays* (Cape 1974), p. 15.

30   The full meaning and implications of revisionism's 'equality' are best stated in Crosland, *The Future of Socialism.*

31   ibid., p. 142. The exception, apparently, was Bernard Shaw who, however, changed his mind in later life.

32   ibid., p. 77.

33   ibid., pp. 195-8.

34   Jenkins, *The Labour Case,* p. 96.

35   Crosland, *The Future of Socialism,* p. 202.

36   Jenkins, *The Labour Case,* pp. 96-7.

37   Brian Simon, *Intelligence, Psychology and Education: A Marxist Critique* (Lawrence & Wishart 1978, first published, in part, in 1953), pp. 112-16.

38   For a more extended account of the late 1950s and early 1960s (on which we draw) see Hall *et al., Policing the Crisis* and Vernon Bogdanor and Robert Skidelsky, *The Age of Affluence 1951-64* (Macmillan 1970). For 'youth' see A. C. H. Smith, *Paper Voices* (Chatto & Windus 1975) and Stuart Hall and Tony Jefferson (eds.), *Resistance Through Rituals* (Hutchinson 1976).

39   Jenkins, *The Labour Case,* p. 96.

40   John Vaizey, *The Costs of Education* (Allen & Unwin 1958), p. 68.

41   John Vaizey, *The Control of Education* (Faber & Faber 1963), p. 34.

42   John Vaizey, *Education for Tomorrow* (Penguin 1971, first published 1962).

43   E. A. G. Robinson and J. E. Vaizey (eds.), *The Economics of Education: Proceedings of a Conference held by the International Economic Association* (Macmillan 1963), p. 713.

44   Vaizey, *The Control of Education,* p. 240.

45   ibid., p. 95.

46   John Vaizey and Michael Debeauvais, 'Economic aspects of educational development' in A. H. Halsey, Jean Floud and C. Arnold Anderson, *Education, Economy and Society: A Reader in the Sociology of Education* (Macmillan 1961), pp. 39-40.

47   ibid., p. 42.

48   ibid., pp. 38 and 40.

49   Later we will argue that this is indeed the 'logic' of the development of
      'manpower' requirements under late capitalist conditions. See especially
      Chapter 7.

50   Vaizey, *The Control of Education*, pp. 230-1.

51   Vaizey, *Education for Tomorrow*, p. 15.

52   Vaizey and Debeauvais, 'Economic aspects', p. 38.

53   Vaizey, *Education for Tomorrow*, p. 27.

54   Vaizey, *The Control of Education*, pp. 246-9; *Education for Tomorrow*,
      p. 28. The preface to *The Control of Education* promises 'an essay on religion
      and education', a subject 'that interests me, as I am a practising churchman and
      hold strong views on the subject'.

55   Vaizey, *Education for Tomorrow*, p. 19.

56   ibid.

57   A. H. Halsey, A. F. Heath and J. M. Ridge, *Origins and Destinations: Family,
      Class and Education in Modern Britain* (Clarendon Press 1980), p. 1. It is this
      sense of 'a tradition' that warrants the label 'the old sociology of education'.
      We include here the predominantly 'socio-graphic' studies of the 1940s,
      1950s and 1960s, especially those deriving from the social-mobility studies
      at the LSE. But we include too the early studies of the school—home relation
      and, for reasons examined below, studies which broke from the methods of
      the 'old sociology' but stayed within its problematic (for example, the studies
      of Lacey and Hargreaves discussed in more detail in Chapter 6). There are
      obvious dangers of neglecting alternative or untypical strands within early
      pre-1970s educational sociology. Most important here, from our point of view,
      was the coexistence of quantitative social surveys with a strong (but minority)
      interest in the social history of education, early represented in the work of
      Olive Banks: see especially *Parity and Prestige in English Secondary Education:
      A Study in Educational Sociology* (Routledge & Kegan Paul 1955), but see
      also Asher Tropp, *The School Teachers: The Growth of the Teaching
      Profession in England and Wales* (Heinemann 1957), and, later, G. Bernbaum,
      Social Change and the Schools 1918-1944 (Routledge & Kegan Paul 1967).

58   Bernstein, *Class, Codes and Control,* vol. 3 (Routledge & Kegan Paul 1977),
      p. 161.

59   For useful histories and critiques of the old sociology see Bernstein, *Class,
      Codes and Control;* J. Karabel and A. H. Halsey (eds.), *Power and Ideology*
      (Oxford University Press 1977); Bill Williamson, 'Continuities and dis-
      continuities in the sociology of education', in Michael Flude and John Ahier
      (eds.), *Educability, Schools and Ideology* (Croom Helm 1974).

60   See especially Jean Floud and A. H. Halsey, 'The sociology of education:
      a trend report and bibliography', *Current Sociology*, vol. 7, no. 3 (1958),
      Paul Halmos (ed.), *The Teaching of Sociology to Students of Education
      and Social Work* (Sociological Review Monography No. 4, Keele, July

1961); Halsey, Floud and Anderson, *Education, Economy and Society.*

61   Floud and Halsey, 'The sociology of education', pp. 170-1.
62   This is most evident in the introduction to *Education, Economy and Society.*
63   Floud and Halsey, 'The sociology of education', pp. 169-72.
64   Much of this is caught in the following: 'Sociologists, already committed to the study of our outmoded but by no means moribund class structure, have been fascinated by the spectacle of educational institutions struggling to respond to the new purposes of an advanced industrial economy . . .', Jean Floud, 'Sociology and education' in Halmos (ed.), *The Teaching of Sociology,* p. 60.
65   Floud and Halsey, 'The sociology of education', p. 170.
66   The collection includes T. W. Schultz's famous announcement of the theme of education and economic growth (summary), articles by Vaizey and by American economists, and is announced as a book about the interrelationships between formal educational institutions and the economy in advanced industrial societies. Halsey's and Floud's own contributions are clearly deeply influenced by this 'economic' problematic.
67   Bernstein, *Class, Codes and Control,* vol. 3, p. 162.
68   Kogan (ed.), *The Politics of Education,* pp. 46-7.
69   ibid., p. 186.
70   Department of Education and Science, *Children and Their Primary Schools,* vol. 1 (HMSO 1967), p. 1.
71   See especially David H. Hargreaves, *Social Relations in a Secondary School* (Routledge & Kegan Paul 1967) and C. Lacey, *Hightown Grammar: The School as a Social System* (Manchester University Press 1970).
72   D. V. Glass (ed.), *Social Mobility in Britain* (Routledge & Kegan Paul 1954), pp. 5 and 10.
73   ibid., p. v.
74   ibid., p. 10.
75   ibid., p. 5.
76   Similarly, the movement between 'class' and 'status' categories in F. M. Martin 'Some subjective aspects of social stratification' in Glass (ed.) *Social Mobility.* Here 'status' appears to designate subjective aspects of individual evaluation of class positions (ibid., pp. 51 ff).
77   J. E. Floud, A. H. Halsey and F. M. Martin, *Social Class and Educational Opportunity* (Heinemann 1956) in which the mobility studies are referred to as 'a national investigation . . . into the movement between the *social classes* in this country' (emphasis supplied), p. xiii.
78   Anne-Marie Wolpe, 'Education and the sexual division of labour' in Annette Kulm and Anne-Marie Wolpe (eds.), *Feminism and, Materialism: Women and Modes of Production* (Routledge & Kegan Paul 1978).
79   Halsey, Heath and Ridge, *Origins and Destinations,* especially pp. 17-19.
80   T. H. Marshall, 'Social selection in the welfare state' in Halsey, Floud and

Anderson, *Education, Economy and Society,* p. 162.

81   Glass (ed.), *Social Mobility in Britain,* pp. 24-5.

82   A. H. Halsey, *Change in British Society* (Oxford University Press 1978), pp. 10-14, 55-7 (on Marshall), 138-59 (the problem of social order) and ch. 8 ('the third alternative' — 'through fraternity as citizenship').

83   J. Klein, *Samples from English Culture* (Routledge & Kegan Paul 1965), p. 7.

84   Floud, Halsey and Martin, *Social Class and Educational Opportunity,* p. 93.

85   ibid., pp. 75-83.

86   For example Glass (ed.), *Social Mobility in Britain,* pp. 154-8.

87   This calculation — in terms of 'class chances' — is already employed in the 1956 study.

88   Glass (ed.), *Social Mobility in Britain,* p. 22.

89   J. W. B. Douglas, *The Home and the School: A Study of Ability and Attainment in the Primary School* (Panther 1967, first published 1964).

90   ibid., pp. 11-26, and for a formidable and characteristic marshalling of the results of research to make a political case D. V. Glass, 'Education and social change in modern England', in M. Ginsberg (ed.), *Law and Opinion in England in the Twentieth Century* (Stevens & Sons 1959) reprinted in *Education, Economy and Society.* The footnotes to this piece form a kind of roll-call of Glass-influenced research to date and of intellectual and political allies!

91   See especially Crosland's judgement quoted on p. 82.

92   See especially Brian Simon, *Intelligence Testing and the Comprehensive School* (Lawrence & Wishart 1953).

93   Halsey, Heath and Ridge, *Origins and Destinations,* pp. 65 and 79-81.

94   Kogan, *Politics of Education,* p. 185.

95   For a discussion of the EPA experiment see pp. 125-7.

96   A. H. Stewart, 'A comment on "sociology and education" ', in Halmos (ed.), *The Teaching of Sociology,* p. 75.

97   Vaizey, *The Control of Education,* pp. 222-3.

98   ibid., p. 218.

99   See V. Burke, *Teachers in Turmoil* (Penguin 1971), especially p. 49.

100   A term coined by David Eccles when Minister of Education.

101   Kogan, *Politics of Education,* p. 173.

102   Robin Pedley, 'Sociology and education' in Halmos (ed.), *The Teaching of Sociology,* p. 69.

103   ibid., pp. 69-70. Pedley was an influential campaigner for and definer of comprehensives in this phase.

104   For these images see Vaizey, *Education for Tommorow;* the comparison with the trade union route is explicitly made in *The Control of Education.*

105   For a longer history of professional struggles see Asher Tropp, *The School Teachers,* and for an interesting interpretation of the failure of this strategy see Noel and José Parry, 'Teachers and professionalism: the failure of an occupational strategy' in Flude and Ahier (eds.), *Educability, Schools and Ideology.*

106   Fenwick, *The Comprehensive School,* especially ch. 3.
107   For the theme of progressivism and control see Rachel Sharp and Anthony
        Green, *Education and Social Control: A Study in Progressive Primary
        Education* (Routledge & Kegan Paul 1975).
108   Quoted in Mark Ginsburg, Robert Meyenn and Henry Miller, 'Teachers,
        professionalism and trade unionism' (paper to SSRC Conference on
        'Teacher and pupil strategies', September 1978), p. 16. We are grateful to the
        authors for early access to and discussion of their findings.
109   ibid., p. 7.
110   One largely hidden story in this, surfacing mainly in occasional Conservative
        panics, is the role of communists and other left groups within the profession
        and within successive organizations of left teachers.
111   For radical teachers and the Conservative press see Chapters 9 and 10.
112   Raymond Williams, 'Education and social democracy' (paper given at a
        conference organized by the Socialist Teachers' Alliance, 1978).
113   Tawney, *Equality* (Allen & Unwin 1969), ch. 3.
114   ibid., p. 105.
115   ibid., p. 111.
116   Tawney, *An Experiment in Democratic Education,* pp. 8-9. Tawney's
        translation here is, however, interesting: why 'universality of *provision'*
        rather than, say, equality of condition?
117   For example, in his Reith Lectures.
118   A. H. Halsey, 'Sociology and the equality debate', *Oxford Review of
        Education*, vol. 1, no. 1 (1975), pp. 9-23.
119   ibid.
120   See also our earlier argument in Finn, Grant and Johnson, 'Social democracy,
        education and the crisis'. Some of this argument is repeated here, but with
        a more critical appraisal of some elements within the 'egalitarian' side of the
        repertoire.
121   Part of this story (without the principal antagonists is told in Raymond
        Williams, *Culture and Society.*
122   The classic statement here is in the work of T. H. Marshall.
123   Marshall, 'Social selection in the welfare state' in Halsey, Floud and Anderson,
        Education, Economy and Society, p. 154.
124   For a discussion see Simon, *Education and the Labour Movement,* ch. 5.
125   For example, B. Jackson, *Streaming: An Education System in Miniature*
        (Routledge & Kegan Paul, 1964); E. Midwinter, *Priority Education* (Penguin
        1971).
126   For example, E. Robinson, *The New Polytechnics* (Penguin 1968).
127   Crosland, *Socialism Now,* p. 206.
128   Harold Wilson, *Purpose in Politics: Selected Speeches* (Weidenfeld &
        Nicolson 1964), p. 19.
129   ibid., p. 27.
130   'Well, what I mean by Socialism is a condition of society in which there
        should be neither rich nor poor, neither master nor master's man, neither

idle nor overworked, neither brain-sick brain workers, nor heart-sick hand workers, in a word, in which all men [and women! Education Group] would be living in equality of condition, and would manage their affairs unwastefully, and with the full consciousness that harm to one would mean harm to all — the realization at last of the meaning of the word COMMONWEALTH'. William Morris, 'How I became a socialist', *Justice,* 16 June 1894 in Asa Briggs (ed.), *William Morris: Selected Writings and Designs* (Penguin 1962), pp. 33-4.

131   ibid., p. 35.

Introduction

1   For sharply different views on these matters see G. R. Elton, *The Practice of History* (Sydney University Press 1967) and E. H. Carr, *What is History?* (Penguin 1961). Also interesting on the past—present relation is Jean Chesneaux, *Pasts and Futures or What is History for?* (Thames & Hudson 1978).

2   Harry Braverman, *Labor and Monopoly Capital* (Monthly Review Press 1974).

3   See Andrew L. Friedman, *Industry and Labour: Class Struggle at Work and Monopoly Capitalism* (Macmillan 1977); the essays in Theo Nicholls (ed.), *Capital and Labour* (Fontana 1980), especially that by Bill Schwarz and Tony Elger; Tony Elger, 'Valorisation and "deskilling". . : a critique of Braverman', *Capital and Class,* no. 7 (Spring 1979).

4   See the positive evaluation of Braverman's openness to questions of gender, compared with subsequent Marxist debate, in Veronica Beechey, 'Some notes on female wage labour in capitalist production', *Capital and Class,* no. 3 (Autumn 1977) especially n. 3, p. 61. For a very interesting feminist development out of Braverman's work see Jane Barker and Hazel Downing, 'Word processing and the transformation of the patriarchal relations of control in the office', *Capital and Class,* no. 10 (Spring 1980) pp. 64-99.

5   For accounts see Stuart Hall's review of the development of cultural studies in *Culture, Media and Language* (Hutchinson 1980); Richard Johnson, 'Culture and the historians' and 'The three problematics' in John Clarke, Chas Critcher, Richard Johnson, *Working Class Culture* (Hutchinson 1979); Michèle Barratt *et al.,* 'Representation and cultural production' in Barrett *et al., Ideology and Cultural Production* (Croom Helm 1979). See also *Screen Education,* no. 34 (Spring 1980), which contains articles on the definition of 'popular culture', on cultural studies in relation to educational practice and on the sociology of sub-cultures.

Chapter 5   Great expectations: the noise and practice of reform

1   William Paul, *The State: Its Origins and Functions* (Proletarian Publishing 1974, first published 1917), pp. 179-80.

2　D. Rubinstein and D. Simon, *The Evolution of the Comprehensive School 1926-72*, 2nd edn (Routledge & Kegan Paul 1973); R. A. Butler, *The Art of the Possible* (Hamish Hamilton 1971); Edward Boyle, 'The politics of secondary school reorganisation: some reflections', *Journal of Educational and Administrative History*, vol. 4, no. 2 (June 1972), pp. 28-38; Basil Bernstein 'Education cannot compensate for society', *New Society,* vol. 387 (February 1970), pp. 344-7.

3　Ernesto Laclau, *Politics and Ideology in Marxist Theory* (New Left Books 1977), pp. 158 and 161.

4　*Fifteen to Eighteen* (The Crowther Report) (HMSO 1959).

5　M. Kogan, *The Politics of Education* (Penguin 1971), p. 17.

6　T. Whiteside, *The Sociology of Educational Innovation* (Methuen 1978), p. 11; M. Kogan, *The Politics of Educational Change* (Fontana/Collins 1978), p. 16.

7　John Vaizey and John Sheehan, *Resources for Education* (Allen & Unwin 1968), p. 2.

8　Anne Corbett, *Much To Do about Education,* 2nd edn (Council for Educational Advance 1972), p. 1.

9　A. H. Halsey, *New Society* (25 July 1968).

10　Cited in *Education in the National Plan,* DES Report on Education no. 25 (1965), p. 4.

11　*Half our Future* (The Newsom Report) (HMSO 1963).

12　Boyle, 'The politics of secondary school reorganisation', p. 33.

13　*The Growth of Comprehensive Education,* DES Report on Education no. 87 (1977), p. 3.

14　The Newsom Report, p. iv.

15　A. H. Halsey, 'Sociology and the equality debate', *Oxford Review of Education,* vol. 1, no. 1 (1975).

16　The Newsom Report, p. xiv.

17　*Report of The Committee on Higher Education* (The Robbins Report), Cmnd 2154 (HMSO 1963), para. 25.

18　C. A. R. Crosland, *The Conservative Enemy* (Cape 1962), p. 159; House of Commons Expenditure Committee Tenth Report, *Policy Making in the Department of Education and Science* (HMSO 1976), paras. 381 and 376; Elizabeth Halsall, *The Comprehensive School* (Pergamon 1973), p. 33.

19　I. G. K. Fenwick, *The Comprehensive School 1940-1970* (Methuen 1976), p. 60.

20　Dennis Marsden, *Politicians, Equality and Comprehensives* (Fabian Society 1971), p. 19.

21　D. E. Butler and A. King, *The British General Election of 1964* (Macmillan 1964), and *The British General Election of 1966* (Macmillan 1966).

22　Elizabeth Wilson, *Women and the Welfare State* (Tavistock 1977), p. 39; Cynthia Cockburn, *The Local State* (Pluto 1977), p. 55.

23　Richard Hoggart, *The Uses of Literacy* (Chatto 1957); Brian Jackson and

Dennis Marsden, *Education and the Working Class* (Routledge & Kegan Paul 1962).

24   The Newsom Report, para. 251.

25   A. H. Halsey, *Educational Priority*, vol. 1: *EPA Problems and Policies* (HMSO 1972), p. 11.

26   Boyle, 'The politics of secondary school reorganization', p. 36.

27   P. Bellaby, *The Sociology of Comprehensive Schooling* (Methuen 1977), p. 46.

28   N. Poulantzas, *Classes in Contemporary Capitalism* (New Left Books 1975), p. 3, ch. 4.

29   *Children and their Primary Schools* (The Plowden Report) (HMSO 1967).

30   Corbett, *Much to do about Education*, 4th edn (Macmillan 1978), p. ix.

31   Expenditure Committee Tenth Report, *Policy Making*, p. 49 and para. 191 and p. 191.

32   K. Kogan and Packwood, *Advisory Councils and Committees in Education* (Routledge & Kegan Paul 1974), p. 22.

33   OECD National Reviews, *Educational Strategy in England and Wales* (OECD 1975).

34   *Education* (18 December 1959); The Newsom Report, p. 26.

35   Cockburn, *The Local State*, p. 55.

36   The Crowther Report, para. 59.

37   *The Youth Service in England and Wales* (The Albermarle Report), Cmnd. 929 (HMSO 1960), para. 65.

38   The Crowther Report, para. 27.

39   ibid., para. 197.

40   K. Marx, *Capital*, vol. 3 (Lawrence & Wishart 1972), pp. 196 and 300.

41   The Crowther Report, para. 664; The Newsom Report, para. 11; The Plowden Report, para. 1174.

42   The Crowther Report, para. 663.

43   ibid., para. 195.

44   ibid., paras. 58 and 262.

45   The Albermarle Report, para. 55.

46   ibid., para. 350.

47   *Report of the Committee on Local Authority and Allied Personal Social Services* (The Seebohm Report), Cmnd. 3703 (HMSO 1968).

48   The Seebohm Report, para. 497.

49   Laclau, *Politics and Ideology*, p. 158.

50   The Crowther Report, para. 167.

51   The Albermarle Report, para. 112.

52   Boyle, 'The politics of secondary school reorganisation', p. 29.

53   The Plowden Report, para. 64.

54   The Newsom Report, para. 618.

55   The Plowden Report, para. 37.

56   ibid., para. 63.

57   The Crowther Report, para. 107.

58 ibid., para. 543.
59 The Newsom Report, para. 16.
60 The Plowden Report, para. 37.
61 ibid., para. 84.
62 The Newsom Report, ch. 22.
63 *Educational Disadvantage* (DES 1975), p. 21.
64 The Plowden Report, para. 37.
65 ibid.
66 ibid., para. 85.
67 ibid.
68 ibid., para. 823.
69 The Crowther Report, para. 51.
70 The Newsom Report, para. 113.
71 ibid., para. 391.
72 ibid., para. 397; The Crowther Report, para. 457.
73 The Newsom Report, para. 113.
74 ibid., para. 80.
75 See Expenditure Committee Tenth Report, *Policy Making,* p. 170.
76 The Plowden Report, paras. 173 and 174.
77 Kogan, *Politics of Education,* p. 197.
78 Halsey, *Educational Priority.*
79 The Newsom Report, ch. 10.
80 F. Musgrove and P. H. Taylor, *Society and the Teacher's Role* (Routledge & Kegan Paul 1969), p. 79.
81 Schools Council Paper 27, *Cross'd With Adversity* (Schools Council 1970).
82 Halsey, *Educational Priority,* p. 7.
83 David Hencke, *Colleges in Crisis* (Penguin 1978).
84 Halsey, *Educational Priority.*
85 Cockburn, *The Local State, passim.*
86 Society of Education Officers, *Management in the Education Service* (Routledge & Kegan Paul 1974), p. 8.
87 Maurice Kogan, *The Government of the Social Services* (Russell Memorial Lecture, Bristol, 1969), p. 8.
88 ibid., p. 13.
89 This may even have been illegal. See Expenditure Committee Tenth Report, *Policy Making,* p. xxxii.
90 Marsden, *Politicians, Equality and Comprehensives,* p. 20.
91 Rubinstein and Simon, *The Evolution of the Comprehensive School,* p. 96.
92 The Crowther Report, para. 614.
93 *Crossbow* (October–December 1964), p. 10.
94 Rubinstein and Simon, *The Evolution of the Comprehensive School, passim.*
95 Dennis Marsden, 'How comprehensives missed the tide' in David Rubinstein and Colin Stoneman (eds.), *Education for Democracy* (Penguin 1970), p. 144.
96 Expenditure Committee Tenth Report, *Policy Making, passim.*

97　Halsey, 'Sociology and the equality debate', p. 14.
98　Elizabeth Halsall (ed.), *Becoming Comprehensive; Case Histories* (Pergamon 1970).
99　Boyle, 'The politics of secondary school reorganization', p. 36.

Chapter 6　The sociology of education: a critique

1　For an explanation of this fact see A. H. Halsey, A. F. Heath and J. M. Ridge, *Origins and Destinations: Family, Class and Education in Modern Britain* (Clarendon Press 1980), pp. 19-20. This seems to boil down to the need to keep existing categories and methods intact and to secure comparability with earlier studies.

2　For a review of work of this kind see Anne-Marie Wolpe, 'Education and the sexual division of labour' in Annette Kuhn and Anne-Marie Wolpe (eds.), *Feminism and Materialism: Women and Modes of Production* (Routledge & Kegan Paul 1978).

3　Halsey, Heath and Ridge, *Origins and Destinations,* pp. 86-8.

4　Jean Floud, A. H. Halsey and C. Arnold Anderson, *Economy and Society: A Reader in the Sociology of Education,* p. 7 (Macmillan 1961).

5　J. W. B. Douglas, *The Home and the School: A Study of Ability and Attainment in the Primary School* (Panther 1967, first published 1964).

6　J. W. B. Douglas, *All Our Future* (Peter Davies 1968), p. 186.

7　*Report of the Committee on Higher Education* (The Robbins Report, Cmnd 2154 (HMSO 1963), p. 268.

8　*Half our Future* (The Newsom Report) (HMSO 1963), p. 3.

9　*Children and their Primary Schools* (The Plowden Report), vol. 1 (HMSO 1967), p. 1.

10　ibid., p. 461.

11　*Social Trends No. 9* (HMSO 1979), p. 76.

12　*General Household Survey for 1975* (HMSO 1978), p. 123.

13　Halsey, Heath and Ridge, *Origins and Destinations,* pp. 213-19.

14　ibid., p. 205.

15　The chapter on education in Sue Sharpe, *'Just Like a Girl': How Girls Learn to be Women* (Penguin 1976), is an excellent introduction.

16　Mica Nava, 'Gender and education', *Feminist Review,* no. 5, p. 70; Eileen Byrne, *Women and Education* (Tavistock 1978).

17　Rosemary Deem, *Women and Schooling* (Routledge & Kegan Paul 1978).

18　Byrne, *Women and Education,* p. 180.

19　Deem, *Women and Schooling,* especially ch. 4.

20　Jean Floud and A. H. Halsey, 'The sociology of education : a trend report and bibliography', *Current Sociology,* vol. 7, no. 3 (1958), p. 183.

21　David H. Hargreaves, *Social Relations in the Secondary School* (Routledge & Kegan Paul 1967) and C. Lacey, *Hightown Grammar: The School as a Social System* (Manchester University Press 1970).

22 Douglas, *The Home and the School,* p. 28.
23 Lacey, *Hightown Grammar,* p. xi.
24 Hargreaves, *Social Relations,* p. ix.
25 Problematic in our view because of the distance of the interpreter of research from the point of research practice itself (a common condition of large scale surveys), and because of the largely official and middle-class character of informants, the insertion of research within the activities of state organizations themselves. One consequence is that reports like Douglas's are invariably more revealing of the official and unofficial beliefs of officials, teachers and researchers than of the object of their research. For the conditions of research in this case see Douglas, *The Home and the School,* pp. 11-15 and ch.
26 Lacey, *Hightown Grammar,* pp. xii-xvi: Hargreaves, *Social Relations,* pp. 182-3.
27 Lacey, *Hightown Grammar,* chs. 4 and 5 and pp. 186-8; *Social Relations,* chs. 6, 7 and 8.
28 Lacey, *Hightown Grammar,* pp. 148-52 and 192.
29 ibid., p. 193.
30 Hargreaves, *Social Relations,* pp. 184-92.
31 ibid., p. 187.
32 ibid., p. 192.
33 Lacey, *Hightown Grammar,* p. xvi. The point, however, is little developed.
34 Hargreaves, *Social Relations,* pp. 186-7.
35 Douglas, *The Home and the School,* pp. 28-9.
36 Anne-Marie Wolpe, 'Education and the sexual division of labour'.
37 Douglas, *The Home and the School,* chs. 6 and 8.
38 B. Sugarman, 'Social class and values as related to achievement and conduct in schools', *Sociological Review,* vol. 14, no. 3 (1966), p. 287.
39 The more or less radical drawing of implications depends in part on the balance between two explanatory moves: explanation in terms of the *deficiencies* of working-class culture or family life and in terms of the 'codes' or 'values' in operation in the school and their more or less discriminatory or dominative character. Bernstein's stress on codes and on 'control' seems to us to remove him from the 1960s' social democratic orthodoxies. The similarities between Bernstein and Bourdieu include their common pessimism 'about orthodox forms of educational reform'. This is not to say that Bernstein's work cannot be appropriated in a thoroughly conservative way. For some of these debates see Diana Adlam and Angie Salfield, 'The diversion of language: a critical assessment of the concept of linguistic diversity', *Screen Education,* no. 34, pp. 71-86, and the sources cited there.
40 In earlier versions we might call these the 'poverty' and 'apathy' stereotypes. For nineteenth-century examples, see Richard Johnson, 'Elementary education' in Gillian Sutherland *et al., Government and Society in Nineteenth-Century Britain: Commentaries on British Parliamentary Papers* (Irish University Press 1977), pp. 13-15.

Chapter 7   Schooling, skilling and social relations

1   See p. 31 above.

2   pp. 24-5 above.

3   Despite or perhaps because of the inter-war economic logic of decreasing the supply of labour to reduce unemployment through expanding formal education and training. On this issue in the inter-war period, see R. H. Tawney, *The School Leaving Age and Juvenile Unemployment* (Workers' Educational Association n.d. [1932-3]); R.H. Tawney, *Juvenile Employment and Education* (Oxford University Press 1934).

4   See pp. 215-16.

5   'Utopian' here in the usual common sense meaning as unrealizable. We don't mean to imply that we can do without utopias – possible visions of the future – especially if we are socialists.

6   See pp. 228 *passim.*

7   André Gorz, 'Technology, technicians and class struggle', in André Gorz (ed.), *The Division of Labour* (Harvester Press 1976).

8   Louis Althusser, 'Ideological state apparatuses' in *Lenin and Philosophy and other Essays* (New Left Books 1971). See also Ted Benton, 'Education and politics' in D. Holly (ed.), *Education or Domination* (Arrow 1974), p. 25; and, in relation to technical education, the similar argument in D. Gleeson and G. Mardle, *Further Education or Training? A Case Study in the Theory and Practice of Day Release Education* (forthcoming 1981).

9   Harry Braverman, *Labor and Monopoly Capital: The Degradation of Work in the Twentieth Century* (Monthly Review Press 1974), p. 193.

10   ibid., pp. 315-16.

11   See sources cited on p. 284, n. 3 above.

12   ibid., pp. 26-7.

13   Much of what follows is drawn from Michael Mann, 'The concept of skill' (paper presented to a meeting of the BSA Industrial Sociology Group, LSE, November 1977), but see also the full version in R. M. Blackburn and Michael Mann, *The Working Class in the Labour Market* (Macmillan 1979).

14   ibid., p. 12.

15   ibid., p. 292.

16   One of the most interesting historical studies of struggles over skill (in the crucial engineering sector) is James Hinton, *The First Shop Steward's Movement* (Allen & Unwin 1973). See especially the excellent discussion of craftism on pages 56-102. For the *locus classicus* of the discussion of skill and struggle in Marx see *Capital,* vol. 1, chs. 14 and 15, especially pp. 547-9.

17   Athar Hussain, 'The economy and the educational system in capitalist societies', *Economy and Society*, vol. 5, no. 4 (November 1976). What follows draws heavily on this article.

18   For a discussion of struggles over qualification and over the division of labour see Pierre Bourdieu and Luc Boltanski, 'Qualifications and jobs', ed. and trans. Richard Nice (CCCS Stencilled Paper, No. 46).

19 Ivor Berg, *Education and Jobs: The Great Training Robbery* (Penguin 1970), p. 89.

20 Blackburn and Mann, *The Working Class in the Labour Market,* pp. 260, 231, and 301.

21 The qualifications and destinations of school leavers can be traced in the DES's annual volumes of statistics. See, for example, DES, *Statistics of Education* (HMSO 1975), vol. 2 (school leavers).

22 It may be replied that most of the young unemployed in the 1970s were drawn from the unqualified. In so far as this is so (and it is what we would predict), it confirms rather than refutes our argument. The obtaining of qualifications *may* constitute an *individual* 'solution' to the problem of unemployment, though not one below a certain level of qualification, that can be relied on. As Berg suggests, employers, finding more workers in possession of certificates will simply 'up' the stakes of competition between them. Education, training and certification, then, cannot solve the problem of unemployment at a *social* level, although it may indeed mitigate the problem by withdrawing youthful labour from the labour market altogether.

23 Braverman, *Labor and Monopoly Capital*, p. 425.

24 For some of these basic forms see Paul Willis, 'Shop-floor culture, masculinity and the wage form' in John Clarke, Chas Critcher and Richard Johnson, *Working Class Culture* (Hutchinson 1979), pp. 185-98.

25 Andrew L. Friedman, *Industry and Labour: Class Struggle at Work and Monopoly Capitalism* (Macmillan 1977).

26 W. W. Daniel, *A National Survey of the Unemployed* (Political and Economic Planning 1974).

27 M. J. Hill, R. M. Harrison, A. V. Sergeant and V. Talbot, *Men Out of Work: A Study of Unemployment in Three English Towns* (Cambridge University Press 1973).

28 'The changing structure of the labour force', *Department of Employment Gazette* (October 1975), Table 4, p. 985.

29 Occupational Census, 1961 and 1971 and *Department of Employment Gazette* (July 1976) quoted in Big Flame, *The Crisis in Education* (Big Flame 1977).

30 For example, the discussion of the workforce in a highly advanced chemical plant in T. Nichols and H. Beynon, *Living With Capitalism: Class Relations and the Modern Factory* (Routledge & Kegan Paul 1977). See also H. Beynon, *Working for Ford* (Penguin 1973) and T. Nichols and H. Beynon, *Workers Divided: A Study in Shopfloor Politics* (Fontana 1976).

31 What follows is based on Braverman, *Labor and Monopoly Capital,* ch. 15 and Barker and Downing, 'Word processing and the transformation of the patriarchal relations of control in the office', *Capital and Class,* no. 10 (Spring 1980). We are grateful for discussions with Hazel Downing on these themes.

32 Braverman, *Labor and Monopoly Capital*, p. 373.

33 For an early emergence of this distinction see a Ministry of Education circular of 1960 quoted in P. J. Perry, *The Evolution of British Manpower Policy* (BACIE 1977), paras. 292-4.

34   John Brown, *Sermons on Various Subjects* (London 1764) p. 8.
35   In what follows we draw on the modern debate about the reserve army
      especially as it affects women. See especially, Veronica Beechey, 'Some notes
      on female wage labour', *Capital and Class*, no. 3 (Autumn 1977), pp. 45-6;
      Lucy Bland *et al.*, 'Women "inside" and "outside" the relations of production' in
      CCCS Women's Studies Group, *Women Take Issue: Aspects of Women's
      Subordination* (Hutchinson 1978), pp. 35-78; Floya Anthias, 'Women and the
      reserve army of labour: a critique of Veronica Beechey', *Capital and Class*, no.
      10 (Spring 1980), pp. 50-63. The starting point of the discussion is Marx,
      Capital, vol. 1, ch. 25.
36   *Department of Employment Gazette* (HMSO October 1975), Table 1, p. 982.
37   D. F. Harris and F. J. Taylor, *The Service Sector: Its Changing Role as a Source
      of Employment* (CES Research Service 25, 1978).
38   Bland *et al.*, 'Women "inside" and "outside" the relations of production', pp.
      63-4 in which various categories of the reserve army are matched to particular
      moments in the life experience of women.
39   Rosemary Deem, *Women and Schooling* (Routledge & Kegan Paul 1978), ch. 3.
40   Debates on the economic status of domestic labour may not help much here,
      but see Ann Oakley, *The Sociology of Housework* (Martin Robertson 1974)
      and *Housewife* (Penguin 1976).
41   This is interestingly and movingly explored in Dorothy Hobson, 'Housewives:
      isolation as oppression' in CCCS Women's Studies Group, *Women Take Issue*,
      pp. 79-95.
42   For this argument in relation to women's 'leisure' see D. Hobson, C. Griffin,
      T. McCabe and S. MacIntosh, 'Women and leisure' (Paper given to conference
      on Leisure Studies, CCCS 1979).
43   Paul Willis, *Learning to Labour: How Working-Class Kids Get Working-Class
      Jobs* (Saxon House 1977); Angela McRobbie, 'Working class girls and the
      culture of femininity', *Women Take Issue*, pp. 96-108; McRobbie, 'Jackie: an
      ideology of adolescent femininity' (CCCS Stencilled Paper No. 53); McRobbie,
      'Settling accounts with subcultures: a feminist critique', *Screen Education*,
      no. 34 (Spring 1980), pp. 37-49. Eagerly anticipated is McRobbie, *Young
      Women and Leisure: How Working-Class Girls Get Working-Class Husbands*
      (forthcoming, cited in 'Settling accounts'). We have learnt much also from
      other on-going work on girls, work, leisure and schooling at CCCS, especially
      that of Christine Griffin and Trish McCabe.
44   Paul Corrigan, *Schooling the Smash Street Kids* (Macmillan 1979), p. 70.
45   McRobbie, 'Working class girls', p. 99.
46   Willis, *Learning to Labour*, pp. 43-7.
47   McRobbie, 'Working class girls', p. 107.

Conclusion

48   B. Hindess, *The Decline of Working Class Politics* (MacGibbon & Kee 1971),
      especially pp. 78 and 136-46.

49   A. H. Halsey, A. F. Heath and J. M. Ridge, *Origins and Destinations: Family, Class and Education in Modern Britain* (Clarendon Press 1980), pp. 216-18.

Chapter 8   Recession, protest and the absent defence

1   *Education: A Framework for Expansion,* Cmnd 5174 (HMSO 1972).
2   Figures derived from *Department of Employment Gazette,* vol. 84, no. 1 (January 1976), p. 70, and vol. 87, no. 12 (December 1979), pp. 1282 and 1290.
3   See David Yaffee, 'The crisis of profitability: a critique of the Glyn-Sutcliffe thesis', *New Left Review,* no. 80 (1973), pp. 54 and 56; Andrew Gamble and Paul Walton, *Capitalism in Crisis* (Macmillan 1976), p. 9.
4   *Department of Employment Gazette,* vol. 87, no. 12 (December 1979), p. 1312.
5   See Ben Fine and Laurence Harris, 'The British economy May 1975 – January 1976', *Bulletin of the Conference of Socialist Economists* (October 1976), p. 6; Andrew Glyn and Bob Sutcliffe, *British Capitalism, Workers and the Profit Squeeze* (Penguin 1972), p. 66; John Harrison, 'British capitalism in 1973 and 1974: the deepening crisis', *Bulletin of the Conference of Socialist Economists* (Spring 1974), p. 46.
6   *The Sunday Times,* 2 November ('Armies'), and 9 and 19 November; 14 December 1975.
7   David Hencke, *Colleges in Crisis* (Penguin 1978), p. 58.
8   Stuart Hall *et al., Policing the Crisis* (Macmillan 1978), p. 237.
9   Harrison, *British Capitalism,* p. 55.
10   J. Karabel and A. H. Halsey, 'Educational research; a review and an interpretation' in J. Karabel and A.H. Halsey (eds.), *Power and Ideology in Education* (Oxford University Press 1977), p. 13.
11   *Educational Disadvantage* (DES 1975), p. 21.
12   Raymond Boudon, *Education, Opportunity and Social Inequality: Changing Prospects in Western Society* (Halsted Press 1974).
13   Christopher Jencks, *Inequality: Reassessment of the Effects of Family and Schooling in America* (Peregrine Books 1975), p. 1.
14   A. H. Halsey, *Educational Priority,* vol. 1: *EPA Problems and Policies* (HMSO 1972), p. 3.
15   ibid., p. 7.
16   ibid., p. 11.
17   ibid., p. 12.
18   ibid., p. 198.
19   Anne Corbett, *Much To Do about Education,* 4th edn (Council for Educational Advance/Macmillan 1978), p. 39.
20   Raymond Williams, *Politics and Letters* (New Left Books 1979), p. 371. Williams's further comment on the Open University is unclear due to a misprint.
21   House of Commons Expenditure Committee Tenth Report, *Policy Making in*

the Department of Education and Science (HMSO 1976).

22   Maurice Kogan, *The Politics of Educational Change* (Fontana/Collins 1978), p. 145.

23   Society of Education Officers, *Management in the Education Service* (Routledge & Kegan Paul 1974), p. 33.

24   Expenditure Committee Tenth Report, *Policy Making,* p. xvii.

25   OECD National Reviews, *Educational Strategy in England and Wales* (OECD 1975).

26   Society of Education Officers, *Management in the Education Service,* p. 35.

27   Expenditure Committee Tenth Report, *Policy Making,* p. 9.

28   Hencke, *Colleges in Crisis,* pp. 126-7.

29   Expenditure Committee Tenth Report, *Policy Making* , para. 191.

30   ibid., para. 30.

31   ibid., Lord Alexander of Potterhill, p. 260 and para. 876.

32   ibid., p. 238.

33   ibid., p. 125.

34   ibid., p. xxviii.

35   Cynthia Cockburn, *The Local State* (Pluto 1977), p. 12.

36   ibid., p. 13.

37   Society of Education Officers, *Management in the Education Service,* p. 7.

38   B. Simon in 'Marx and the crisis in education', *Marxism Today,* vol. 21, no. 7 (July 1977), pp. 195-205.

39   Ian Lister (ed.), *Deschooling: A Reader* (Cambridge University Press 1974), p. 1.

40   L. Althusser, 'Ideology and ideological state apparatuses' in *Lenin and Philosophy and Other Essays* (New Left Books 1971), p. 157.

41   M. F. D. Young (ed.), *Knowledge and Control* (Collier, Macmillan 1971).

42   J. Karabel and A. H. Halsey, 'Educational research', pp. 52-3.

43   Antonio Gramsci, *Selections from the Prison Notebooks* (Lawrence & Wishart 1971); Raymond Williams, *The Long Revolution* (Chatto 1961).

44   Basil Bernstein, *Class, Codes and Control,* vol. 1 (Routledge & Kegan Paul 1974) and vol. 3 (Routledge & Kegan Paul 1975); Pierre Bourdieu and Jean-Claude Passeron, *Reproduction in Education, Society and Culture,* trans. R. Nice (Sage 1977), p. 67; Samuel Bowles and Herbert Gintis, *Schooling in Capitalist America: Educational Reform and the Contradictions of Economic Life* (Routledge & Kegan Paul 1976).

45   Bourdieu, *Reproduction,* p. 67.

46   Bowles and Gintis, *Schooling in Capitalist America,* p. 6.

47   ibid., p. 53.

48   ibid., p. 125.

49   ibid., p. 56.

50   Gerald Grace, *Teachers, Ideology and Control* (Routledge & Kegan Paul 1978), p. 217.

Chapter 9 Turning the tables: the Conservative education offensive

1 House of Commons Expenditure Committee Tenth Report, *Policy Making in the Department of Education and Science* (HMSO 1976), *passim.*

2 R. A. Butler, *The Education Act of 1944 and After* (University of Essex 1966), p. 2.

3 R. A. Butler, *The Art of the Possible* (Hamish Hamilton 1971), p. 94.

4 A. Maude, *The Common Problem* (Constable 1969), p. 120.

5 M. Kogan, *The Politics of Education* (Penguin 1971), p. 17.

6 R. Bell, G. Fowler and K. Little (eds.), *Education in Great Britain and Ireland* (Routledge & Kegan Paul 1973), p. 131.

7 Cited in A. Gamble, *Conservative Nation* (Routledge & Kegan Paul 1974), p. 107; this and N. Harris, *Competition and the Corporate Society: British Conservatives, the State and Industry 1945-64* (Methuen 1972).

8 *Crossbow* (October–December 1970), p. 27.

9 *Education: A Framework for Expansion,* Cmnd 5174 (HMSO 1972).

10 E. Halsall, *The Comprehensive School* (Pergamon 1973), p. 69.

11 There has been a cluster of studies on Tyndale. For Risinghill, see Leila Berg, *Risinghill: Death of a Comprehensive School* (Pelican 1968).

12 Schools Council Working Paper No. 2, *Raising the School Leaving Age* (HMSO 1965), para. 2.

13 J. Webb, 'The sociology of a school', *British Journal of Sociology*, vol. 13 (1962), pp. 264-72.

14 Schools Council Welsh Committee, *Another Year – to Endure or Enjoy?* (HMSO 1967).

15 Sir A. Clegg, 'Problem authorities, problem children' in B. Turner (ed.), *Raising the School Leaving Age – a Seminar* (Encyclopaedia Britannica 1971), pp. 16-17.

16 Cited in University of Nottingham, School of Education, ROSLA Discussion Paper No. 2, J. Bastiani (ed.), *Work Experience Schemes* (University of Nottingham 1977), p. 4.

17 Halsall, *The Comprehensive School,* p. 76.

18 Much of this information and all that concerning Coventry from D. J. Finn, *Education, Class, Experience and the Former 'Early School Leaver'* (unpublished ms.).

19 C. B. Cox and A. E. Dyson (eds.), *Fight for Education: A Black Paper* (Critical Quarterly Society 1969), p. 6.

20 K. B. Start and B. K. Wells, *The Trend of Reading Standards* (National Foundation for Educational Research 1972).

21 *A Language for Life* (The Bullock Report) (HMSO 1975).

22 See Michael Rutter in *Dimensions of Parenthood* (DHSS 1974).

23 Quoted in *The Sunday Times*, 27 October 1974.

24 ibid.

25 *Daily Mail,* 19 February 1975.

26   N. Bennett, *Teaching Styles and Pupil Progress* (Open Books 1976).
27   R. Boyson, *The Crisis in Education* (Woburn Press 1975).
28   C. B. Cox and A. E. Dyson (eds.), *Black Paper 2: The Crisis in Education* (Critical Quarterly Society 1970), p. 1.
29   C. B. Cox and R. Boyson (eds.), *Black Paper 5: The Fight for Education* (Dent 1975), p. 1.
30   ibid., p. 3.
31   Boyson, *The Crisis in Education,* Introduction.
32   N. Wright, *Progress in Education* (Croom Helm 1977).
33   R. Boyson, *The Crisis in Education,* Introduction.
34   V. Bogdanor, 'Education' in Lord R. Blake and J. Patten (eds.), *The Conservative Opportunity* (Macmillan 1976), p. 117.
35   Cox and Dyson (eds.), *Black Paper 2*, p. 85.
36   But studies of many other schools and circumstances are needed.
37   Gamble, *Conservative Nation*, p. 75.
38   C. B. Cox and A. E. Dyson (eds.), *Black Paper 3 : Goodbye Mr Short* (Critical Quarterly Society 1970), pp. 9-10.
39   Bogdanor, 'Education', p. 131.

Chapter 10   Labour's appropriation: the Great Debate and after

1   Renewed thanks to Marilyn Crutcher, whose work on the media coverage of education has served as a basis for this chapter's discussion of the *Daily Mail* and *Daily Mirror*; also to Stuart Hall who wrote a valuable commentary on this section.
2   A BBC *Panorama* film, by Angela Pope, *The Best Days?*, broadcast March 1977.
3   N. Wright, *Progress in Education* (Croom Helm 1977).
4   R. Boyson, *The Crisis in Education* (Woburn Press 1976).
5   N. Bennett, *Teaching Styles and Pupil Progress* (Open Books 1976).
6   *A Language for Life* (The Bullock Report) (HMSO 1975).
7   DES, *Education in Schools*: *A Consultative Document* (Green Paper), Cmnd 6869 (HMSO 1977).
8   J. Callaghan, Ruskin College speech (18 October 1976). From *The Times Educational Supplement,* 22 October 1979.
9   Quoted in V. Burke, *Teachers in Turmoil* (Penguin 1971), p. 49.
10   *Guardian,* 13 October 1976.
11   ibid.
12   Quoted in *The Times Educational Supplement,* October 1976.
13   *Guardian,* 23 October 1976.
14   *Guardian,* 13 February 1977.
15   *The Times Educational Supplement,* 30 December 1977.
16   *Guardian,* 20 October 1976.
17   J. Donald, 'Green Paper: noise of crisis' in *Screen Education*, no. 30 (Spring 1979).

18 DES, *Education in Schools,* p. 12.
19 ibid., p. 22.
20 See the 1974-6 publications of the Hansard Society, 12 Gower Street, London WC1.
21 DES, *Education in Schools,* p. 43.
22 See *The Times Educational Supplement,* 4 March 1977.
23 House of Commons Expenditure Committee Tenth Report, *The Attainments of the School Leaver* (HMSO July 1977), p. lvii.
24 DES and Welsh Office, *A New Partnership for our Schools* (The Taylor Report), (HMSO 1977).
25 Quoted from NUT, *Partnership in Education* in *The Times Educational Supplement,* 7 July 1978.
26 *The Times Educational Supplement,* 10 February 1978.
27 *The Times Educational Supplement,* 19 November 1977.
28 DES, *Education in Schools,* p. 35.
29 Expenditure Committee Tenth Report, *The Attainments of the School Leaver,* p. li.

Chapter 11   The rise of the Manpower Services Commission

1   Manpower Services Commission, *Young People and Work* (The Holland Report), (MSC May 1977).
2   Training Services Agency, *Vocational Preparation for Young People* (MSC 1975).
3   M. Simon, *Youth into Industry: A Study of Young People's Attitudes to Work at a Large Midlands Factory* (National Youth Bureau October 1977).
4   National Youth Employment Council, *Unqualified, Untrained and Unemployed* (HMSO 1974), p. 29.
5   Training Services Agency, *Vocational Preparation,* p. 15.
6   Quoted in Conference of Socialist Economists Social Policy Group, *Bulletin on Social Policy No. 1* (Spring 1978).
7   Quoted in S. Frith, *The Sociology of Rock* (Constable 1978), p. 35.
8   Central Advisory Council for England and Wales, *Fifteen to Eighteen* (The Crowther Report) (HMSO 1959), p. 4.
9   National Youth Employment Council, *Unqualified, Untrained and Unemployed,* p. 1.
10 Commission for Racial Equality, *Looking for Work: Black and White School Leavers in Lewisham* (CRE 1978).
11 National Youth Employment Council, *Unqualified, Untrained and Unemployed,* p. 15.
12 S. Frith, *Education, Training and the Labour Process* (unpublished, CSE Education Group November 1977).
13 ibid., p. 4.
14 P. Corrigan and P. Corrigan, *Labour and the State* (unpublished paper given at BSA Annual Conference 1977).

15   British Youth Council, *Youth Unemployment: Causes and Cures* (BYC March 1977), p. 12.
16   Further Education Curriculum Review and Development Unit, *Experience, Reflection, Learning: Suggestions for Organisers of Schemes of UVP* (DES April 1978), section on Coventry.
17   Quoted in R. Gorringe, *Why Vocationally Oriented Courses?*, General Studies Workshop Dayschool (unpublished July 1978).
18   Paper Products ITB, *Outline of Suggested Pilot Scheme of Career Preparation for Young People in the N.W. Area of Greater Manchester* (Paper Products ITB 1978), appendix 1, p. 1.
19   ibid., pp. 1-2.
20   ibid., appendix 1, p. 1.
21   M. A. Pirie, *Identifying Common Skills,* BACIE Journal, vol. 30, no. 10 (November 1976).
22   ibid.
23   Department of Education and Science, *16 to 18: Education and Training for 16-18 year olds: A Consultative Paper,* HMSO (February 1979), p. 10.
24   Further Education Curriculum Review and Development Unit, *Principles and Guidelines for Colleges Contributing to the Youth Opportunities Programme,* DES (February 1978), p. 35.
25   Manpower Services Commission, *Annual Report 1976-7* (MSC 1977), p. 24.
26   Manpower Services Commission, *Towards a Comprehensive Manpower Policy* (MCS October 1976), p.6.
27   ibid., p. 7.
28   In December 1980, James Prior, the Employment Secretary, announced changes in both YOP and schemes for the adult unemployed. While the number of YOP places was to be expanded to 440,000 in 1981-2, 50 per cent more than the 1980-1 figure, and the duration of many courses was to be extended to nine months, the money paid to trainees was to be frozen at 1979 levels, and the vast majority of places was to be concentrated on employers' premises. Conservative policy now aims at the gradual removal of the 16-18 age group from the labour market, although the role of the MSC and education sector in this process will not be fully established until a major review of provision in 1984, when the current Youth Opportunities Programme comes to an end.

By no means concluded

1   G. C. T. Giles, *The New School Tie* (Pilot Press 1946), p. 105.
2   ibid.
3   ibid.
4   ibid., p. 107.
5   ibid., p. 108.
6   ibid., p. 109.
7   ibid., p. 110.

8   ibid., p. 104.
9   Neville Bennett, *Teaching Styles and Pupil Progress* (Open Books 1976).
10   See report on work of Dr L. Lowenstein in *Daily Mail* (24 October 1975).
11   L. C. Comber and R. C. Whitfield, *Action on Indiscipline* (NAS/UWT, Department of Educational Enquiry, University of Aston 1979).
12   See, for instance, Nigel Wright, *Progress in Education* (Croom Helm 1977); John Gray and David Satterly, 'A chapter of errors: teaching styles and pupil progress in retrospect', *Educational Research,* vol. 20, no. 2 (1977), pp. 137-42; Donald McIntyre, 'Review of teaching styles and pupil progress', *British Journal of Teacher Education,* vol. 2, no. 3 (October 1976), pp. 291-7.
13   Antonio Gramsci, *Selections from the Prison Notebooks* (Lawrence & Wishart 1971), p. 12.
14   We are indebted here to various comments by Stuart Hall.
15   Gramsci, *Selections from the Prison Notebooks*, p. 324.
16   ibid., p. 330.
17   ibid., pp. 330-1.
18   See Ann Phillips and Tim Putnam, 'Education for working class education 1908-1928' in *Capital and Class*, no. 10 (Spring 1980), pp. 18-42.

Index

Centre for Contemporary Cultural Studies

The Centre is a research and largely postgraduate unit in the Faculty of Arts of the University of Birmingham (though a new undergraduate Combined Honours half degree will be offered from October 1982). It is concerned, across a broad front, with theoretically informed concrete analyses of contemporary culture. While main emphasis is placed upon Britain, comparative studies are encouraged where possible. The Centre has tried to break down some traditional divisions and hierarchies of labour within research and to pioneer styles of collective work; and to take up seriously issues raised by feminism. Work in the Centre typically combines membership of a research group with progress on an MA, MLitt., or Ph.D degree by thesis. A taught MA course is also offered. A report on the Centre's work is available annually from the Centre Secretary, Cultural Studies Centre, Arts Faculty, University of Birmingham, PO Box 363, Birmingham B15 2TT (Tel. 021 472 1301 ext. 3549).

Comradely publications

We list here related radical magazines and jornals. The list will be amended in future Centre publications. We would welcome corrections, or the omission of journals or groups, being brought to our notice.

English Magazine   A magazine for English, media studies and humanities teachers.

Radical Education Dossier   A journal of radical educational discussion, published in Australia.

Schooling and Culture   A journal of cultural studies in secondary teaching.

Screen Education   A journal of media and cultural studies and education.

Socialism and Education   The journal of the Socialist Educational Association of the Labour Party.

Socialist Teacher   A magazine of news and debate for socialist teachers.

Teachers Action   A magazine of a strategy for educational politics.

Teaching London Kids   A magazine for English teachers, not confined to London.

Block   A journal of art, design and representation.
Camerawork   A journal of radical photography.
Capital and Class   Journal of the Conference of Socialist Economists.
Counter-Information Services   Radical research reports.
Critique of Anthropology   Concrete and theoretical studies in social sciences.
Feminist Review   A journal of feminist studies, politics and theory.
Film and Poster Collective   Publishers of radical and educational posters.
Head and Hand   A socialist review of books, published by the CSE.
History Workshop Journal   A journal of socialist historians.
Ideology and Consciousness   Marxist and feminist studies.
Leveller   Independent magazine of socialist news and debate.
M/F   A journal of Marxist and feminist theory.

Manushi   Feminist journal produced by Asian women.
Marxism Today   Analysis and discussion journal of the CP.
Media, Culture and Society   A journal of media and cultural studies.
New Left Review   Independent journal of socialist theory and debate.
News from Neasden   Annotated catalogue of radical publications.
Race and Class   A journal of black liberation.
Race Today   Discussion and analysis of politics of race.
Radical Bookseller   A magazine of news on radical publications.
Radical Science Journal   A journal of radical analyses of science and technology.
Radical Philosophy   A journal of radical critique and debate within philosophy.
Rebecca   Welsh independent socialist news magazine.
Red Letters   CP journal of politics of writing and culture.
Red Rag   A feminist discussion magazine.
Screen   A journal of media theory and analysis, especially film.
Social History   A journal of debates and studies in social history.
Spare Rib   A feminist news and discussion magazine.
Voice   A journal of the Federation of Worker Writers.

Most of these publications are available from Full Time Distribution,
27 Clerkenwell Close, London EC1 (Tel. 01 251 4976).

Many may be purchased through alternative bookshops, either a local radical
bookshop or contact the Federation of Radical Booksellers, York Community
Books, 73 Walmgate, York (Tel. 0904 37355).

Published abroad

Cine-Tract   A journal of film and cultural studies. Institute of Cinema Studies,
    4227 Esplanade Avenue, Montreal, Quebec, Canada
Insurgent Sociologist   Radical studies in social science. Department of
    Sociology, University of Oregon, Eugene, Oregon, USA
Monthly Review   An independent socialist journal. 62 West 14th Street,
    New York, NY 10011, USA
Praxis   Radical arts journal. PO Box 207, Galeta, Ca. 93017, USA
Radical America   Radical analysis and debate. PO Box B, North Cambridge,
    Mass. 02140, USA
Radical History Review   Journal of American radical historians. John Jay
    College, 445 West 59th Street, New York, NY 10019, USA
Science for the People   A journal of radical science. Science Resources Centre
    Inc., 897 Main Street, Cambridge, Mass. 02139, USA
Social Text   A journal of Marxist perspectives on culture, theory and ideology.
    700 West Badger Road, Suite 101, Madison, Wis. 153713, USA
Socialist Review   A journal of socialist discussion and analysis. New Front
    Publishing, 4228 Telegraph Avenue, Oakland, Ca.94609, USA
Telos   A journal of Marxist theory and analysis, with review sections.
    Department of Sociology, Washington University, St Louis, Miss. 63139, USA
Working Papers   Papers in Marxist theory of culture and ideology. Feral
    Publications, PO Box 83, Wentworth Building, Sydney University, Australia 2006

Occasional stencilled papers

The Centre publishes a series of stencilled occasional papers of work in progress.

Forthcoming

Janet Batsleer and Rebecca O'Rourke: Feminism, Women and Writing in the '30s
Brian Doyle: Some Uses of English: Denys Thompson and English in Secondary Schools, now available 65p
Janice Winship: Woman Becomes an 'Individual': Femininity and Consumption in Women's Magazines 1954–69, now available 65p

Payment with orders is requested. Postage is charged on overseas orders, which will be sent by surface mail unless air mail is requested. Please make cheques payable to CCCS, not the University of Birmingham. Orders should be sent to Stencilled Papers, CCCS, Arts Faculty, University of Birmingham, Birmingham B15 2TT.